Preface

Django is a powerful Python web framework that encourages rapid development and clean, pragmatic design, offering a relatively shallow learning curve. This makes it attractive to both novice and expert programmers.

This book will guide you through the entire process of developing professional web applications with Django. The book not only covers the most relevant aspects of the framework, but also teaches you how to integrate other popular technologies into your Django projects.

The book will walk you through the creation of real-world applications, solving common problems, and implementing best practices with a step-by-step approach that is easy to follow.

After reading this book, you will have a good understanding of how Django works and how to build practical, advanced web applications.

Who this book is for

This book is intended for developers with Python knowledge who wish to learn Django in a pragmatic way. Perhaps you are completely new to Django, or you already know a little but you want to get the most out of it. This book will help you master the most relevant areas of the framework by building practical projects from scratch. You need to have familiarity with programming concepts in order to read this book. Some previous knowledge of HTML and JavaScript is assumed.

What this book covers

Chapter 1, *Building a Blog Application*, introduces you to the framework by creating a blog application. You will create the basic blog models, views, templates, and URLs to display blog posts. You will learn how to build QuerySets with the Django ORM, and you will configure the Django administration site.

Chapter 2, *Enhancing Your Blog with Advanced Features*, teaches you how to handle forms and model forms, send emails with Django, and integrate third-party applications. You will implement a comment system for your blog posts and allow your users to share posts via email. The chapter also guides you through the process of creating a tagging system.

Chapter 3, *Extending Your Blog Application,* explores how to create custom template tags and filters. The chapter also shows you how to use the sitemap framework and create an RSS feed for your posts. You will complete your blog application by building a search engine with PostgreSQL's full-text search capabilities.

Chapter 4, *Building a Social Website,* explains how to build a social website. You will use the Django authentication framework to create user account views. You will learn how to create a custom user profile model and build social authentication into your project using major social networks.

Chapter 5, *Sharing Content in Your Website,* teaches you how to transform your social application into an image bookmarking website. You will define many-to-many relationships for models, and you will create an AJAX bookmarklet in JavaScript and integrate it into your project. The chapter shows you how to generate image thumbnails and create custom decorators for your views.

Chapter 6, *Tracking User Actions,* shows you how to build a follower system for users. You will complete your image bookmarking website by creating a user activity stream application. You will learn how to optimize QuerySets, and you will work with signals. You will integrate Redis into your project to count image views.

Chapter 7, *Building an Online Shop,* explores how to create an online shop. You will build catalog models, and you will create a shopping cart using Django sessions. You will build a context processor for the shopping cart, and you will learn how to implement sending asynchronous notifications to users using Celery.

Chapter 8, *Managing Payments and Orders,* explains how to integrate a payment gateway into your shop. You will also customize the administration site to export orders to CSV files, and you will generate PDF invoices dynamically.

Chapter 9, *Extending Your Shop,* teaches you how to create a coupon system to apply discounts to orders. The chapter shows you how to add internationalization to your project and how to translate models. You will also build a product recommendation engine using Redis.

Chapter 10, *Building an E-Learning Platform,* guides you through creating an e-learning platform. You will add fixtures to your project, use model inheritance, create custom model fields, use class-based views, and manage groups and permissions. You will create a content management system and handle formsets.

Chapter 11, *Rendering and Caching Content,* shows you how to create a student registration system and manage student enrollment on courses. You will render diverse course content and you will learn how to use the cache framework.

Chapter 12, *Building an API*, explores building a RESTful API for your project using the Django REST framework.

Chapter 13, *Going Live*, shows how to set up a production environment using uWSGI and NGINX, and how to secure it with SSL. The chapter explains how to build a custom middleware and create custom management commands.

To get the most out of this book

To get the most out of this book, it is recommended that you have good working knowledge of Python. You should also be comfortable with HTML and JavaScript. Before reading this book, it is recommended that you read parts 1 to 3 of the official Django documentation tutorial at https://docs.djangoproject.com/en/2.0/intro/tutorial01/.

Download the example code files

You can download the example code files for this book from your account at www.packtpub.com. If you purchased this book elsewhere, you can visit www.packtpub.com/support and register to have the files emailed directly to you.

You can download the code files by following these steps:

1. Log in or register at www.packtpub.com.
2. Select the **SUPPORT** tab.
3. Click on **Code Downloads & Errata**.
4. Enter the name of the book in the **Search** box and follow the onscreen instructions.

Once the file is downloaded, please make sure that you unzip or extract the folder using the latest version of:

- WinRAR/7-Zip for Windows
- Zipeg/iZip/UnRarX for Mac
- 7-Zip/PeaZip for Linux

The code bundle for the book is also hosted on GitHub at https://github.com/PacktPublishing/Django-2-by-Example. In case there's an update to the code, it will be updated on the existing GitHub repository.

We also have other code bundles from our rich catalog of books and videos available at https://github.com/PacktPublishing/. Check them out!

Conventions used

There are a number of text conventions used throughout this book.

CodeInText: Indicates code words in text, database table names, folder names, filenames, file extensions, pathnames, dummy URLs, user input, and Twitter handles. Here is an example: "You can deactivate your environment at any time with the deactivate command."

A block of code is set as follows:

```
from django.contrib import admin
from .models import Post

admin.site.register(Post)
```

When we wish to draw your attention to a particular part of a code block, the relevant lines or items are set in bold:

```
INSTALLED_APPS = [
    'django.contrib.admin',
    'django.contrib.auth',
    'django.contrib.contenttypes',
    'django.contrib.sessions',
    'django.contrib.messages',
    'django.contrib.staticfiles',
    'blog.apps.BlogConfig',
]
```

Any command-line input or output is written as follows:

```
$ python manage.py startapp blog
```

Bold: Indicates a new term, an important word, or words that you see onscreen. For example, words in menus or dialog boxes appear in the text like this. Here is an example: "Fill in the form and click on the **SAVE** button."

Warnings or important notes appear like this.

Tips and tricks appear like this.

Get in touch

Feedback from our readers is always welcome.

General feedback: Email `feedback@packtpub.com` and mention the book title in the subject of your message. If you have questions about any aspect of this book, please email us at `questions@packtpub.com`.

Errata: Although we have taken every care to ensure the accuracy of our content, mistakes do happen. If you have found a mistake in this book, we would be grateful if you would report this to us. Please visit `www.packtpub.com/submit-errata`, selecting your book, clicking on the Errata Submission Form link, and entering the details.

Piracy: If you come across any illegal copies of our works in any form on the Internet, we would be grateful if you would provide us with the location address or website name. Please contact us at `copyright@packtpub.com` with a link to the material.

If you are interested in becoming an author: If there is a topic that you have expertise in and you are interested in either writing or contributing to a book, please visit `authors.packtpub.com`.

Reviews

Please leave a review. Once you have read and used this book, why not leave a review on the site that you purchased it from? Potential readers can then see and use your unbiased opinion to make purchase decisions, we at Packt can understand what you think about our products, and our authors can see your feedback on their book. Thank you!

For more information about Packt, please visit `packtpub.com`.

Building a Blog Application 1

In this book, you will learn how to build complete Django projects, ready for production use. In case you haven't installed Django yet, you will learn how to do it in the first part of this chapter. This chapter covers how to create a simple blog application using Django. The purpose of this chapter is to get a general idea of how the framework works, understand how the different components interact with each other, and provide you with the skills to easily create Django projects with a basic functionality. You will be guided through the creation of a complete project without elaborating upon all the details. The different framework components will be covered in detail throughout this book.

This chapter will cover the following topics:

- Installing Django and creating your first project
- Designing models and generating model migrations
- Creating an administration site for your models
- Working with QuerySet and managers
- Building views, templates, and URLs
- Adding pagination to list views
- Using Django's class-based views

Installing Django

If you have already installed Django, you can skip this section and jump directly to the *Creating your first project* section. Django comes as a Python package and thus can be installed in any Python environment. If you haven't installed Django yet, the following is a quick guide to install Django for local development.

Django 2.0 requires Python version 3.4 or higher. In the examples for this book, we will use Python 3.6.5. If you're using Linux or macOS X, you probably have Python installed. If you are using Windows, you can download a Python installer at `https://www.python.org/downloads/windows/`.

If you are not sure whether Python is installed on your computer, you can verify it by typing `python` in the shell. If you see something like the following, then Python is installed on your computer:

```
Python 3.6.5 (v3.6.5:f59c0932b4, Mar 28 2018, 03:03:55)
[GCC 4.2.1 (Apple Inc. build 5666) (dot 3)] on darwin
Type "help", "copyright", "credits" or "license" for more information.
>>>
```

If your installed Python version is lower than 3.4, or if Python is not installed on your computer, download Python 3.6.5 from `https://www.python.org/downloads/` and install it.

Since you will use Python 3, you don't have to install a database. This Python version comes with a built-in SQLite database. SQLite is a lightweight database that you can use with Django for development. If you plan to deploy your application in a production environment, you should use an advanced database, such as PostgreSQL, MySQL, or Oracle. You can get more information about how to get your database running with Django at `https://docs.djangoproject.com/en/2.0/topics/install/#database-installation`.

Creating an isolated Python environment

It is recommended that you use `virtualenv` to create isolated Python environments, so that you can use different package versions for different projects, which is far more practical than installing Python packages system-wide. Another advantage of using `virtualenv` is that you won't need any administration privileges to install Python packages. Run the following command in your shell to install `virtualenv`:

```
pip install virtualenv
```

After you install `virtualenv`, create an isolated environment with the following command:

```
virtualenv my_env
```

This will create a `my_env/` directory, including your Python environment. Any Python libraries you install while your virtual environment is active will go into the `my_env/lib/python3.6/site-packages` directory.

 If your system comes with Python 2.X and you have installed Python 3.X, you have to tell `virtualenv` to use the latter.

You can locate the path where Python 3 is installed and use it to create the virtual environment with the following commands:

```
zenx$ which python3
/Library/Frameworks/Python.framework/Versions/3.6/bin/python3
zenx$ virtualenv my_env -p
/Library/Frameworks/Python.framework/Versions/3.6/bin/python3
```

Run the following command to activate your virtual environment:

```
source my_env/bin/activate
```

The shell prompt will include the name of the active virtual environment enclosed in parentheses, as follows:

```
(my_env) laptop:~ zenx$
```

You can deactivate your environment at any time with the `deactivate` command.

You can find more information about `virtualenv` at `https://virtualenv.pypa.io/en/latest/`.

On top of `virtualenv`, you can use `virtualenvwrapper`. This tool provides wrappers that make it easier to create and manage your virtual environments. You can download it from `https://virtualenvwrapper.readthedocs.io/en/latest/`.

Installing Django with pip

The `pip` package management system is the preferred method for installing Django. Python 3.6 comes with `pip` preinstalled, but you can find `pip` installation instructions at `https://pip.pypa.io/en/stable/installing/`.

Run the following command at the shell prompt to install Django with `pip`:

```
pip install Django==2.0.5
```

Django will be installed in the Python `site-packages/` directory of your virtual environment.

Now, check whether Django has been successfully installed. Run `python` on a terminal, import Django, and check its version, as follows:

```
>>> import django
>>> django.get_version()
'2.0.5'
```

If you get the preceding output, Django has been successfully installed on your machine.

 Django can be installed in several other ways. You can find a complete installation guide at https://docs.djangoproject.com/en/2.0/topics/install/.

Creating your first project

Our first Django project will be building a complete blog. Django provides a command that allows you to create an initial project file structure. Run the following command from your shell:

```
django-admin startproject mysite
```

This will create a Django project with the name `mysite`.

 Avoid naming projects after built-in Python or Django modules in order to avoid conflicts.

Let's take a look at the project structure generated:

```
mysite/
   manage.py
   mysite/
      __init__.py
      settings.py
      urls.py
      wsgi.py
```

These files are as follows:

- `manage.py`: This is a command-line utility used to interact with your project. It is a thin wrapper around the `django-admin.py` tool. You don't need to edit this file.
- `mysite/`: This is your project directory, which consists of the following files:
  - `__init__.py`: An empty file that tells Python to treat the `mysite` directory as a Python module.
  - `settings.py`: This indicates settings and configuration for your project and contains initial default settings.
  - `urls.py`: This is the place where your URL patterns live. Each URL defined here is mapped to a view.
  - `wsgi.py`: This is the configuration to run your project as a **Web Server Gateway Interface** (**WSGI**) application.

The generated `settings.py` file contains the project settings, including a basic configuration to use an SQLite 3 database and a list named `INSTALLED_APPS`, which contains common Django applications that are added to your project by default. We will go through these applications later in the *Project settings* section.

To complete the project setup, we will need to create the tables in the database required by the applications listed in `INSTALLED_APPS`. Open the shell and run the following commands:

```
cd mysite
python manage.py migrate
```

You will note an output that ends with the following lines:

```
Applying contenttypes.0001_initial... OK
Applying auth.0001_initial... OK
Applying admin.0001_initial... OK
Applying admin.0002_logentry_remove_auto_add... OK
```

```
Applying contenttypes.0002_remove_content_type_name... OK
Applying auth.0002_alter_permission_name_max_length... OK
Applying auth.0003_alter_user_email_max_length... OK
Applying auth.0004_alter_user_username_opts... OK
Applying auth.0005_alter_user_last_login_null... OK
Applying auth.0006_require_contenttypes_0002... OK
Applying auth.0007_alter_validators_add_error_messages... OK
Applying auth.0008_alter_user_username_max_length... OK
Applying auth.0009_alter_user_last_name_max_length... OK
Applying sessions.0001_initial... OK
```

The preceding lines are the database migrations that are applied by Django. By applying migrations, the tables for the initial applications are created in the database. You will learn about the `migrate` management command in the *Creating and applying migrations* section of this chapter.

Running the development server

Django comes with a lightweight web server to run your code quickly, without needing to spend time configuring a production server. When you run the Django development server, it keeps checking for changes in your code. It reloads automatically, freeing you from manually reloading it after code changes. However, it might not notice some actions, such as adding new files to your project, so you will have to restart the server manually in these cases.

Start the development server by typing the following command from your project's root folder:

```
python manage.py runserver
```

You should see something like this:

```
Performing system checks...

System check identified no issues (0 silenced).
May 06, 2018 - 17:17:31
Django version 2.0.5, using settings 'mysite.settings'
Starting development server at http://127.0.0.1:8000/
Quit the server with CONTROL-C.
```

Now, open `http://127.0.0.1:8000/` in your browser. You should see a page stating that the project is successfully running, as shown in the following screenshot:

The preceding screenshot indicates that Django is running. If you take a look at your console, you will see the GET request performed by your browser:

```
[06/May/2018 17:20:30] "GET / HTTP/1.1" 200 16348
```

Each HTTP request is logged in the console by the development server. Any error that occurs while running the development server will also appear in the console.

You can indicate Django to run the development server on a custom host and port or tell it to run your project, loading a different settings file, as follows:

```
python manage.py runserver 127.0.0.1:8001 \
--settings=mysite.settings
```

When you have to deal with multiple environments that require different configurations, you can create a different settings file for each environment.

Remember that this server is only intended for development and is not suitable for production use. In order to deploy Django in a production environment, you should run it as a WSGI application using a real web server, such as Apache, Gunicorn, or uWSGI. You can find more information on how to deploy Django with different web servers at `https://docs.djangoproject.com/en/2.0/howto/deployment/wsgi/`.

`Chapter 13`, *Going Live*, explains how to set up a production environment for your Django projects.

Project settings

Let's open the `settings.py` file and take a look at the configuration of our project. There are several settings that Django includes in this file, but these are only a part of all the Django settings available. You can see all settings and their default values in `https://docs.djangoproject.com/en/2.0/ref/settings/`.

The following settings are worth looking at:

- `DEBUG` is a boolean that turns the debug mode of the project on and off. If it is set to `True`, Django will display detailed error pages when an uncaught exception is thrown by your application. When you move to a production environment, remember that you have to set it to `False`. Never deploy a site into production with `DEBUG` turned on because you will expose sensitive project-related data.

- `ALLOWED_HOSTS` is not applied while debug mode is on, or when the tests are run. Once you move your site to production and set `DEBUG` to `False`, you will have to add your domain/host to this setting in order to allow it to serve your Django site.

- `INSTALLED_APPS` is a setting you will have to edit for all projects. This setting tells Django which applications are active for this site. By default, Django includes the following applications:
    - `django.contrib.admin`: An administration site
    - `django.contrib.auth`: An authentication framework
    - `django.contrib.contenttypes`: A framework for handling content types
    - `django.contrib.sessions`: A session framework
    - `django.contrib.messages`: A messaging framework
    - `django.contrib.staticfiles`: A framework for managing static files

- MIDDLEWARE is a list that contains middleware to be executed.
- ROOT_URLCONF indicates the Python module where the root URL patterns of your application are defined.
- DATABASES is a dictionary that contains the settings for all the databases to be used in the project. There must always be a default database. The default configuration uses an SQLite3 database.
- LANGUAGE_CODE defines the default language code for this Django site.
- USE_TZ tells Django to activate/deactivate timezone support. Django comes with support for timezone-aware datetime. This setting is set to True when you create a new project using the startproject management command.

Don't worry if you don't understand much about what you are seeing. You will learn the different Django settings in the following chapters.

Projects and applications

Throughout this book, you will encounter the terms project and application over and over. In Django, a project is considered a Django installation with some settings. An application is a group of models, views, templates, and URLs. Applications interact with the framework to provide some specific functionalities and may be reused in various projects. You can think of the project as your website, which contains several applications such as a blog, wiki, or forum, that can be used by other projects also.

Creating an application

Now, let's create our first Django application. We will create a blog application from scratch. From the project's root directory, run the following command:

```
python manage.py startapp blog
```

This will create the basic structure of the application, which looks like this:

```
blog/
    __init__.py
    admin.py
    apps.py
    migrations/
        __init__.py
    models.py
    tests.py
```

```
views.py
```

These files are as follows:

- `admin.py`: This is where you register models to include them in the Django administration site—using the Django admin site is optional.
- `apps.py`: This includes the main configuration of the `blog` application.
- `migrations`: This directory will contain database migrations of your application. Migrations allow Django to track your model changes and synchronize the database accordingly.
- `models.py`: Data models of your application—all Django applications need to have a `models.py` file, but this file can be left empty.
- `tests.py`: This is where you can add tests for your application.
- `views.py`: The logic of your application goes here; each view receives an HTTP request, processes it, and returns a response.

Designing the blog data schema

We will start designing our blog data schema by defining the data models for our blog. A model is a Python class that subclasses `django.db.models.Model`, in which each attribute represents a database field. Django will create a table for each model defined in the `models.py` file. When you create a model, Django provides you with a practical API to query objects in the database easily.

First, we will define a `Post` model. Add the following lines to the `models.py` file of the `blog` application:

```python
from django.db import models
from django.utils import timezone
from django.contrib.auth.models import User

class Post(models.Model):
    STATUS_CHOICES = (
        ('draft', 'Draft'),
        ('published', 'Published'),
    )
    title = models.CharField(max_length=250)
    slug = models.SlugField(max_length=250,
                            unique_for_date='publish')
    author = models.ForeignKey(User,
                               on_delete=models.CASCADE,
```

```
                              related_name='blog_posts')
body = models.TextField()
publish = models.DateTimeField(default=timezone.now)
created = models.DateTimeField(auto_now_add=True)
updated = models.DateTimeField(auto_now=True)
status = models.CharField(max_length=10,
                          choices=STATUS_CHOICES,
                          default='draft')

class Meta:
    ordering = ('-publish',)

def __str__(self):
    return self.title
```

This is our data model for blog posts. Let's take a look at the fields we just defined for this model:

- `title`: This is the field for the post title. This field is `CharField`, which translates into a `VARCHAR` column in the SQL database.
- `slug`: This is a field intended to be used in URLs. A slug is a short label that contains only letters, numbers, underscores, or hyphens. We will use the `slug` field to build beautiful, SEO-friendly URLs for our blog posts. We have added the `unique_for_date` parameter to this field so that we can build URLs for posts using their publish date and `slug`. Django will prevent multiple posts from having the same `slug` for a given date.
- `author`: This field is a foreign key. It defines a many-to-one relationship. We are telling Django that each post is written by a user, and a user can write any number of posts. For this field, Django will create a foreign key in the database using the primary key of the related model. In this case, we are relying on the `User` model of the Django authentication system. The `on_delete` parameter specifies the behavior to adopt when the referenced object is deleted. This is not specific to Django; it is an SQL standard. Using `CASCADE`, we specify that when the referenced user is deleted, the database will also delete its related blog posts. You can take a look at all possible options at `https://docs.djangoproject.com/en/2.0/ref/models/fields/#django.db.models.ForeignKey.on_delete`. We specify the name of the reverse relationship, from `User` to `Post`, with the `related_name` attribute. This will allow us to access related objects easily. We will learn more about this later.
- `body`: This is the body of the post. This field is a text field, which translates into a `TEXT` column in the SQL database.

- `publish`: This datetime indicates when the post was published. We use Django's timezone `now` method as the default value. This returns the current datetime in a timezone-aware format. You can think of it as a timezone-aware version of the standard Python `datetime.now` method.
- `created`: This datetime indicates when the post was created. Since we are using `auto_now_add` here, the date will be saved automatically when creating an object.
- `updated`: This datetime indicates the last time the post was updated. Since we are using `auto_now` here, the date will be updated automatically when saving an object.
- `status`: This field shows the status of a post. We use a `choices` parameter, so the value of this field can only be set to one of the given choices.

Django comes with different types of fields that you can use to define your models. You can find all field types at `https://docs.djangoproject.com/en/2.0/ref/models/fields/`.

The `Meta` class inside the model contains metadata. We tell Django to sort results in the `publish` field in descending order by default when we query the database. We specify descending order using the negative prefix. By doing so, posts published recently will appear first.

The `__str__()` method is the default human-readable representation of the object. Django will use it in many places, such as the administration site.

 If you come from using Python 2.X, note that in Python 3, all strings are natively considered Unicode, and therefore, we only use the `__str__()` method. The `__unicode__()` method is obsolete.

Activating your application

In order for Django to keep track of our application and be able to create database tables for its models, we have to activate it. To do this, edit the `settings.py` file and add `blog.apps.BlogConfig` to the `INSTALLED_APPS` setting. It should look like this:

```
INSTALLED_APPS = [
    'django.contrib.admin',
    'django.contrib.auth',
    'django.contrib.contenttypes',
    'django.contrib.sessions',
    'django.contrib.messages',
```

```
    'django.contrib.staticfiles',
    'blog.apps.BlogConfig',
]
```

The BlogConfig class is your application configuration. Now Django knows that our application is active for this project and will be able to load its models.

Creating and applying migrations

Now that we have a data model for our blog posts, we will need a database table for it. Django comes with a migration system that tracks the changes done to models and allows to propagate them into the database. The migrate command applies migrations for all applications listed in INSTALLED_APPS; it synchronizes the database with the current models and existing migrations.

First, you will need to create an initial migration for our Post model. In the root directory of your project, run the following command:

```
python manage.py makemigrations blog
```

You should get the following output:

```
Migrations for 'blog':
  blog/migrations/0001_initial.py
    - Create model Post
```

Django just created the 0001_initial.py file inside the migrations directory of the blog application. You can open that file to see how a migration appears. A migration specifies dependencies on other migrations and operations to perform in the database to synchronize it with model changes.

Let's take a look at the SQL code that Django will execute in the database to create the table for our model. The sqlmigrate command takes migration names and returns their SQL without executing it. Run the following command to inspect the SQL output of our first migration:

```
python manage.py sqlmigrate blog 0001
```

The output should look as follows:

```
BEGIN;
--
-- Create model Post
--
```

```
CREATE TABLE "blog_post" ("id" integer NOT NULL PRIMARY KEY AUTOINCREMENT,
"title" varchar(250) NOT NULL, "slug" varchar(250) NOT NULL, "body" text
NOT NULL, "publish" datetime NOT NULL, "created" datetime NOT NULL,
"updated" datetime NOT NULL, "status" varchar(10) NOT NULL, "author_id"
integer NOT NULL REFERENCES "auth_user" ("id"));
CREATE INDEX "blog_post_slug_b95473f2" ON "blog_post" ("slug");
CREATE INDEX "blog_post_author_id_dd7a8485" ON "blog_post" ("author_id");
COMMIT;
```

The exact output depends on the database you are using. The preceding output is generated for SQLite. As you can see in the preceding output, Django generates the table names by combining the app name and the lowercase name of the model (blog_post), but you can also specify a custom database name for your model in the Meta class of the model using the db_table attribute. Django creates a primary key automatically for each model, but you can also override this by specifying primary_key=True in one of your model fields. The default primary key is an id column, which consists of an integer that is incremented automatically. This column corresponds to the id field that is automatically added to your models.

Let's sync our database with the new model. Run the following command to apply existing migrations:

```
python manage.py migrate
```

You will get an output that ends with the following line:

```
Applying blog.0001_initial... OK
```

We just applied migrations for the applications listed in INSTALLED_APPS, including our blog application. After applying migrations, the database reflects the current status of our models.

If you edit your models.py file in order to add, remove, or change fields of existing models, or if you add new models, you will have to create a new migration using the makemigrations command. The migration will allow Django to keep track of model changes. Then, you will have to apply it with the migrate command to keep the database in sync with your models.

Creating an administration site for your models

Now that we have defined the Post model, we will create a simple administration site to manage your blog posts. Django comes with a built-in administration interface that is very useful for editing content. The Django admin site is built dynamically by reading your model metadata and providing a production-ready interface for editing content. You can use it out of the box, configuring how you want your models to be displayed in it.

The django.contrib.admin application is already included in the INSTALLED_APPS setting, so we don't need to add it.

Creating a superuser

First, we will need to create a user to manage the administration site. Run the following command:

```
python manage.py createsuperuser
```

You will see the following output; enter your desired username, email, and password, as follows:

```
Username (leave blank to use 'admin'): admin
Email address: admin@admin.com
Password: ********
Password (again): ********
Superuser created successfully.
```

The Django administration site

Now, start the development server with the `python manage.py runserver` command and open `http://127.0.0.1:8000/admin/` in your browser. You should see the administration login page, as shown in the following screenshot:

Log in using the credentials of the user you created in the preceding step. You will see the admin site index page, as shown in the following screenshot:

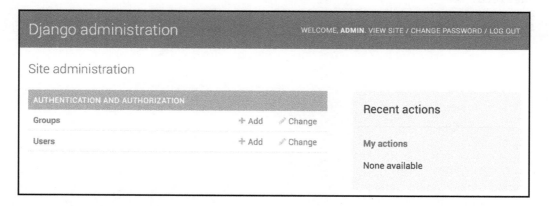

The `Group` and `User` models you see in the preceding screenshot are part of the Django authentication framework located in `django.contrib.auth`. If you click on **Users**, you will see the user you created previously. The `Post` model of your `blog` application has a relationship with this `User` model. Remember that it is a relationship defined by the `author` field.

Adding your models to the administration site

Let's add your blog models to the administration site. Edit the `admin.py` file of your `blog` application and make it look like this:

```
from django.contrib import admin
from .models import Post

admin.site.register(Post)
```

Now, reload the admin site in your browser. You should see your `Post` model on the admin site, as follows:

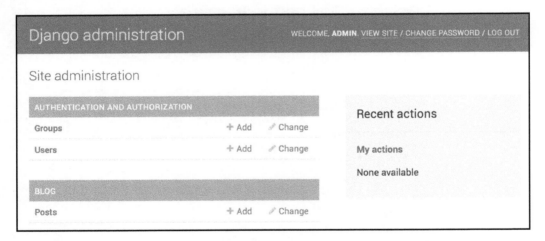

That was easy, right? When you register a model in the Django admin site, you get a user-friendly interface generated by introspecting your models that allows you to list, edit, create, and delete objects in a simple way.

Click on the **Add** link beside **Posts** to add a new post. You will note the create form that Django has generated dynamically for your model, as shown in the following screenshot:

Django uses different form widgets for each type of field. Even complex fields, such as DateTimeField, are displayed with an easy interface, such as a JavaScript date picker.

Fill in the form and click on the **SAVE** button. You should be redirected to the post list page with a successful message and the post you just created, as shown in the following screenshot:

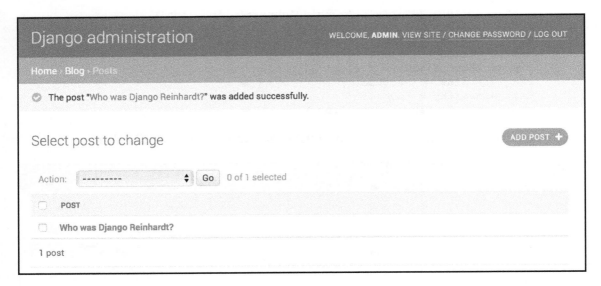

Customizing the way models are displayed

Now, we will take a look at how to customize the admin site. Edit the admin.py file of your blog application and change it, as follows:

```
from django.contrib import admin
from .models import Post

@admin.register(Post)
class PostAdmin(admin.ModelAdmin):
    list_display = ('title', 'slug', 'author', 'publish',
                    'status')
```

We are telling the Django admin site that our model is registered in the admin site using a custom class that inherits from ModelAdmin. In this class, we can include information about how to display the model in the admin site and how to interact with it. The list_display attribute allows you to set the fields of your model that you want to display in the admin object list page. The @admin.register() decorator performs the same function as the admin.site.register() function we have replaced, registering the ModelAdmin class that it decorates.

Let's customize the admin model with some more options, using the following code:

```python
@admin.register(Post)
class PostAdmin(admin.ModelAdmin):
    list_display = ('title', 'slug', 'author', 'publish',
                    'status')
    list_filter = ('status', 'created', 'publish', 'author')
    search_fields = ('title', 'body')
    prepopulated_fields = {'slug': ('title',)}
    raw_id_fields = ('author',)
    date_hierarchy = 'publish'
    ordering = ('status', 'publish')
```

Return to your browser and reload the post list page. Now, it will look like this:

You can see that the fields displayed on the post list page are the ones you specified in the `list_display` attribute. The list page now includes a right sidebar that allows you to filter the results by the fields included in the `list_filter` attribute. A **Search** bar has appeared on the page. This is because we have defined a list of searchable fields using the `search_fields` attribute. Just below the **Search** bar, there are navigation links to navigate through a date hierarchy: this has been defined by the `date_hierarchy` attribute. You can also see that the posts are ordered by **Status** and **Publish** columns by default. We have specified the default order using the `ordering` attribute.

Now, click on the **Add Post** link. You will also note some changes here. As you type the title of a new post, the `slug` field is filled in automatically. We have told Django to prepopulate the `slug` field with the input of the `title` field using the `prepopulated_fields` attribute. Also, now, the `author` field is displayed with a lookup widget that can scale much better than a drop-down select input when you have thousands of users, as shown in the following screenshot:

With a few lines of code, we have customized the way our model is displayed on the admin site. There are plenty of ways to customize and extend the Django administration site. You will learn more about this later in this book.

Working with QuerySet and managers

Now that you have a fully functional administration site to manage your blog's content, it's time to learn how to retrieve information from the database and interact with it. Django comes with a powerful database abstraction API that lets you create, retrieve, update, and delete objects easily. The Django **Object-relational mapper** is compatible with MySQL, PostgreSQL, SQLite, and Oracle. Remember that you can define the database of your project in the DATABASES setting of your project's `settings.py` file. Django can work with multiple databases at a time, and you can program database routers to create custom routing schemes.

Once you have created your data models, Django gives you a free API to interact with them. You can find the data model reference of the official documentation at `https://docs.djangoproject.com/en/2.0/ref/models/`.

Creating objects

Open the terminal and run the following command to open the Python shell:

```
python manage.py shell
```

Then, type the following lines:

```
>>> from django.contrib.auth.models import User
>>> from blog.models import Post
>>> user = User.objects.get(username='admin')
>>> post = Post(title='Another post',
                slug='another-post',
                body='Post body.',
                author=user)
>>> post.save()
```

Let's analyze what this code does. First, we will retrieve the user object with the username admin:

```
user = User.objects.get(username='admin')
```

The get() method allows you to retrieve a single object from the database. Note that this method expects a result that matches the query. If no results are returned by the database, this method will raise a DoesNotExist exception, and if the database returns more than one result, it will raise a MultipleObjectsReturned exception. Both exceptions are attributes of the model class that the query is being performed on.

Then, we create a Post instance with a custom title, slug, and body, and we set the user we previously retrieved as the author of the post:

```
post = Post(title='Another post', slug='another-post', body='Post body.',
author=user)
```

 This object is in memory and is not persisted to the database.

Finally, we save the Post object to the database using the save() method:

```
post.save()
```

The preceding action performs an INSERT SQL statement behind the scenes. We have seen how to create an object in memory first and then persist it to the database, but we can also create the object and persist it into the database in a single operation using the create() method, as follows:

```
Post.objects.create(title='One more post', slug='one-more-post', body='Post
body.', author=user)
```

Updating objects

Now, change the title of the post to something different and save the object again:

```
>>> post.title = 'New title'
>>> post.save()
```

This time, the save() method performs an UPDATE SQL statement.

 The changes you make to the object are not persisted to the database until you call the save() method.

Retrieving objects

The Django **object-relational mapping (ORM)** is based on QuerySets. A QuerySet is a collection of objects from your database that can have several filters to limit the results. You already know how to retrieve a single object from the database using the get() method. We have accessed this method using Post.objects.get(). Each Django model has at least one manager, and the default manager is called **objects**. You get a QuerySet object using your model manager. To retrieve all objects from a table, you just use the all() method on the default objects manager, like this:

```
>>> all_posts = Post.objects.all()
```

This is how we create a QuerySet that returns all objects in the database. Note that this QuerySet has not been executed yet. Django QuerySets are *lazy*; they are only evaluated when they are forced to. This behavior makes QuerySets very efficient. If we don't set the QuerySet to a variable, but instead write it directly on the Python shell, the SQL statement of the QuerySet is executed because we force it to output results:

```
>>> Post.objects.all()
```

Using the filter() method

To filter a QuerySet, you can use the `filter()` method of the manager. For example, we can retrieve all posts published in the year 2017 using the following QuerySet:

```
Post.objects.filter(publish__year=2017)
```

You can also filter by multiple fields. For example, we can retrieve all posts published in 2017 by the author with the username `admin`:

```
Post.objects.filter(publish__year=2017, author__username='admin')
```

This equates to building the same QuerySet chaining multiple filters:

```
Post.objects.filter(publish__year=2017) \
            .filter(author__username='admin')
```

 Queries with field lookup methods are built using two underscores, for example, `publish__year`, but the same notation is also used for accessing fields of related models, such as `author__username`.

Using exclude()

You can exclude certain results from your QuerySet using the `exclude()` method of the manager. For example, we can retrieve all posts published in 2017 whose titles don't start with `Why`:

```
Post.objects.filter(publish__year=2017) \
            .exclude(title__startswith='Why')
```

Using order_by()

You can order results by different fields using the `order_by()` method of the manager. For example, you can retrieve all objects ordered by their `title`, as follows:

```
Post.objects.order_by('title')
```

Ascending order is implied. You can indicate descending order with a negative sign prefix, like this:

```
Post.objects.order_by('-title')
```

Deleting objects

If you want to delete an object, you can do it from the object instance using the `delete()` method:

```
post = Post.objects.get(id=1)
post.delete()
```

 Note that deleting objects will also delete any dependent relationships for `ForeignKey` objects defined with `on_delete` set to `CASCADE`.

When QuerySets are evaluated

You can concatenate as many filters as you like to a QuerySet, and you will not hit the database until the QuerySet is evaluated. QuerySets are only evaluated in the following cases:

- The first time you iterate over them
- When you slice them, for instance, `Post.objects.all()[:3]`
- When you pickle or cache them
- When you call `repr()` or `len()` on them
- When you explicitly call `list()` on them
- When you test them in a statement, such as `bool()`, `or`, `and`, or `if`

Creating model managers

As we previously mentioned, `objects` is the default manager of every model that retrieves all objects in the database. However, we can also define custom managers for our models. We will create a custom manager to retrieve all posts with the `published` status.

There are two ways to add managers to your models: you can add extra manager methods or modify initial manager QuerySets. The first method provides you with a QuerySet API such as `Post.objects.my_manager()`, and the latter provides you with `Post.my_manager.all()`. The manager will allow us to retrieve posts using `Post.published.all()`.

Edit the `models.py` file of your `blog` application to add the custom manager:

```
class PublishedManager(models.Manager):
    def get_queryset(self):
        return super(PublishedManager,
                      self).get_queryset()\
                            .filter(status='published')

class Post(models.Model):
    # ...
    objects = models.Manager() # The default manager.
    published = PublishedManager() # Our custom manager.
```

The `get_queryset()` method of a manager returns the QuerySet that will be executed. We override this method to include our custom filter in the final QuerySet. We have defined our custom manager and added it to the `Post` model; we can now use it to perform queries. Let's test it.

Start the development server again with the following command:

```
python manage.py shell
```

Now, you can retrieve all published posts whose title starts with `Who` using the following command:

```
Post.published.filter(title__startswith='Who')
```

Building list and detail views

Now that you have knowledge of how to use the ORM, you are ready to build the views of the blog application. A Django view is just a Python function that receives a web request and returns a web response. All the logic to return the desired response goes inside the view.

First, we will create our application views, then we will define a URL pattern for each view, and finally, we will create HTML templates to render the data generated by the views. Each view will render a template passing variables to it and will return an HTTP response with the rendered output.

Creating list and detail views

Let's start by creating a view to display the list of posts. Edit the `views.py` file of your `blog` application and make it look like this:

```
from django.shortcuts import render, get_object_or_404
from .models import Post

def post_list(request):
    posts = Post.published.all()
    return render(request,
                  'blog/post/list.html',
                  {'posts': posts})
```

You just created your first Django view. The `post_list` view takes the `request` object as the only parameter. Remember that this parameter is required by all views. In this view, we are retrieving all the posts with the `published` status using the `published` manager we created previously.

Finally, we are using the `render()` shortcut provided by Django to render the list of posts with the given template. This function takes the `request` object, the template path, and the context variables to render the given template. It returns an `HttpResponse` object with the rendered text (normally, HTML code). The `render()` shortcut takes the request context into account, so any variable set by template context processors is accessible by the given template. Template context processors are just callables that set variables into the context. You will learn how to use them in `Chapter 3`, *Extending Your Blog Application*.

Let's create a second view to display a single post. Add the following function to the `views.py` file:

```
def post_detail(request, year, month, day, post):
    post = get_object_or_404(Post, slug=post,
                                   status='published',
                                   publish__year=year,
                                   publish__month=month,
                                   publish__day=day)
    return render(request,
                  'blog/post/detail.html',
                  {'post': post})
```

This is the post detail view. This view takes `year`, `month`, `day`, and `post` parameters to retrieve a published post with the given slug and date. Note that when we created the `Post` model, we added the `unique_for_date` parameter to the `slug` field. This way, we ensure that there will be only one post with a slug for a given date, and thus, we can retrieve single posts using date and slug. In the detail view, we use the `get_object_or_404()` shortcut to retrieve the desired post. This function retrieves the object that matches the given parameters or launches an HTTP 404 (not found) exception if no object is found. Finally, we use the `render()` shortcut to render the retrieved post using a template.

Adding URL patterns for your views

URL patterns allow you to map URLs to views. A URL pattern is composed of a string pattern, a view, and, optionally, a name that allows you to name the URL project-wide. Django runs through each URL pattern and stops at the first one that matches the requested URL. Then, Django imports the view of the matching URL pattern and executes it, passing an instance of the `HttpRequest` class and keyword or positional arguments.

Create an `urls.py` file in the directory of the `blog` application and add the following lines to it:

```
from django.urls import path
from . import views

app_name = 'blog'

urlpatterns = [
    # post views
    path('', views.post_list, name='post_list'),
    path('<int:year>/<int:month>/<int:day>/<slug:post>/',
        views.post_detail,
        name='post_detail'),
]
```

In the preceding code, we define an application namespace with the `app_name` variable. This allows us to organize URLs by application and use the name when referring to them. We define two different patterns using the `path()` function. The first URL pattern doesn't take any arguments and is mapped to the `post_list` view. The second pattern takes the following four arguments and is mapped to the `post_detail` view:

- `year`: Requires an integer
- `month`: Requires an integer
- `day`: Requires an integer
- `post`: Can be composed of words and hyphens

We use angle brackets to capture the values from the URL. Any value specified in the URL pattern as `<parameter>` is captured as a string. We use path converters, such as `<int:year>`, to specifically match and return an integer and `<slug:post>` to specifically match a slug (a string consisting of ASCII letters or numbers, plus the hyphen and underscore characters). You can see all path converters provided by Django at `https:/` `/docs.djangoproject.com/en/2.0/topics/http/urls/#path-converters`.

If using `path()` and converters isn't sufficient for you, you can use `re_path()` instead to define complex URL patterns with Python regular expressions. You can learn more about defining URL patterns with regular expressions at `https://docs.djangoproject.com/en/2.0/ref/urls/#django.urls.re_path`. If you haven't worked with regular expressions before, you might want to take a look at the *Regular Expression HOWTO* located at `https://docs.python.org/3/howto/regex.html` first.

 Creating a `urls.py` file for each app is the best way to make your applications reusable by other projects.

Now, you have to include the URL patterns of the `blog` application in the main URL patterns of the project. Edit the `urls.py` file located in the `mysite` directory of your project and make it look like the following:

```python
from django.urls import path, include
from django.contrib import admin

urlpatterns = [
    path('admin/', admin.site.urls),
    path('blog/', include('blog.urls', namespace='blog')),
]
```

The new URL pattern defined with `include` refers to the URL patterns defined in the blog application so that they are included under the `blog/` path. We include these patterns under the namespace `blog`. Namespaces have to be unique across your entire project. Later, we will refer to our blog URLs easily by including the namespace, building them, for example, `blog:post_list` and `blog:post_detail`. You can learn more about URL namespaces at `https://docs.djangoproject.com/en/2.0/topics/http/urls/#url-namespaces`.

Canonical URLs for models

You can use the `post_detail` URL that you have defined in the preceding section to build the canonical URL for `Post` objects. The convention in Django is to add a `get_absolute_url()` method to the model that returns the canonical URL of the object. For this method, we will use the `reverse()` method that allows you to build URLs by their name and passing optional parameters. Edit your `models.py` file and add the following:

```
from django.urls import reverse

class Post(models.Model):
    # ...
    def get_absolute_url(self):
        return reverse('blog:post_detail',
                       args=[self.publish.year,
                             self.publish.month,
                             self.publish.day,
                             self.slug])
```

We will use the `get_absolute_url()` method in our templates to link to specific posts.

Creating templates for your views

We have created views and URL patterns for the `blog` application. Now, it's time to add templates to display posts in a user-friendly manner.

Create the following directories and files inside your `blog` application directory:

```
templates/
    blog/
        base.html
        post/
            list.html
```

```
detail.html
```

The preceding structure will be the file structure for our templates. The base.html file will include the main HTML structure of the website and divide the content into the main content area and a sidebar. The list.html and detail.html files will inherit from the base.html file to render the blog post list and detail views, respectively.

Django has a powerful template language that allows you to specify how data is displayed. It is based on *template tags*, *template variables,* and *template filters*:

- Template tags control the rendering of the template and look like {% tag %}.
- Template variables get replaced with values when the template is rendered and look like {{ variable }}.
- Template filters allow you to modify variables for display and look like {{ variable|**filter** }}.

You can see all built-in template tags and filters in https://docs.djangoproject.com/en/2.0/ref/templates/builtins/.

Let's edit the base.html file and add the following code:

```
{% load static %}
<!DOCTYPE html>
<html>
<head>
  <title>{% block title %}{% endblock %}</title>
  <link href="{% static "css/blog.css" %}" rel="stylesheet">
</head>
<body>
  <div id="content">
    {% block content %}
    {% endblock %}
  </div>
  <div id="sidebar">
    <h2>My blog</h2>
      <p>This is my blog.</p>
  </div>
</body>
</html>
```

`{% load static %}` tells Django to load the `static` template tags that are provided by the `django.contrib.staticfiles` application, which is contained in the `INSTALLED_APPS` setting. After loading it, you are able to use the `{% static %}` template filter throughout this template. With this template filter, you can include static files, such as the `blog.css` file, that you will find in the code of this example under the `static/` directory of the `blog` application. Copy the `static/` directory from the code that comes along with this chapter into the same location of your project to apply the CSS style sheets.

You can see that there are two `{% block %}` tags. These tell Django that we want to define a block in that area. Templates that inherit from this template can fill in the blocks with content. We have defined a block called `title` and a block called `content`.

Let's edit the `post/list.html` file and make it look like the following:

```
{% extends "blog/base.html" %}

{% block title %}My Blog{% endblock %}

{% block content %}
  <h1>My Blog</h1>
  {% for post in posts %}
    <h2>
      <a href="{{ post.get_absolute_url }}">
        {{ post.title }}
      </a>
    </h2>
    <p class="date">
      Published {{ post.publish }} by {{ post.author }}
    </p>
    {{ post.body|truncatewords:30|linebreaks }}
  {% endfor %}
{% endblock %}
```

With the `{% extends %}` template tag, we tell Django to inherit from the `blog/base.html` template. Then, we are filling the `title` and `content` blocks of the base template with content. We iterate through the posts and display their title, date, author, and body, including a link in the title to the canonical URL of the post. In the body of the post, we are applying two template filters: `truncatewords` truncates the value to the number of words specified, and `linebreaks` converts the output into HTML line breaks. You can concatenate as many template filters as you wish; each one will be applied to the output generated by the preceding one.

Open the shell and execute the `python manage.py runserver` command to start the development server. Open `http://127.0.0.1:8000/blog/` in your browser, and you will see everything running. Note that you need to have some posts with the **Published** status to show them here. You should see something like this:

Then, let's edit the `post/detail.html` file:

```
{% extends "blog/base.html" %}

{% block title %}{{ post.title }}{% endblock %}

{% block content %}
  <h1>{{ post.title }}</h1>
  <p class="date">
    Published {{ post.publish }} by {{ post.author }}
  </p>
  {{ post.body|linebreaks }}
{% endblock %}
```

Now, you can return to your browser and click on one of the post titles to take a look at the detail view of a post. You should see something like this:

Take a look at the URL—it should be `/blog/2017/12/14/who-was-django-reinhardt/`. We have designed SEO-friendly URLs for our blog posts.

Adding pagination

When you start adding content to your blog, you will soon realize you need to split the list of posts across several pages. Django has a built-in pagination class that allows you to manage paginated data easily.

Edit the `views.py` file of the `blog` application to import the Django paginator classes and modify the `post_list` view, as follows:

```
from django.core.paginator import Paginator, EmptyPage,\
                                  PageNotAnInteger

def post_list(request):
    object_list = Post.published.all()
    paginator = Paginator(object_list, 3) # 3 posts in each page
    page = request.GET.get('page')
    try:
        posts = paginator.page(page)
    except PageNotAnInteger:
        # If page is not an integer deliver the first page
        posts = paginator.page(1)
    except EmptyPage:
        # If page is out of range deliver last page of results
        posts = paginator.page(paginator.num_pages)
    return render(request,
                  'blog/post/list.html',
                  {'page': page,
                   'posts': posts})
```

This is how pagination works:

1. We instantiate the `Paginator` class with the number of objects we want to display on each page.
2. We get the `page` `GET` parameter that indicates the current page number.
3. We obtain the objects for the desired page calling the `page()` method of `Paginator`.
4. If the `page` parameter is not an integer, we retrieve the first page of results. If this parameter is a number higher than the last page of results, we will retrieve the last page.
5. We pass the page number and retrieved objects to the template.

Now, we have to create a template to display the paginator so that it can be included in any template that uses pagination. In the `templates/` folder of the `blog` application, create a new file and name it `pagination.html`. Add the following HTML code to the file:

```
<div class="pagination">
  <span class="step-links">
    {% if page.has_previous %}
      <a href="?page={{ page.previous_page_number }}">Previous</a>
    {% endif %}
    <span class="current">
      Page {{ page.number }} of {{ page.paginator.num_pages }}.
    </span>
      {% if page.has_next %}
        <a href="?page={{ page.next_page_number }}">Next</a>
      {% endif %}
  </span>
</div>
```

The pagination template expects a `Page` object in order to render previous and next links and to display the current page and total pages of results. Let's return to the `blog/post/list.html` template and include the `pagination.html` template at the bottom of the `{% content %}` block, as follows:

```
{% block content %}
  ...
  {% include "pagination.html" with page=posts %}
{% endblock %}
```

Since the `Page` object we are passing to the template is called `posts`, we include the pagination template in the post list template, passing the parameters to render it correctly. You can follow this method to reuse your pagination template in paginated views of different models.

Now, open `http://127.0.0.1:8000/blog/` in your browser. You should see the pagination at the bottom of the post list and should be able to navigate through pages:

Using class-based views

Class-based views are an alternative way to implement views as Python objects instead of functions. Since a view is a callable that takes a web request and returns a web response, you can also define your views as class methods. Django provides base view classes for this. All of them inherit from the `View` class, which handles HTTP method dispatching and other common functionalities.

Class-based views offer advantages over function-based views for some use cases. They have the following features:

- Organizing code related to HTTP methods, such as GET, POST, or PUT, in separate methods instead of using conditional branching
- Using multiple inheritance to create reusable view classes (also known as *mixins*)

You can take a look at an introduction to class-based views at https://docs.djangoproject.com/en/2.0/topics/class-based-views/intro/.

We will change our post_list view into a class-based view to use the generic ListView offered by Django. This base view allows you to list objects of any kind.

Edit the views.py file of your blog application and add the following code:

```
from django.views.generic import ListView

class PostListView(ListView):
    queryset = Post.published.all()
    context_object_name = 'posts'
    paginate_by = 3
    template_name = 'blog/post/list.html'
```

This class-based view is analogous to the previous post_list view. In the preceding code, we are telling ListView to do the following things:

- Use a specific QuerySet instead of retrieving all objects. Instead of defining a queryset attribute, we could have specified model = Post and Django would have built the generic Post.objects.all() QuerySet for us.
- Use the context variable posts for the query results. The default variable is object_list if we don't specify any context_object_name.
- Paginate the result displaying three objects per page.
- Use a custom template to render the page. If we don't set a default template, ListView will use blog/post_list.html.

Now, open the `urls.py` file of your `blog` application, comment the preceding `post_list` URL pattern, and add a new URL pattern using the `PostListView` class, as follows:

```
urlpatterns = [
    # post views
    # path('', views.post_list, name='post_list'),
    path('', views.PostListView.as_view(), name='post_list'),
    path('<int:year>/<int:month>/<int:day>/<slug:post>/',
        views.post_detail,
        name='post_detail'),
]
```

In order to keep pagination working, we have to use the right page object that is passed to the template. Django's `ListView` generic view passes the selected page in a variable called `page_obj`, so you have to edit your `post/list.html` template accordingly to include the paginator using the right variable, as follows:

```
{% include "pagination.html" with page=page_obj %}
```

Open `http://127.0.0.1:8000/blog/` in your browser and verify that everything works the same way as with the previous `post_list` view. This is a simple example of a class-based view that uses a generic class provided by Django. You will learn more about class-based views in `Chapter 10`, *Building an E-Learning Platform*, and successive chapters.

Summary

In this chapter, you have learned the basics of the Django web framework by creating a basic blog application. You have designed the data models and applied migrations to your project. You have created the views, templates, and URLs for your blog, including object pagination.

In the next chapter, you will learn how to enhance your blog application with a comment system and tagging functionality and allow your users to share posts by email.

2
Enhancing Your Blog with Advanced Features

In the preceding chapter, you created a basic blog application. Now, you will turn your application into a fully functional blog with advanced features, such as sharing posts by email, adding comments, tagging posts, and retrieving posts by similarity. In this chapter, you will learn the following topics:

- Sending emails with Django
- Creating forms and handling them in views
- Creating forms from models
- Integrating third-party applications
- Building complex QuerySets

Sharing posts by email

First, we will allow users to share posts by sending them emails. Take a short time to think how you would use *views*, *URLs*, and *templates* to create this functionality using what you have learned in the preceding chapter. Now, check what you need in order to allow your users to send posts by email. You will need to do the following things:

- Create a form for users to fill in their name and email, the email recipient, and optional comments
- Create a view in the `views.py` file that handles the posted data and sends the email
- Add a URL pattern for the new view in the `urls.py` file of the blog application
- Create a template to display the form

Creating forms with Django

Let's start by building the form to share posts. Django has a built-in forms framework that allows you to create forms in an easy manner. The forms framework allows you to define the fields of your form, specify how they have to be displayed, and indicate how they have to validate input data. The Django forms framework offers a flexible way to render forms and handle the data.

Django comes with two base classes to build forms:

- Form: Allows you to build standard forms
- ModelForm: Allows you to build forms tied to model instances

First, create a forms.py file inside the directory of your blog application and make it look like this:

```python
from django import forms

class EmailPostForm(forms.Form):
    name = forms.CharField(max_length=25)
    email = forms.EmailField()
    to = forms.EmailField()
    comments = forms.CharField(required=False,
                               widget=forms.Textarea)
```

This is your first Django form. Take a look at the code. We have created a form by inheriting the base Form class. We use different field types for Django to validate fields accordingly.

 Forms can reside anywhere in your Django project. The convention is to place them inside a forms.py file for each application.

The name field is CharField. This type of field is rendered as an `<input type="text">` HTML element. Each field type has a default widget that determines how the field is rendered in HTML. The default widget can be overridden with the widget attribute. In the comments field, we use a Textarea widget to display it as a `<textarea>` HTML element instead of the default `<input>` element.

Field validation also depends on the field type. For example, the email and to fields are EmailField fields. Both fields require a valid email address, otherwise, the field validation will raise a forms.ValidationError exception and the form will not validate. Other parameters are also taken into account for form validation: we define a maximum length of 25 characters for the name field and make the comments field optional with required=False. All of this is also taken into account for field validation. The field types used in this form are only a part of Django form fields. For a list of all form fields available, you can visit https://docs.djangoproject.com/en/2.0/ref/forms/fields/.

Handling forms in views

You have to create a new view that handles the form and sends an email when it's successfully submitted. Edit the views.py file of your blog application and add the following code to it:

```python
from .forms import EmailPostForm

def post_share(request, post_id):
    # Retrieve post by id
    post = get_object_or_404(Post, id=post_id, status='published')

    if request.method == 'POST':
        # Form was submitted
        form = EmailPostForm(request.POST)
        if form.is_valid():
            # Form fields passed validation
            cd = form.cleaned_data
            # ... send email
    else:
        form = EmailPostForm()
    return render(request, 'blog/post/share.html', {'post': post,
                                                    'form': form})
```

This view works as follows:

- We define the post_share view that takes the request object and the post_id variable as parameters.
- We use the get_object_or_404() shortcut to retrieve the post by ID and make sure that the retrieved post has a published status.

- We use the same view for both displaying the initial form and processing the submitted data. We differentiate whether the form was submitted or not based on the `request` method and submit the form using `POST`. We assume that if we get a `GET` request, an empty form has to be displayed, and if we get a `POST` request, the form is submitted and needs to be processed. Therefore, we use `request.method == 'POST'` to distinguish between the two scenarios.

The following is the process to display and handle the form:

1. When the view is loaded initially with a `GET` request, we create a new `form` instance that will be used to display the empty form in the template:

   ```
   form = EmailPostForm()
   ```

2. The user fills in the form and submits it via `POST`. Then, we create a form instance using the submitted data that is contained in `request.POST`:

   ```
   if request.method == 'POST':
       # Form was submitted
       form = EmailPostForm(request.POST)
   ```

3. After this, we validate the submitted data using the form's `is_valid()` method. This method validates the data introduced in the form and returns `True` if all fields contain valid data. If any field contains invalid data, then `is_valid()` returns `False`. You can see a list of validation errors by accessing `form.errors`.

4. If the form is not valid, we render the form in the template again with the submitted data. We will display validation errors in the template.

5. If the form is valid, we retrieve the validated data accessing `form.cleaned_data`. This attribute is a dictionary of form fields and their values.

 If your form data does not validate, `cleaned_data` will contain only the valid fields.

Now, let's learn how to send emails using Django to put everything together.

Sending emails with Django

Sending emails with Django is pretty straightforward. First, you will need to have a local SMTP server or define the configuration of an external SMTP server by adding the following settings in the `settings.py` file of your project:

- `EMAIL_HOST`: The SMTP server host; the default is `localhost`
- `EMAIL_PORT`: The SMTP port; the default is `25`
- `EMAIL_HOST_USER`: Username for the SMTP server
- `EMAIL_HOST_PASSWORD`: Password for the SMTP server
- `EMAIL_USE_TLS`: Whether to use a TLS secure connection
- `EMAIL_USE_SSL`: Whether to use an implicit TLS secure connection

If you cannot use an SMTP server, you can tell Django to write emails to the console by adding the following setting to the `settings.py` file:

```
EMAIL_BACKEND = 'django.core.mail.backends.console.EmailBackend'
```

By using this setting, Django will output all emails to the shell. This is very useful for testing your application without an SMTP server.

If you want to send emails, but you don't have a local SMTP server, you can probably use the SMTP server of your email service provider. The following sample configuration is valid for sending emails via Gmail servers using a Google account:

```
EMAIL_HOST = 'smtp.gmail.com'
EMAIL_HOST_USER = 'your_account@gmail.com'
EMAIL_HOST_PASSWORD = 'your_password'
EMAIL_PORT = 587
EMAIL_USE_TLS = True
```

Run the `python manage.py shell` command to open the Python shell and send an email, as follows:

```
>>> from django.core.mail import send_mail
>>> send_mail('Django mail', 'This e-mail was sent with Django.',
'your_account@gmail.com', ['your_account@gmail.com'], fail_silently=False)
```

The `send_mail()` function takes the subject, message, sender, and list of recipients as required arguments. By setting the optional argument `fail_silently=False`, we are telling it to raise an exception if the email couldn't be sent correctly. If the output you see is `1`, then your email was successfully sent.

If you are sending emails by Gmail with the preceding configuration, you might have to enable access for less secured apps at `https://myaccount.google.com/lesssecureapps`, as follows:

Some apps and devices use less secure sign-in technology, which makes your account more vulnerable. You can **turn off** access for these apps, which we recommend, or **turn on** access if you want to use them despite the risks. Learn more

Allow less secure apps: ON

Now, we will add this functionality to our view.

Edit the `post_share` view in the `views.py` file of the `blog` application as follows:

```python
from django.core.mail import send_mail

def post_share(request, post_id):
    # Retrieve post by id
    post = get_object_or_404(Post, id=post_id, status='published')
    sent = False

    if request.method == 'POST':
        # Form was submitted
        form = EmailPostForm(request.POST)
        if form.is_valid():
            # Form fields passed validation
            cd = form.cleaned_data
            post_url = request.build_absolute_uri(
                                        post.get_absolute_url())
            subject = '{} ({}) recommends you reading "
{}"'.format(cd['name'], cd['email'], post.title)
            message = 'Read "{}" at {}\n\n{}\'s comments:
{}'.format(post.title, post_url, cd['name'], cd['comments'])
            send_mail(subject, message, 'admin@myblog.com',
 [cd['to']])
            sent = True
    else:
        form = EmailPostForm()
    return render(request, 'blog/post/share.html', {'post': post,
                                        'form': form,
                                        'sent': sent})
```

We declare a `sent` variable and set it to `True` when the post was sent. We will use that variable later in the template to display a success message when the form is successfully submitted. Since we have to include a link to the post in the email, we will retrieve the absolute path of the post using its `get_absolute_url()` method. We use this path as an input for `request.build_absolute_uri()` to build a complete URL, including HTTP schema and hostname. We build the subject and the message body of the email using the cleaned data of the validated form and finally send the email to the email address contained in the `to` field of the form.

Now that your view is complete, remember to add a new URL pattern for it. Open the `urls.py` file of your `blog` application and add the `post_share` URL pattern, as follows:

```
urlpatterns = [
    # ...
    path('<int:post_id>/share/',
        views.post_share, name='post_share'),
]
```

Rendering forms in templates

After creating the form, programming the view, and adding the URL pattern, we are only missing the template for this view. Create a new file in the `blog/templates/blog/post/` directory and name it `share.html`; add the following code to it:

```
{% extends "blog/base.html" %}

{% block title %}Share a post{% endblock %}

{% block content %}
  {% if sent %}
    <h1>E-mail successfully sent</h1>
    <p>
      "{{ post.title }}" was successfully sent to {{ form.cleaned_data.to }}.
    </p>
  {% else %}
    <h1>Share "{{ post.title }}" by e-mail</h1>
    <form action="." method="post">
      {{ form.as_p }}
      {% csrf_token %}
      <input type="submit" value="Send e-mail">
    </form>
  {% endif %}
{% endblock %}
```

This is the template to display the form or a success message when it's sent. As you would notice, we create the HTML form element, indicating that it has to be submitted by the POST method:

```
<form action="." method="post">
```

Then, we include the actual form instance. We tell Django to render its fields in HTML paragraph <p> elements with the as_p method. We can also render the form as an unordered list with as_ul or as an HTML table with as_table. If we want to render each field, we can also iterate through the fields, as in the following example:

```
{% for field in form %}
  <div>
    {{ field.errors }}
    {{ field.label_tag }} {{ field }}
  </div>
{% endfor %}
```

The {% csrf_token %} template tag introduces a hidden field with an autogenerated token to avoid **cross-site request forgery** (CSRF) attacks. These attacks consist of a malicious website or program performing an unwanted action for a user on your site. You can find more information about this at https://www.owasp.org/index.php/Cross-Site_Request_Forgery_(CSRF).

The preceding tag generates a hidden field that looks like this:

```
<input type='hidden' name='csrfmiddlewaretoken'
value='26JjKo21cEtYkGoV9z4XmJIEHLXN5LDR' />
```

 By default, Django checks for the CSRF token in all POST requests. Remember that you include the csrf_token tag in all forms that are submitted via POST.

Edit your blog/post/detail.html template and add the following link to the share post URL after the {{ post.body|linebreaks }} variable:

```
<p>
  <a href="{% url "blog:post_share" post.id %}">
    Share this post
  </a>
</p>
```

Remember that we are building the URL dynamically using the `{% url %}` template tag provided by Django. We are using the namespace called `blog` and the URL named `post_share`, and we are passing the post ID as a parameter to build the absolute URL.

Now, start the development server with the `python manage.py runserver` command and open `http://127.0.0.1:8000/blog/` in your browser. Click on any post title to view its detail page. Under the post body, you should see the link we just added, as shown in the following screenshot:

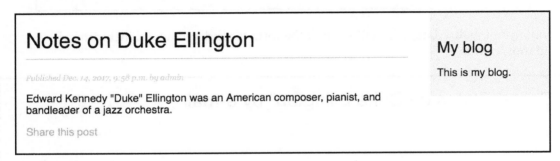

Click on **Share this post**, and you should see the page including the form to share this post by email, as follows:

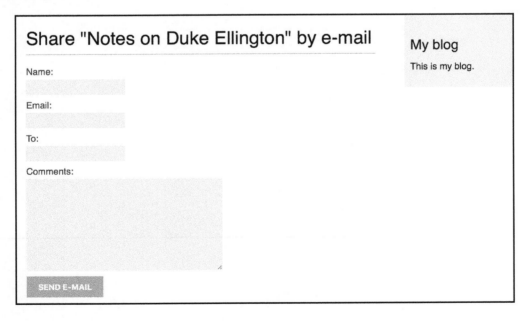

CSS styles for the form are included in the example code in the `static/css/blog.css` file. When you click on the **SEND E-MAIL** button, the form is submitted and validated. If all fields contain valid data, you will get a success message, as follows:

If you input invalid data, you will see that the form is rendered again, including all validation errors:

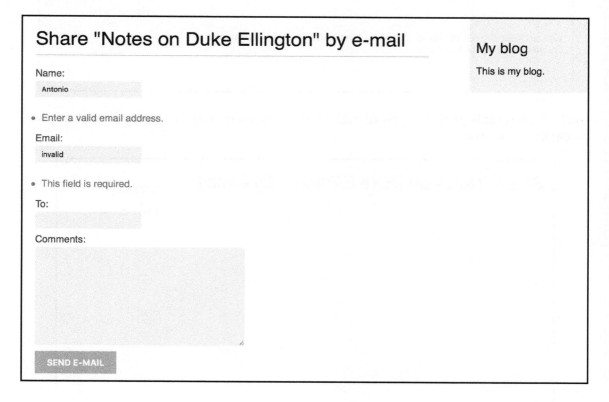

Note that some modern browsers will prevent you from submitting the form with empty or erroneous fields. This is because of form validation done by the browser based on field types and restrictions per field. In this case, the form won't be submitted and the browser will display an error message for the fields that are wrong.

Our form for sharing posts by email is now complete. Let's create a comment system for our blog.

Creating a comment system

Now, we will build a comment system for the blog, wherein the users will be able to comment on posts. To build the comment system, you will need to do the following steps:

1. Create a model to save comments
2. Create a form to submit comments and validate the input data
3. Add a view that processes the form and saves the new comment to the database
4. Edit the post detail template to display the list of comments and the form to add a new comment

First, let's build a model to store comments. Open the `models.py` file of your `blog` application and add the following code:

```python
class Comment(models.Model):
    post = models.ForeignKey(Post,
                             on_delete=models.CASCADE,
                             related_name='comments')
    name = models.CharField(max_length=80)
    email = models.EmailField()
    body = models.TextField()
    created = models.DateTimeField(auto_now_add=True)
    updated = models.DateTimeField(auto_now=True)
    active = models.BooleanField(default=True)

    class Meta:
        ordering = ('created',)

    def __str__(self):
        return 'Comment by {} on {}'.format(self.name, self.post)
```

This is our `Comment` model. It contains `ForeignKey` to associate the comment with a single post. This many-to-one relationship is defined in the `Comment` model because each comment will be made on one post, and each post may have multiple comments. The `related_name` attribute allows us to name the attribute that we use for the relation from the related object back to this one. After defining this, we can retrieve the post of a comment object using `comment.post` and retrieve all comments of a post using `post.comments.all()`. If you don't define the `related_name` attribute, Django will use the name of the model in lowercase, followed by `_set` (that is, `comment_set`) to name the manager of the related object back to this one.

You can learn more about many-to-one relationships at `https://docs.djangoproject.com/en/2.0/topics/db/examples/many_to_one/`.

We have included an `active` boolean field that we will use to manually deactivate inappropriate comments. We use the `created` field to sort comments in a chronological order by default.

The new `Comment` model you just created is not yet synchronized into the database. Run the following command to generate a new migration that reflects the creation of the new model:

```
python manage.py makemigrations blog
```

You should see the following output:

```
Migrations for 'blog':
  blog/migrations/0002_comment.py
    - Create model Comment
```

Django has generated a `0002_comment.py` file inside the `migrations/` directory of the `blog` application. Now, you will need to create the related database schema and apply the changes to the database. Run the following command to apply existing migrations:

```
python manage.py migrate
```

You will get an output that includes the following line:

```
Applying blog.0002_comment... OK
```

The migration we just created has been applied, and, now, a `blog_comment` table exists in the database.

Now, we can add our new model to the administration site in order to manage comments through a simple interface. Open the `admin.py` file of the `blog` application, import the `Comment` model, and add the following `ModelAdmin` class:

```
from .models import Post, Comment

@admin.register(Comment)
class CommentAdmin(admin.ModelAdmin):
    list_display = ('name', 'email', 'post', 'created', 'active')
    list_filter = ('active', 'created', 'updated')
    search_fields = ('name', 'email', 'body')
```

Start the development server with the `python manage.py runserver` command and open `http://127.0.0.1:8000/admin/` in your browser. You should see the new model included in the **BLOG** section, as shown in the following screenshot:

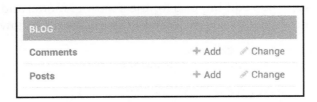

The model is now registered in the admin site, and we can manage `Comment` instances using a simple interface.

Creating forms from models

We will still need to build a form to let our users comment on blog posts. Remember that Django has two base classes to build forms, `Form` and `ModelForm`. You used the first one previously to let your users share posts by email. In the present case, you will need to use `ModelForm` because you have to build a form dynamically from your `Comment` model. Edit the `forms.py` file of your `blog` application and add the following lines:

```
from .models import Comment

class CommentForm(forms.ModelForm):
    class Meta:
        model = Comment
        fields = ('name', 'email', 'body')
```

To create a form from a model, we will just need to indicate which model to use to build the form in the Meta class of the form. Django introspects the model and builds the form dynamically for us. Each model field type has a corresponding default form field type. The way we define our model fields is taken into account for form validation. By default, Django builds a form field for each field contained in the model. However, you can explicitly tell the framework which fields you want to include in your form using a fields list or define which fields you want to exclude using an exclude list of fields. For our CommentForm form, we will just use the name, email, and body fields because those are the only fields our users will be able to fill in.

Handling ModelForms in views

We will use the post detail view to instantiate the form and process it in order to keep it simple. Edit the views.py file, add imports for the Comment model and the CommentForm form, and modify the post_detail view to make it look like the following:

```python
from .models import Post, Comment
from .forms import EmailPostForm, CommentForm

def post_detail(request, year, month, day, post):
    post = get_object_or_404(Post, slug=post,
                                   status='published',
                                   publish__year=year,
                                   publish__month=month,
                                   publish__day=day)

    # List of active comments for this post
    comments = post.comments.filter(active=True)

    new_comment = None

    if request.method == 'POST':
        # A comment was posted
        comment_form = CommentForm(data=request.POST)
        if comment_form.is_valid():
            # Create Comment object but don't save to database yet
            new_comment = comment_form.save(commit=False)
            # Assign the current post to the comment
            new_comment.post = post
            # Save the comment to the database
            new_comment.save()
    else:
        comment_form = CommentForm()
    return render(request,
```

```
'blog/post/detail.html',
{'post': post,
 'comments': comments,
 'new_comment': new_comment,
 'comment_form': comment_form})
```

Let's review what we have added to our view. We used the `post_detail` view to display the post and its comments. We added a QuerySet to retrieve all active comments for this post, as follows:

```
comments = post.comments.filter(active=True)
```

We build this QuerySet, starting from the `post` object. We use the manager for related objects we defined as `comments` using the `related_name` attribute of the relationship in the `Comment` model.

We also use the same view to let our users add a new comment. Therefore, we initialize the `new_comment` variable by setting it to `None`. We will use this variable when a new comment is created. We build a form instance with `comment_form = CommentForm()` if the view is called by a `GET` request. If the request is done via `POST`, we instantiate the form using the submitted data and validate it using the `is_valid()` method. If the form is invalid, we render the template with the validation errors. If the form is valid, we take the following actions:

1. We create a new `Comment` object by calling the form's `save()` method and assign it to the `new_comment` variable as follows:

   ```
   new_comment = comment_form.save(commit=False)
   ```

   The `save()` method creates an instance of the model that the form is linked to and saves it to the database. If you call it using `commit=False`, you create the model instance, but you don't save it to the database yet. This comes in handy when you want to modify the object before finally saving it, which is what we do next.

 The `save()` method is available for `ModelForm` but not for `Form` instances, since they are not linked to any model.

2. We assign the current post to the comment we just created:

```
new_comment.post = post
```

By doing this, we are specifying that the new comment belongs to this post.

3. Finally, we save the new comment to the database by calling its `save()` method:

```
new_comment.save()
```

Our view is now ready to display and process new comments.

Adding comments to the post detail template

We have created the functionality to manage comments for a post. Now, we will need to adapt our `post/detail.html` template to do the following things:

- Display the total number of comments for the post
- Display the list of comments
- Display a form for users to add a new comment

First, we will add the total comments. Open the `post/detail.html` template and append the following code to the `content` block:

```
{% with comments.count as total_comments %}
  <h2>
    {{ total_comments }} comment{{ total_comments|pluralize }}
  </h2>
{% endwith %}
```

We are using the Django ORM in the template, executing the QuerySet `comments.count()`. Note that Django template language doesn't use parentheses for calling methods. The `{% with %}` tag allows us to assign a value to a new variable that will be available to be used until the `{% endwith %}` tag.

 The `{% with %}` template tag is useful to avoid hitting the database or accessing *expensive* methods multiple times.

We use the `pluralize` template filter to display a plural suffix for the word *comment*, depending on the `total_comments` value. Template filters take the value of the variable they are applied to as their input and return a computed value. We will discuss template filters in `Chapter 3`, *Extending Your Blog Application*.

The `pluralize` template filter returns a string with the letter *"s"* if the value is different from 1. The preceding text will be rendered as *0 comments, 1 comment*, or *N comments*. Django includes plenty of template tags and filters that help you display information in the way you want.

Now, let's include the list of comments. Append the following lines to the `post/detail.html` template below the preceding code:

```
{% for comment in comments %}
  <div class="comment">
    <p class="info">
      Comment {{ forloop.counter }} by {{ comment.name }}
      {{ comment.created }}
    </p>
    {{ comment.body|linebreaks }}
  </div>
{% empty %}
  <p>There are no comments yet.</p>
{% endfor %}
```

We use the `{% for %}` template tag to loop through comments. We display a default message if the `comments` list is empty, informing our users that there are no comments on this post yet. We enumerate comments with the `{{ forloop.counter }}` variable, which contains the loop counter in each iteration. Then, we display the name of the user who posted the comment, the date, and the body of the comment.

Finally, you need to render the form or display a successful message instead when it is successfully submitted. Add the following lines just below the preceding code:

```
{% if new_comment %}
  <h2>Your comment has been added.</h2>
{% else %}
  <h2>Add a new comment</h2>
  <form action="." method="post">
    {{ comment_form.as_p }}
    {% csrf_token %}
    <p><input type="submit" value="Add comment"></p>
  </form>
{% endif %}
```

The code is pretty straightforward: if the `new_comment` object exists, we display a success message because the comment was successfully created. Otherwise, we render the form with a paragraph <p> element for each field and include the CSRF token required for POST requests. Open `http://127.0.0.1:8000/blog/` in your browser and click on a post title to take a look at its detail page. You will see something like the following screenshot:

Add a couple of comments using the form. They should appear under your post in chronological order, as follows:

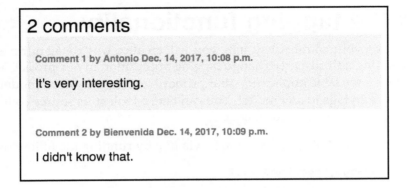

Open `http://127.0.0.1:8000/admin/blog/comment/` in your browser. You will see the admin page with the list of comments you created. Click on one of them to edit it, uncheck the **Active** checkbox, and click on the **Save** button. You will be redirected to the list of comments again, and the **Active** column will display an inactive icon for the comment. It should look like the first comment in the following screenshot:

If you return to the post detail view, you will note that the deleted comment is not displayed any more; neither is it being counted for the total number of comments. Thanks to the `active` field, you can deactivate inappropriate comments and avoid showing them in your posts.

Adding the tagging functionality

After implementing your comment system, you will create a way to tag our posts. You will do this by integrating a third-party Django tagging application in our project. The django-taggit module is a reusable application that primarily offers you a Tag model and a manager to easily add tags to any model. You can take a look at its source code at https://github.com/alex/django-taggit.

First, you will need to install django-taggit via pip by running the following command:

```
pip install django_taggit==0.22.2
```

Then, open the settings.py file of the mysite project and add taggit to your INSTALLED_APPS setting, as follows:

```
INSTALLED_APPS = [
    # ...
    'blog.apps.BlogConfig',
    'taggit',
]
```

Open the models.py file of your blog application and add the TaggableManager manager provided by django-taggit to the Post model using the following code:

```
from taggit.managers import TaggableManager

class Post(models.Model):
    # ...
    tags = TaggableManager()
```

The tags manager will allow you to add, retrieve, and remove tags from Post objects.

Run the following command to create a migration for your model changes:

```
python manage.py makemigrations blog
```

You should get the following output:

```
Migrations for 'blog':
  blog/migrations/0003_post_tags.py
    - Add field tags to post
```

Now, run the following command to create the required database tables for django-taggit models and to synchronize your model changes:

```
python manage.py migrate
```

You will see an output indicating that migrations have been applied, as follows:

```
Applying taggit.0001_initial... OK
Applying taggit.0002_auto_20150616_2121... OK
Applying blog.0003_post_tags... OK
```

Your database is now ready to use django-taggit models. Let's learn how to use the tags manager. Open the terminal with the python manage.py shell command and enter the following code; first, we will retrieve one of our posts (the one with the 1 ID):

```
>>> from blog.models import Post
>>> post = Post.objects.get(id=1)
```

Then, add some tags to it and retrieve its tags to check whether they were successfully added:

```
>>> post.tags.add('music', 'jazz', 'django')
>>> post.tags.all()
<QuerySet [<Tag: jazz>, <Tag: music>, <Tag: django>]>
```

Finally, remove a tag and check the list of tags again:

```
>>> post.tags.remove('django')
>>> post.tags.all()
<QuerySet [<Tag: jazz>, <Tag: music>]>
```

That was easy, right? Run the `python manage.py runserver` command to start the development server again and open `http://127.0.0.1:8000/admin/taggit/tag/` in your browser. You will see the admin page with the list of `Tag` objects of the `taggit` application:

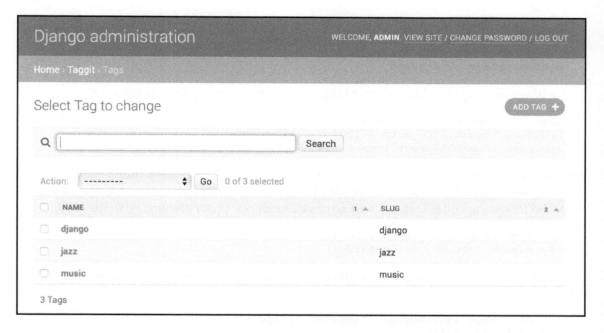

Navigate to `http://127.0.0.1:8000/admin/blog/post/` and click on a post to edit it. You will see that posts now include a new **Tags** field, as follows, where you can easily edit tags:

Now, we will edit our blog posts to display tags. Open the `blog/post/list.html` template and add the following HTML code below the post title:

```
<p class="tags">Tags: {{ post.tags.all|join:", " }}</p>
```

The `join` template filter works as the Python string `join()` method to concatenate elements with the given string. Open `http://127.0.0.1:8000/blog/` in your browser. You should be able to see the list of tags under each post title:

> # Who was Django Reinhardt?
>
> Tags: jazz, music
>
> Published Dec. 14, 2017, 8:54 a.m. by admin

Now, we will edit our `post_list` view to let users list all posts tagged with a specific tag. Open the `views.py` file of your `blog` application, import the `Tag` model form `django-taggit`, and change the `post_list` view to optionally filter posts by a tag, as follows:

```python
from taggit.models import Tag

def post_list(request, tag_slug=None):
    object_list = Post.published.all()
    tag = None

    if tag_slug:
        tag = get_object_or_404(Tag, slug=tag_slug)
        object_list = object_list.filter(tags__in=[tag])

    paginator = Paginator(object_list, 3) # 3 posts in each page
    # ...
```

The `post_list` view now works as follows:

1. It takes an optional `tag_slug` parameter that has a `None` default value. This parameter will come in the URL.
2. Inside the view, we build the initial QuerySet, retrieving all published posts, and if there is a given tag slug, we get the `Tag` object with the given slug using the `get_object_or_404()` shortcut.
3. Then, we filter the list of posts by the ones that contain the given tag. Since this is a many-to-many relationship, we have to filter by tags contained in a given list, which, in our case, contains only one element.

Remember that QuerySets are lazy. The QuerySets to retrieve posts will only be evaluated when we loop over the post list when rendering the template.

Finally, modify the render() function at the bottom of the view to pass the tag variable to the template. The view should finally look like this:

```
def post_list(request, tag_slug=None):
    object_list = Post.published.all()
    tag = None

    if tag_slug:
        tag = get_object_or_404(Tag, slug=tag_slug)
        object_list = object_list.filter(tags__in=[tag])

    paginator = Paginator(object_list, 3) # 3 posts in each page
    page = request.GET.get('page')
    try:
        posts = paginator.page(page)
    except PageNotAnInteger:
        # If page is not an integer deliver the first page
        posts = paginator.page(1)
    except EmptyPage:
        # If page is out of range deliver last page of results
        posts = paginator.page(paginator.num_pages)
    return render(request, 'blog/post/list.html', {'page': page,
                                                   'posts': posts,
                                                   'tag': tag})
```

Open the urls.py file of your blog application, comment out the class-based PostListView URL pattern, and uncomment the post_list view, like this:

```
path('', views.post_list, name='post_list'),
# path('', views.PostListView.as_view(), name='post_list'),
```

Add the following additional URL pattern to list posts by tag:

```
path('tag/<slug:tag_slug>/',
     views.post_list, name='post_list_by_tag'),
```

As you can see, both patterns point to the same view, but we are naming them differently. The first pattern will call the `post_list` view without any optional parameters, whereas the second pattern will call the view with the `tag_slug` parameter. We use a `slug` path converter for matching the parameter as a lowercase string with ASCII letters or numbers, plus the hyphen and underscore characters.

Since we are using the `post_list` view, edit the `blog/post/list.html` template and modify the pagination to use the `posts` object:

```
{% include "pagination.html" with page=posts %}
```

Add the following lines above the `{% for %}` loop:

```
{% if tag %}
  <h2>Posts tagged with "{{ tag.name }}"</h2>
{% endif %}
```

If the user is accessing the blog, they will see the list of all posts. If they filter by posts tagged with a specific tag, they will see the tag that they are filtering by. Now, change the way tags are displayed, as follows:

```
<p class="tags">
  Tags:
  {% for tag in post.tags.all %}
    <a href="{% url "blog:post_list_by_tag" tag.slug %}">
      {{ tag.name }}
    </a>
    {% if not forloop.last %}, {% endif %}
  {% endfor %}
</p>
```

Now, we loop through all the tags of a post displaying a custom link to the URL to filter posts by that tag. We build the URL with `{% url "blog:post_list_by_tag" tag.slug %}`, using the name of the URL and the `slug` tag as its parameter. We separate the tags by commas.

Open `http://127.0.0.1:8000/blog/` in your browser and click on any tag link. You will see the list of posts filtered by that tag, like this:

My Blog

Posts tagged with "jazz"

Who was Django Reinhardt?

Tags: jazz , music

Published Dec. 14, 2017, 8:54 a.m. by admin

Who was Django Reinhardt.

Page 1 of 1.

Retrieving posts by similarity

Now that we have implemented tagging for our blog posts, we can do many interesting things with them. Using tags, we can classify our blog posts very well. Posts about similar topics will have several tags in common. We will build a functionality to display similar posts by the number of tags they share. In this way, when a user reads a post, we can suggest to them that they read other related posts.

In order to retrieve similar posts for a specific post, we need to perform the following steps:

1. Retrieve all tags for the current post
2. Get all posts that are tagged with any of those tags
3. Exclude the current post from that list to avoid recommending the same post
4. Order the results by the number of tags shared with the current post
5. In case of two or more posts with the same number of tags, recommend the most recent post
6. Limit the query to the number of posts we want to recommend

These steps are translated into a complex QuerySet that we will include in our `post_detail` view. Open the `views.py` file of your blog application and add the following import at the top of it:

```
from django.db.models import Count
```

This is the `Count` aggregation function of the Django ORM. This function will allow us to perform aggregated counts of tags. `django.db.models` includes the following aggregation functions:

- `Avg`: The value average
- `Max`: The maximum value
- `Min`: The minimum value
- `Count`: The objects count

You can learn about aggregation at `https://docs.djangoproject.com/en/2.0/topics/db/aggregation/`.

Add the following lines inside the `post_detail` view before the `render()` function, with the same indentation level:

```
# List of similar posts
post_tags_ids = post.tags.values_list('id', flat=True)
similar_posts = Post.published.filter(tags__in=post_tags_ids)\
                            .exclude(id=post.id)
similar_posts = similar_posts.annotate(same_tags=Count('tags'))\
                            .order_by('-same_tags','-publish')[:4]
```

The preceding code is as follows:

1. We retrieve a Python list of IDs for the tags of the current post. The `values_list()` QuerySet returns tuples with the values for the given fields. We pass `flat=True` to it to get a flat list like `[1, 2, 3, ...]`.
2. We get all posts that contain any of these tags, excluding the current post itself.
3. We use the `Count` aggregation function to generate a calculated field—`same_tags`—that contains the number of tags shared with all the tags queried.
4. We order the result by the number of shared tags (descending order) and by `publish` to display recent posts first for the posts with the same number of shared tags. We slice the result to retrieve only the first four posts.

Add the `similar_posts` object to the context dictionary for the `render()` function, as follows:

```
return render(request,
              'blog/post/detail.html',
              {'post': post,
               'comments': comments,
               'new_comment': new_comment,
               'comment_form': comment_form,
               'similar_posts': similar_posts})
```

Now, edit the `blog/post/detail.html` template and add the following code before the post comments list:

```
<h2>Similar posts</h2>
{% for post in similar_posts %}
  <p>
    <a href="{{ post.get_absolute_url }}">{{ post.title }}</a>
  </p>
{% empty %}
  There are no similar posts yet.
{% endfor %}
```

Now, your post detail page should look like this:

Who was Django Reinhardt?

Published Dec. 14, 2017, 8:54 a.m. by admin

Who was Django Reinhardt.

Share this post

Similar posts

Miles Davis favourite songs

Notes on Duke Ellington

You are now able to successfully recommend similar posts to your users. `django-taggit` also includes a `similar_objects()` manager that you can use to retrieve objects by shared tags. You can take a look at all `django-taggit` managers at `https://django-taggit.readthedocs.io/en/latest/api.html`.

You can also add the list of tags to your post detail template the same way we did in the `blog/post/list.html` template.

Summary

In this chapter, you learned how to work with Django forms and model forms. You created a system to share your site's content by email and created a comment system for your blog. You added tagging to your blog posts, integrating a reusable application, and built complex QuerySets to retrieve objects by similarity.

In the next chapter, you will learn how to create custom template tags and filters. You will also build a custom sitemap and feed for your blog posts and implement the full text search functionality for your blog posts.

3
Extending Your Blog Application

The preceding chapter went through the basics of forms, and you learned how to integrate third-party applications into your project. This chapter will cover the following points:

- Creating custom template tags and filters
- Adding a sitemap and post feed
- Implementing full text search with PostgreSQL

Creating custom template tags and filters

Django offers a variety of built-in template tags, such as `{% if %}` or `{% block %}`. You have used several in your templates. You can find a complete reference of built-in template tags and filters at `https://docs.djangoproject.com/en/2.0/ref/templates/builtins/`.

However, Django also allows you to create your own template tags to perform custom actions. Custom template tags come in very handy when you need to add a functionality to your templates that is not covered by the core set of Django template tags.

Creating custom template tags

Django provides the following helper functions that allow you to create your own template tags in an easy manner:

- `simple_tag`: Processes the data and returns a string
- `inclusion_tag`: Processes the data and returns a rendered template

Template tags must live inside Django applications.

Inside your `blog` application directory, create a new directory, name it `templatetags`, and add an empty `__init__.py` file to it. Create another file in the same folder and name it `blog_tags.py`. The file structure of the blog application should look like the following:

```
blog/
    __init__.py
    models.py
    ...
    templatetags/
        __init__.py
        blog_tags.py
```

The way you name the file is important. You will use the name of this module to load tags in templates.

We will start by creating a simple tag to retrieve the total posts published in the blog. Edit the `blog_tags.py` file you just created and add the following code:

```python
from django import template
from ..models import Post

register = template.Library()

@register.simple_tag
def total_posts():
    return Post.published.count()
```

We have created a simple template tag that returns the number of posts published so far. Each template tags module needs to contain a variable called `register` to be a valid tag library. This variable is an instance of `template.Library`, and it's used to register our own template tags and filters. Then, we define a tag called `total_posts` with a Python function and use the `@register.simple_tag` decorator to register the function as a simple tag. Django will use the function's name as the tag name. If you want to register it using a different name, you can do it by specifying a `name` attribute, such as `@register.simple_tag(name='my_tag')`.

After adding a new template tags module, you will need to restart the Django development server in order to use the new tags and filters in templates.

Before using custom template tags, you have to make them available for the template using the {% load %} tag. As mentioned before, you need to use the name of the Python module containing your template tags and filters. Open the blog/templates/base.html template and add {% load blog_tags %} at the top of it to load your template tags module. Then, use the tag you created to display your total posts. Just add {% total_posts %} to your template. The template should finally look like this:

```
{% load blog_tags %}
{% load static %}
<!DOCTYPE html>
<html>
<head>
  <title>{% block title %}{% endblock %}</title>
  <link href="{% static "css/blog.css" %}" rel="stylesheet">
</head>
<body>
  <div id="content">
    {% block content %}
    {% endblock %}
  </div>
  <div id="sidebar">
    <h2>My blog</h2>
    <p>This is my blog. I've written {% total_posts %} posts so far.</p>
  </div>
</body>
</html>
```

We will need to restart the server to keep track of the new files added to the project. Stop the development server with *Ctrl + C* and run it again using the following command:

```
python manage.py runserver
```

Open http://127.0.0.1:8000/blog/ in your browser. You should see the number of total posts in the sidebar of the site, as follows:

The power of custom template tags is that you can process any data and add it to any template regardless of the view executed. You can perform QuerySets or process any data to display results in your templates.

Now, we will create another tag to display the latest posts in the sidebar of our blog. This time, we will use an inclusion tag. Using an inclusion tag, you can render a template with context variables returned by your template tag. Edit the `blog_tags.py` file and add the following code:

```
@register.inclusion_tag('blog/post/latest_posts.html')
def show_latest_posts(count=5):
    latest_posts = Post.published.order_by('-publish')[:count]
    return {'latest_posts': latest_posts}
```

In the preceding code, we register the template tag using `@register.inclusion_tag` and specify the template that has to be rendered with the returned values using `blog/post/latest_posts.html`. Our template tag will accept an optional `count` parameter that defaults to 5. This parameter allows us to specify the number of posts we want to display. We use this variable to limit the results of the query `Post.published.order_by('-publish')[:count]`. Note that the function returns a dictionary of variables instead of a simple value. Inclusion tags have to return a dictionary of values, which is used as the context to render the specified template. The template tag we just created allows you to specify the optional number of posts to display as `{% show_latest_posts 3 %}`.

Now, create a new template file under `blog/post/` and name it `latest_posts.html`. Add the following code to it:

```
<ul>
{% for post in latest_posts %}
  <li>
    <a href="{{ post.get_absolute_url }}">{{ post.title }}</a>
  </li>
{% endfor %}
</ul>
```

In the preceding code, we display an unordered list of posts using the `latest_posts` variable returned by our template tag. Now, edit the `blog/base.html` template and add the new template tag to display the last three posts. The sidebar code should look like the following:

```
<div id="sidebar">
  <h2>My blog</h2>
  <p>This is my blog. I've written {% total_posts %} posts so far.</p>

  <h3>Latest posts</h3>
  {% show_latest_posts 3 %}
</div>
```

The template tag is called, passing the number of posts to display, and the template is rendered in place with the given context.

Now, return to your browser and refresh the page. The sidebar should now look like this:

My blog

This is my blog. I've written 4 posts so far.

Latest posts

- Miles Davis favourite songs
- Notes on Duke Ellington
- Another post

Finally, we will create a simple template tag that stores the result in a variable that can be reused rather than directly outputting it. We will create a tag to display the most commented posts. Edit the `blog_tags.py` file and add the following import and template tag in it:

```
from django.db.models import Count

@register.simple_tag
def get_most_commented_posts(count=5):
    return Post.published.annotate(
            total_comments=Count('comments')
        ).order_by('-total_comments')[:count]
```

In the preceding template tag, we build a QuerySet using the `annotate()` function to aggregate the total number of comments for each post. We use the `Count` aggregation function to store the number of comments in the computed field `total_comments` for each `Post` object. We order the QuerySet by the computed field in descending order. We also provide an optional `count` variable to limit the total number of objects returned.

In addition to `Count`, Django offers the aggregation functions `Avg`, `Max`, `Min`, and `Sum`. You can read more about aggregation functions at https://docs.djangoproject.com/en/2.0/topics/db/aggregation/.

Edit the `blog/base.html` template and append the following code to the sidebar `<div>` element:

```
<h3>Most commented posts</h3>
{% get_most_commented_posts as most_commented_posts %}
```

```
<ul>
{% for post in most_commented_posts %}
  <li>
    <a href="{{ post.get_absolute_url }}">{{ post.title }}</a>
  </li>
{% endfor %}
</ul>
```

We store the result in a custom variable using the `as` argument followed by the variable name. For our template tag, we use `{% get_most_commented_posts as most_commented_posts %}` to store the result of the template tag in a new variable named `most_commented_posts`. Then, we display the returned posts using an unordered list.

Now, open your browser and refresh the page to see the final result. It should look like the following:

You have now a clear idea about how to build custom template tags. You can read more about them at `https://docs.djangoproject.com/en/2.0/howto/custom-template-tags/`.

Creating custom template filters

Django has a variety of built-in template filters that allow you to modify variables in templates. These are Python functions that take one or two parameters—the value of the variable it's being applied to, and an optional argument. They return a value that can be displayed or treated by another filter. A filter looks like {{ variable|**my_filter** }}. Filters with an argument look like {{ variable|**my_filter:"foo"** }}. You can apply as many filters as you like to a variable, for example, {{ variable|filter1|filter2 }}, and each of them will be applied to the output generated by the preceding filter.

We will create a custom filter to be able to use markdown syntax in our blog posts and then convert the post contents to HTML in the templates. Markdown is a plain text formatting syntax that is very simple to use, and it's intended to be converted into HTML. You can learn the basics of this format at
https://daringfireball.net/projects/markdown/basics.

First, install the Python markdown module via pip using the following command:

```
pip install Markdown==2.6.11
```

Then, edit the blog_tags.py file and include the following code:

```
from django.utils.safestring import mark_safe
import markdown

@register.filter(name='markdown')
def markdown_format(text):
    return mark_safe(markdown.markdown(text))
```

We register template filters in the same way as template tags. To avoid a collision between our function name and the markdown module, we name our function markdown_format and name the filter markdown for usage in templates, such as {{ variable|markdown }}. Django escapes the HTML code generated by filters. We use the mark_safe function provided by Django to mark the result as safe HTML to be rendered in the template. By default, Django will not trust any HTML code and will escape it before placing it in the output. The only exceptions are variables that are marked as safe from escaping. This behavior prevents Django from outputting potentially dangerous HTML and allows you to create exceptions for returning safe HTML.

Now, load your template tags module in the post list and detail templates. Add the following line at the top of the `blog/post/list.html` and `blog/post/detail.html` templates after the `{% extends %}` tag:

```
{% load blog_tags %}
```

In the `post/detail.html` templates, take a look at the following line:

```
{{ post.body|linebreaks }}
```

Replace it with the following one:

```
{{ post.body|markdown }}
```

Then, in the `post/list.html` file, replace the following line:

```
{{ post.body|truncatewords:30|linebreaks }}
```

Then, swap it with the following one:

```
{{ post.body|markdown|truncatewords_html:30 }}
```

The `truncatewords_html` filter truncates a string after a certain number of words, avoiding unclosed HTML tags.

Now, open `http://127.0.0.1:8000/admin/blog/post/add/` in your browser and add a post with the following body:

```
This is a post formatted with markdown
---------------------------------------

*This is emphasized* and **this is more emphasized**.

Here is a list:

* One
* Two
* Three

And a [link to the Django website](https://www.djangoproject.com/)
```

Open your browser and take a look at how the post is rendered. You should see the following output:

Markdown post

Published Dec. 15, 2017, 8:42 a.m. by admin

This is a post formatted with markdown

This is emphasized and **this is more emphasized**.

Here is a list:

- One
- Two
- Three

And a link to the Django website

As you can see in the preceding screenshot, custom template filters are very useful to customize formatting. You can find more information about custom filters at `https://docs.djangoproject.com/en/2.0/howto/custom-template-tags/#writing-custom-template-filters`.

Adding a sitemap to your site

Django comes with a sitemap framework, which allows you to generate sitemaps for your site dynamically. A sitemap is an XML file that tells search engines the pages of your website, their relevance, and how frequently they are updated. Using a sitemap, you will help crawlers that index your website's content.

The Django sitemap framework depends on `django.contrib.sites`, which allows you to associate objects to particular websites that are running with your project. This comes handy when you want to run multiple sites using a single Django project. To install the sitemap framework, you will need to activate both the sites and the sitemap applications in our project. Edit the `settings.py` file of your project and add `django.contrib.sites` and `django.contrib.sitemaps` to the `INSTALLED_APPS` setting. Also, define a new setting for the site ID, as follows:

```
SITE_ID = 1

# Application definition
INSTALLED_APPS = [
    # ...
    'django.contrib.sites',
    'django.contrib.sitemaps',
]
```

Now, run the following command to create the tables of the Django site application in the database:

```
python manage.py migrate
```

You should see an output that contains the following lines:

```
Applying sites.0001_initial... OK
Applying sites.0002_alter_domain_unique... OK
```

The `sites` application is now synced with the database. Now, create a new file inside your `blog` application directory and name it `sitemaps.py`. Open the file and add the following code to it:

```python
from django.contrib.sitemaps import Sitemap
from .models import Post

class PostSitemap(Sitemap):
    changefreq = 'weekly'
    priority = 0.9

    def items(self):
        return Post.published.all()

    def lastmod(self, obj):
        return obj.updated
```

We create a custom sitemap by inheriting the Sitemap class of the sitemaps module. The changefreq and priority attributes indicate the change frequency of your post pages and their relevance in your website (the maximum value is 1). The items() method returns the QuerySet of objects to include in this sitemap. By default, Django calls the get_absolute_url() method on each object to retrieve its URL. Remember that we created this method in Chapter 1, *Building a Blog Application*, to retrieve the canonical URL for posts. If you want to specify the URL for each object, you can add a location method to your sitemap class. The lastmod method receives each object returned by items() and returns the last time the object was modified. Both changefreq and priority methods can also be either methods or attributes. You can take a look at the complete sitemap reference in the official Django documentation located at https://docs.djangoproject.com/en/2.0/ref/contrib/sitemaps/.

Finally, you will just need to add your sitemap URL. Edit the main urls.py file of your project and add the sitemap, as follows:

```
from django.urls import path, include
from django.contrib import admin
from django.contrib.sitemaps.views import sitemap
from blog.sitemaps import PostSitemap

sitemaps = {
    'posts': PostSitemap,
}

urlpatterns = [
    path('admin/', admin.site.urls),
    path('blog/', include('blog.urls', namespace='blog')),
    path('sitemap.xml', sitemap, {'sitemaps': sitemaps},
        name='django.contrib.sitemaps.views.sitemap')
]
```

In the preceding code, we included the required imports and defined a dictionary of sitemaps. We defined a URL pattern that matches with sitemap.xml and uses the sitemap view. The sitemaps dictionary is passed to the sitemap view. Now, run the development server and open http://127.0.0.1:8000/sitemap.xml in your browser. You will note the following XML output:

```
<?xml version="1.0" encoding="utf-8"?>
<urlset xmlns="http://www.sitemaps.org/schemas/sitemap/0.9">
  <url>
    <loc>http://example.com/blog/2017/12/15/markdown-post/</loc>
    <lastmod>2017-12-15</lastmod>
    <changefreq>weekly</changefreq>
```

```
      <priority>0.9</priority>
    </url>
    <url>
      <loc>
  http://example.com/blog/2017/12/14/who-was-django-reinhardt/
  </loc>
      <lastmod>2017-12-14</lastmod>
      <changefreq>weekly</changefreq>
      <priority>0.9</priority>
    </url>
  </urlset>
```

The URL for each post has been built calling its `get_absolute_url()` method.
The `lastmod` attribute corresponds to the post `updated` date field, as we specified in our
sitemap, and the `changefreq` and `priority` attributes are also taken from our
`PostSitemap` class. You can see that the domain used to build the URLs is `example.com`.
This domain comes from a `Site` object stored in the database. This default object has been
created when we synced the site's framework with our database. Open
`http://127.0.0.1:8000/admin/sites/site/` in your browser. You should see
something like this:

The preceding screenshot contains the list display admin view for the site's framework.
Here, you can set the domain or host to be used by the site's framework and the
applications that depend on it. In order to generate URLs that exist in our local
environment, change the domain name to `localhost:8000`, as shown in the following
screenshot, and save it:

The URLs displayed in your feed will now be built using this hostname. In a production environment, you will have to use your own domain name for the site's framework.

Creating feeds for your blog posts

Django has a built-in syndication feed framework that you can use to dynamically generate RSS or Atom feeds in a similar manner to creating sitemaps using the site's framework. A web feed is a data format (usually XML) that provides users with frequently updated content. Users will be able to subscribe to your feed using a feed aggregator, a software that is used to read feeds and get new content notifications.

Create a new file in your `blog` application directory and name it `feeds.py`. Add the following lines to it:

```python
from django.contrib.syndication.views import Feed
from django.template.defaultfilters import truncatewords
from .models import Post

class LatestPostsFeed(Feed):
    title = 'My blog'
    link = '/blog/'
    description = 'New posts of my blog.'

    def items(self):
        return Post.published.all()[:5]

    def item_title(self, item):
        return item.title

    def item_description(self, item):
        return truncatewords(item.body, 30)
```

First, we subclass the `Feed` class of the syndication framework. The `title`, `link`, and `description` attributes correspond to the `<title>`, `<link>`, and `<description>` RSS elements, respectively.

The `items()` method retrieves the objects to be included in the feed. We are retrieving only the last five published posts for this feed. The `item_title()` and `item_description()` methods receive each object returned by `items()` and return the title and description for each item. We use the `truncatewords` built-in template filter to build the description of the blog post with the first 30 words.

Now, edit the `blog/urls.py` file, import `LatestPostsFeed` you just created, and instantiate the feed in a new URL pattern:

```
from .feeds import LatestPostsFeed

urlpatterns = [
    # ...
    path('feed/', LatestPostsFeed(), name='post_feed'),
]
```

Navigate to `http://127.0.0.1:8000/blog/feed/` in your browser. You should now see the RSS feed, including the last five blog posts:

```
<?xml version="1.0" encoding="utf-8"?>
<rss xmlns:atom="http://www.w3.org/2005/Atom" version="2.0">
  <channel>
    <title>My blog</title>
    <link>http://localhost:8000/blog/</link>
    <description>New posts of my blog.</description>
    <atom:link href="http://localhost:8000/blog/feed/" rel="self"/>
    <language>en-us</language>
    <lastBuildDate>Fri, 15 Dec 2017 09:56:40 +0000</lastBuildDate>
    <item>
      <title>Who was Django Reinhardt?</title>
      <link>http://localhost:8000/blog/2017/12/14/who-was-django-
      reinhardt/</link>
      <description>Who was Django Reinhardt.</description>
      <guid>http://localhost:8000/blog/2017/12/14/who-was-django-
      reinhardt/</guid>
    </item>
    ...
  </channel>
</rss>
```

If you open the same URL in an RSS client, you will be able to see your feed with a user-friendly interface.

The final step is to add a feed subscription link to the blog's sidebar. Open the `blog/base.html` template and add the following line under the number of total posts inside the sidebar `div`:

```
<p><a href="{% url "blog:post_feed" %}">Subscribe to my RSS feed</a></p>
```

Now, open `http://127.0.0.1:8000/blog/` in your browser and take a look at the sidebar. The new link should take you to your blog's feed:

My blog

This is my blog. I've written 5 posts so far.

Subscribe to my RSS feed

Adding full-text search to your blog

Now, you will add search capabilities to your blog. The Django ORM allows you to perform simple matching operations using, for example, the `contains` filter (or its case-insensitive version, `icontains`). You can use the following query to find posts that contain the word `framework` in their body:

```
from blog.models import Post
Post.objects.filter(body__contains='framework')
```

However, if you want to perform complex search lookups, retrieving results by similarity or by weighting terms, you will need to use a full-text search engine.

Django provides a powerful search functionality built on top of PostgreSQL full-text search features. The `django.contrib.postgres` module provides functionalities offered by PostgreSQL that are not shared by the other databases that Django supports. You can learn about PostgreSQL full-text search at `https://www.postgresql.org/docs/10/static/textsearch.html`.

Although Django is a database-agnostic web framework, it provides a
module that supports part of the rich feature set offered by PostgreSQL,
not shared by other databases that Django supports.

Installing PostgreSQL

You are currently using SQLite for your `blog` project. This is sufficient for development
purposes. However, for a production environment, you will need a more powerful
database, such as PostgreSQL, MySQL, or Oracle. We will change our database to
PostgreSQL to benefit from its full-text search features.

If you are using Linux, install dependencies for PostgreSQL to work with Python, like this:

```
sudo apt-get install libpq-dev python-dev
```

Then, install PostgreSQL with the following command:

```
sudo apt-get install postgresql postgresql-contrib
```

If you are using macOS X or Windows, download PostgreSQL from `https://www.`
`postgresql.org/download/` and install it.

You also need to install the Psycopg2 PostgreSQL adapter for Python. Run the following
command in the shell to install it:

```
pip install psycopg2==2.7.4
```

Let's create a user for our PostgreSQL database. Open the shell and run the following
commands:

```
su postgres
createuser -dP blog
```

You will be prompted a password for the new user. Enter the desired password and then
create the `blog` database and give the ownership to the `blog` user you just created with the
following command:

```
createdb -E utf8 -U blog blog
```

Then, edit the `settings.py` file of your project and modify the `DATABASES` setting to make it look as follows:

```
DATABASES = {
    'default': {
        'ENGINE': 'django.db.backends.postgresql',
        'NAME': 'blog',
        'USER': 'blog',
        'PASSWORD': '*****',
    }
}
```

Replace the preceding data with the database name and credentials for the user you created. The new database is empty. Run the following command to apply all database migrations:

```
python manage.py migrate
```

Finally, create a superuser with the following command:

```
python manage.py createsuperuser
```

You can now run the development server and access the administration site at `http://127.0.0.1:8000/admin/` with the new superuser.

Since we switched the database, there are no posts stored in it. Populate your new database with a couple of sample blog posts so that you can perform searches against the database.

Simple search lookups

Edit the `settings.py` file of your project and add `django.contrib.postgres` to the `INSTALLED_APPS` setting, as follows:

```
INSTALLED_APPS = [
    # ...
    'django.contrib.postgres',
]
```

Now, you can search against a single field using the `search` QuerySet lookup, like this:

```
from blog.models import Post
Post.objects.filter(body__search='django')
```

This query uses PostgreSQL to create a search vector for the `body` field and a search query from the term `django`. Results are obtained by matching the query with the vector.

Searching against multiple fields

You might want to search against multiple fields. In this case, you will need to define `SearchVector`. Let's build a vector that allows us to search against the `title` and `body` fields of the `Post` model:

```
from django.contrib.postgres.search import SearchVector
from blog.models import Post

Post.objects.annotate(
    search=SearchVector('title', 'body'),
).filter(search='django')
```

Using annotate and defining `SearchVector` with both fields, we provide a functionality to match the query against both the title and body of the posts.

 Full-text search is an intensive process. If you are searching for more than a few hundred rows, you should define a functional index that matches the search vector you are using. Django provides a `SearchVectorField` field for your models. You can read more about this at `https://docs.djangoproject.com/en/2.0/ref/contrib/postgres/search/#performance`.

Building a search view

Now, we will create a custom view to allow our users to search posts. First, we will need a search form. Edit the `forms.py` file of the `blog` application and add the following form:

```
class SearchForm(forms.Form):
    query = forms.CharField()
```

We will use the `query` field to let the users introduce search terms. Edit the `views.py` file of the `blog` application and add the following code to it:

```python
from django.contrib.postgres.search import SearchVector
from .forms import EmailPostForm, CommentForm, SearchForm

def post_search(request):
    form = SearchForm()
    query = None
    results = []
    if 'query' in request.GET:
        form = SearchForm(request.GET)
        if form.is_valid():
            query = form.cleaned_data['query']
            results = Post.objects.annotate(
                search=SearchVector('title', 'body'),
            ).filter(search=query)
    return render(request,
                  'blog/post/search.html',
                  {'form': form,
                   'query': query,
                   'results': results})
```

In the preceding view, first, we instantiate the `SearchForm` form. We plan to submit the form using the GET method so that the resulting URL includes the `query` parameter. To check whether the form is submitted, we look for the `query` parameter in the `request.GET` dictionary. When the form is submitted, we instantiate it with the submitted GET data, and we verify that the form data is valid. If the form is valid, we search for posts with a custom `SearchVector` instance built with the `title` and `body` fields.

The search view is ready now. We need to create a template to display the form and the results when the user performs a search. Create a new file inside the `/blog/post/` template directory, name it `search.html`, and add the following code to it:

```html
{% extends "blog/base.html" %}

{% block title %}Search{% endblock %}

{% block content %}
  {% if query %}
    <h1>Posts containing "{{ query }}"</h1>
    <h3>
      {% with results.count as total_results %}
        Found {{ total_results }} result{{ total_results|pluralize }}
      {% endwith %}
```

```
    </h3>
    {% for post in results %}
        <h4><a href="{{ post.get_absolute_url }}">{{ post.title }}</a></h4>
        {{ post.body|truncatewords:5 }}
    {% empty %}
      <p>There are no results for your query.</p>
    {% endfor %}
    <p><a href="{% url "blog:post_search" %}">Search again</a></p>
  {% else %}
    <h1>Search for posts</h1>
    <form action="." method="get">
      {{ form.as_p }}
      <input type="submit" value="Search">
    </form>
  {% endif %}
{% endblock %}
```

As in the search view, we can distinguish whether the form has been submitted by the presence of the query parameter. Before the post is submitted, we display the form and a submit button. After the post is submitted, we display the query performed, the total number of results, and the list of posts returned.

Finally, edit the urls.py file of your blog application and add the following URL pattern:

```
path('search/', views.post_search, name='post_search'),
```

Now, open http://127.0.0.1:8000/blog/search/ in your browser. You should see the following search form:

Enter a query and click on the **Search** button. You will see the results of the search query, as follows:

Congratulations! You have created a basic search engine for your blog.

Stemming and ranking results

Django provides a `SearchQuery` class to translate the terms into a search query object. By default, the terms are passed through stemming algorithms, which helps you to obtain better matches. You also may want to order results by relevancy. PostgreSQL provides a ranking function that orders results based on how often the query terms appear and how close together they are. Edit the `views.py` file of your `blog` application and add the following imports:

```
from django.contrib.postgres.search import SearchVector, SearchQuery,
SearchRank
```

Then, take a look at the following lines:

```
results = Post.objects.annotate(
            search=SearchVector('title', 'body'),
        ).filter(search=query)
```

Replace them with the following ones:

```
search_vector = SearchVector('title', 'body')
search_query = SearchQuery(query)
results = Post.objects.annotate(
            search=search_vector,
            rank=SearchRank(search_vector, search_query)
        ).filter(search=search_query).order_by('-rank')
```

In the preceding code, we created a `SearchQuery` object, filtered results by it, and used `SearchRank` to order the results by relevancy. You can open `http://127.0.0.1:8000/blog/search/` in your browser and test different searches to test stemming and ranking. The following is an example of ranking by the number of occurrences for the word `django` in the title and body of the posts:

Posts containing "django"

Found 3 results

Django, Django, Django

Django is the Web Framework ...

Django twice

Django offers full text search ...

Django once

A Python web framework.

Search again

Weighting queries

You can boost specific vectors so that more weight is attributed to them when ordering results by relevancy. For example, you can use this to give more relevance to posts that are matched by title rather than by content. Edit the previous lines of the `views.py` file of your `blog` application and make them look like this:

```
search_vector = SearchVector('title', weight='A') + SearchVector('body',
weight='B')
search_query = SearchQuery(query)
```

```
results = Post.objects.annotate(
 rank=SearchRank(search_vector, search_query)
 ).filter(rank__gte=0.3).order_by('-rank')
```

In the preceding code, we apply different weights to the search vectors built using the title and body fields. The default weights are D, C, B, and A that refer to the numbers 0.1, 0.2, 0.4, and 1.0, respectively. We apply a weight of 1.0 to the title search vector and a weight of 0.4 to the body vector: title matches will prevail over body content matches. We filter the results to display only the ones with a rank higher than 0.3.

Searching with trigram similarity

Another search approach is trigram similarity. A trigram is a group of three consecutive characters. You can measure the similarity of two strings by counting the number of trigrams they share. This approach turns out to be very effective for measuring the similarity of words in many languages.

In order to use trigrams in PostgreSQL, you will need to install the pg_trgm extension first. Execute the following command from the shell to connect to your database:

psql blog

Then, execute the following command to install the pg_trgm extension:

CREATE EXTENSION pg_trgm;

Let's edit our view and modify it to search for trigrams. Edit the views.py file of your blog application and add the following import:

```
from django.contrib.postgres.search import TrigramSimilarity
```

Then, replace Post search query with the following lines:

```
results = Post.objects.annotate(
    similarity=TrigramSimilarity('title', query),
).filter(similarity__gt=0.3).order_by('-similarity')
```

Open `http://127.0.0.1:8000/blog/search/` in your browser and test different searches for trigrams. The following example displays a hypothetical typo in the `django` term, showing search results for `yango`:

Posts containing "yango"

Found 1 result

Django Django

A Python web framework.

Now, you have a powerful search engine built into your project. You can find more information about full-text search at `https://docs.djangoproject.com/en/2.0/ref/contrib/postgres/search/`.

Other full-text search engines

You may want to use a full-text search engine different from PostgreSQL. If you want to use Solr or Elasticsearch, you can integrate them into your Django project using Haystack. Haystack is a Django application that works as an abstraction layer for multiple search engines. It offers a simple search API very similar to Django QuerySets. You can find more information about Haystack at `http://haystacksearch.org/`.

Summary

In this chapter, you learned how to create custom Django template tags and filters to provide templates with a custom functionality. You also created a sitemap for search engines to crawl your site and an RSS feed for users to subscribe to your blog. You also built a search engine for your blog using the full-text search engine of PostgreSQL.

In the next chapter, you will learn how to build a social website using the Django authentication framework, create custom user profiles, and build social authentication.

Building a Social Website

4

In the preceding chapter, you learned how to create sitemaps and feeds and built a search engine for your blog application. In this chapter, you will develop a social application. You will create a functionality for users to log in, log out, edit, and reset their password. You will learn how to create a custom profile for your users, and you will add social authentication to your site.

This chapter will cover the following topics:

- Using the Django authentication framework
- Creating user registration views
- Extending the user model with a custom profile model
- Adding social authentication with python-social-auth

Let's start by creating our new project.

Creating a social website project

We will create a social application that will allow users to share images they find on the internet. We will need to build the following elements for this project:

- An authentication system for users to register, log in, edit their profile, and change or reset their password
- A followers' system to allow users to follow each other
- A functionality to display shared images and implement a bookmarklet for users to share images from any website
- An activity stream for each user that allows users to see the content uploaded by the people they follow

This chapter addresses the first point mentioned in the preceding list.

Starting your social website project

Open the terminal, and use the following commands to create a virtual environment for your project and activate it:

```
mkdir env
virtualenv env/bookmarks
source env/bookmarks/bin/activate
```

The shell prompt will display your active virtual environment, as follows:

```
(bookmarks) laptop:~ zenx$
```

Install Django in your virtual environment with the following command:

```
pip install Django==2.0.5
```

Run the following command to create a new project:

```
django-admin startproject bookmarks
```

After creating the initial project structure, use the following commands to get into your project directory and create a new application named account:

```
cd bookmarks/
django-admin startapp account
```

Remember that you should activate the new application in your project by adding it to the INSTALLED_APPS setting in the settings.py file. Place it in the INSTALLED_APPS list before any of the other installed apps:

```
INSTALLED_APPS = [
    'account.apps.AccountConfig',
    # ...
]
```

We will define Django authentication templates later on. By placing our app first in the INSTALLED_APPS setting, we ensure that our authentication templates will be used by default instead of any other authentication templates contained in other apps. Django looks for templates by order of app appearance in the INSTALLED_APPS setting.

Run the next command to sync the database with the models of the default applications included in the INSTALLED_APPS setting:

```
python manage.py migrate
```

You will see that all initial Django database migrations get applied. We will build an authentication system into our project using the Django authentication framework.

Using the Django authentication framework

Django comes with a built-in authentication framework that can handle user authentication, sessions, permissions, and user groups. The authentication system includes views for common user actions such as login, logout, password change, and password reset.

The authentication framework is located at django.contrib.auth and is used by other Django contrib packages. Remember that you have already used the authentication framework in Chapter 1, *Building a Blog Application*, to create a superuser for your blog application to access the administration site.

When you create a new Django project using the startproject command, the authentication framework is included in the default settings of your project. It consists of the django.contrib.auth application and the following two middleware classes found in the MIDDLEWARE setting of your project:

- AuthenticationMiddleware: Associates users with requests using sessions
- SessionMiddleware: Handles the current session across requests

A middleware is a class with methods that are globally executed during the request or response phase. You will use middleware classes on several occasions throughout this book, and you will learn to create custom middleware in Chapter 13, *Going Live*.

The authentication framework also includes the following models:

- User: A user model with basic fields; the main fields of this model are username, password, email, first_name, last_name, and is_active
- Group: A group model to categorize users
- Permission: Flags for users or groups to perform certain actions

The framework also includes default authentication views and forms that we will use later.

Creating a login view

We will start this section by using the Django authentication framework to allow users to log in to our website. Our view should perform the following actions to log in a user:

1. Get the username and password by posting a form
2. Authenticate the user against the data stored in the database
3. Check whether the user is active
4. Log the user into the website and start an authenticated session

First, we will create a login form. Create a new `forms.py` file in your `account` application directory and add the following lines to it:

```python
from django import forms

class LoginForm(forms.Form):
    username = forms.CharField()
    password = forms.CharField(widget=forms.PasswordInput)
```

This form will be used to authenticate users against the database. Note that we use the `PasswordInput` widget to render its HTML `input` element, including a `type="password"` attribute, so that the browser treats it as a password input. Edit the `views.py` file of your `account` application and add the following code to it:

```python
from django.http import HttpResponse
from django.shortcuts import render
from django.contrib.auth import authenticate, login
from .forms import LoginForm

def user_login(request):
    if request.method == 'POST':
        form = LoginForm(request.POST)
        if form.is_valid():
            cd = form.cleaned_data
            user = authenticate(request,
                                username=cd['username'],
                                password=cd['password'])
            if user is not None:
                if user.is_active:
                    login(request, user)
                    return HttpResponse('Authenticated '\
                                        'successfully')
                else:
                    return HttpResponse('Disabled account')
            else:
```

```
                    return HttpResponse('Invalid login')
    else:
        form = LoginForm()
    return render(request, 'account/login.html', {'form': form})
```

This is what our basic login view does: when the `user_login` view is called with a GET request, we instantiate a new login form with `form = LoginForm()` to display it in the template. When the user submits the form via POST, we perform the following actions:

1. Instantiate the form with the submitted data with `form = LoginForm(request.POST)`.
2. Check whether the form is valid with `form.is_valid()`. If it is not valid, we display the form errors in our template (for example, if the user didn't fill in one of the fields).
3. If the submitted data is valid, we authenticate the user against the database using the `authenticate()` method. This method takes the `request` object, the `username`, and the `password` parameters and returns the `User` object if the user has been successfully authenticated, or `None` otherwise. If the user has not been authenticated, we return a raw `HttpResponse`, displaying the **Invalid login** message.
4. If the user was successfully authenticated, we check whether the user is active, accessing its `is_active` attribute. This is an attribute of Django's user model. If the user is not active, we return an `HttpResponse` that displays the **Disabled account** message.
5. If the user is active, we log the user into the website. We set the user in the session by calling the `login()` method and return the **Authenticated successfully** message.

 Note the difference between `authenticate` and `login`: `authenticate()` checks user credentials and returns a `User` object if they are right; `login()` sets the user in the current session.

Now, you will need to create a URL pattern for this view. Create a new `urls.py` file in your `account` application directory and add the following code to it:

```
from django.urls import path
from . import views

urlpatterns = [
    # post views
    path('login/', views.user_login, name='login'),
```

]

Edit the main `urls.py` file located in your `bookmarks` project directory, import `include`, and add the URL patterns of the `account` application, as follows:

```
from django.conf.urls import path, include
from django.contrib import admin

urlpatterns = [
    path('admin/', admin.site.urls),
    path('account/', include('account.urls')),
]
```

The login view can now be accessed by a URL. It is time to create a template for this view. Since you don't have any templates for this project, you can start by creating a base template that can be extended by the login template. Create the following files and directories inside the `account` application directory:

```
templates/
    account/
        login.html
    base.html
```

Edit the `base.html` file and add the following code to it:

```
{% load staticfiles %}
<!DOCTYPE html>
<html>
<head>
  <title>{% block title %}{% endblock %}</title>
  <link href="{% static "css/base.css" %}" rel="stylesheet">
</head>
<body>
  <div id="header">
    <span class="logo">Bookmarks</span>
  </div>
  <div id="content">
    {% block content %}
    {% endblock %}
  </div>
</body>
</html>
```

This will be the base template for the website. As we did in our previous project, we include the CSS styles in the main template. You can find these static files in the code that comes along with this chapter. Copy the static/ directory of the account application from the chapter's source code to the same location in your project so that you can use the static files.

The base template defines a title block and a content block that can be filled with content by the templates that extend from it.

Let's fill in the template for our login form. Open the account/login.html template and add the following code to it:

```
{% extends "base.html" %}

{% block title %}Log-in{% endblock %}

{% block content %}
  <h1>Log-in</h1>
  <p>Please, use the following form to log-in:</p>
  <form action="." method="post">
    {{ form.as_p }}
    {% csrf_token %}
    <p><input type="submit" value="Log in"></p>
  </form>
{% endblock %}
```

This template includes the form that is instantiated in the view. Since our form will be submitted via POST, we will include the {% csrf_token %} template tag for CSRF protection. You learned about CSRF protection in Chapter 2, *Enhancing Your Blog with Advanced Features*.

There are no users in your database, yet. You will need to create a superuser first in order to be able to access the administration site to manage other users. Open the command line and execute python manage.py createsuperuser. Fill in the desired username, email, and password. Then, run the development server using the python manage.py runserver command and open http://127.0.0.1:8000/admin/ in your browser. Access the administration site using the credentials of the user you just created. You will see the Django administration site, including the User and Group models of the Django authentication framework.

It will look as follows:

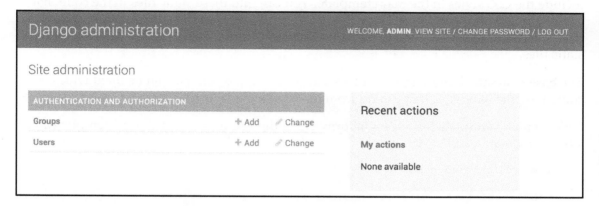

Create a new user using the administration site and open
`http://127.0.0.1:8000/account/login/` in your browser. You should see the rendered template, including the login form:

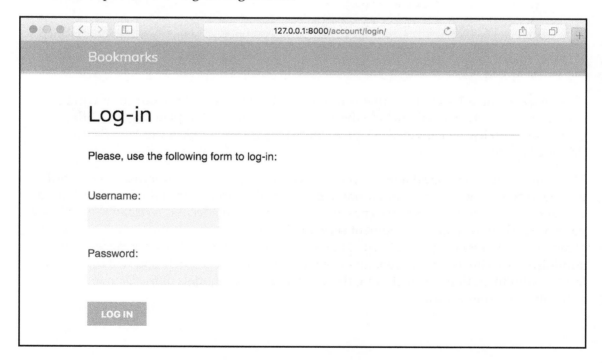

Now, submit the form, leaving one of the fields empty. In this case, you will see that the form is not valid and displays errors, as follows:

Note that some modern browsers will prevent you from submitting the form with empty or erroneous fields. This is because of form validation done by the browser based on field types and restrictions per field. In this case, the form won't be submitted and the browser will display an error message for the fields that are wrong.

If you enter a non-existing user or a wrong password, you will get an **Invalid login** message.

If you enter valid credentials, you will get an **Authenticated successfully** message, like this:

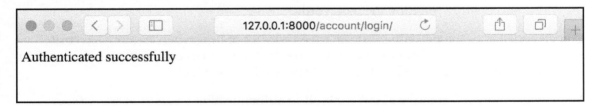

Using Django authentication views

Django includes several forms and views in the authentication framework that you can use straight away. The login view you have created is a good exercise to understand the process of user authentication in Django. However, you can use the default Django authentication views in most cases.

Django provides the following class-based views to deal with authentication. All of them are located in django.contrib.auth.views:

- LoginView: Handles a login form and logs in a user
- LogoutView: Logs out a user

Django provides the following views to handle password changes:

- PasswordChangeView: Handles a form to change the user password
- PasswordChangeDoneView: The success view the user is redirected to after a successful password change

Django also includes the following views to allow users to reset their password:

- PasswordResetView: Allows users to reset their password. It generates a one-time use link with a token and sends it to the user's email account.
- PasswordResetDoneView: Tells users that an email—including a link to reset their password—has been sent to them.
- PasswordResetConfirmView: Allows users to set a new password.
- PasswordResetCompleteView: The success view the user is redirected to after successfully resetting the password.

The views listed in the preceding list can save you a lot of time when creating a website with user accounts. The views use default values that you can override, such as the location of the template to be rendered, or the form to be used by the view.

You can get more information about the built-in authentication views at https://docs.djangoproject.com/en/2.0/topics/auth/default/#all-authentication-views.

Login and logout views

Edit the `urls.py` of your account application, like this:

```
from django.urls import path
from django.contrib.auth import views as auth_views
from . import views

urlpatterns = [
    # previous login view
    # path('login/', views.user_login, name='login'),
    path('login/', auth_views.LoginView.as_view(), name='login'),
    path('logout/', auth_views.LogoutView.as_view(), name='logout'),
]
```

We comment out the URL pattern for the `user_login` view we have created previously to use the `LoginView` view of Django's authentication framework. We also add a URL pattern for the `LogoutView` view.

Create a new directory inside the `templates` directory of your `account` application and name it `registration`. This is the default path where the Django authentication views expect your authentication templates to be.

The `django.contrib.admin` module includes some of the authentication templates that are used for the administration site. We have placed the `account` application at the top of the `INSTALLED_APPS` setting so that Django uses our templates by default instead of any authentication templates defined in other apps.

Create a new file inside the `templates/registration` directory, name it `login.html`, and add the following code to it:

```
{% extends "base.html" %}

{% block title %}Log-in{% endblock %}

{% block content %}
  <h1>Log-in</h1>
  {% if form.errors %}
    <p>
      Your username and password didn't match.
      Please try again.
    </p>
  {% else %}
    <p>Please, use the following form to log-in:</p>
  {% endif %}
```

```
<div class="login-form">
  <form action="{% url 'login' %}" method="post">
    {{ form.as_p }}
    {% csrf_token %}
    <input type="hidden" name="next" value="{{ next }}" />
    <p><input type="submit" value="Log-in"></p>
  </form>
</div>
{% endblock %}
```

This login template is quite similar to the one we created before. Django uses the AuthenticationForm form located at django.contrib.auth.forms by default. This form tries to authenticate the user and raises a validation error if login was unsuccessful. In this case, we can look for errors using {% if form.errors %} in the template to check whether the credentials provided are wrong. Note that we have added a hidden HTML <input> element to submit the value of a variable called next. This variable is first set by the login view when you pass a next parameter in the request (for example, http://127.0.0.1:8000/account/login/?next=/account/).

The next parameter has to be a URL. If this parameter is given, the Django login view will redirect the user to the given URL after a successful login.

Now, create a logged_out.html template inside the registration template directory and make it look like this:

```
{% extends "base.html" %}

{% block title %}Logged out{% endblock %}

{% block content %}
  <h1>Logged out</h1>
  <p>You have been successfully logged out. You can <a href="{% url
  "login" %}">log-in again</a>.</p>
{% endblock %}
```

This is the template that Django will display after the user logs out.

After adding the URL patterns and the templates for login and logout views, your website is ready for users to log in using Django authentication views.

Now, we will create a new view to display a dashboard when users log in to their account. Open the `views.py` file of your `account` application and add the following code to it:

```
from django.contrib.auth.decorators import login_required

@login_required
def dashboard(request):
    return render(request,
                  'account/dashboard.html',
                  {'section': 'dashboard'})
```

We decorate our view with the `login_required` decorator of the authentication framework. The `login_required` decorator checks whether the current user is authenticated. If the user is authenticated, it executes the decorated view; if the user is not authenticated, it redirects the user to the login URL with the originally requested URL as a `GET` parameter named `next`. By doing so, the login view redirects users to the URL they were trying to access after they successfully log in. Remember that we added a hidden input in the form of our login template for this purpose.

We also define a `section` variable. We will use this variable to track the site's section that the user is browsing. Multiple views may correspond to the same section. This is a simple way to define the section that each view corresponds to.

Now, you will need to create a template for the dashboard view. Create a new file inside the `templates/account/` directory and name it `dashboard.html`. Make it look like this:

```
{% extends "base.html" %}

{% block title %}Dashboard{% endblock %}

{% block content %}
  <h1>Dashboard</h1>
  <p>Welcome to your dashboard.</p>
{% endblock %}
```

Then, add the following URL pattern for this view in the `urls.py` file of the `account` application:

```
urlpatterns = [
    # ...
    path('', views.dashboard, name='dashboard'),
]
```

Edit the `settings.py` file of your project and add the following code to it:

```
LOGIN_REDIRECT_URL = 'dashboard'
LOGIN_URL = 'login'
LOGOUT_URL = 'logout'
```

The settings mentioned in the preceding code are as follows:

- `LOGIN_REDIRECT_URL`: Tells Django which URL to redirect after a successful login if no `next` parameter is present in the request
- `LOGIN_URL`: The URL to redirect the user to log in (for example, views using the `login_required` decorator)
- `LOGOUT_URL`: The URL to redirect the user to log out

We are using the names of the URL patterns we previously defined using the `name` attribute of the `path()` function. Hardcoded URLs instead of URL names can also be used for these settings.

Let's summarize what you have done so far:

- You have added the built-in Django authentication login and logout views to your project
- You have created custom templates for both views and defined a simple dashboard view to redirect users after they log in
- Finally, you have configured your settings for Django to use these URLs by default

Now, we will add login and logout links to our base template to put everything together. In order to do this, we have to determine whether the current user is logged in or not in order to display the appropriate link for each case. The current user is set in the `HttpRequest` object by the authentication middleware. You can access it with `request.user`. You will find a `User` object in the request even if the user is not authenticated. A non-authenticated user is set in the request as an instance of `AnonymousUser`. The best way to check whether the current user is authenticated is by accessing its read-only attribute `is_authenticated`.

Edit your `base.html` template and modify the `<div>` element with a `header` ID, like this:

```
<div id="header">
  <span class="logo">Bookmarks</span>
  {% if request.user.is_authenticated %}
    <ul class="menu">
      <li {% if section == "dashboard" %}class="selected"{% endif %}>
        <a href="{% url "dashboard" %}">My dashboard</a>
```

```
      </li>
      <li {% if section == "images" %}class="selected"{% endif %}>
        <a href="#">Images</a>
      </li>
      <li {% if section == "people" %}class="selected"{% endif %}>
        <a href="#">People</a>
      </li>
    </ul>
  {% endif %}

  <span class="user">
    {% if request.user.is_authenticated %}
      Hello {{ request.user.first_name }},
      <a href="{% url "logout" %}">Logout</a>
    {% else %}
      <a href="{% url "login" %}">Log-in</a>
    {% endif %}
  </span>
</div>
```

As you can see in the preceding code, we only display the site's menu to authenticated users. We also check the current section to add a `selected` class attribute to the corresponding `<li>` item in order to highlight the current section in the menu using CSS. We also display the user's first name and a link to log out if the user is authenticated, or a link to log in otherwise.

Now, open `http://127.0.0.1:8000/account/login/` in your browser. You should see the login page. Enter a valid username and password and click on the **Log-in** button. You should see the following output:

You can see that the **My dashboard** section is highlighted with CSS because it has a `selected` class. Since the user is authenticated, the first name of the user is displayed on the right side of the header. Click on the **Logout** link. You should see the following page:

In the page mentioned in the preceding screenshot, you can see that the user is logged out, and, therefore, the menu of the website is not being displayed anymore. Now, the link on the right side of the header shows **Log-in**.

If you see the logout page of the Django administration site instead of your own log out page, check the `INSTALLED_APPS` setting of your project and make sure that `django.contrib.admin` comes after the `account` application. Both templates are located in the same relative path, and the Django template loader will use the first one it finds.

Changing password views

We also need our users to be able to change their password after they log in to our site. We will integrate Django authentication views for password change. Open the `urls.py` file of the `account` application and add the following URL patterns to it:

```python
# change password urls
path('password_change/',
    auth_views.PasswordChangeView.as_view(),
    name='password_change'),
path('password_change/done/',
    auth_views.PasswordChangeDoneView.as_view(),
    name='password_change_done'),
```

The `PasswordChangeView` view will handle the form to change the password, and the `PasswordChangeDoneView` view will display a success message after the user has successfully changed his password. Let's create a template for each view.

Add a new file inside the `templates/registration/` directory of your account application and name it `password_change_form.html`. Add the following code to it:

```
{% extends "base.html" %}

{% block title %}Change you password{% endblock %}

{% block content %}
  <h1>Change you password</h1>
  <p>Use the form below to change your password.</p>
  <form action="." method="post">
    {{ form.as_p }}
    <p><input type="submit" value="Change"></p>
    {% csrf_token %}
  </form>
{% endblock %}
```

The `password_change_form.html` template includes the form to change the password. Now, create another file in the same directory and name it `password_change_done.html`. Add the following code to it:

```
{% extends "base.html" %}

{% block title %}Password changed{% endblock %}

{% block content %}
  <h1>Password changed</h1>
  <p>Your password has been successfully changed.</p>
{% endblock %}
```

The `password_change_done.html` template only contains the success message to be displayed when the user has successfully changed their password.

Open `http://127.0.0.1:8000/account/password_change/` in your browser. If your user is not logged in, the browser will redirect you to the login page. After you are successfully authenticated, you will see the following change password page:

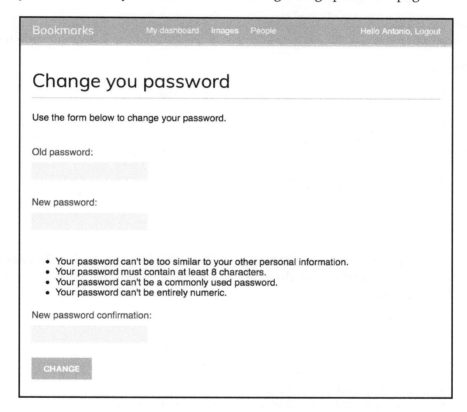

Fill in the form with your current password and your new password, and click on the **CHANGE** button. You will see the following success page:

Log out and log in again using your new password to verify that everything works as expected.

Resetting password views

Add the following URL patterns for password restoration to the `urls.py` file of the `account` application:

```
# reset password urls
path('password_reset/',
     auth_views.PasswordResetView.as_view(),
     name='password_reset'),
path('password_reset/done/',
     auth_views.PasswordResetDoneView.as_view(),
     name='password_reset_done'),
path('reset/<uidb64>/<token>/',
     auth_views.PasswordResetConfirmView.as_view(),
     name='password_reset_confirm'),
path('reset/done/',
     auth_views.PasswordResetCompleteView.as_view(),
     name='password_reset_complete'),
```

Add a new file in the `templates/registration/` directory of your `account` application and name it `password_reset_form.html`. Add the following code to it:

```
{% extends "base.html" %}

{% block title %}Reset your password{% endblock %}

{% block content %}
  <h1>Forgotten your password?</h1>
  <p>Enter your e-mail address to obtain a new password.</p>
  <form action="." method="post">
    {{ form.as_p }}
    <p><input type="submit" value="Send e-mail"></p>
    {% csrf_token %}
  </form>
{% endblock %}
```

Now, create another file in the same directory and name it `password_reset_email.html`. Add the following code to it:

```
Someone asked for password reset for email {{ email }}. Follow the link
below:
{{ protocol }}://{{ domain }}{% url "password_reset_confirm" uidb64=uid
token=token %}
Your username, in case you've forgotten: {{ user.get_username }}
```

The `password_reset_email.html` template will be used to render the email sent to users to reset their password.

Create another file in the same directory and name it `password_reset_done.html`. Add the following code to it:

```
{% extends "base.html" %}

{% block title %}Reset your password{% endblock %}

{% block content %}
  <h1>Reset your password</h1>
  <p>We've emailed you instructions for setting your password.</p>
  <p>If you don't receive an email, please make sure you've entered the
address you registered with.</p>
{% endblock %}
```

Create another template in the same directory and name it `password_reset_confirm.html`. Add the following code to it:

```
{% extends "base.html" %}

{% block title %}Reset your password{% endblock %}

{% block content %}
  <h1>Reset your password</h1>
  {% if validlink %}
    <p>Please enter your new password twice:</p>
    <form action="." method="post">
      {{ form.as_p }}
      {% csrf_token %}
      <p><input type="submit" value="Change my password" /></p>
    </form>
  {% else %}
    <p>The password reset link was invalid, possibly because it has
    already been used. Please request a new password reset.</p>
  {% endif %}
{% endblock %}
```

We check whether the provided link is valid. The view `PasswordResetConfirmView` sets this variable and puts it in the context of the `password_reset_confirm.html` template. If the link is valid, we display the user password reset form.

Create another template and name it `password_reset_complete.html`. Enter the following code into it:

```
{% extends "base.html" %}

{% block title %}Password reset{% endblock %}

{% block content %}
  <h1>Password set</h1>
  <p>Your password has been set. You can <a href="{% url "login" %}">log in
now</a></p>
{% endblock %}
```

Finally, edit the `registration/login.html` template of the `account` application, and add the following code after the `<form>` element:

```
<p><a href="{% url "password_reset" %}">Forgotten your
  password?</a></p>
```

Now, open `http://127.0.0.1:8000/account/login/` in your browser and click on the **Forgotten your password?** link. You should see the following page:

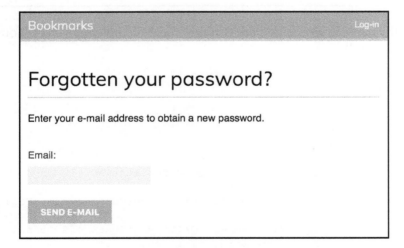

At this point, you need to add an SMTP configuration to the `settings.py` file of your project so that Django is able to send emails. You learned how to add email settings to your project in Chapter 2, *Enhancing Your Blog with Advanced Features*. However, during development, you can configure Django to write emails to the standard output instead of sending them through an SMTP server. Django provides an email backend to write emails to the console. Edit the `settings.py` file of your project, and add the following line:

```
EMAIL_BACKEND = 'django.core.mail.backends.console.EmailBackend'
```

The `EMAIL_BACKEND` setting indicates the class to use to send emails.

Return to your browser, enter the email address of an existing user, and click on the **SEND E-MAIL** button. You should see the following page:

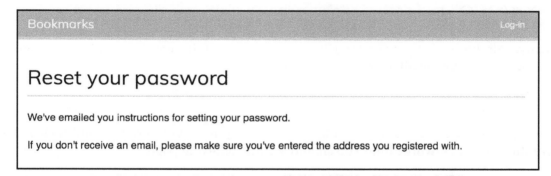

Take a look at the console where you are running the development server. You will see the generated email, as follows:

```
Content-Type: text/plain; charset="utf-8"
MIME-Version: 1.0
Content-Transfer-Encoding: 7bit
Subject: Password reset on 127.0.0.1:8000
From: webmaster@localhost
To: user@domain.com
Date: Fri, 15 Dec 2017 14:35:08 -0000
Message-ID: <20150924143508.62996.55653@zenx.local>

Someone asked for password reset for email user@domain.com. Follow the link
below:
http://127.0.0.1:8000/account/reset/MQ/45f-9c3f30caafd523055fcc/
Your username, in case you've forgotten: zenx
```

The email is rendered using the `password_reset_email.html` template we created earlier. The URL to reset your password includes a token that was generated dynamically by Django. Copy the URL and open it in your browser. You should see the following page:

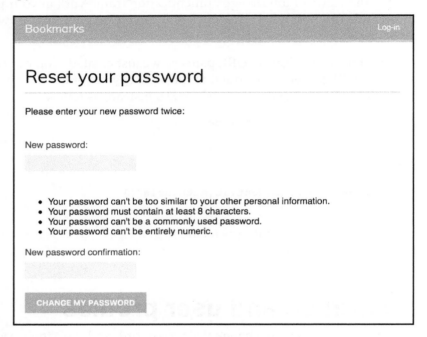

The page to set a new password corresponds to the `password_reset_confirm.html` template. Fill in a new password and click on the **CHANGE MY PASSWORD** button. Django creates a new encrypted password and saves it in the database. You will see the following success page:

Now, you can log back into your account using your new password.

Each token to set a new password can be used only once. If you open the link you received again, you will get a message stating that the token is invalid.

You have integrated the views of the Django authentication framework in your project. These views are suitable for most cases. However, you can create your own views if you need a different behavior.

Django also provides the authentication URL patterns we just created. You can comment out the authentication URL patterns we added to the `urls.py` file of the `account` application and include `django.contrib.auth.urls` instead, as follows:

```
from django.urls import path, include
# ...

urlpatterns = [
    # ...
    path('', include('django.contrib.auth.urls')),
]
```

You can see the authentication URL patterns included at https://github.com/django/django/blob/stable/2.0.x/django/contrib/auth/urls.py.

User registration and user profiles

Existing users can now log in, log out, change their password, and reset their password. Now, we will need to build a view to allow visitors to create a user account.

User registration

Let's create a simple view to allow user registration on our website. Initially, we have to create a form to let the user enter a username, their real name, and a password. Edit the `forms.py` file located inside the `account` application directory and add the following code to it:

```
from django.contrib.auth.models import User

class UserRegistrationForm(forms.ModelForm):
    password = forms.CharField(label='Password',
                               widget=forms.PasswordInput)
    password2 = forms.CharField(label='Repeat password',
                                widget=forms.PasswordInput)
```

```
class Meta:
    model = User
    fields = ('username', 'first_name', 'email')

def clean_password2(self):
    cd = self.cleaned_data
    if cd['password'] != cd['password2']:
        raise forms.ValidationError('Passwords don\'t match.')
    return cd['password2']
```

We have created a model form for the user model. In our form, we include only the username, first_name, and email fields of the model. These fields will be validated based on their corresponding model fields. For example, if the user chooses a username that already exists, they will get a validation error because username is a field defined with unique=True. We have added two additional fields—password and password2—for users to set their password and confirm it. We have defined a clean_password2() method to check the second password against the first one and not let the form validate if the passwords don't match. This check is done when we validate the form calling its is_valid() method. You can provide a clean_<fieldname>() method to any of your form fields in order to clean the value or raise form validation errors for a specific field. Forms also include a general clean() method to validate the entire form, which is useful to validate fields that depend on each other.

Django also provides a UserCreationForm form that you can use, which resides in django.contrib.auth.forms and is very similar to the one we have created.

Edit the views.py file of the account application and add the following code to it:

```
from .forms import LoginForm, UserRegistrationForm

def register(request):
    if request.method == 'POST':
        user_form = UserRegistrationForm(request.POST)
        if user_form.is_valid():
            # Create a new user object but avoid saving it yet
            new_user = user_form.save(commit=False)
            # Set the chosen password
            new_user.set_password(
                user_form.cleaned_data['password'])
            # Save the User object
            new_user.save()
            return render(request,
                          'account/register_done.html',
                          {'new_user': new_user})
    else:
```

```
      user_form = UserRegistrationForm()
  return render(request,
                'account/register.html',
                {'user_form': user_form})
```

The view for creating user accounts is quite simple. Instead of saving the raw password entered by the user, we use the set_password() method of the user model that handles encryption to save for safety reasons.

Now, edit the urls.py file of your account application and add the following URL pattern:

```
path('register/', views.register, name='register'),
```

Finally, create a new template in the account/ template directory, name it register.html, and make it look as follows:

```
{% extends "base.html" %}

{% block title %}Create an account{% endblock %}

{% block content %}
  <h1>Create an account</h1>
  <p>Please, sign up using the following form:</p>
  <form action="." method="post">
    {{ user_form.as_p }}
    {% csrf_token %}
    <p><input type="submit" value="Create my account"></p>
  </form>
{% endblock %}
```

Add a template file in the same directory and name it register_done.html. Add the following code to it:

```
{% extends "base.html" %}

{% block title %}Welcome{% endblock %}

{% block content %}
  <h1>Welcome {{ new_user.first_name }}!</h1>
  <p>Your account has been successfully created. Now you can <a href="{%
url "login" %}">log in</a>.</p>
{% endblock %}
```

Now, open `http://127.0.0.1:8000/account/register/` in your browser. You will see the registration page you have created:

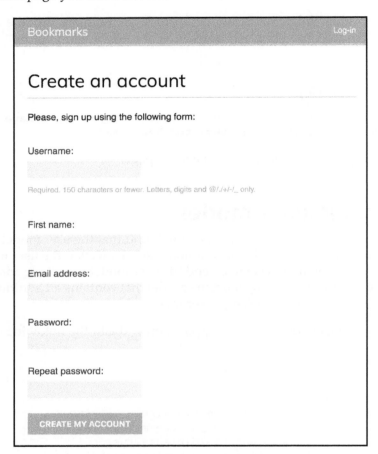

Fill in the details for a new user and click on the **CREATE MY ACCOUNT** button. If all fields are valid, the user will be created, and you will get the following success message:

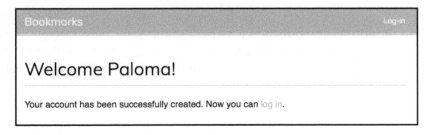

Click on the **log in** link and enter your username and password to verify that you can access your account.

Now, you can also add a link to registration in your login template. Edit the `registration/login.html` template; take a look at the following line:

```
<p>Please, use the following form to log-in:</p>
```

Replace it with the following:

```
<p>Please, use the following form to log-in. If you don't have an account
<a href="{% url "register" %}">register here</a></p>
```

We made the signup page accessible from the login page.

Extending the user model

When you have to deal with user accounts, you will find that the user model of the Django authentication framework is suitable for common cases. However, the user model comes with very basic fields. You may wish to extend the user model to include additional data. The best way to do this is by creating a profile model that contains all additional fields and a one-to-one relationship with the Django user model.

Edit the `models.py` file of your `account` application and add the following code to it:

```
from django.db import models
from django.conf import settings

class Profile(models.Model):
    user = models.OneToOneField(settings.AUTH_USER_MODEL,
                                on_delete=models.CASCADE)
    date_of_birth = models.DateField(blank=True, null=True)
    photo = models.ImageField(upload_to='users/%Y/%m/%d/',
                              blank=True)

    def __str__(self):
        return 'Profile for user {}'.format(self.user.username)
```

 In order to keep your code generic, use the `get_user_model()` method to retrieve the user model and the `AUTH_USER_MODEL` setting to refer to it when defining a model's relations to the user model, instead of referring to the auth user model directly.

The user one-to-one field allows you to associate profiles with users. We use CASCADE for the on_delete parameter so that its related profile also gets deleted when a user is deleted. The photo field is an ImageField field. You will need to install the Pillow library to handle images. Install Pillow by running the following command in your shell:

```
pip install Pillow==5.1.0
```

For Django to serve media files uploaded by users with the development server, add the following settings to the settings.py file of your project:

```
MEDIA_URL = '/media/'
MEDIA_ROOT = os.path.join(BASE_DIR, 'media/')
```

MEDIA_URL is the base URL to serve the media files uploaded by users, and MEDIA_ROOT is the local path where they reside. We build the path dynamically relative to our project path to make our code more generic.

Now, edit the main urls.py file of the bookmarks project and modify the code, as follows:

```
from django.contrib import admin
from django.urls import path, include
from django.conf import settings
from django.conf.urls.static import static

urlpatterns = [
    path('admin/', admin.site.urls),
    path('account/', include('account.urls')),
]

if settings.DEBUG:
    urlpatterns += static(settings.MEDIA_URL,
                          document_root=settings.MEDIA_ROOT)
```

In this way, the Django development server will be in charge of serving the media files during development (that is when the DEBUG setting is set to True).

 The static() helper function is suitable for development, but not for production use. Never serve your static files with Django in a production environment.

Open the shell and run the following command to create the database migration for the new model:

```
python manage.py makemigrations
```

You will get the following output:

```
Migrations for 'account':
  account/migrations/0001_initial.py
    - Create model Profile
```

Next, sync the database with the following command:

```
python manage.py migrate
```

You will see an output that includes the following line:

```
Applying account.0001_initial... OK
```

Edit the admin.py file of the account application and register the Profile model in the administration site, like this:

```
from django.contrib import admin
from .models import Profile

@admin.register(Profile)
class ProfileAdmin(admin.ModelAdmin):
    list_display = ['user', 'date_of_birth', 'photo']
```

Run the development server using the python manage.py runserver command and open http://127.0.0.1:8000/admin/ in your browser. Now, you should be able to see the **Profiles** model in the administration site of your project, as follows:

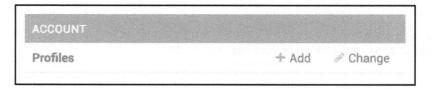

Now, we will let users edit their profile on the website. Add the following import and model forms to the forms.py file of the account application:

```
from .models import Profile

class UserEditForm(forms.ModelForm):
    class Meta:
        model = User
        fields = ('first_name', 'last_name', 'email')

class ProfileEditForm(forms.ModelForm):
    class Meta:
```

```
model = Profile
fields = ('date_of_birth', 'photo')
```

These forms are as follows:

- `UserEditForm`: This will allow users to edit their first name, last name, and email, which are attributes of the built-in Django user model.
- `ProfileEditForm`: This will allow users to edit the profile data we save in the custom `Profile` model. Users will be able to edit their date of birth and upload a picture for their profile.

Edit the `views.py` file of the `account` application and import the `Profile` model, like this:

```
from .models import Profile
```

Then, add the following lines to the `register` view below `new_user.save()`:

```
# Create the user profile
Profile.objects.create(user=new_user)
```

When users register on our site, we will create an empty profile associated with them. You should create a `Profile` object manually using the administration site for the users you created before.

Now, we will let users edit their profile. Add the following code to the same file:

```
from .forms import LoginForm, UserRegistrationForm, \
                    UserEditForm, ProfileEditForm

@login_required
def edit(request):
    if request.method == 'POST':
        user_form = UserEditForm(instance=request.user,
                                 data=request.POST)
        profile_form = ProfileEditForm(
                                instance=request.user.profile,
                                data=request.POST,
                                files=request.FILES)
        if user_form.is_valid() and profile_form.is_valid():
            user_form.save()
            profile_form.save()
    else:
        user_form = UserEditForm(instance=request.user)
        profile_form = ProfileEditForm(
                                instance=request.user.profile)
    return render(request,
```

```
        'account/edit.html',
        {'user_form': user_form,
         'profile_form': profile_form})
```

We use the `login_required` decorator because users have to be authenticated to edit their profile. In this case, we are using two model forms: `UserEditForm` to store the data of the built-in user model and `ProfileEditForm` to store the additional profile data in the custom `Profile` model. To validate the submitted data, we will execute the `is_valid()` method of both forms. If both forms contain valid data, we will save both forms, calling the `save()` method to update the corresponding objects in the database.

Add the following URL pattern to the `urls.py` file of the `account` application:

```
path('edit/', views.edit, name='edit'),
```

Finally, create a template for this view in `templates/account/` and name it `edit.html`. Add the following code to it:

```
{% extends "base.html" %}

{% block title %}Edit your account{% endblock %}

{% block content %}
  <h1>Edit your account</h1>
  <p>You can edit your account using the following form:</p>
  <form action="." method="post" enctype="multipart/form-data">
    {{ user_form.as_p }}
    {{ profile_form.as_p }}
    {% csrf_token %}
    <p><input type="submit" value="Save changes"></p>
  </form>
{% endblock %}
```

We include `enctype="multipart/form-data"` in our form to enable file uploads. We use an HTML form to submit both the `user_form` and the `profile_form` forms.

Register a new user and open `http://127.0.0.1:8000/account/edit/`. You should see the following page:

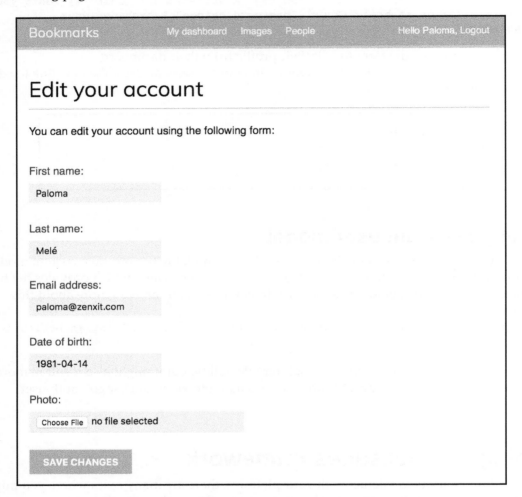

Now, you can also edit the dashboard page and include links to the edit profile and change password pages. Open the `account/dashboard.html` template:

```
<p>Welcome to your dashboard.</p>
```

Replace the preceding line with the following one:

```
<p>Welcome to your dashboard. You can <a href="{% url "edit" %}">edit your
profile</a> or <a href="{% url "password_change" %}">change your
password</a>.</p>
```

Users can now access the form to edit their profile from their dashboard.
Open `http://127.0.0.1:8000/account/` in your browser and test the new link to edit
the user's profile:

Dashboard

Welcome to your dashboard. You can edit your profile or change your password.

Using a custom user model

Django also offers a way to substitute the whole user model with your own custom model.
Your user class should inherit from Django's `AbstractUser` class, which provides the full
implementation of the default user as an abstract model. You can read more about this
method
at `https://docs.djangoproject.com/en/2.0/topics/auth/customizing/#substituting-a-custom-user-model`.

Using a custom user model will give you more flexibility, but it might also result in more
difficult integration with pluggable applications that interact with Django's auth user
model.

Using the messages framework

When allowing users to interact with your platform, there are many cases where you might
want to inform them about the result of their actions. Django has a built-in messages
framework that allows you to display one-time notifications to your users.

The messages framework is located at `django.contrib.messages` and is included in the
default `INSTALLED_APPS` list of the `settings.py` file when you create new projects using
`python manage.py startproject`. You will note that your settings file contains a
middleware named `django.contrib.messages.middleware.MessageMiddleware` in
the `MIDDLEWARE` settings.

The messages framework provides a simple way to add messages to users. Messages are stored in a cookie by default (falling back to session storage), and they are displayed in the next request the user does. You can use the messages framework in your views by importing the `messages` module and adding new messages with simple shortcuts, as follows:

```
from django.contrib import messages
messages.error(request, 'Something went wrong')
```

You can create new messages using the `add_message()` method or any of the following shortcut methods:

- `success()`: Success messages to be displayed after an action was successful
- `info()`: Informational messages
- `warning()`: Something has not yet failed but may fail imminently
- `error()`: An action was not successful, or something failed
- `debug()`: Debug messages that will be removed or ignored in a production environment

Let's add messages to our platform. Since the messages framework applies globally to the project, we can display messages for the user in our base template. Open the `base.html` template of the `account` application and add the following code between the `<div>` element with the `header` ID and the `<div>` element with the `content` ID:

```
{% if messages %}
  <ul class="messages">
    {% for message in messages %}
      <li class="{{ message.tags }}">
        {{ message|safe }}
          <a href="#" class="close">x</a>
      </li>
    {% endfor %}
  </ul>
{% endif %}
```

The messages framework includes the context processor `django.contrib.messages.context_processors.messages` that adds a `messages` variable to the request context. You can find it in the `context_processors` list of the `TEMPLATES` setting of your project. You can use this variable in your templates to display all existing messages to the user.

Now, let's modify our edit view to use the messages framework. Edit the `views.py` file of the `account` application, import `messages`, and make the `edit` view look as follows:

```python
from django.contrib import messages

@login_required
def edit(request):
    if request.method == 'POST':
        # ...
        if user_form.is_valid() and profile_form.is_valid():
            user_form.save()
            profile_form.save()
            messages.success(request, 'Profile updated '\
                                      'successfully')
        else:
            messages.error(request, 'Error updating your profile')
    else:
        user_form = UserEditForm(instance=request.user)
        # ...
```

We add a success message when the user successfully updates their profile. If any of the forms contain invalid data, we add an error message instead.

Open `http://127.0.0.1:8000/account/edit/` in your browser and edit your profile. When the profile is successfully updated, you should see the following message:

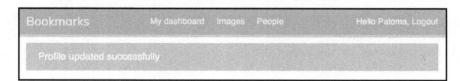

When data is not valid, for example, using an incorrectly formatted date for the **Date of birth** field, you should see the following message:

You can learn more about the messages framework at `https://docs.djangoproject.com/en/2.0/ref/contrib/messages/`.

Building a custom authentication backend

Django allows you to authenticate against different sources. The `AUTHENTICATION_BACKENDS` setting includes the list of authentication backends for your project. By default, this setting is set as follows:

```
['django.contrib.auth.backends.ModelBackend']
```

The default `ModelBackend` authenticates users against the database using the user model of `django.contrib.auth`. This will suit most of your projects. However, you can create custom backends to authenticate your user against other sources, such as an LDAP directory or any other system.

You can read more information about customizing authentication at `https://docs.djangoproject.com/en/2.0/topics/auth/customizing/#other-authentication-sources`.

Whenever you use the `authenticate()` function of `django.contrib.auth`, Django tries to authenticate the user against each of the backends defined in `AUTHENTICATION_BACKENDS` one by one, until one of them successfully authenticates the user. Only if all of the backends fail to authenticate will the user not be authenticated into your site.

Django provides a simple way to define your own authentication backends. An authentication backend is a class that provides the following two methods:

- `authenticate()`: It takes the `request` object and user credentials as parameters. It has to return a `user` object that matches those credentials if the credentials are valid, or `None` otherwise. The `request` parameter is an `HttpRequest` object, or `None` if it's not provided to `authenticate()`.
- `get_user()`: Takes a user ID parameter and has to return a `user` object.

Creating a custom authentication backend is as simple as writing a Python class that implements both methods. We will create an authentication backend to let users authenticate in our site using their email address instead of their username.

Create a new file inside your `account` application directory and name it `authentication.py`. Add the following code to it:

```
from django.contrib.auth.models import User

class EmailAuthBackend(object):
    """
```

```
Authenticate using an e-mail address.
"""
def authenticate(self, request, username=None, password=None):
    try:
        user = User.objects.get(email=username)
        if user.check_password(password):
            return user
        return None
    except User.DoesNotExist:
        return None

def get_user(self, user_id):
    try:
        return User.objects.get(pk=user_id)
    except User.DoesNotExist:
        return None
```

The preceding code is a simple authentication backend. The `authenticate()` method receives a `request` object and the `username` and `password` optional parameters. We could use different parameters, but we use `username` and `password` to make our backend work with the authentication framework views straight away. The preceding code works as follows:

- `authenticate()`: We try to retrieve a user with the given email address and check the password using the built-in `check_password()` method of the user model. This method handles the password hashing to compare the given password against the password stored in the database.
- `get_user()`: We get a user through the ID set in the `user_id` parameter. Django uses the backend that authenticated the user to retrieve the `User` object for the duration of the user session.

Edit the `settings.py` file of your project and add the following setting:

```
AUTHENTICATION_BACKENDS = [
    'django.contrib.auth.backends.ModelBackend',
    'account.authentication.EmailAuthBackend',
]
```

In the preceding setting, we kept the default `ModelBackend` that is used to authenticate with username and password and included our own email-based authentication backend. Now, open `http://127.0.0.1:8000/account/login/` in your browser. Remember that Django will try to authenticate the user against each of the backends, so now we should be able to log in seamlessly using your username or email account. User credentials will be checked using the `ModelBackend` authentication backend, and if no user is returned, credentials will be checked using our custom `EmailAuthBackend` backend.

 The order of the backends listed in the `AUTHENTICATION_BACKENDS` setting matters. If the same credentials are valid for multiple backends, Django will stop at the first backend that successfully authenticates the user.

Adding social authentication to your site

You might also want to add social authentication to your site using services such as Facebook, Twitter, or Google. Python Social Auth is a Python module that simplifies the process of adding social authentication to our website. Using this module, you can let your users log in to your website using their account of other services. You can find the code of this module at `https://github.com/python-social-auth`.

This module comes with authentication backends for different Python frameworks, including Django. To install the Django package via `pip`, open the console and run the following command:

```
pip install social-auth-app-django==2.1.0
```

Then, add `social_django` to the `INSTALLED_APPS` setting in the `settings.py` file of your project:

```
INSTALLED_APPS = [
    #...
    'social_django',
]
```

This is the default application to add python-social-auth to Django projects. Now, run the following command to sync python-social-auth models with your database:

```
python manage.py migrate
```

You should see that the migrations for the default application are applied as follows:

```
Applying social_django.0001_initial... OK
Applying social_django.0002_add_related_name... OK
...
Applying social_django.0008_partial_timestamp... OK
```

Python-social-auth includes backends for multiple services. You can see a list of all backends at https://python-social-auth.readthedocs.io/en/latest/backends/index.html#supported-backends.

We will include authentication backends for Facebook, Twitter, and Google.

You will need to add social login URL patterns to your project. Open the main urls.py file of the bookmarks project and include the social_django URL patterns as follows:

```
urlpatterns = [
    path('admin/', admin.site.urls),
    path('account/', include('account.urls')),
    path('social-auth/',
        include('social_django.urls', namespace='social')),
]
```

Several social services will not allow the redirecting of users to 127.0.0.1 or localhost after a successful authentication. In order to make social authentication work, you will need a domain. In order to fix this, under Linux or macOS X, edit your /etc/hosts file and add the following line to it:

```
127.0.0.1 mysite.com
```

This will tell your computer to point the mysite.com hostname to your own machine. If you are using Windows, your hosts file is located at C:\Windows\System32\Drivers\etc\hosts.

To verify that your host redirection worked, start the development server with python manage.py runserver and open http://mysite.com:8000/account/login/ in your browser. You will see the following error:

DisallowedHost at /account/login/

Invalid HTTP_HOST header: 'mysite.com:8000'. You may need to add 'mysite.com' to ALLOWED_HOSTS.

Django controls the hosts able to serve your application using the ALLOWED_HOSTS setting. This is a security measure to prevent HTTP host header attacks. Django will only allow the hosts included in this list to serve the application. You can learn more about the ALLOWED_HOSTS setting at https://docs.djangoproject.com/en/2.0/ref/settings/#allowed-hosts.

Edit the settings.py file of your project and edit the ALLOWED_HOSTS setting as follows:

```
ALLOWED_HOSTS = ['mysite.com', 'localhost', '127.0.0.1']
```

Besides the mysite.com host, we explicitly include localhost and 127.0.0.1. We do this to be able to access the site through localhost, which is the default Django's behavior when DEBUG is True and ALLOWED_HOSTS is empty. Now, you should be able to open http://mysite.com:8000/account/login/ in your browser.

Authentication using Facebook

In order to let your users log in with their Facebook account to your site, add the following line to the AUTHENTICATION_BACKENDS setting in the settings.py file of your project:

```
'social_core.backends.facebook.FacebookOAuth2',
```

In order to add social authentication with Facebook, you will need a Facebook developer account and to create a new Facebook application. Open https://developers.facebook.com/apps/ in your browser. You will see the following header in the site:

Click on the **Add a New App** button. You will see the following form to create a new app ID:

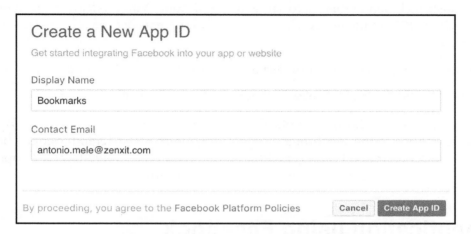

Enter `Bookmarks` as **Display Name**, add a contact email address, and click on **Create App ID**. You will see a dashboard for your new app that displays different features you can set up for your app. Look for the following **Facebook Login** box and click on **Set Up**:

You will be asked to choose the platform, as follows:

Select the **Web** platform. You will see the following form:

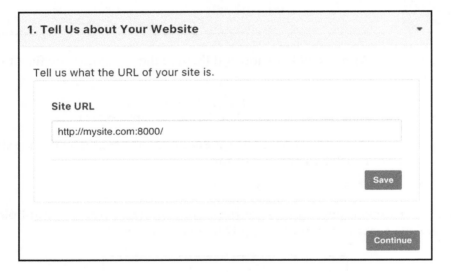

Enter `http://mysite.com:8000/` as your **Site URL** and click on the **Save** button. You can skip the rest of the quickstart process. In the left-hand menu, click on **Dashboard**. You will see something similar to the following:

Copy the **App ID** and **App Secret** keys and add them to the `settings.py` file of your project, as follows:

```
SOCIAL_AUTH_FACEBOOK_KEY = 'XXX' # Facebook App ID
SOCIAL_AUTH_FACEBOOK_SECRET = 'XXX' # Facebook App Secret
```

Optionally, you can define a `SOCIAL_AUTH_FACEBOOK_SCOPE` setting with the extra permissions you want to ask Facebook users for:

```
SOCIAL_AUTH_FACEBOOK_SCOPE = ['email']
```

Now, go back to Facebook and click on **Settings**. You will see a form with multiple settings for your app. Add `mysite.com` under **App Domains**, as follows:

Click on **Save Changes**. Then, in the left-hand menu, click on **Facebook Login**. Ensure that only the following settings are active:

- **Client OAuth Login**
- **Web OAuth Login**
- **Embedded Browser OAuth Login**

Enter `http://mysite.com:8000/social-auth/complete/facebook/` under **Valid OAuth redirect URIs**. The selection should look like this:

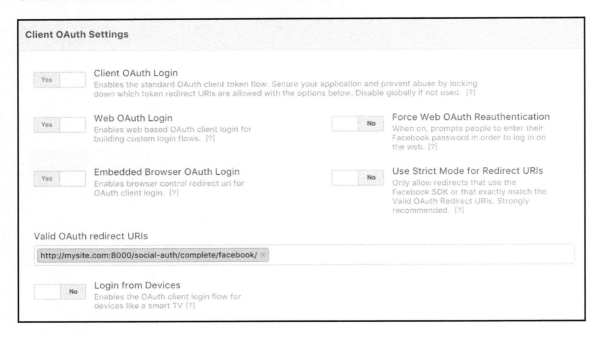

Open the `registration/login.html` template of your `account` application and append the following code at the bottom of the `content` block:

```
<div class="social">
  <ul>
    <li class="facebook"><a href="{% url "social:begin" "facebook" %}">Sign
in with Facebook</a></li>
  </ul>
</div>
```

Open `http://mysite.com:8000/account/login/` in your browser. Now, the login page will look as follows:

Click on the **Sign in with Facebook** button. You will be redirected to Facebook, and you will see a modal dialog asking for your permission to let the *Bookmarks* application access your public Facebook profile:

Click on the **Continue as ...** button. You will be logged in and redirected to the dashboard page of your site. Remember that we have set this URL in the LOGIN_REDIRECT_URL setting. As you can see, adding social authentication to your site is pretty straightforward.

Authentication using Twitter

For social authentication using Twitter, add the following line to the AUTHENTICATION_BACKENDS setting in the settings.py file of your project:

```
'social_core.backends.twitter.TwitterOAuth',
```

You will need to create a new application in your Twitter account. Open https://apps.twitter.com/app/new in your browser. You will see the following form:

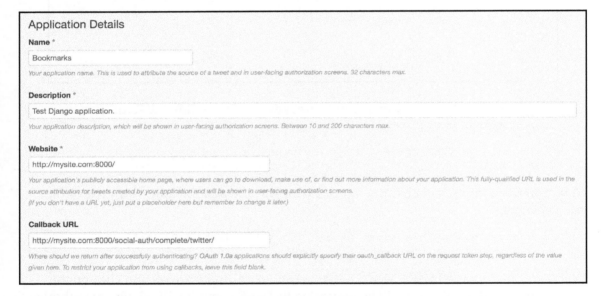

Enter the details of your application, including the following settings:

- **Website**: http://mysite.com:8000/
- **Callback URL**:
  http://mysite.com:8000/social-auth/complete/twitter/

Then, click on **Create your Twitter application**. You will see the application details. Click on **Keys and Access Tokens**. You should see the following information:

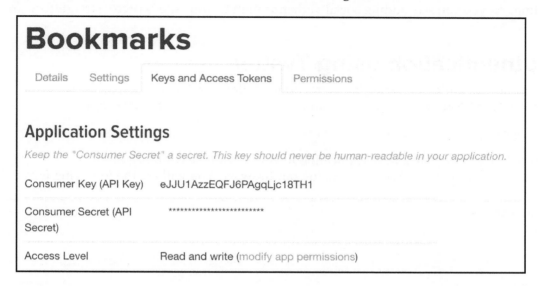

Copy the **Consumer Key** and **Consumer Secret** keys into the following settings in the `settings.py` file of your project:

```
SOCIAL_AUTH_TWITTER_KEY = 'XXX' # Twitter Consumer Key
SOCIAL_AUTH_TWITTER_SECRET = 'XXX' # Twitter Consumer Secret
```

Now, edit the `registration/login.html` template and add the following code to the `<ul>` element:

```
<li class="twitter"><a href="{% url "social:begin" "twitter"
 %}">Login with Twitter</a></li>
```

Open `http://mysite.com:8000/account/login/` in your browser and click on the **Login with Twitter** link. You will be redirected to Twitter, and it will ask you to authorize the application as follows:

**Authorize Bookmarks Test to use
your account?**

Authorize app   Cancel

Bookmarks

mysite.com:8000/

Test Django application.

This application will be able to:

- Read Tweets from your timeline.
- See who you follow.

Will not be able to:

- Follow new people.
- Update your profile.
- Post Tweets for you.
- Access your direct messages.
- See your email address.
- See your Twitter password.

Click on **Authorize app**. You will be logged in and redirected to the dashboard page of
your site.

Authentication using Google

Google offers OAuth2 authentication. You can read about Google's OAuth2
implementation at `https://developers.google.com/identity/protocols/OAuth2`.

To implement authentication using Google, add the following line to
the AUTHENTICATION_BACKENDS setting in the settings.py file of your project:

```
'social_core.backends.google.GoogleOAuth2',
```

First, you will need to create an API key in your Google Developer Console. Open `https://console.developers.google.com/apis/credentials` in your browser. Click on **Select a project** and create a new project, as follows:

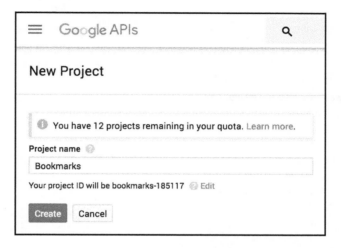

After the project is created, under **Credentials**, click on **Create credentials** and choose **OAuth client ID**, as follows:

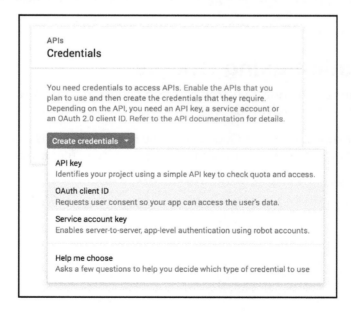

Google will ask you to configure the consent screen first:

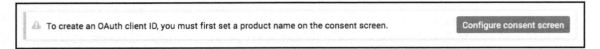

The preceding page is the page that will be shown to users to give their consent to access your site with their Google account. Click on the **Configure consent screen** button. Select your email address, enter `Bookmarks` under **Product name**, and click on the **Save** button. The consent screen for your application will be configured, and you will be redirected to finish creating your client ID.

Fill in the form with the following information:

- **Application type**: Select **Web application**
- **Name**: Enter `Bookmarks`
- **Authorized redirect URIs**: Add
  `http://mysite.com:8000/social-auth/complete/google-oauth2/`

The form should look like this:

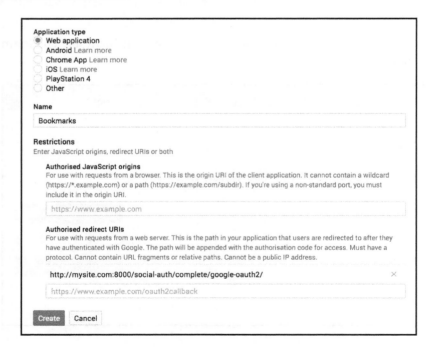

Click on the **Create** button. You will get the **Client ID** and **Client Secret** keys. Add them to your `settings.py` file, like this:

```
SOCIAL_AUTH_GOOGLE_OAUTH2_KEY = 'XXX' # Google Consumer Key
SOCIAL_AUTH_GOOGLE_OAUTH2_SECRET = 'XXX' # Google Consumer Secret
```

In the left-hand menu of the Google Developers Console, under the **APIs & Services** section, click on the **Library** link. You will see a list that contains all Google APIs. Click on **Google+ API** and then click on the **ENABLE** button in the following page:

Edit the `login.html` template and add the following code to the `<ul>` element:

```
<li class="google"><a href="{% url "social:begin" "google-oauth2" %}">Login
with Google</a></li>
```

Open `http://mysite.com:8000/account/login/` in your browser. The login page should now look as follows:

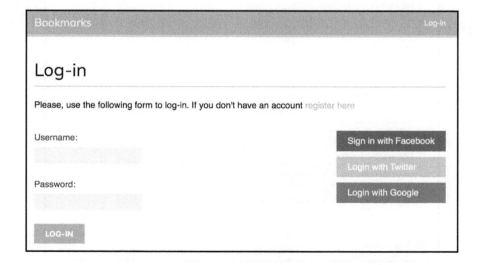

Click on the **Login with Google** button. You will be logged in and redirected to the dashboard page of your website.

You have added social authentication to your project. You can easily implement social authentication with other popular online services using Python Social Auth.

Summary

In this chapter, you learned how to build an authentication system into your site and created custom user profiles. You also added social authentication to your site.

In the next chapter, you will learn how to create an image bookmarking system, generate image thumbnails, and build AJAX views.

5
Sharing Content in Your Website

In the preceding chapter, you built user registration and authentication into your website. You learned how to create a custom profile model for your users and added social authentication to your site with major social networks.

In this chapter, you will learn how to create a JavaScript bookmarklet to share content from other sites into your website, and you will implement AJAX features into your project using jQuery and Django.

This chapter will cover the following points:

- Creating many-to-many relationships
- Customizing behavior for forms
- Using jQuery with Django
- Building a jQuery bookmarklet
- Generating image thumbnails using sorl-thumbnail
- Implementing AJAX views and integrating them with jQuery
- Creating custom decorators for views
- Building AJAX pagination

Creating an image bookmarking website

We will allow users to bookmark and share images they find on other websites and on our site. For this, we will need to do the following tasks:

1. Define a model to store images and their information

2. Create a form and a view to handle image uploads
3. Build a system for users to be able to post images they find on external websites

First, create a new application inside your `bookmarks` project directory with the following command:

```
django-admin startapp images
```

Add the new app to the INSTALLED_APPS setting in the `settings.py` file, as follows:

```
INSTALLED_APPS = [
    # ...
    'images.apps.ImagesConfig',
]
```

We have activated the `images` application in the project.

Building the image model

Edit the `models.py` file of the `images` application and add the following code to it:

```
from django.db import models
from django.conf import settings

class Image(models.Model):
    user = models.ForeignKey(settings.AUTH_USER_MODEL,
                             related_name='images_created',
                             on_delete=models.CASCADE)
    title = models.CharField(max_length=200)
    slug = models.SlugField(max_length=200,
                            blank=True)
    url = models.URLField()
    image = models.ImageField(upload_to='images/%Y/%m/%d/')
    description = models.TextField(blank=True)
    created = models.DateField(auto_now_add=True,
                               db_index=True)

    def __str__(self):
        return self.title
```

This is the model we will use to store images bookmarked from different sites. Let's take a look at the fields of this model:

- user: This indicates the User object that bookmarked this image. This is a foreign key field because it specifies a one-to-many relationship. A user can post multiple images, but each image is posted by a single user. We use CASCADE for the on_delete parameter so that related images are also deleted when a user is deleted.
- title: A title for the image.
- slug: A short label that contains only letters, numbers, underscores, or hyphens to be used for building beautiful SEO-friendly URLs.
- url: The original URL for this image.
- image: The image file.
- description: An optional description for the image.
- created: The date and time that indicate when the object has been created in the database. Since we use auto_now_add, this datetime is automatically set when the object is created. We use db_index=True so that Django creates an index in the database for this field.

 Database indexes improve query performance. Consider setting db_index=True for fields that you frequently query using filter(), exclude(), or order_by(). ForeignKey fields or fields with unique=True imply the creation of an index. You can also use Meta.index_together to create indexes for multiple fields.

We will override the save() method of the Image model to automatically generate the slug field based on the value of the title field. Import the slugify() function and add a save() method to the Image model, as follows:

```
from django.utils.text import slugify

class Image(models.Model):
    # ...
    def save(self, *args, **kwargs):
    if not self.slug:
        self.slug = slugify(self.title)
    super(Image, self).save(*args, **kwargs)
```

In the preceding code, we use the `slugify()` function provided by Django to automatically generate the image slug for the given title when no slug is provided. Then, we save the object. We will generate slugs for images automatically so that users don't have to manually enter a slug for each image.

Creating many-to-many relationships

We will add another field to the `Image` model to store the users who like an image. We will need a many-to-many relationship in this case because a user might like multiple images and each image can be liked by multiple users.

Add the following field to the `Image` model:

```
users_like = models.ManyToManyField(settings.AUTH_USER_MODEL,
                                     related_name='images_liked',
                                     blank=True)
```

When you define a `ManyToManyField`, Django creates an intermediary join table using the primary keys of both models. The `ManyToManyField` can be defined in any of the two related models.

As with `ForeignKey` fields, the `related_name` attribute of `ManyToManyField` allows us to name the relationship from the related object back to this one. The `ManyToManyField` fields provide a many-to-many manager that allows us to retrieve related objects, such as `image.users_like.all()`, or from a `user` object, such as `user.images_liked.all()`.

Open the command line and run the following command to create an initial migration:

```
python manage.py makemigrations images
```

You should see the following output:

```
Migrations for 'images':
  images/migrations/0001_initial.py
    - Create model Image
```

Now, run the following command to apply your migration:

```
python manage.py migrate images
```

You will get an output that includes the following line:

```
Applying images.0001_initial... OK
```

The Image model is now synced to the database.

Registering the image model in the administration site

Edit the `admin.py` file of the `images` application and register the Image model into the administration site, as follows:

```python
from django.contrib import admin
from .models import Image

@admin.register(Image)
class ImageAdmin(admin.ModelAdmin):
    list_display = ['title', 'slug', 'image', 'created']
    list_filter = ['created']
```

Start the development server with the `python manage.py runserver` command. Open `http://127.0.0.1:8000/admin/` in your browser, and you will see the Image model in the administration site, like this:

Posting content from other websites

We will allow users to bookmark images from external websites. The user will provide the URL of the image, a title, and optional description. Our application will download the image and create a new Image object in the database.

Let's start by building a form to submit new images. Create a new `forms.py` file inside the `Images` application directory and add the following code to it:

```
from django import forms
from .models import Image

class ImageCreateForm(forms.ModelForm):
    class Meta:
        model = Image
        fields = ('title', 'url', 'description')
        widgets = {
            'url': forms.HiddenInput,
        }
```

As you would notice in this preceding code, this form is a `ModelForm` form built from the `Image` model, including only the `title`, `url`, and `description` fields. Users will not enter the image URL directly in the form. Instead, we will provide them with a JavaScript tool to choose an image from an external site, and our form will receive its URL as a parameter. We override the default widget of the `url` field to use a `HiddenInput` widget. This widget is rendered as an HTML `input` element with a `type="hidden"` attribute. We use this widget because we don't want this field to be visible to users.

Cleaning form fields

In order to verify that the provided image URL is valid, we will check that the filename ends with a `.jpg` or `.jpeg` extension to only allow JPEG files. As you saw in the preceding chapter, Django allows you to define form methods to clean specific fields using the `clean_<fieldname>()` notation. This method is executed for each field, if present, when you call `is_valid()` on a form instance. In the clean method, you can alter the field's value or raise any validation errors for this specific field when needed. Add the following method to `ImageCreateForm`:

```
def clean_url(self):
    url = self.cleaned_data['url']
    valid_extensions = ['jpg', 'jpeg']
    extension = url.rsplit('.', 1)[1].lower()
    if extension not in valid_extensions:
        raise forms.ValidationError('The given URL does not ' \
                                    'match valid image extensions.')
    return url
```

In the preceding code, we define a `clean_url()` method to clean the `url` field. The code works as follows:

1. We get the value of the `url` field by accessing the `cleaned_data` dictionary of the form instance.
2. We split the URL to get the file extension and check whether it is one of the valid extensions. If the extension is invalid, we raise `ValidationError` and the form instance will not be validated. Here, we are performing a very simple validation. You could use more advanced methods to check whether the given URL provides a valid image file.

In addition to validating the given URL, we will also need to download the image file and save it. We could, for example, use the view that handles the form to download the image file. Instead, we will take a more general approach by overriding the `save()` method of our model form to perform this task every time the form is saved.

Overriding the save() method of a ModelForm

As you know, `ModelForm` provides a `save()` method to save the current model instance to the database and return the object. This method receives a boolean `commit` parameter, which allows you to specify whether the object has to be persisted to the database. If `commit` is `False`, the `save()` method will return a model instance but will not save it to the database. We will override the `save()` method of our form in order to retrieve the given image and save it.

Add the following imports at the top of the `forms.py` file:

```
from urllib import request
from django.core.files.base import ContentFile
from django.utils.text import slugify
```

Then, add the following `save()` method to the `ImageCreateForm` form:

```
def save(self, force_insert=False,
              force_update=False,
              commit=True):
    image = super(ImageCreateForm, self).save(commit=False)
    image_url = self.cleaned_data['url']
    image_name = '{}.{}'.format(slugify(image.title),
                                image_url.rsplit('.', 1)[1].lower())

    # download image from the given URL
    response = request.urlopen(image_url)
```

```
image.image.save(image_name,
                 ContentFile(response.read()),
                 save=False)
if commit:
    image.save()
return image
```

We override the `save()` method, keeping the parameters required by `ModelForm`. The preceding code is explained as follows:

1. We create a new `image` instance by calling the `save()` method of the form with `commit=False`.
2. We get the URL from the `cleaned_data` dictionary of the form.
3. We generate the image name by combining the `image` title slug with the original file extension.
4. We use the Python `urllib` module to download the image and then we call the `save()` method of the image field, passing it a `ContentFile` object that is instantiated with the downloaded file content. In this way, we save the file to the media directory of our project. We also pass the `save=False` parameter to avoid saving the object to the database, yet.
5. In order to maintain the same behavior as the `save()` method we override, we save the form to the database only when the `commit` parameter is `True`.

Now, we will need a view for handling the form. Edit the `views.py` file of the images application and add the following code to it:

```
from django.shortcuts import render, redirect
from django.contrib.auth.decorators import login_required
from django.contrib import messages
from .forms import ImageCreateForm

@login_required
def image_create(request):
    if request.method == 'POST':
        # form is sent
        form = ImageCreateForm(data=request.POST)
        if form.is_valid():
            # form data is valid
            cd = form.cleaned_data
            new_item = form.save(commit=False)

            # assign current user to the item
            new_item.user = request.user
            new_item.save()
```

```
                messages.success(request, 'Image added successfully')

                # redirect to new created item detail view
                return redirect(new_item.get_absolute_url())
        else:
            # build form with data provided by the bookmarklet via GET
            form = ImageCreateForm(data=request.GET)

    return render(request,
                  'images/image/create.html',
                  {'section': 'images',
                   'form': form})
```

We add a `login_required` decorator to the `image_create` view to prevent access for unauthenticated users. This is how this view works:

1. We expect initial data via `GET` in order to create an instance of the form. This data will consist of the `url` and `title` attributes of an image from an external website and will be provided via `GET` by the JavaScript tool we will create later. For now, we just assume that this data will be there initially.
2. If the form is submitted, we check whether it is valid. If the form data is valid, we create a new `Image` instance, but prevent the object from being saved to the database yet by passing `commit=False` to the form's `save()` method.
3. We assign the current user to the new `image` object. This is how we can know who uploaded each image.
4. We save the `image` object to the database.
5. Finally, we create a success message using the Django messaging framework and redirect the user to the canonical URL of the new image. We haven't yet implemented the `get_absolute_url()` method of the `Image` model; we will do that later.

Create a new `urls.py` file inside the `images` application and add the following code to it:

```
from django.urls import path
from . import views

app_name = 'images'

urlpatterns = [
    path('create/', views.image_create, name='create'),
]
```

Edit the main `urls.py` file of the `bookmarks` project to include the patterns for the `images` application, as follows:

```
urlpatterns = [
    path('admin/', admin.site.urls),
    path('account/', include('account.urls')),
    path('social-auth/',
        include('social_django.urls', namespace='social')),
    path('images/', include('images.urls', namespace='images')),
]
```

Finally, you will need to create a template to render the form. Create the following directory structure inside the `images` application directory:

```
templates/
   images/
      image/
         create.html
```

Edit the new `create.html` template and add the following code to it:

```
{% extends "base.html" %}

{% block title %}Bookmark an image{% endblock %}

{% block content %}
  <h1>Bookmark an image</h1>
  <img src="{{ request.GET.url }}" class="image-preview">
  <form action="." method="post">
    {{ form.as_p }}
    {% csrf_token %}
    <input type="submit" value="Bookmark it!">
  </form>
{% endblock %}
```

Now, open `http://127.0.0.1:8000/images/create/?title=...&url=...` in your browser, including a `title` and `url` GET parameters, providing an existing JPEG image URL in the latter.

For example, you can use the following URL:
`http://127.0.0.1:8000/images/create/?title=%20Django%20and%20Duke&url=h ttp://upload.wikimedia.org/wikipedia/commons/8/85/Django_Reinhardt_and_ Duke_Ellington_%28Gottlieb%29.jpg`.

You will see the form with an image preview, like the following one:

Add a description and click on the **BOOKMARK IT!** button. A new Image object will be saved in your database. However, you will get an error that indicates that the Image model has no get_absolute_url() method, as follows:

> ### AttributeError at /images/create/
> 'Image' object has no attribute 'get_absolute_url'

Don't worry about this for now; we are going to add this method later. Open
http://127.0.0.1:8000/admin/images/image/ in your browser and verify that the
new image object has been saved, like this:

Building a bookmarklet with jQuery

A bookmarklet is a bookmark stored in a web browser that contains JavaScript code to extend the browser's functionality. When you click on the bookmark, the JavaScript code is executed on the website being displayed in the browser. This is very useful to build tools that interact with other websites.

Some online services, such as Pinterest, implement their own bookmarklets to let users share content from other sites onto their platform. We will create a bookmarklet, in a similar way, to let users share images from other sites in our website.

We will use jQuery to build our bookmarklet. jQuery is a popular JavaScript framework that allows you to develop client-side functionality faster. You can read more about jQuery at its official website, `https://jquery.com/`.

This is how your users will add a bookmarklet to their browser and use it:

1. The user drags a link from your site to his browser's bookmarks. The link contains JavaScript code in its `href` attribute. This code will be stored in the bookmark.
2. The user navigates to any website and clicks on the bookmark. The JavaScript code of the bookmark is executed.

Since the JavaScript code will be stored as a bookmark, you will not be able to update it later. This is an important drawback that you can solve by implementing a launcher script to load the actual JavaScript bookmarklet from a URL. Your users will save this launcher script as a bookmark, and you will be able to update the code of the bookmarklet at any time. This is the approach we will take to build our bookmarklet. Let's start!

Create a new template under `images/templates/` and name it `bookmarklet_launcher.js`. This will be the launcher script. Add the following JavaScript code to this file:

```
(function(){
    if (window.myBookmarklet !== undefined){
        myBookmarklet();
    }
    else {
document.body.appendChild(document.createElement('script')).src='http://127
.0.0.1:8000/static/js/bookmarklet.js?r='+Math.floor(Math.random()*999999999
99999999999);
    }
})();
```

The preceding script discovers whether the bookmarklet has been already loaded by checking whether the myBookmarklet variable is defined. By doing so, we avoid loading it again if the user clicks on the bookmarklet repeatedly. If myBookmarklet is not defined, we load another JavaScript file by adding a <script> element to the document. The script tag loads the bookmarklet.js script using a random number as a parameter to prevent loading the file from the browser's cache.

The actual bookmarklet code will reside in the bookmarklet.js static file. This will allow us to update our bookmarklet code without requiring our users to update the bookmark they previously added to their browser. Let's add the bookmarklet launcher to the dashboard pages so that our users can copy it to their bookmarks.

Edit the account/dashboard.html template of the account application and make it look like the following:

```
{% extends "base.html" %}

{% block title %}Dashboard{% endblock %}

{% block content %}
  <h1>Dashboard</h1>

  {% with total_images_created=request.user.images_created.count %}
    <p>Welcome to your dashboard. You have bookmarked {{
total_images_created }} image{{ total_images_created|pluralize }}.</p>
  {% endwith %}

  <p>Drag the following button to your bookmarks toolbar to bookmark images
from other websites → <a href="javascript:{% include
"bookmarklet_launcher.js" %}" class="button">Bookmark it</a><p>

  <p>You can also <a href="{% url "edit" %}">edit your profile</a> or <a
href="{% url "password_change" %}">change your password</a>.<p>
{% endblock %}
```

The dashboard now displays the total number of images bookmarked by the user. We use the {% with %} template tag to set a variable with the total number of images bookmarked by the current user. We also include a link with an href attribute that contains the bookmarklet launcher script. We will include this JavaScript code from the bookmarklet_launcher.js template.

Open `http://127.0.0.1:8000/account/` in your browser. You should see the following page:

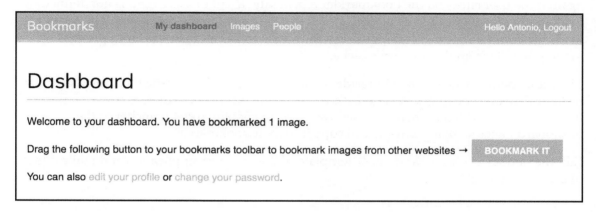

Now, create the following directories and files inside the `images` application directory:

```
static/
  js/
    bookmarklet.js
```

You will find a `static/css/` directory under the `images` application directory, in the code that comes along with this chapter. Copy the `css/` directory into the `static/` directory of your code. The `css/bookmarklet.css` file provides the styles for our JavaScript bookmarklet.

Edit the `bookmarklet.js` static file and add the following JavaScript code to it:

```
(function(){
  var jquery_version = '3.3.1';
  var site_url = 'http://127.0.0.1:8000/';
  var static_url = site_url + 'static/';
  var min_width = 100;
  var min_height = 100;

  function bookmarklet(msg) {
    // Here goes our bookmarklet code
  };

  // Check if jQuery is loaded
  if(typeof window.jQuery != 'undefined') {
    bookmarklet();
  } else {
```

```
    // Check for conflicts
    var conflict = typeof window.$ != 'undefined';
    // Create the script and point to Google API
    var script = document.createElement('script');
    script.src = '//ajax.googleapis.com/ajax/libs/jquery/' +
      jquery_version + '/jquery.min.js';
    // Add the script to the 'head' for processing
    document.head.appendChild(script);
    // Create a way to wait until script loading
    var attempts = 15;
    (function(){
      // Check again if jQuery is undefined
      if(typeof window.jQuery == 'undefined') {
        if(--attempts > 0) {
          // Calls himself in a few milliseconds
          window.setTimeout(arguments.callee, 250)
        } else {
          // Too much attempts to load, send error
          alert('An error ocurred while loading jQuery')
        }
      } else {
        bookmarklet();
      }
    })();
  }
})()
```

This is the main jQuery loader script. It takes care of using jQuery if it has already been
loaded on the current website. If jQuery is not loaded, the script loads jQuery from
Google's content delivery network, which hosts popular JavaScript frameworks. When
jQuery is loaded, it executes the `bookmarklet()` function that will contain our
bookmarklet code. We also set some variables at the top of the file:

- `jquery_version`: The jQuery version to load
- `site_url` and `static_url`: The base URL for our website and base static files'
  URL
- `min_width` and `min_height`: Minimum width and height in pixels for the
  images our bookmarklet will try to find on the site

Now, let's implement the `bookmarklet` function. Edit the `bookmarklet()` function to
make it look like this:

```
function bookmarklet(msg) {
  // load CSS
  var css = jQuery('<link>');
```

```
    css.attr({
        rel: 'stylesheet',
        type: 'text/css',
        href: static_url + 'css/bookmarklet.css?r=' +
Math.floor(Math.random()*9999999999999999999)
    });
    jQuery('head').append(css);

    // load HTML
    box_html = '<div id="bookmarklet"><a href="#"
id="close">&times;</a><h1>Select an image to bookmark:</h1><div
class="images"></div></div>';
    jQuery('body').append(box_html);

    // close event
    jQuery('#bookmarklet #close').click(function(){
        jQuery('#bookmarklet').remove();
    });
};
```

The preceding code works as follows:

1. We load the `bookmarklet.css` stylesheet using a random number as a parameter to prevent the browser from returning a cached file.

2. We add custom HTML to the document `<body>` element of the current website. This consists of a `<div>` element that will contain the images found on the current website.

3. We add an event that removes our HTML from the document when the user clicks on the close link of our HTML block. We use the `#bookmarklet #close` selector to find the HTML element with an ID named `close`, which has a parent element with an ID named `bookmarklet`. jQuery selectors allow you to find HTML elements. A jQuery selector returns all elements found by the given CSS selector. You can find a list of jQuery selectors at `https://api.jquery.com/category/selectors/`.

After loading the CSS styles and the HTML code for the bookmarklet, we will need to find the images on the website. Add the following JavaScript code at the bottom of the `bookmarklet()` function:

```
// find images and display them
jQuery.each(jQuery('img[src$="jpg"]'), function(index, image) {
    if (jQuery(image).width() >= min_width && jQuery(image).height()
    >= min_height)
    {
        image_url = jQuery(image).attr('src');
```

```
jQuery('#bookmarklet .images').append('<a href="#"><img src="'+
image_url +'" /></a>');
  }
});
```

The preceding code uses the `img[src$="jpg"]` selector to find all `<img>` HTML elements, whose `src` attribute finishes with a `jpg` string. This means that we will search all JPEG images displayed on the current website. We iterate over the results using the `each()` method of jQuery. We add the images with a size larger than the one specified with the `min_width` and `min_height` variables to our `<div class="images">` HTML container.

You will need to be able to load the bookmarklet on any site, including sites served through HTTPS. SSL has become widely used, and most websites serve content through HTTPS nowadays. For security reasons, your browser will prevent you from running the bookmarklet over HTTP on a site served through HTTPS.

The Django development server is intended only for development and doesn't support HTTPS. To test the bookmarklet over HTTPS, we will use Ngrok. Ngrok is a tool that creates a tunnel to expose your localhost to the internet through HTTP and HTTPS.

Download Ngrok for your operating system from `https://ngrok.com/download` and run it from the shell using the following command:

`./ngrok http 8000`

With the preceding command, you tell Ngrok to create a tunnel to your localhost on the `8000` port and assign an internet-accessible hostname for it. You should see an output similar to this one:

```
Session Status        online
Version               2.2.8
Region                United States (us)
Web Interface         http://127.0.0.1:4040
Forwarding            http://3f6ad53c.ngrok.io -> localhost:8000
Forwarding            https://3f6ad53c.ngrok.io -> localhost:8000

Connnections          ttl    opn    rt1    rt5    p50    p90
                      0      0      0.00   0.00   0.00   0.00
```

Ngrok tells us that our site, running locally at localhost on the 8000 port using Django's development server, is made available on the internet through the http://3f6ad53c.ngrok.io and https://3f6ad53c.ngrok.io URLs using the HTTP and HTTPS protocols, respectively. Ngrok also provides a URL to access a web interface that displays information about requests sent to the server in the localhost at the 4040 port.

Edit the settings.py file of your project and add the host provided by Ngrok to the ALLOWED_HOSTS setting, as follows:

```
ALLOWED_HOSTS = [
    'mysite.com',
    'localhost',
    '127.0.0.1',
    '3f6ad53c.ngrok.io'
]
```

This will allow you to serve the application through the new hostname. Then, open the URL https://3f6ad53c.ngrok.io/account/login/ in your browser, replacing the host with the one provided by Ngrok. You will be able to see the login site.

Edit the bookmarklet_launcher.js template and replace the http://127.0.0.1:8000/ URL with the HTTPS URL provided by Ngrok, as follows:

```
(function(){
    if (window.myBookmarklet !== undefined){
        myBookmarklet();
    }
    else {
document.body.appendChild(document.createElement('script')).src='https://3f
6ad53c.ngrok.io/static/js/bookmarklet.js?r='+Math.floor(Math.random()*99999
999999999999);
    }
})();
```

Edit the js/bookmarklet.js static file, and take a look at the following line:

```
var site_url = 'http://127.0.0.1:8000/';
```

Replace the preceding line with the following one, including the HTTPS URL provided by Ngrok:

```
var site_url = 'https://3f6ad53c.ngrok.io/';
```

Open `https://3f6ad53c.ngrok.io/account/` in your browser, replacing the host with the one provided by Ngrok. Log in with an existing user and then drag the **BOOKMARK IT** button to the bookmarks toolbar of your browser as follows:

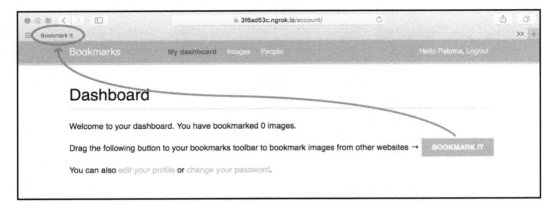

Open a website of your own choice in your browser and click on your bookmarklet. You will see that a new white box appears on the website, displaying all JPEG images found with dimensions higher than 100 x 100 pixels. It should look like the following example:

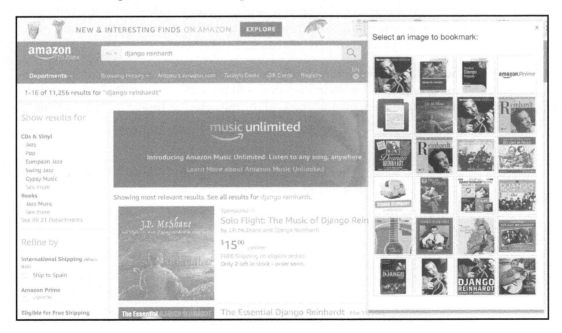

The HTML container includes the images that can be bookmarked. We want the user to click on the desired image and bookmark it. Edit the `js/bookmarklet.js` static file and add the following code at the bottom of the `bookmarklet()` function:

```
// when an image is selected open URL with it
jQuery('#bookmarklet .images a').click(function(e){
  selected_image = jQuery(this).children('img').attr('src');
  // hide bookmarklet
  jQuery('#bookmarklet').hide();
  // open new window to submit the image
  window.open(site_url +'images/create/?url='
              + encodeURIComponent(selected_image)
              + '&title='
              + encodeURIComponent(jQuery('title').text()),
              '_blank');
});
```

The preceding code works as follows:

1. We attach a `click()` event to the images' link elements.
2. When a user clicks on an image, we set a new variable called `selected_image` that contains the URL of the selected image.
3. We hide the bookmarklet and open a new browser window with the URL for bookmarking a new image on our site. We pass the `<title>` element of the website and the selected image URL as GET parameters.

Open a new URL with your browser and click on your bookmarklet again to display the image selection box. If you click on an image, you will be redirected to the image create page, passing the title of the website and the URL of the selected image as GET parameters:

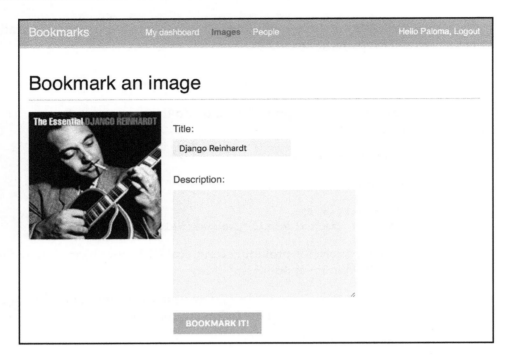

Congratulations! This is your first JavaScript bookmarklet, and it is fully integrated into your Django project.

Creating a detail view for images

We will now create a simple detail view to display an image that has been saved into our site. Open the `views.py` file of the `images` application and add the following code to it:

```
from django.shortcuts import get_object_or_404
from .models import Image

def image_detail(request, id, slug):
    image = get_object_or_404(Image, id=id, slug=slug)
    return render(request,
                  'images/image/detail.html',
                  {'section': 'images',
                   'image': image})
```

This is a simple view to display an image. Edit the `urls.py` file of the `images` application and add the following URL pattern:

```
path('detail/<int:id>/<slug:slug>/',
    views.image_detail, name='detail'),
```

Edit the `models.py` file of the `images` application and add the `get_absolute_url()` method to the `Image` model, as follows:

```
from django.urls import reverse

class Image(models.Model):
    # ...
    def get_absolute_url(self):
        return reverse('images:detail', args=[self.id, self.slug])
```

Remember that the common pattern for providing canonical URLs for objects is to define a `get_absolute_url()` method in the model.

Finally, create a template inside the `/images/image/` template directory of the `images` application and name it `detail.html`. Add the following code to it:

```
{% extends "base.html" %}

{% block title %}{{ image.title }}{% endblock %}

{% block content %}
  <h1>{{ image.title }}</h1>
  <img src="{{ image.image.url }}" class="image-detail">
  {% with total_likes=image.users_like.count %}
    <div class="image-info">
      <div>
        <span class="count">
          {{ total_likes }} like{{ total_likes|pluralize }}
        </span>
      </div>
      {{ image.description|linebreaks }}
    </div>
    <div class="image-likes">
      {% for user in image.users_like.all %}
        <div>
          <img src="{{ user.profile.photo.url }}">
          <p>{{ user.first_name }}</p>
        </div>
      {% empty %}
        Nobody likes this image yet.
      {% endfor %}
```

```
    </div>
  {% endwith %}
{% endblock %}
```

This is the template to display the detail of a bookmarked image. We make use of the `{% with %}` tag to store the result of the QuerySet, counting all user likes in a new variable called `total_likes`. By doing so, we avoid evaluating the same QuerySet twice. We also include the image description and iterate over `image.users_like.all` to display all the users who like this image.

 Using the `{% with %}` template tag is useful to prevent Django from evaluating QuerySets multiple times.

Now, bookmark a new image using the bookmarklet. You will be redirected to the image detail page after you post the image. The page will include a success message, as follows:

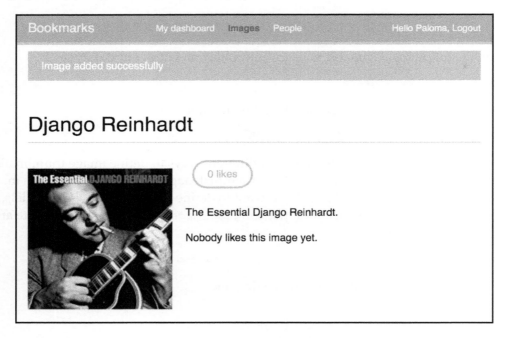

Creating image thumbnails using sorl-thumbnail

We display the original image on the detail page, but dimensions for different images may vary a lot. Also, the original files for some images might be huge, and loading them might take too long. The best way to display optimized images in a uniform way is to generate thumbnails. We will use a Django application called `sorl-thumbnail` for this purpose.

Open the terminal and install `sorl-thumbnail` using the following command:

```
pip install sorl-thumbnail==12.4.1
```

Edit the `settings.py` file of the bookmarks project and add `sorl.thumbnail` to the `INSTALLED_APPS` setting, as follows:

```
INSTALLED_APPS = [
    # ...
    'sorl.thumbnail',
]
```

Then, run the following command to sync the application with your database:

```
python manage.py migrate
```

You should see an output that includes the following line:

```
Applying thumbnail.0001_initial... OK
```

The `sorl-thumbnail` application offers you different ways to define image thumbnails. The application provides a `{% thumbnail %}` template tag to generate thumbnails in templates and a custom `ImageField` if you want to define thumbnails in your models. We will use the template tag approach. Edit the `images/image/detail.html` template and replace the following line:

```
<img src="{{ image.image.url }}" class="image-detail">
```

The following lines should replace the preceding one:

```
{% load thumbnail %}
{% thumbnail image.image "300" as im %}
  <a href="{{ image.image.url }}">
    <img src="{{ im.url }}" class="image-detail">
  </a>
{% endthumbnail %}
```

Here, we define a thumbnail with a fixed width of 300 pixels. The first time a user loads this page, a thumbnail image will be created. The generated thumbnail will be served in the following requests. Start the development server with the `python manage.py runserver` command and access the image detail page for an existing image. The thumbnail will be generated and displayed on the site.

The `sorl-thumbnail` application offers several options to customize your thumbnails, including cropping algorithms and different effects that can be applied. If you have any difficulty generating thumbnails, you can add `THUMBNAIL_DEBUG = True` to your `settings.py` file in order to obtain debug information. You can read the full documentation of the `sorl-thumbnail` application at `https://sorl-thumbnail.readthedocs.io/`.

Adding AJAX actions with jQuery

Now, we will add AJAX actions to our application. AJAX comes from **Asynchronous JavaScript and XML**. This term encompasses a group of techniques to make asynchronous HTTP requests. It consists of sending and retrieving data from the server asynchronously, without reloading the whole page. Despite the name, XML is not required. You can send or retrieve data in other formats, such as JSON, HTML, or plain text.

We will add a link to the image detail page to let users click on it in order to like an image. We will perform this action with an AJAX call to avoid reloading the whole page. First, we will create a view for users to like/unlike images. Edit the `views.py` file of the `images` application and add the following code to it:

```
from django.http import JsonResponse
from django.views.decorators.http import require_POST

@login_required
@require_POST
def image_like(request):
    image_id = request.POST.get('id')
    action = request.POST.get('action')
    if image_id and action:
        try:
            image = Image.objects.get(id=image_id)
            if action == 'like':
                image.users_like.add(request.user)
            else:
                image.users_like.remove(request.user)
            return JsonResponse({'status':'ok'})
```

```
        except:
            pass
    return JsonResponse({'status':'ko'})
```

We will use two decorators for our view. The `login_required` decorator prevents users that are not logged in from accessing this view. The `require_POST` decorator returns an `HttpResponseNotAllowed` object (status code `405`) if the HTTP request is not done via `POST`. This way, we only allow `POST` requests for this view. Django also provides a `require_GET` decorator to only allow `GET` requests and a `require_http_methods` decorator to which you can pass a list of allowed methods as an argument.

In this view, we use two `GET` parameters:

- `image_id`: The ID of the image object on which the user is performing the action
- `action`: The action that the user wants to perform, which we assume to be a string with the value `like` or `unlike`

We use the manager provided by Django for the `users_like` many-to-many field of the `Image` model in order to add or remove objects from the relationship using the `add()` or `remove()` methods. Calling `add()`, that is, passing an object that is already present in the related object set does not duplicate it, and thus, calling `remove()`, passing an object that is not in the related object set does nothing. Another useful method of the many-to-many manager is `clear()`, which removes all objects from the related object set.

Finally, we use the `JsonResponse` class provided by Django, which returns an HTTP response with an `application/json` content type, converting the given object into a JSON output.

Edit the `urls.py` file of the `images` application and add the following URL pattern to it:

```
path('like/', views.image_like, name='like'),
```

Loading jQuery

We will need to add the AJAX functionality to our image detail template. In order to use jQuery in our templates, we will include it in the `base.html` template of our project first. Edit the `base.html` template of the `account` application and include the following code before the closing `</body>` HTML tag:

```
<script
src="https://ajax.googleapis.com/ajax/libs/jquery/3.2.1/jquery.min.js"></sc
ript>
```

```
<script>
  $(document).ready(function(){
    {% block domready %}
    {% endblock %}
  });
</script>
```

We load the jQuery framework from Google's CDN. You can also download jQuery from `https://jquery.com/` and add it to the `static` directory of your application instead.

We add a `<script>` tag to include JavaScript code. `$(document).ready()` is a jQuery function that takes a handler that is executed when the DOM hierarchy has been fully constructed. **DOM** comes from **Document Object Model**. The DOM is created by the browser when a web page is loaded, and is constructed as a tree of objects. By including our code inside this function, we will make sure that all HTML elements we are going to interact with are loaded in the DOM. Our code will only be executed once the DOM is ready.

Inside the document-ready handler function, we include a Django template block called `domready`, in which templates that extend the base template will be able to include specific JavaScript.

Don't get confused with the JavaScript code and Django template tags. Django template language is rendered on the server side outputting the final HTML document and JavaScript is executed on the client side. In some cases, it is useful to generate JavaScript code dynamically using Django.

In the examples in this chapter, we include JavaScript code in Django templates. The preferred way to include JavaScript code is by loading `.js` files, which are served as static files, especially when they are large scripts.

Cross-Site Request Forgery in AJAX requests

You have learned *Cross-Site Request Forgery* in `Chapter 2`, *Enhancing Your Blog with Advanced Features*. With the CSRF protection active, Django checks for a CSRF token in all `POST` requests. When you submit forms, you can use the `{% csrf_token %}` template tag to send the token along with the form. However, it is a bit inconvenient for AJAX requests to pass the CSRF token as a `POST` data in with every `POST` request. Therefore, Django allows you to set a custom `X-CSRFToken` header in your AJAX requests with the value of the CSRF token. This allows you to set up jQuery or any other JavaScript library to automatically set the `X-CSRFToken` header in every request.

In order to include the token in all requests, you need to take the following steps:

1. Retrieve the CSRF token from the `csrftoken` cookie, which is set if CSRF protection is active
2. Send the token in the AJAX request using the `X-CSRFToken` header

You can find more information about CSRF protection and AJAX at https://docs. djangoproject.com/en/2.0/ref/csrf/#ajax.

Edit the last code you included in your `base.html` template and make it look like the following:

```
<script
src="https://ajax.googleapis.com/ajax/libs/jquery/3.2.1/jquery.min.js"></sc
ript>
<script
src="https://cdn.jsdelivr.net/npm/js-cookie@2/src/js.cookie.min.js"></scrip
t>
<script>
  var csrftoken = Cookies.get('csrftoken');
  function csrfSafeMethod(method) {
    // these HTTP methods do not require CSRF protection
    return (/^(GET|HEAD|OPTIONS|TRACE)$/.test(method));
  }
  $.ajaxSetup({
    beforeSend: function(xhr, settings) {
      if (!csrfSafeMethod(settings.type) && !this.crossDomain) {
        xhr.setRequestHeader("X-CSRFToken", csrftoken);
      }
    }
  });
  $(document).ready(function(){
    {% block domready %}
    {% endblock %}
  });
</script>
```

The preceding code is as follows:

1. We load the JS Cookie plugin from a public CDN so that we can easily interact with cookies. JS Cookie is a lightweight JavaScript for handling cookies. You can learn more about it at https://github.com/js-cookie/js-cookie.
2. We read the value of the `csrftoken` cookie with `Cookies.get()`.

3. We define the `csrfSafeMethod()` function to check whether an HTTP method is safe. Safe methods don't require CSRF protection—these are `GET`, `HEAD`, `OPTIONS`, and `TRACE`.

4. We set up jQuery AJAX requests using `$.ajaxSetup()`. Before each AJAX request is performed, we check whether the request method is safe and the current request is not cross-domain. If the request is unsafe, we set the `X-CSRFToken` header with the value obtained from the cookie. This setup will apply to all AJAX requests performed with jQuery.

The CSRF token will be included in all AJAX requests that use unsafe HTTP methods, such as `POST` or `PUT`.

Performing AJAX requests with jQuery

Edit the `images/image/detail.html` template of the `images` application, and consider the following line:

```
{% with total_likes=image.users_like.count %}
```

Replace the preceding one with the following one:

```
{% with total_likes=image.users_like.count users_like=image.users_like.all %}
```

Then, modify the `<div>` element with the `image-info` class, as follows:

```
<div class="image-info">
  <div>
    <span class="count">
      <span class="total">{{ total_likes }}</span>
      like{{ total_likes|pluralize }}
    </span>
    <a href="#" data-id="{{ image.id }}" data-action="{% if
    request.user in users_like %}un{% endif %}like"
    class="like button">
      {% if request.user not in users_like %}
        Like
      {% else %}
        Unlike
      {% endif %}
    </a>
  </div>
  {{ image.description|linebreaks }}
</div>
```

First, we added another variable to the `{% with %}` template tag in order to store the results of the `image.users_like.all` query and avoid executing it twice. We display the total number of users that like this image and include a link to like/unlike the image: we check whether the user is in the related object set of `users_like` to display either *like* or *unlike*, based on the current relationship between the user and this image. We add the following attributes to the `<a>` HTML element:

- `data-id`: The ID of the image displayed
- `data-action`: The action to run when the user clicks on the link. This can be `like` or `unlike`

We will send the value of both attributes in the AJAX request to the `image_like` view. When a user clicks on the `like`/`unlike` link, we will need to perform the following actions on the client side:

1. Call the AJAX view, passing the image ID and the action parameters to it.
2. If the AJAX request is successful, update the `data-action` attribute of the `<a>` HTML element with the opposite action (`like` / `unlike`), and modify its display text accordingly.
3. Update the total number of `likes` that is displayed.

Add the `domready` block at the bottom of the `images/image/detail.html` template with the following JavaScript code:

```
{% block domready %}
  $('a.like').click(function(e){
    e.preventDefault();
    $.post('{% url "images:like" %}',
      {
        id: $(this).data('id'),
        action: $(this).data('action')
      },
      function(data){
        if (data['status'] == 'ok')
        {
          var previous_action = $('a.like').data('action');

          // toggle data-action
          $('a.like').data('action', previous_action == 'like' ?
          'unlike' : 'like');
          // toggle link text
          $('a.like').text(previous_action == 'like' ? 'Unlike' :
          'Like');
```

```
        // update total likes
        var previous_likes = parseInt($('span.count .total').text());
        $('span.count .total').text(previous_action == 'like' ?
        previous_likes + 1 : previous_likes - 1);
      }
    }
  );
});
{% endblock %}
```

The preceding code works as follows:

1. We use the $('a.like') jQuery selector to find all <a> elements of the HTML document with the like class.

2. We define a handler function for the click event. This function will be executed every time the user clicks on the like/unlike link.

3. Inside the handler function, we use e.preventDefault() to avoid the default behavior of the <a> element. This will prevent the link from taking us anywhere.

4. We use $.post() to perform an asynchronous POST request to the server. jQuery also provides a $.get() method to perform GET requests and a low-level $.ajax() method.

5. We use Django's {% url %} template tag to build the URL for the AJAX request.

6. We build the POST parameters dictionary to send in the request. These are the ID and action parameters expected by our Django view. We retrieve these values from the <a> element's data-id and data-action attributes.

7. We define a callback function that is executed when the HTTP response is received; it takes a data attribute that contains the content of the response.

8. We access the status attribute of the data received and check whether it equals ok. If the returned data is as expected, we toggle the data-action attribute of the link and its text. This allows the user to undo their action.

9. We increase or decrease the total likes count by one, depending on the action performed.

Open the image detail page in your browser for an image you have uploaded. You should be able to see the following initial likes count and the **LIKE** button, as follows:

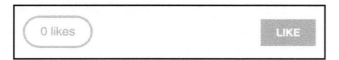

Click on the **UNLIKE** button. You will note that the total likes count decreases by one and the button text changes to **UNLIKE**, as follows:

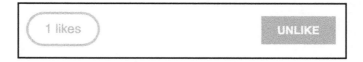

When you click on the **UNLIKE** button, the action is performed, the button's text changes back to **LIKE**, and the total count changes accordingly.

When programming JavaScript, especially when performing AJAX requests, it is recommended that you use a tool for debugging JavaScript and HTTP requests. Most modern browsers include developer tools to debug JavaScript. Usually, you can right-click anywhere on the website and click on **Inspect element** to access the web developer tools.

Creating custom decorators for your views

We will restrict our AJAX views to allow only requests generated via AJAX. The Django request object provides an `is_ajax()` method that checks whether the request is being made with `XMLHttpRequest`, which means it is an AJAX request. This value is set in the `HTTP_X_REQUESTED_WITH` HTTP header, which is included in AJAX requests by most JavaScript libraries.

We will create a decorator for checking the `HTTP_X_REQUESTED_WITH` header in our views. A decorator is a function that takes another function and extends the behavior of the latter without explicitly modifying it. If the concept of decorators is foreign to you, you might like to take a look at `https://www.python.org/dev/peps/pep-0318/` before you continue reading.

Since our decorator will be generic and could be applied to any view, we will create a `common` Python package in our project. Create the following directory and files inside the `bookmarks` project directory:

```
common/
    __init__.py
    decorators.py
```

Edit the `decorators.py` file and add the following code to it:

```
from django.http import HttpResponseBadRequest

def ajax_required(f):
    def wrap(request, *args, **kwargs):
        if not request.is_ajax():
            return HttpResponseBadRequest()
        return f(request, *args, **kwargs)
    wrap.__doc__=f.__doc__
    wrap.__name__=f.__name__
    return wrap
```

The preceding code is our custom `ajax_required` decorator. It defines a wrap function that returns an `HttpResponseBadRequest` object (HTTP 400 code) if the request is not AJAX. Otherwise, it returns the decorated function.

Now, you can edit the `views.py` file of the `images` application and add this decorator to your `image_like` AJAX view, as follows:

```
from common.decorators import ajax_required

@ajax_required
@login_required
@require_POST
def image_like(request):
    # ...
```

If you try to access `http://127.0.0.1:8000/images/like/` directly with your browser, you will get an HTTP 400 response.

 Build custom decorators for your views if you find that you are repeating the same checks in multiple views.

Adding AJAX pagination to your list views

We will need to list all bookmarked images on our website. We will use AJAX pagination to build infinite scroll functionality. Infinite scroll is achieved by loading the next results automatically when the user scrolls to the bottom of the page.

We will implement an image list view that will handle both standard browser requests and AJAX requests, including pagination. When the user initially loads the image list page, we will display the first page of images. When they scroll to the bottom of the page, we load the following page of items via AJAX and append it to the bottom of the main page.

The same view will handle both standard and AJAX pagination. Edit the `views.py` file of the `images` application and add the following code to it:

```python
from django.http import HttpResponse
from django.core.paginator import Paginator, EmptyPage, \
                                   PageNotAnInteger

@login_required
def image_list(request):
    images = Image.objects.all()
    paginator = Paginator(images, 8)
    page = request.GET.get('page')
    try:
        images = paginator.page(page)
    except PageNotAnInteger:
        # If page is not an integer deliver the first page
        images = paginator.page(1)
    except EmptyPage:
        if request.is_ajax():
            # If the request is AJAX and the page is out of range
            # return an empty page
            return HttpResponse('')
        # If page is out of range deliver last page of results
        images = paginator.page(paginator.num_pages)
    if request.is_ajax():
        return render(request,
                      'images/image/list_ajax.html',
                      {'section': 'images', 'images': images})
    return render(request,
                  'images/image/list.html',
                  {'section': 'images', 'images': images})
```

In this view, we create a QuerySet to return all images from the database. Then, we build a `Paginator` object to paginate the results, retrieving eight images per page. We get an `EmptyPage` exception if the requested page is out of range. If this is the case and the request is done via AJAX, we return an empty `HttpResponse` that will help us stop the AJAX pagination on the client side. We render the results to two different templates:

- For AJAX requests, we render the `list_ajax.html` template. This template will only contain the images of the requested page.
- For standard requests, we render the `list.html` template. This template will extend the `base.html` template to display the whole page and will include the `list_ajax.html` template to include the list of images.

Edit the `urls.py` file of the `images` application and add the following URL pattern to it:

```
path('', views.image_list, name='list'),
```

Finally, we will need to create the templates mentioned here. Inside the `images/image/` template directory, create a new template and name it `list_ajax.html`. Add the following code to it:

```
{% load thumbnail %}

{% for image in images %}
  <div class="image">
    <a href="{{ image.get_absolute_url }}">
      {% thumbnail image.image "300x300" crop="100%" as im %}
        <a href="{{ image.get_absolute_url }}">
          <img src="{{ im.url }}">
        </a>
      {% endthumbnail %}
    </a>
    <div class="info">
      <a href="{{ image.get_absolute_url }}" class="title">
        {{ image.title }}
      </a>
    </div>
  </div>
{% endfor %}
```

The preceding template displays the list of images. We will use it to return results for AJAX requests. Create another template in the same directory and name it `list.html`. Add the following code to it:

```
{% extends "base.html" %}

{% block title %}Images bookmarked{% endblock %}

{% block content %}
  <h1>Images bookmarked</h1>
  <div id="image-list">
    {% include "images/image/list_ajax.html" %}
  </div>
{% endblock %}
```

The list template extends the `base.html` template. To avoid repeating code, we included the `list_ajax.html` template for displaying images. The `list.html` template will hold the JavaScript code for loading additional pages when scrolling to the bottom of the page.

Add the following code to the `list.html` template:

```
{% block domready %}
  var page = 1;
  var empty_page = false;
  var block_request = false;

  $(window).scroll(function() {
    var margin = $(document).height() - $(window).height() - 200;
    if  ($(window).scrollTop() > margin && empty_page == false &&
    block_request == false) {
     block_request = true;
      page += 1;
      $.get('?page=' + page, function(data) {
       if(data == '') {
          empty_page = true;
        }
        else {
          block_request = false;
          $('#image-list').append(data);
        }
      });
    }
  });
{% endblock %}
```

The preceding code provides the infinite scroll functionality. We include the JavaScript code in the `domready` block that we defined in the `base.html` template. The code is as follows:

1. We define the following variables:
   - `page`: Stores the current page number.
   - `empty_page`: Allows us to know whether the user is on the last page and retrieves an empty page. As soon as we get an empty page, we will stop sending additional AJAX requests because we will assume that there are no more results.
   - `block_request`: Prevents us from sending additional requests while an AJAX request is in progress.

2. We use `$(window).scroll()` to capture the scroll event and also to define a handler function for it.

3. We calculate the `margin` variable to get the difference between the total document height and the window height, because that's the height of the remaining content for the user to scroll. We subtract a value of 200 from the result so that we load the next page when the user is closer than 200 pixels to the bottom of the page.

4. We only send an AJAX request if no other AJAX request is being done (`block_request` has to be `false`) and the user didn't get to the last page of results (`empty_page` is also `false`).

5. We set `block_request` to `true` to avoid a situation whereby the scroll event triggers additional AJAX requests, and increase the `page` counter by one, in order to retrieve the next page.

6. We perform an AJAX GET request using `$.get()` and receive the HTML response in a variable called `data`. The following are the two scenarios:
   - **The response has no content**: We got to the end of the results, and there are no more pages to load. We set `empty_page` to true to prevent additional AJAX requests.
   - **The response contains data**: We append the data to the HTML element with the `image-list` ID. The page content expands vertically appending results when the user approaches the bottom of the page.

Open `http://127.0.0.1:8000/images/` in your browser. You will see the list of images you have bookmarked so far. It should look similar to this:

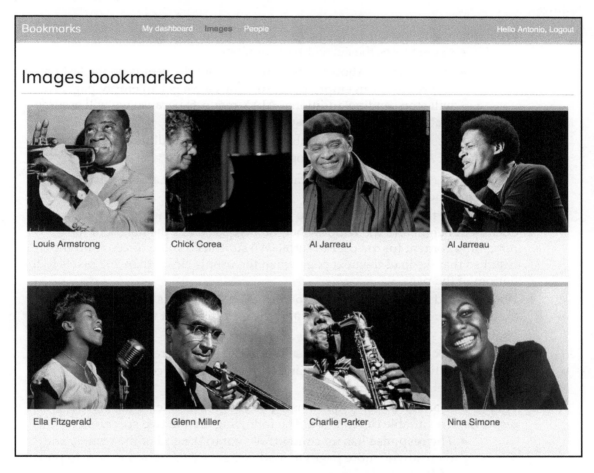

Scroll to the bottom of the page to load additional pages. Ensure that you have bookmarked more than eight images using the bookmarklet because that's the number of images we are displaying per page. Remember that you can use Firebug or a similar tool to track the AJAX requests and debug your JavaScript code.

Finally, edit the `base.html` template of the `account` application and add the URL for the images item of the main menu, as follows:

```
<li {% if section == "images" %}class="selected"{% endif %}>
  <a href="{% url "images:list" %}">Images</a>
</li>
```

Now you can access the image list from the main menu.

Summary

In this chapter, we have built a JavaScript bookmarklet to share images from other websites into our site. You have implemented AJAX views with jQuery and added AJAX pagination.

In the next chapter, we will teach you how to build a follower system and an activity stream. You will work with generic relations, signals, and denormalization. You will also learn how to use Redis with Django.

6
Tracking User Actions

In the preceding chapter, you implemented AJAX views into your project using jQuery and built a JavaScript bookmarklet to share content from other websites on your platform.

In this chapter, you will learn how to build a follower system and create a user activity stream. You will discover how Django signals work and integrate Redis's fast I/O storage into your project to store item views.

This chapter will cover the following points:

- Creating many-to-many relationships with an intermediary model
- Building a follower system
- Creating an activity stream application
- Adding generic relations to models
- Optimizing QuerySets for related objects
- Using signals for denormalizing counts
- Storing item views in Redis

Building a follower system

We will build a follower system into our project. Our users will be able to follow each other and track what other users share on the platform. The relationship between users is a many-to-many relationship. A user can follow multiple users and they, in turn, can be followed by multiple users.

Creating many-to-many relationships with an intermediary model

In previous chapters, you created many-to-many relationships by adding `ManyToManyField` to one of the related models and letting Django create the database table for the relationship. This is suitable for most of the cases, but sometimes you may need to create an intermediate model for the relation. Creating an intermediary model is necessary when you want to store additional information for the relationship, for example, the date when the relation was created, or a field that describes the nature of the relationship.

We will create an intermediary model to build relationships between users. There are two reasons why we want to use an intermediate model:

- We are using the `User` model provided by Django, and we want to avoid altering it
- We want to store the time when the relation is created

Edit the `models.py` file of your `account` application and add the following code to it:

```python
class Contact(models.Model):
    user_from = models.ForeignKey('auth.User',
                                  related_name='rel_from_set',
                                  on_delete=models.CASCADE)
    user_to = models.ForeignKey('auth.User',
                                related_name='rel_to_set',
                                on_delete=models.CASCADE)
    created = models.DateTimeField(auto_now_add=True,
                                   db_index=True)

    class Meta:
        ordering = ('-created',)

    def __str__(self):
        return '{} follows {}'.format(self.user_from,
                                      self.user_to)
```

The preceding code shows the `Contact` model we will use for user relationships. It contains the following fields:

- `user_from`: `ForeignKey` for the user that creates the relationship
- `user_to`: `ForeignKey` for the user being followed
- `created`: A `DateTimeField` field with `auto_now_add=True` to store the time when the relationship was created

A database index is automatically created on the `ForeignKey` fields. We use `db_index=True` to create a database index for the `created` field. This will improve query performance when ordering QuerySets by this field.

Using the ORM, we could create a relationship for a user—`user1`—following another user, `user2`, like this:

```
user1 = User.objects.get(id=1)
user2 = User.objects.get(id=2)
Contact.objects.create(user_from=user1, user_to=user2)
```

The related managers `rel_from_set` and `rel_to_set` will return a QuerySet for the `Contact` model. In order to access the end side of the relationship from the `User` model, it would be desirable that `User` contained `ManyToManyField`, as follows:

```
following = models.ManyToManyField('self',
                                   through=Contact,
                                   related_name='followers',
                                   symmetrical=False)
```

In the preceding example, we tell Django to use our custom intermediary model for the relationship by adding `through=Contact` to the `ManyToManyField`. This is a many-to-many relationship from the `User` model to itself: we refer to `'self'` in the `ManyToManyField` field to create a relationship to the same model.

 When you need additional fields in a many-to-many relationship, create a custom model with `ForeignKey` for each side of the relationship. Add `ManyToManyField` in one of the related models and indicate to Django that your intermediary model should be used by including it in the `through` parameter.

If the User model was part of our application, we could add the previous field to the model. However, we cannot alter the User class directly because it belongs to the django.contrib.auth application. We will take a slightly different approach by adding this field dynamically to the User model. Edit the models.py file of the account application and add the following lines:

```
from django.contrib.auth.models import User

# Add following field to User dynamically
User.add_to_class('following',
                  models.ManyToManyField('self',
                                         through=Contact,
                                         related_name='followers',
                                         symmetrical=False))
```

In the preceding code, we use the add_to_class() method of Django models to monkey patch the User model. Be aware that using add_to_class() is not the recommended way of adding fields to models. However, we take advantage of using it in this case because of the following reasons:

- We simplify the way we retrieve related objects using the Django ORM with user.followers.all() and user.following.all(). We use the intermediary Contact model and avoid complex queries that would involve additional database joins, as it would have been, had we defined the relationship in our custom Profile model.
- The table for this many-to-many relationship will be created using the Contact model. Thus, the ManyToManyField added dynamically will not imply any database changes for the Django User model.
- We avoid creating a custom user model, keeping all the advantages of Django's built-in User.

Keep in mind that, in most cases, it is preferable to add fields to the Profile model we created before, instead of monkey-patching the User model. Django also allows you to use custom user models. If you want to use your custom user model, take a look at the documentation at https://docs.djangoproject.com/en/2.0/topics/auth/customizing/#specifying-a-custom-user-model.

You can note that the relationship includes symmetrical=False. When you define a ManyToManyField to the model itself, Django forces the relationship to be symmetrical. In this case, we are setting symmetrical=False to define a non-symmetric relation. This is, if I follow you, it doesn't mean that you automatically follow me.

When you use an intermediate model for many-to-many relationships, some of the related manager's methods are disabled, such as `add()`, `create()`, or `remove()`. You need to create or delete instances of the intermediate model instead.

Run the following command to generate the initial migrations for the `account` application:

```
python manage.py makemigrations account
```

You will obtain the following output:

```
Migrations for 'account':
  account/migrations/0002_contact.py
    - Create model Contact
```

Now, run the following command to sync the application with the database:

```
python manage.py migrate account
```

You should see an output that includes the following line:

```
Applying account.0002_contact... OK
```

The `Contact` model is now synced to the database, and we are able to create relationships between users. However, our site doesn't offer a way to browse users or see a particular user profile yet. Let's build list and detail views for the `User` model.

Creating list and detail views for user profiles

Open the `views.py` file of the `account` application and add the following code to it:

```python
from django.shortcuts import get_object_or_404
from django.contrib.auth.models import User

@login_required
def user_list(request):
    users = User.objects.filter(is_active=True)
    return render(request,
                  'account/user/list.html',
                  {'section': 'people',
                   'users': users})

@login_required
def user_detail(request, username):
    user = get_object_or_404(User,
```

```
                         username=username,
                         is_active=True)
    return render(request,
               'account/user/detail.html',
               {'section': 'people',
                'user': user})
```

These are simple list and detail views for `user` objects. The `user_list` view gets all active users. The Django `User` model contains an `is_active` flag to designate whether the user account is considered active. We filter the query by `is_active=True` to return only active users. This view returns all results, but you can improve it by adding pagination the same way as we did for the `image_list` view.

The `user_detail` view uses the `get_object_or_404()` shortcut to retrieve the active user with the given username. The view returns an HTTP 404 response if no active user with the given username is found.

Edit the `urls.py` file of the `account` application, and add a URL pattern for each view, as follows:

```
urlpatterns = [
    # ...
    path('users/', views.user_list, name='user_list'),
    path('users/<username>/', views.user_detail, name='user_detail'),
]
```

We will use the `user_detail` URL pattern to generate the canonical URL for users. You have already defined a `get_absolute_url()` method in a model to return the canonical URL for each object. Another way to specify an URL for a model is by adding the `ABSOLUTE_URL_OVERRIDES` setting to your project.

Edit the `settings.py` file of your project and add the following code to it:

```
from django.urls import reverse_lazy

ABSOLUTE_URL_OVERRIDES = {
    'auth.user': lambda u: reverse_lazy('user_detail',
                                        args=[u.username])
}
```

Django adds a `get_absolute_url()` method dynamically to any models that appear in the `ABSOLUTE_URL_OVERRIDES` setting. This method returns the corresponding URL for the given model specified in the setting. We return the `user_detail` URL for the given user. Now, you can use `get_absolute_url()` on a `User` instance to retrieve its corresponding URL.

Open the Python shell with the `python manage.py shell` command and run the following code to test it:

```
>>> from django.contrib.auth.models import User
>>> user = User.objects.latest('id')
>>> str(user.get_absolute_url())
'/account/users/ellington/'
```

The returned URL is as expected. We will need to create templates for the views we just built. Add the following directory and files to the `templates/account/` directory of the `account` application:

```
/user/
    detail.html
    list.html
```

Edit the `account/user/list.html` template and add the following code to it:

```
{% extends "base.html" %}
{% load thumbnail %}

{% block title %}People{% endblock %}

{% block content %}
  <h1>People</h1>
  <div id="people-list">
    {% for user in users %}
      <div class="user">
        <a href="{{ user.get_absolute_url }}">
          {% thumbnail user.profile.photo "180x180" crop="100%"
            as im %}
            <img src="{{ im.url }}">
          {% endthumbnail %}
        </a>
        <div class="info">
          <a href="{{ user.get_absolute_url }}" class="title">
            {{ user.get_full_name }}
          </a>
        </div>
      </div>
    {% endfor %}
  </div>
{% endblock %}
```

The preceding template allows us to list all the active users in the site. We iterate over the given users and use sorl-thumbnail's `{% thumbnail %}` template tag to generate profile image thumbnails.

Open the `base.html` template of your project and include the `user_list` URL in the `href` attribute of the following menu item:

```
<li {% if section == "people" %}class="selected"{% endif %}>
  <a href="{% url "user_list" %}">People</a>
</li>
```

Start the development server with the `python manage.py runserver` command and open `http://127.0.0.1:8000/account/users/` in your browser. You should see a list of users like the following one:

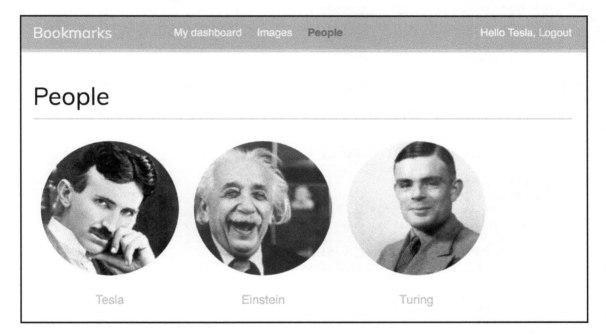

Remember that if you have any difficulty generating thumbnails, you can add `THUMBNAIL_DEBUG = True` to your `settings.py` file in order to obtain debug information in the shell.

Edit the `account/user/detail.html` template of the `account` application and add the following code to it:

```
{% extends "base.html" %}
{% load thumbnail %}

{% block title %}{{ user.get_full_name }}{% endblock %}
```

```
{% block content %}
  <h1>{{ user.get_full_name }}</h1>
  <div class="profile-info">
    {% thumbnail user.profile.photo "180x180" crop="100%" as im %}
      <img src="{{ im.url }}" class="user-detail">
    {% endthumbnail %}
  </div>
  {% with total_followers=user.followers.count %}
    <span class="count">
      <span class="total">{{ total_followers }}</span>
      follower{{ total_followers|pluralize }}
    </span>
    <a href="#" data-id="{{ user.id }}" data-action="{% if request.user
    in user.followers.all %}un{% endif %}follow" class="follow button">
      {% if request.user not in user.followers.all %}
        Follow
      {% else %}
        Unfollow
      {% endif %}
    </a>
    <div id="image-list" class="image-container">
      {% include "images/image/list_ajax.html" with
      images=user.images_created.all %}
    </div>
  {% endwith %}
{% endblock %}
```

In the detail template, we will display the user profile and use the `{% thumbnail %}` template tag to display the profile image. We show the total number of followers and a link to follow or unfollow the user. We will perform an AJAX request to follow/unfollow a particular user. We add `data-id` and `data-action` attributes to the <a> HTML element, including the user ID and the initial action to perform when it's clicked, `follow` or `unfollow`, that depends on the user requesting the page being a follower of this other user or not, as the case may be. We display the images bookmarked by the user, including the `images/image/list_ajax.html` template.

Open your browser again and click on a user that has bookmarked some images. You will see profile details, as follows:

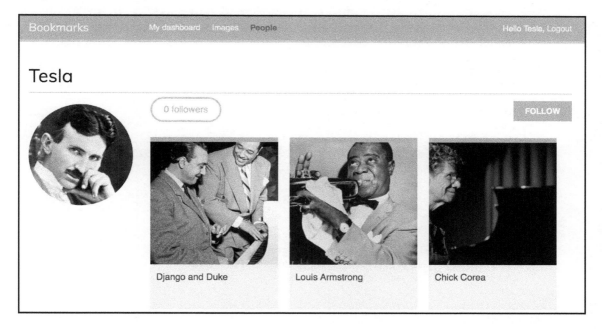

Building an AJAX view to follow users

We will create a simple view to follow/unfollow a user using AJAX. Edit the `views.py` file of the `account` application and add the following code to it:

```
from django.http import JsonResponse
from django.views.decorators.http import require_POST
from common.decorators import ajax_required
from .models import Contact

@ajax_required
@require_POST
@login_required
def user_follow(request):
    user_id = request.POST.get('id')
    action = request.POST.get('action')
    if user_id and action:
        try:
            user = User.objects.get(id=user_id)
```

```
        if action == 'follow':
            Contact.objects.get_or_create(
                user_from=request.user,
                user_to=user)
        else:
            Contact.objects.filter(user_from=request.user,
                                   user_to=user).delete()
        return JsonResponse({'status':'ok'})
    except User.DoesNotExist:
        return JsonResponse({'status':'ko'})
return JsonResponse({'status':'ko'})
```

The `user_follow` view is quite similar to the `image_like` view we created before. Since we are using a custom intermediary model for the users' many-to-many relationship, the default `add()` and `remove()` methods of the automatic manager of `ManyToManyField` are not available. We use the intermediary `Contact` model to create or delete user relationships.

Edit the `urls.py` file of the `account` application and add the following URL pattern to it:

```
path('users/follow/', views.user_follow, name='user_follow'),
```

Ensure that you place the preceding pattern before the `user_detail` URL pattern. Otherwise, any requests to `/users/follow/` will match the regular expression of the `user_detail` pattern and that view will be executed instead. Remember that, in every HTTP request, Django checks the requested URL against each pattern in order of appearance and stops at the first match.

Edit the `user/detail.html` template of the `account` application and append the following code to it:

```
{% block domready %}
  $('a.follow').click(function(e){
    e.preventDefault();
    $.post('{% url "user_follow" %}',
      {
        id: $(this).data('id'),
        action: $(this).data('action')
      },
      function(data){
        if (data['status'] == 'ok') {
          var previous_action = $('a.follow').data('action');

          // toggle data-action
          $('a.follow').data('action',
            previous_action == 'follow' ? 'unfollow' : 'follow');
```

```
                    // toggle link text
                    $('a.follow').text(
                      previous_action == 'follow' ? 'Unfollow' : 'Follow');

                    // update total followers
                    var previous_followers = parseInt(
                      $('span.count .total').text());
                    $('span.count .total').text(previous_action == 'follow' ?
                    previous_followers + 1 : previous_followers - 1);
                }
            }
        );
    });
{% endblock %}
```

The preceding code is the JavaScript code to perform the AJAX request to follow or unfollow a particular user and also to toggle the follow/unfollow link. We use jQuery to perform the AJAX request and set both the `data-action` attribute and the text of the HTML `<a>` element based on its previous value. When the AJAX action is performed, we also update the total followers count displayed on the page. Open the user detail page of an existing user and click on the **FOLLOW** link to test the functionality we just built. You will see that the follower's count gets increased:

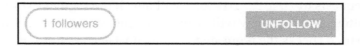

Building a generic activity stream application

Many social websites display an activity stream to their users so that they can track what other users do on the platform. An activity stream is a list of recent activities performed by a user or a group of users. For example, Facebook's News Feed is an activity stream. Sample actions can be *user X bookmarked image Y* or *user X is now following user Y*. We will build an activity stream application so that every user can see recent interactions of the users they follow. To do so, we will need a model to save the actions performed by users on the website and a simple way to add actions to the feed.

Create a new application named `actions` inside your project with the following command:

```
python manage.py startapp actions
```

Add the new application to INSTALLED_APPS in the settings.py file of your project to activate the application in your project:

```
INSTALLED_APPS = [
    # ...
    'actions.apps.ActionsConfig',
]
```

Edit the models.py file of the actions application and add the following code to it:

```
from django.db import models

class Action(models.Model):
    user = models.ForeignKey('auth.User',
                             related_name='actions',
                             db_index=True,
                             on_delete=models.CASCADE)
    verb = models.CharField(max_length=255)
    created = models.DateTimeField(auto_now_add=True,
                                   db_index=True)

    class Meta:
        ordering = ('-created',)
```

The preceding code shows the Action model that will be used to store user activities. The fields of this model are as follows:

- user: The user that performed the action; this is ForeignKey to the Django User model.
- verb: The verb describing the action that the user has performed.
- created: The date and time when this action was created. We use auto_now_add=True to automatically set this to the current datetime when the object is saved for the first time in the database.

With this basic model, we can only store actions, such as *user X did something*. We need an extra ForeignKey field in order to save actions that involve a target object, such as *user X bookmarked image Y* or *user X is now following user Y*. As you already know, a normal ForeignKey can point to only one model. Instead, we will need a way for the action's target object to be an instance of an existing model. This is where the Django content types framework comes on the scene.

Using the contenttypes framework

Django includes a contenttypes framework located at `django.contrib.contenttypes`. This application can track all models installed in your project and provides a generic interface to interact with your models.

The `django.contrib.contenttypes` application is included in the `INSTALLED_APPS` setting by default when you create a new project using the `startproject` command. It is used by other `contrib` packages, such as the authentication framework and the admin application.

The `contenttypes` application contains a `ContentType` model. Instances of this model represent the actual models of your application, and new instances of `ContentType` are automatically created when new models are installed in your project. The `ContentType` model has the following fields:

- `app_label`: This indicates the name of the application the model belongs to. This is automatically taken from the `app_label` attribute of the model `Meta` options. For example, our `Image` model belongs to the `images` application.
- `model`: The name of the model class.
- `name`: This indicates the human-readable name of the model. This is automatically taken from the `verbose_name` attribute of the model `Meta` options.

Let's take a look at how we can interact with `ContentType` objects. Open the shell using the `python manage.py shell` command. You can obtain the `ContentType` object corresponding to a specific model by performing a query with the `app_label` and `model` attributes, as follows:

```
>>> from django.contrib.contenttypes.models import ContentType
>>> image_type = ContentType.objects.get(app_label='images', model='image')
>>> image_type
<ContentType: image>
```

You can also retrieve the model class from a `ContentType` object by calling its `model_class()` method:

```
>>> image_type.model_class()
<class 'images.models.Image'>
```

It's also common to get the `ContentType` object for a particular model class, as follows:

```
>>> from images.models import Image
>>> ContentType.objects.get_for_model(Image)
<ContentType: image>
```

These are just some examples of using content types. Django offers more ways to work with them. You can find the official documentation about the content types framework at `https://docs.djangoproject.com/en/2.0/ref/contrib/contenttypes/`.

Adding generic relations to your models

In generic relations, `ContentType` objects play the role of pointing to the model used for the relationship. You will need three fields to set up a generic relation in a model:

- **A `ForeignKey` field to `ContentType`:** This will tell us the model for the relationship
- **A field to store the primary key of the related object:** This will usually be a `PositiveIntegerField` to match Django's automatic primary key fields
- **A field to define and manage the generic relation using the two previous fields:** The content types framework offers a `GenericForeignKey` field for this purpose

Edit the `models.py` file of the `actions` application and make it look like this:

```python
from django.db import models
from django.contrib.contenttypes.models import ContentType
from django.contrib.contenttypes.fields import GenericForeignKey

class Action(models.Model):
    user = models.ForeignKey('auth.User',
                             related_name='actions',
                             db_index=True,
                             on_delete=models.CASCADE)
    verb = models.CharField(max_length=255)
    target_ct = models.ForeignKey(ContentType,
                                  blank=True,
                                  null=True,
                                  related_name='target_obj',
                                  on_delete=models.CASCADE)
    target_id = models.PositiveIntegerField(null=True,
                                            blank=True,
                                            db_index=True)
    target = GenericForeignKey('target_ct', 'target_id')
```

```
created = models.DateTimeField(auto_now_add=True,
                               db_index=True)

class Meta:
    ordering = ('-created',)
```

We have added the following fields to the `Action` model:

- `target_ct`: A `ForeignKey` field that points to the `ContentType` model
- `target_id`: A `PositiveIntegerField` for storing the primary key of the related object
- `target`: A `GenericForeignKey` field to the related object based on the combination of the two previous fields

Django does not create any field in the database for `GenericForeignKey` fields. The only fields that are mapped to database fields are `target_ct` and `target_id`. Both fields have `blank=True` and `null=True` attributes so that a `target` object is not required when saving `Action` objects.

 You can make your applications more flexible by using generic relationships instead of foreign keys when it makes sense to have a generic relation.

Run the following command to create initial migrations for this application:

python manage.py makemigrations actions

You should see the following output:

**Migrations for 'actions':
  actions/migrations/0001_initial.py
    - Create model Action**

Then, run the next command to sync the application with the database:

python manage.py migrate

The output of the command should indicate that the new migrations have been applied, as follows:

Applying actions.0001_initial... OK

Let's add the `Action` model to the administration site. Edit the `admin.py` file of the actions application and add the following code to it:

```
from django.contrib import admin
from .models import Action

@admin.register(Action)
class ActionAdmin(admin.ModelAdmin):
    list_display = ('user', 'verb', 'target', 'created')
    list_filter = ('created',)
    search_fields = ('verb',)
```

You just registered the `Action` model in the administration site. Run the `python manage.py runserver` command to initialize the development server and open `http://127.0.0.1:8000/admin/actions/action/add/` in your browser. You should see the page for creating a new `Action` object, as follows:

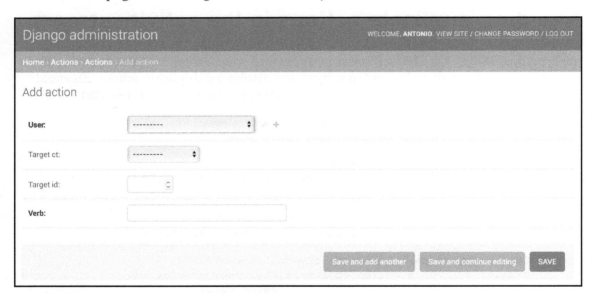

As you would notice in the preceding screenshot, only the `target_ct` and `target_id` fields that are mapped to actual database fields are shown. The `GenericForeignKey` field does not appear in the form. The `target_ct` field allows you to select any of the registered models of your Django project. You can restrict the content types to choose from a limited set of models using the `limit_choices_to` attribute in the `target_ct` field: the `limit_choices_to` attribute allows you to restrict the content of `ForeignKey` fields to a specific set of values.

Create a new file inside the `actions` application directory and name it `utils.py`. We will define a shortcut function that will allow us to create new `Action` objects in a simple way. Edit the new `utils.py` file and add the following code to it:

```
from django.contrib.contenttypes.models import ContentType
from .models import Action

def create_action(user, verb, target=None):
    action = Action(user=user, verb=verb, target=target)
    action.save()
```

The `create_action()` function allows us to create actions that optionally include a `target` object. We can use this function anywhere in our code as a shortcut to add new actions to the activity stream.

Avoiding duplicate actions in the activity stream

Sometimes, your users might perform an action multiple times. They might click several times on the **LIKE** or **UNLIKE** buttons or perform the same action multiple times in a short period of time. This will easily lead to storing and displaying duplicate actions. To avoid this, we will improve the `create_action()` function to skip obvious duplicated actions.

Edit the `utils.py` file of the `actions` application, as follows:

```
import datetime
from django.utils import timezone
from django.contrib.contenttypes.models import ContentType
from .models import Action

def create_action(user, verb, target=None):
    # check for any similar action made in the last minute
    now = timezone.now()
    last_minute = now - datetime.timedelta(seconds=60)
    similar_actions = Action.objects.filter(user_id=user.id,
                                            verb= verb,
                                            created__gte=last_minute)
    if target:
        target_ct = ContentType.objects.get_for_model(target)
        similar_actions = similar_actions.filter(
                                            target_ct=target_ct,
                                            target_id=target.id)
    if not similar_actions:
        # no existing actions found
        action = Action(user=user, verb=verb, target=target)
```

```
        action.save()
    return True
return False
```

We have changed the `create_action()` function to avoid saving duplicate actions and return Boolean to tell whether the action was saved or not. This is how we avoid duplicates:

- First, we get the current time using the `timezone.now()` method provided by Django. This method does the same as `datetime.datetime.now()` but returns a `timezone-aware` object. Django provides a setting called `USE_TZ` to enable or disable time zone support. The default `settings.py` file created using the `startproject` command includes `USE_TZ=True`.
- We use the `last_minute` variable to store the datetime from one minute ago and retrieve any identical actions performed by the user since then.
- We create an `Action` object if no identical action already exists in the last minute. We return `True` if an `Action` object was created, otherwise `False`.

Adding user actions to the activity stream

It's time to add some actions to our views to build the activity stream for our users. We will store an action for each of the following interactions:

- A user bookmarks an image
- A user likes an image
- A user creates an account
- A user starts following another user

Edit the `views.py` file of the `images` application and add the following import:

```
from actions.utils import create_action
```

In the `image_create` view, add `create_action()` after saving the image, like this:

```
new_item.save()
create_action(request.user, 'bookmarked image', new_item)
```

In the `image_like` view, add `create_action()` after adding the user to the `users_like` relationship, as follows:

```
image.users_like.add(request.user)
create_action(request.user, 'likes', image)
```

Now, edit the `views.py` file of the `account` application and add the following import:

```
from actions.utils import create_action
```

In the `register` view, add `create_action()` after creating the `Profile` object, as follows:

```
Profile.objects.create(user=new_user)
create_action(new_user, 'has created an account')
```

In the `user_follow` view, add `create_action()`:

```
Contact.objects.get_or_create(user_from=request.user,
                              user_to=user)
create_action(request.user, 'is following', user)
```

As you can see in the preceding code, thanks to our `Action` model and our helper function, it's very easy to save new actions to the activity stream.

Displaying the activity stream

Finally, we will need a way to display the activity stream for each user. We will include the activity stream in the user's dashboard. Edit the `views.py` file of the `account` application. Import the `Action` model and modify the dashboard view, as follows:

```
from actions.models import Action

@login_required
def dashboard(request):
    # Display all actions by default
    actions = Action.objects.exclude(user=request.user)
    following_ids = request.user.following.values_list('id',
                                                       flat=True)
    if following_ids:
        # If user is following others, retrieve only their actions
        actions = actions.filter(user_id__in=following_ids)
    actions = actions[:10]

    return render(request,
                  'account/dashboard.html',
                  {'section': 'dashboard',
                   'actions': actions})
```

In the preceding view, we retrieve all actions from the database, excluding the ones performed by the current user. By default, we will retrieve the latest actions performed by all users on the platform. If the user is following other users, we restrict the query to retrieve only the actions performed by the users they follow. Finally, we limit the result to the first 10 actions returned. We don't use order_by() in the QuerySet because we rely on the default ordering we provided in the Meta options of the Action model. Recent actions will come first since we have set ordering = ('-created',) in the Action model.

Optimizing QuerySets that involve related objects

Every time you retrieve an Action object, you will usually access its related User object and the user's related Profile object. The Django ORM offers a simple way to retrieve related objects at the same time thereby avoiding additional queries to the database.

Using select_related()

Django offers a QuerySet method called select_related() that allows you to retrieve related objects for one-to-many relationships. This translates to a single, more complex QuerySet, but you avoid additional queries when accessing the related objects. The select_related method is for ForeignKey and OneToOne fields. It works by performing an SQL JOIN and including the fields of the related object in the SELECT statement.

To take advantage of select_related(), edit the following line of the preceding code:

```
actions = actions[:10]
```

Also, add select_related to the fields that you will use, like this:

```
actions = actions.select_related('user', 'user__profile')[:10]
```

We use user__profile to join the Profile table in a single SQL query. If you call select_related() without passing any arguments to it, it will retrieve objects from all ForeignKey relationships. Always limit select_related() to the relationships that will be accessed afterward.

 Using select_related() carefully can vastly improve execution time.

Using prefetch_related()

`select_related()` will help you boost performance for retrieving related objects in one-to-many relationships. However, `select_related()` cannot work for many-to-many or many-to-one relationships (`ManyToMany` or reverse `ForeignKey` fields). Django offers a different QuerySet method called `prefetch_related` that works for many-to-many and many-to-one relations in addition to the relations supported by `select_related()`. The `prefetch_related()` method performs a separate lookup for each relationship and joins the results using Python. This method also supports the prefetching of `GenericRelation` and `GenericForeignKey`.

Edit the `views.py` file of the `application` account and complete your query by adding `prefetch_related()` to it for the target `GenericForeignKey` field, as follows:

```
actions = actions.select_related('user', 'user__profile')\
                 .prefetch_related('target')[:10]
```

This query is now optimized for retrieving the user actions, including related objects.

Creating templates for actions

We will now create the template to display a particular `Action` object. Create a new directory inside the `actions` application directory and name it `templates`. Add the following file structure to it:

```
actions/
    action/
        detail.html
```

Edit the `actions/action/detail.html` template file and add the following lines to it:

```
{% load thumbnail %}

{% with user=action.user profile=action.user.profile %}
<div class="action">
  <div class="images">
    {% if profile.photo %}
      {% thumbnail user.profile.photo "80x80" crop="100%" as im %}
        <a href="{{ user.get_absolute_url }}">
          <img src="{{ im.url }}" alt="{{ user.get_full_name }}"
          class="item-img">
        </a>
      {% endthumbnail %}
    {% endif %}
```

```
      {% if action.target %}
        {% with target=action.target %}
          {% if target.image %}
            {% thumbnail target.image "80x80" crop="100%" as im %}
              <a href="{{ target.get_absolute_url }}">
                <img src="{{ im.url }}" class="item-img">
              </a>
            {% endthumbnail %}
          {% endif %}
        {% endwith %}
      {% endif %}
    </div>
    <div class="info">
      <p>
        <span class="date">{{ action.created|timesince }} ago</span>
        <br />
        <a href="{{ user.get_absolute_url }}">
          {{ user.first_name }}
        </a>
        {{ action.verb }}
        {% if action.target %}
          {% with target=action.target %}
            <a href="{{ target.get_absolute_url }}">{{ target }}</a>
          {% endwith %}
        {% endif %}
      </p>
    </div>
  </div>
{% endwith %}
```

This is the template used to display an Action object. First, we use the `{% with %}` template tag to retrieve the user performing the action and the related Profile object. Then, we display the image of the target object if the Action object has a related target object. Finally, we display the link to the user who performed the action, the verb, and the target object, if any.

Now, edit the `account/dashboard.html` template of the account application and append the following code to the bottom of the content block:

```
<h2>What's happening</h2>
<div id="action-list">
  {% for action in actions %}
    {% include "actions/action/detail.html" %}
  {% endfor %}
</div>
```

Open `http://127.0.0.1:8000/account/` in your browser. Log in with an existing user and perform several actions so that they get stored in the database. Then, log in using another user, follow the previous user, and take a look at the generated action stream on the dashboard page. It should look like the following:

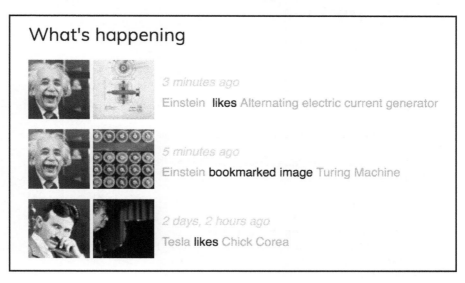

We just created a complete activity stream for our users, and we can easily add new user actions to it. You can also add infinite scroll functionality to the activity stream by implementing the same AJAX paginator you used for the `image_list` view.

Using signals for denormalizing counts

There are some cases when you would like to denormalize your data. Denormalization is making data redundant in a way that it optimizes read performance. You have to be careful about denormalization and only start using it when you really need it. The biggest issue you will find with denormalization is that it's difficult to keep your denormalized data updated.

We will take a look at an example of how to improve our queries by denormalizing counts. The drawback is that we have to keep the redundant data updated. We will denormalize data from our `Image` model and use Django signals to keep the data updated.

Working with signals

Django comes with a signal dispatcher that allows `receiver` functions to get notified when certain actions occur. Signals are very useful when you need your code to do something every time something else happens. You can also create your own signals so that others can get notified when an event happens.

Django provides several signals for models located at `django.db.models.signals`. Some of these signals are as follows:

- `pre_save` and `post_save` are sent before or after calling the `save()` method of a model
- `pre_delete` and `post_delete` are sent before or after calling the `delete()` method of a model or QuerySet
- `m2m_changed` is sent when a `ManyToManyField` on a model is changed

These are just a subset of the signals provided by Django. You can find the list of all built-in signals at `https://docs.djangoproject.com/en/2.0/ref/signals/`.

Let's say you want to retrieve images by popularity. You can use the Django aggregation functions to retrieve images ordered by the number of users who like them. Remember you used Django aggregation functions in `Chapter 3`, *Extending Your Blog Application*. The following code will retrieve images according to their number of likes:

```
from django.db.models import Count
from images.models import Image

images_by_popularity = Image.objects.annotate(
    total_likes=Count('users_like')).order_by('-total_likes')
```

However, ordering images by counting their total `likes` is more expensive in terms of performance than ordering them by a field, which stores total counts. You can add a field to the `Image` model to denormalize the total number of likes to boost performance in queries that involve this field. Now, the issue is how to keep this field updated?

Edit the `models.py` file of the `images` application and add the following `total_likes` field to the `Image` model:

```
class Image(models.Model):
    # ...
    total_likes = models.PositiveIntegerField(db_index=True,
                                              default=0)
```

The `total_likes` field will allow us to store the total count of users that like each image. Denormalizing counts is useful when you want to filter or order QuerySets by them.

 There are several ways to improve performance that you have to take into account before denormalizing fields. Consider database indexes, query optimization, and caching, before starting to denormalize your data.

Run the following command to create the migrations for adding the new field to the database table:

```
python manage.py makemigrations images
```

You should see the following output:

```
Migrations for 'images':
  images/migrations/0002_image_total_likes.py
    - Add field total_likes to image
```

Then, run the following command to apply the migration:

```
python manage.py migrate images
```

The output should include the following line:

```
Applying images.0002_image_total_likes... OK
```

We will attach a `receiver` function to the `m2m_changed` signal. Create a new file inside the `images` application directory and name it `signals.py`. Add the following code to it:

```python
from django.db.models.signals import m2m_changed
from django.dispatch import receiver
from .models import Image

@receiver(m2m_changed, sender=Image.users_like.through)
def users_like_changed(sender, instance, **kwargs):
    instance.total_likes = instance.users_like.count()
    instance.save()
```

First, we register the `users_like_changed` function as a `receiver` function using the `receiver()` decorator, and we attach it to the `m2m_changed` signal. We connect the function to `Image.users_like.through` so that the function is only called if the `m2m_changed` signal has been launched by this sender. There is an alternate method for registering a `receiver` function, which consists of using the `connect()` method of the `Signal` object.

Django signals are synchronous and blocking. Don't confuse signals with asynchronous tasks. However, you can combine both to launch asynchronous tasks when your code gets notified by a signal.

You have to connect your receiver function to a signal so that it gets called every time the signal is sent. The recommended method for registering your signals is by importing them in the ready() method of your application configuration class. Django provides an application registry that allows you to configure and introspect your applications.

Application configuration classes

Django allows you to specify configuration classes for your applications. When you create an application using the startapp command, Django adds an apps.py file to the app directory, including a basic app configuration that inherits from the AppConfig class.

The application configuration class allows you to store metadata and configuration for the application and provides introspection for the app. You can find more information about application configurations at https://docs.djangoproject.com/en/2.0/ref/applications/.

In order to register your signal receiver functions, when you use the receiver() decorator, you just need to import the signals module of your application inside the ready() method of the application configuration class. This method is called as soon as the application registry is fully populated. Any other initializations for your application should also be included in this method.

Edit the apps.py file of the images application and make it look like this:

```
from django.apps import AppConfig

class ImagesConfig(AppConfig):
    name = 'images'

    def ready(self):
        # import signal handlers
        import images.signals
```

We import the signals for this application in the ready() method so that they are imported when the images application is loaded.

Run the development server with the following command:

```
python manage.py runserver
```

Open your browser to view an image detail page and click on the **LIKE** button. Go back to the administration site, navigate to the edit image URL, such as http://127.0.0.1:8000/admin/images/image/1/change/, and take a look at the total_likes attribute. You should see that the total_likes attribute is updated with the total number of users that like the image, as follows:

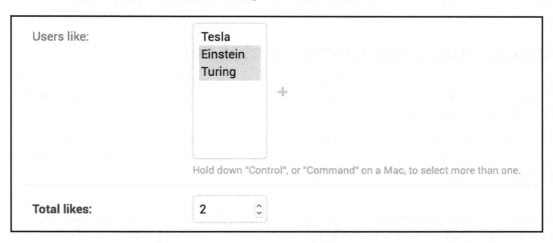

Now, you can use the total_likes attribute to order images by popularity or display the value anywhere, avoiding complex queries to calculate it. Consider the following query to get images ordered according to their like count:

```
from django.db.models import Count

images_by_popularity = Image.objects.annotate(
    likes=Count('users_like')).order_by('-likes')
```

The preceding query can now be written as follows:

```
images_by_popularity = Image.objects.order_by('-total_likes')
```

This results in a less expensive SQL query. This is just an example of how to use Django signals.

Use signals with caution since they make it difficult to know the control flow. In many cases, you can avoid using signals if you know which receivers need to be notified.

You will need to set initial counts to match the current status of the database. Open the shell with the `python manage.py shell` command and run the following code:

```
from images.models import Image
for image in Image.objects.all():
    image.total_likes = image.users_like.count()
    image.save()
```

The likes count for each image is now up to date.

Using Redis for storing item views

Redis is an advanced key/value database that allows you to save different types of data and is extremely fast in I/O operations. Redis stores everything in memory, but the data can be persisted by dumping the dataset to disk every once in a while or by adding each command to a log. Redis is very versatile compared to other key/value stores: it provides a set of powerful commands and supports diverse data structures, such as strings, hashes, lists, sets, ordered sets, and even bitmaps or HyperLogLogs.

Although SQL is best suited to schema-defined persistent data storage, Redis offers numerous advantages when dealing with rapidly changing data, volatile storage, or when a quick cache is needed. Let's take a look at how Redis can be used to build a new functionality into our project.

Installing Redis

Download the latest Redis version from `https://redis.io/download`. Unzip the `tar.gz` file, enter the `redis` directory, and compile Redis using the `make` command, as follows:

```
cd redis-4.0.9
make
```

After installing it, use the following shell command to initialize the Redis server:

```
src/redis-server
```

You should see an output that ends with the following lines:

```
# Server initialized
* Ready to accept connections
```

By default, Redis runs on port 6379. You can specify a custom port using the --port flag, for example, redis-server --port 6655.

Keep the Redis server running and open another shell. Start the Redis client with the following command:

```
src/redis-cli
```

You will see the Redis client shell prompt like this:

```
127.0.0.1:6379>
```

The Redis client allows you to execute Redis commands directly from the shell. Let's try some commands. Enter the SET command in the Redis shell to store a value in a key:

```
127.0.0.1:6379> SET name "Peter"
OK
```

The preceding command creates a name key with the string value "Peter" in the Redis database. The OK output indicates that the key has been saved successfully. Then, retrieve the value using the GET command, as follows:

```
127.0.0.1:6379> GET name
"Peter"
```

You can also check whether a key exists using the EXISTS command. This command returns 1 if the given key exists, 0 otherwise:

```
127.0.0.1:6379> EXISTS name
(integer) 1
```

You can set the time for a key to expire using the EXPIRE command, which allows you to set time to live in seconds. Another option is using the EXPIREAT command that expects a Unix timestamp. Key expiration is useful to use Redis as a cache or to store volatile data:

```
127.0.0.1:6379> GET name
"Peter"
127.0.0.1:6379> EXPIRE name 2
(integer) 1
```

Wait for two seconds and try to get the same key again:

```
127.0.0.1:6379> GET name
(nil)
```

The `(nil)` response is a null response and means that no key has been found. You can also delete any key using the `DEL` command, as follows:

```
127.0.0.1:6379> SET total 1
OK
127.0.0.1:6379> DEL total
(integer) 1
127.0.0.1:6379> GET total
(nil)
```

These are just basic commands for key operations. Redis includes a large set of commands for other data types, such as strings, hashes, sets, and ordered sets. You can take a look at all Redis commands at `https://redis.io/commands` and all Redis data types at `https://redis.io/topics/data-types`.

Using Redis with Python

We will need Python bindings for Redis. Install `redis-py` via `pip` using the following command:

```
pip install redis==2.10.6
```

You can find the `redis-py` docs at `https://redis-py.readthedocs.io/`.

The `redis-py` package offers two classes for interacting with Redis: `StrictRedis` and `Redis`. Both offer the same functionality. The `StrictRedis` class attempts to adhere to the official Redis command syntax. The `Redis` class extends `StrictRedis`, overriding some methods to provide backward compatibility. We will use `StrictRedis` since it follows the Redis command syntax. Open the Python shell and execute the following code:

```
>>> import redis
>>> r = redis.StrictRedis(host='localhost', port=6379, db=0)
```

The preceding code creates a connection with the Redis database. In Redis, databases are identified by an integer index instead of a database name. By default, a client is connected to the database 0. The number of available Redis databases is set to 16, but you can change this in the `redis.conf` configuration file.

Now, set a key using the Python shell:

```
>>> r.set('foo', 'bar')
True
```

The command returns `True`, indicating that the key has been successfully created. Now, you can retrieve the key using the `get()` command:

```
>>> r.get('foo')
b'bar'
```

As you can note from the preceding code, the methods of `StrictRedis` follow the Redis command syntax.

Let's integrate Redis into our project. Edit the `settings.py` file of the `bookmarks` project and add the following settings to it:

```
REDIS_HOST = 'localhost'
REDIS_PORT = 6379
REDIS_DB = 0
```

These are the settings for the Redis server and the database that we will use for our project.

Storing item views in Redis

Let's find a way to store the total number of times an image has been viewed. If we implement this using the Django ORM, it will involve an SQL UPDATE query every time an image is displayed. If we use Redis instead, we just need to increment a counter stored in memory, resulting in a much better performance and less overhead.

Edit the `views.py` file of the `images` application and add the following code to it after the existing `import` statements:

```
import redis
from django.conf import settings

# connect to redis
r = redis.StrictRedis(host=settings.REDIS_HOST,
                      port=settings.REDIS_PORT,
                      db=settings.REDIS_DB)
```

With the preceding code, we establish the Redis connection in order to use it in our views. Edit the `image_detail` view and make it look as follows:

```
def image_detail(request, id, slug):
    image = get_object_or_404(Image, id=id, slug=slug)
    # increment total image views by 1
    total_views = r.incr('image:{}:views'.format(image.id))
    return render(request,
                  'images/image/detail.html',
                  {'section': 'images',
                   'image': image,
                   'total_views': total_views})
```

In this view, we use the `incr` command that increments the value of a given key by 1. If the key doesn't exist, the `incr` command creates it previously. The `incr()` method returns the final value of the key after performing the operation. We store the value in the `total_views` variable and pass it in the template context. We build the Redis key using a notation, such as `object-type:id:field` (for example, `image:33:id`).

> The convention for naming Redis keys is to use a colon sign as a separator for creating namespaced keys. By doing so, the key names are especially verbose and related keys share part of the same schema in their names.

Edit the `images/image/detail.html` template of the `images` application and add the following code to it, after the existing `<span class="count">` element:

```
<span class="count">
  {{ total_views }} view{{ total_views|pluralize }}
</span>
```

Now, open an image detail page in your browser and reload it several times. You will see that each time the view is processed, the total views displayed is incremented by 1. Take a look at the following example:

Great! You have successfully integrated Redis into your project to store item counts.

Storing a ranking in Redis

Let's build something more complex with Redis. We will create a ranking of the most viewed images in our platform. For building this ranking, we will use Redis sorted sets. A sorted set is a non-repeating collection of strings in which every member is associated with a score. Items are sorted by their score.

Edit the `views.py` file of the `images` application and make the `image_detail` view look as follows:

```
def image_detail(request, id, slug):
    image = get_object_or_404(Image, id=id, slug=slug)
    # increment total image views by 1
    total_views = r.incr('image:{}:views'.format(image.id))
    # increment image ranking by 1
    r.zincrby('image_ranking', image.id, 1)
    return render(request,
                  'images/image/detail.html',
                  {'section': 'images',
                   'image': image,
                   'total_views': total_views})
```

We use the `zincrby()` command to store image views in a sorted set with the `image:ranking` key. We will store the image `id` and a related score of 1 that will be added to the total score of this element in the sorted set. This will allow us to keep track of all image views globally and have a sorted set ordered by the total number of views.

Now, create a new view to display the ranking of the most viewed images. Add the following code to the `views.py` file of the `images` application:

```python
@login_required
def image_ranking(request):
    # get image ranking dictionary
    image_ranking = r.zrange('image_ranking', 0, -1,
                             desc=True)[:10]
    image_ranking_ids = [int(id) for id in image_ranking]
    # get most viewed images
    most_viewed = list(Image.objects.filter(
                           id__in=image_ranking_ids))
    most_viewed.sort(key=lambda x: image_ranking_ids.index(x.id))
    return render(request,
                  'images/image/ranking.html',
                  {'section': 'images',
                   'most_viewed': most_viewed})
```

The `image_ranking` view works like this:

1. We use the `zrange()` command to obtain the elements in the sorted set. This command expects a custom range according to the lowest and highest score. Using `0` as the lowest and `-1` as the highest score, we are telling Redis to return all elements in the sorted set. We also specify `desc=True` to retrieve the elements ordered by descending score. Finally, we slice the results using `[:10]` to get the first 10 elements with the highest score.

2. We build a list of returned image IDs and store it in the `image_ranking_ids` variable as a list of integers. We retrieve the `Image` objects for those IDs and force the query to be executed using the `list()` function. It is important to force the QuerySet execution because we will now use the `sort()` list method on it (at this point, we need a list of objects instead of a QuerySet).

3. We sort the `Image` objects by their index of appearance in the image ranking. Now, we can use the `most_viewed` list in our template to display the 10 most viewed images.

Create a new `ranking.html` template inside the `images/image/` template directory of the `images` application and add the following code to it:

```
{% extends "base.html" %}

{% block title %}Images ranking{% endblock %}

{% block content %}
  <h1>Images ranking</h1>
  <ol>
    {% for image in most_viewed %}
      <li>
        <a href="{{ image.get_absolute_url }}">
          {{ image.title }}
        </a>
      </li>
    {% endfor %}
  </ol>
{% endblock %}
```

The template is pretty straightforward. We iterate over the `Image` objects contained in the `most_viewed` list and display their names, including a link to the image detail page.

Finally, you will need to create a URL pattern for the new view. Edit the `urls.py` file of the `images` application and add the following pattern to it:

```
path('ranking/', views.image_ranking, name='create'),
```

Run the development server, access your site in your web browser, and load the image detail multiple times for different images. Then, access `http://127.0.0.1:8000/images/ranking/` from your browser. You should be able to see an images ranking, as follows:

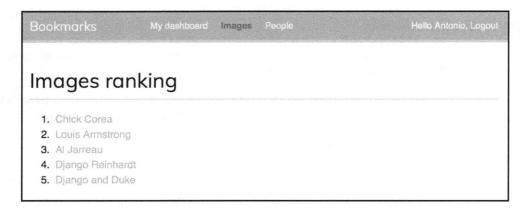

Great! You just created an ranking with Redis.

Next steps with Redis

Redis is not a replacement for your SQL database, but a fast in-memory storage that is more suitable for certain tasks. Add it to your stack and use it when you really feel it's needed. The following are some scenarios in which Redis suits pretty well:

- **Counting**: As you have seen, it is very easy to manage counters with Redis. You can use `incr()` and `incrby()` for counting stuff.
- **Storing latest items**: You can add items to the start/end of a list using `lpush()` and `rpush()`. Remove and return the first/last element using `lpop()` / `rpop()`. You can trim the list length using `ltrim()` to maintain its length.
- **Queues**: In addition to `push` and `pop` commands, Redis offers blocking queue commands.
- **Caching**: Using `expire()` and `expireat()` allows you to use Redis as a cache. You can also find third-party Redis cache backends for Django.
- **Pub/sub**: Redis provides commands for subscribing/unsubscribing and sending messages to channels.
- **Rankings and leaderboards**: Redis sorted sets with scores make it very easy to create leaderboards.
- **Real-time tracking**: Redis's fast I/O makes it perfect for real-time scenarios.

Summary

In this chapter, you have built a follower system and a user activity stream. You learned how Django signals work and integrated Redis into your project.

In the next chapter, you will learn how to build an online shop. You will create a product catalog and build a shopping cart using sessions. You will also learn how to launch asynchronous tasks using Celery.

Building an Online Shop 7

In the previous chapter, you created a follower system and built a user activity stream. You also learned how Django signals work and integrated Redis into your project to count image views. In this chapter, you will learn how to build a basic online shop. You will create a catalog of products and implement a shopping cart using Django sessions. You will also learn how to create custom context processors and launch asynchronous tasks using Celery.

In this chapter, you will learn to:

- Create a product catalog
- Build a shopping cart using Django sessions
- Manage customer orders
- Send asynchronous notifications to customers using Celery

Creating an online shop project

We are going to start with a new Django project to build an online shop. Our users will be able to browse through a product catalog and add products to a shopping cart. Finally, they will be able to check out the cart and place an order. This chapter will cover the following functionalities of an online shop:

- Creating the product catalog models, adding them to the administration site, and building the basic views to display the catalog
- Building a shopping cart system using Django sessions to allow users to keep selected products while they browse the site
- Creating the form and functionality to place orders on the site
- Sending an asynchronous email confirmation to users when they place an order

Open a shell, create a virtual environment for the new project, and activate it with the following commands:

```
mkdir env
virtualenv env/myshop
source env/myshop/bin/activate
```

Install Django in your virtual environment with the following command:

```
pip install Django==2.0.5
```

Start a new project called myshop with an application called shop by opening a shell and running the following commands:

```
django-admin startproject myshop
cd myshop/
django-admin startapp shop
```

Edit the settings.py file of your project and add the shop application to the INSTALLED_APPS setting as follows:

```
INSTALLED_APPS = [
    # ...
    'shop.apps.ShopConfig',
]
```

Your application is now active for this project. Let's define the models for the product catalog.

Creating product catalog models

The catalog of our shop will consist of products that are organized into different categories. Each product will have a name, optional description, optional image, price, and availability. Edit the models.py file of the shop application that you just created and add the following code:

```
from django.db import models

class Category(models.Model):
    name = models.CharField(max_length=200,
                            db_index=True)
    slug = models.SlugField(max_length=200,
                            unique=True)

    class Meta:
```

```
        ordering = ('name',)
        verbose_name = 'category'
        verbose_name_plural = 'categories'

    def __str__(self):
        return self.name

class Product(models.Model):
    category = models.ForeignKey(Category,
                                 related_name='products',
                                 on_delete=models.CASCADE)
    name = models.CharField(max_length=200, db_index=True)
    slug = models.SlugField(max_length=200, db_index=True)
    image = models.ImageField(upload_to='products/%Y/%m/%d',
                              blank=True)
    description = models.TextField(blank=True)
    price = models.DecimalField(max_digits=10, decimal_places=2)
    available = models.BooleanField(default=True)
    created = models.DateTimeField(auto_now_add=True)
    updated = models.DateTimeField(auto_now=True)

    class Meta:
        ordering = ('name',)
        index_together = (('id', 'slug'),)

    def __str__(self):
        return self.name
```

These are the `Category` and `Product` models. The `Category` model consists of a `name` field and a `slug` unique field (`unique` implies the creation of an index). The `Product` model fields are as follows:

- `category`: `ForeignKey` to the `Category` model. This is a many-to-one relationship: a product belongs to one category and a category contains multiple products.
- `name`: The name of the product.
- `slug`: The slug for this product to build beautiful URLs.
- `image`: An optional product image.
- `description`: An optional description of the product.
- `price`: This field uses Python's `decimal.Decimal` type to store a fixed-precision decimal number. The maximum number of digits (including the decimal places) is set using the `max_digits` attribute and decimal places with the `decimal_places` attribute.

- `available`: A boolean value that indicates whether the product is available or not. It will be used to enable/disable the product in the catalog.
- `created`: This field stores when the object was created.
- `updated`: This field stores when the object was last updated.

For the `price` field, we use `DecimalField` instead of `FloatField` to avoid rounding issues.

 Always use `DecimalField` to store monetary amounts. `FloatField` uses Python's `float` type internally, whereas `DecimalField` uses Python's `Decimal` type. By using the `Decimal` type, you will avoid `float` rounding issues.

In the `Meta` class of the `Product` model, we use the `index_together` meta option to specify an index for the `id` and `slug` fields together. We define this index because we plan to query products by both `id` and `slug`. Both fields are indexed together to improve performances for queries that utilize the two fields.

Since we are going to deal with images in our models, open the shell and install `Pillow` with the following command:

```
pip install Pillow==5.1.0
```

Now, run the next command to create initial migrations for your project:

```
python manage.py makemigrations
```

You will see the following output:

```
Migrations for 'shop':
  shop/migrations/0001_initial.py
    - Create model Category
    - Create model Product
    - Alter index_together for product (1 constraint(s))
```

Run the next command to sync the database:

```
python manage.py migrate
```

You will see output that includes the following line:

```
Applying shop.0001_initial... OK
```

The database is now synced with your models.

Registering catalog models on the admin site

Let's add our models to the administration site so that we can easily manage categories and products. Edit the admin.py file of the shop application and add the following code to it:

```
from django.contrib import admin
from .models import Category, Product

@admin.register(Category)
class CategoryAdmin(admin.ModelAdmin):
    list_display = ['name', 'slug']
    prepopulated_fields = {'slug': ('name',)}

@admin.register(Product)
class ProductAdmin(admin.ModelAdmin):
    list_display = ['name', 'slug', 'price',
                    'available', 'created', 'updated']
    list_filter = ['available', 'created', 'updated']
    list_editable = ['price', 'available']
    prepopulated_fields = {'slug': ('name',)}
```

Remember that we use the prepopulated_fields attribute to specify fields where the value is automatically set using the value of other fields. As you have seen before, this is convenient for generating slugs. We use the list_editable attribute in the ProductAdmin class to set the fields that can be edited from the list display page of the administration site. This will allow you to edit multiple rows at once. Any field in list_editable must also be listed in the list_display attribute since only the fields displayed can be edited.

Now, create a superuser for your site using the following command:

```
python manage.py createsuperuser
```

Start the development server with the command `python manage.py runserver`. Open `http://127.0.0.1:8000/admin/shop/product/add/` in your browser and log in with the user that you just created. Add a new category and product using the administration interface. The product change list page of the administration page will then look like this:

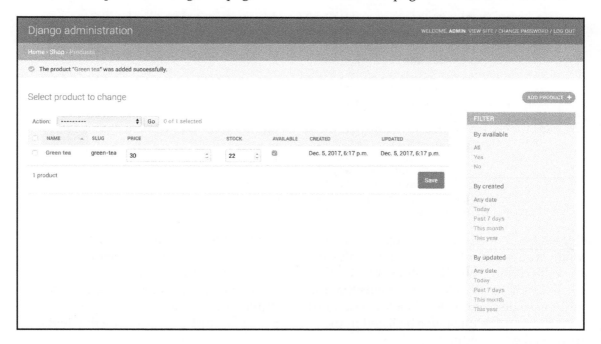

Building catalog views

In order to display the product catalog, we need to create a view to list all the products or filter products by a given category. Edit the `views.py` file of the `shop` application and add the following code to it:

```python
from django.shortcuts import render, get_object_or_404
from .models import Category, Product

def product_list(request, category_slug=None):
    category = None
    categories = Category.objects.all()
    products = Product.objects.filter(available=True)
    if category_slug:
        category = get_object_or_404(Category, slug=category_slug)
        products = products.filter(category=category)
```

```
        return render(request,
                      'shop/product/list.html',
                      {'category': category,
                       'categories': categories,
                       'products': products})
```

We will filter the QuerySet with `available=True` to retrieve only available products. We use an optional `category_slug` parameter to optionally filter products by a given category.

We also need a view to retrieve and display a single product. Add the following view to the `views.py` file:

```
def product_detail(request, id, slug):
    product = get_object_or_404(Product,
                                id=id,
                                slug=slug,
                                available=True)
    return render(request,
                  'shop/product/detail.html',
                  {'product': product})
```

The `product_detail` view expects the `id` and `slug` parameters in order to retrieve the `Product` instance. We can get this instance just through the ID since it's a unique attribute. However, we include the slug in the URL to build SEO-friendly URLs for products.

After building the product list and detail views, we have to define URL patterns for them. Create a new file inside the `shop` application directory and name it `urls.py`. Add the following code to it:

```
from django.urls import path
from . import views

app_name = 'shop'

urlpatterns = [
    path('', views.product_list, name='product_list'),
    path('<slug:category_slug>/', views.product_list,
        name='product_list_by_category'),
    path('<int:id>/<slug:slug>/', views.product_detail,
        name='product_detail'),
]
```

These are the URL patterns for our product catalog. We have defined two different URL patterns for the product_list view: a pattern named product_list, which calls the product_list view without any parameters; and a pattern named product_list_by_category, which provides a category_slug parameter to the view for filtering products according to a given category. We added a pattern for the product_detail view, which passes the id and slug parameters to the view in order to retrieve a specific product.

Edit the urls.py file of the myshop project to make it look like this:

```python
from django.contrib import admin
from django.urls import path, include

urlpatterns = [
    path('admin/', admin.site.urls),
    path('', include('shop.urls', namespace='shop')),
]
```

In the main URL patterns of the project, we will include URLs for the shop application under a custom namespace named shop.

Now, edit the models.py file of the shop application, import the reverse() function, and add a get_absolute_url() method to the Category and Product models as follows:

```python
from django.urls import reverse
# ...
class Category(models.Model):
    # ...
    def get_absolute_url(self):
        return reverse('shop:product_list_by_category',
                       args=[self.slug])

class Product(models.Model):
    # ...
    def get_absolute_url(self):
        return reverse('shop:product_detail',
                       args=[self.id, self.slug])
```

As you already know, get_absolute_url() is the convention to retrieve the URL for a given object. Here, we will use the URLs patterns that we just defined in the urls.py file.

Creating catalog templates

Now, we need to create templates for the product list and detail views. Create the following directory and file structure inside the `shop` application directory:

```
templates/
    shop/
        base.html
        product/
            list.html
            detail.html
```

We need to define a base template, and then extend it in the product list and detail templates. Edit the `shop/base.html` template and add the following code to it:

```
{% load static %}
<!DOCTYPE html>
<html>
<head>
  <meta charset="utf-8" />
  <title>{% block title %}My shop{% endblock %}</title>
  <link href="{% static "css/base.css" %}" rel="stylesheet">
</head>
<body>
  <div id="header">
    <a href="/" class="logo">My shop</a>
  </div>
  <div id="subheader">
    <div class="cart">
      Your cart is empty.
    </div>
  </div>
  <div id="content">
    {% block content %}
    {% endblock %}
  </div>
</body>
</html>
```

This is the base template that we will use for our shop. In order to include the CSS styles and images that are used by the templates, you will need to copy the static files that accompany this chapter, located in the `static/` directory of the `shop` application. Copy them to the same location in your project.

Edit the `shop/product/list.html` template and add the following code to it:

```
{% extends "shop/base.html" %}
{% load static %}

{% block title %}
  {% if category %}{{ category.name }}{% else %}Products{% endif %}
{% endblock %}

{% block content %}
  <div id="sidebar">
    <h3>Categories</h3>
    <ul>
      <li {% if not category %}class="selected"{% endif %}>
        <a href="{% url "shop:product_list" %}">All</a>
      </li>
      {% for c in categories %}
        <li {% if category.slug == c.slug %}class="selected"
        {% endif %}>
          <a href="{{ c.get_absolute_url }}">{{ c.name }}</a>
        </li>
      {% endfor %}
    </ul>
  </div>
  <div id="main" class="product-list">
    <h1>{% if category %}{{ category.name }}{% else %}Products
    {% endif %}</h1>
    {% for product in products %}
      <div class="item">
        <a href="{{ product.get_absolute_url }}">
          <img src="{% if product.image %}{{ product.image.url }}{%
          else %}{% static "img/no_image.png" %}{% endif %}">
        </a>
        <a href="{{ product.get_absolute_url }}">{{ product.name }}</a>
        <br>
        ${{ product.price }}
      </div>
    {% endfor %}
  </div>
{% endblock %}
```

This is the product list template. It extends the shop/base.html template and uses the categories context variable to display all the categories in a sidebar and products to display the products of the current page. The same template is used for both: listing all available products and listing products filtered by a category. Since the image field of the Product model can be blank, we need to provide a default image for the products that don't have an image. The image is located in our static files directory with the relative path img/no_image.png.

Since we are using ImageField to store product images, we need the development server to serve uploaded image files.

Edit the settings.py file of myshop and add the following settings:

```
MEDIA_URL = '/media/'
MEDIA_ROOT = os.path.join(BASE_DIR, 'media/')
```

MEDIA_URL is the base URL that serves media files uploaded by users. MEDIA_ROOT is the local path where these files reside, which we build by dynamically prepending the BASE_DIR variable.

For Django to serve the uploaded media files using the development server, edit the main urls.py file of myshop and add the following code to it:

```
from django.conf import settings
from django.conf.urls.static import static

urlpatterns = [
    # ...
]
if settings.DEBUG:
    urlpatterns += static(settings.MEDIA_URL,
                          document_root=settings.MEDIA_ROOT)
```

Remember that we only serve static files this way during development. In a production environment, you should never serve static files with Django.

Add a couple of products to your shop using the administration site and open `http://127.0.0.1:8000/` in your browser. You will see the product list page, which looks like this:

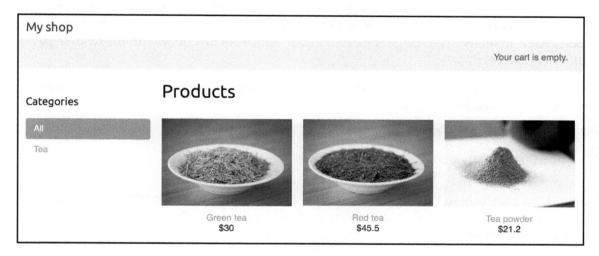

If you create a product using the administration site and don't upload any image for it, the default `no_image.png` image will be displayed instead:

Let's edit the product detail template. Edit the `shop/product/detail.html` template and add the following code to it:

```
{% extends "shop/base.html" %}
{% load static %}

{% block title %}
  {{ product.name }}
```

```
{% endblock %}

{% block content %}
  <div class="product-detail">
    <img src="{% if product.image %}{{ product.image.url }}{% else %}
    {% static "img/no_image.png" %}{% endif %}">
    <h1>{{ product.name }}</h1>
    <h2><a href="{{ product.category.get_absolute_url }}">{{
    product.category }}</a></h2>
    <p class="price">${{ product.price }}</p>
    {{ product.description|linebreaks }}
  </div>
{% endblock %}
```

We call the `get_absolute_url()` method on the related category object to display the available products that belong to the same category. Now, open `http://127.0.0.1:8000/` in your browser and click on any product to see the product detail page. It will look as follows:

You have now created a basic product catalog.

Building a shopping cart

After building the product catalog, the next step is to create a shopping cart so that users can pick the products that they want to purchase. A shopping cart allows users to select products and set the amounts they want to order, and then store this information temporarily, while they browse the site until they eventually place an order. The cart has to be persisted in the session so that the cart items are maintained during the user's visit.

We will use Django's session framework to persist the cart. The cart will be kept in the session until it finishes or the user checks out of the cart. We will also need to build additional Django models for the cart and its items.

Using Django sessions

Django provides a session framework that supports anonymous and user sessions. The session framework allows you to store arbitrary data for each visitor. Session data is stored on the server side, and cookies contain the session ID unless you use the cookie-based session engine. The session middleware manages the sending and receiving of cookies. The default session engine stores session data in the database, but you can choose between different session engines.

To use sessions, you have to make sure that the MIDDLEWARE setting of your project contains 'django.contrib.sessions.middleware.SessionMiddleware'. This middleware manages sessions. It's added by default to the MIDDLEWARE setting when you create a new project using the startproject command.

The session middleware makes the current session available in the request object. You can access the current session using request.session, treating it like a Python dictionary to store and retrieve session data. The session dictionary accepts any Python object by default that can be serialized to JSON. You can set a variable in the session like this:

```
request.session['foo'] = 'bar'
```

Retrieve a session key as follows:

```
request.session.get('foo')
```

Delete a key you previously stored in the session as follows:

```
del request.session['foo']
```

You can just treat `request.session` like a standard Python dictionary.

When users log in to the site, their anonymous session is lost and a new session is created for the authenticated users. If you store items in an anonymous session that you need to keep after the user logs in, you will have to copy the old session data into the new session.

Session settings

There are several settings you can use to configure sessions for your project. The most important is `SESSION_ENGINE`. This setting allows you to set the place where sessions are stored. By default, Django stores sessions in the database using the `Session` model of the `django.contrib.sessions` application.

Django offers the following options for storing session data:

- **Database sessions**: Session data is stored in the database. This is the default session engine.
- **File-based sessions**: Session data is stored in the filesystem.
- **Cached sessions**: Session data is stored in a cache backend. You can specify cache backends using the `CACHES` setting. Storing session data in a cache system provides the best performance.
- **Cached database sessions**: Session data is stored in a write-through cache and database. Reads-only use the database if the data is not already in the cache.
- **Cookie-based sessions**: Session data is stored in the cookies that are sent to the browser.

For better performance, use a cache-based session engine. Django supports Memcached out of the box and you can find third-party cache backends for Redis and other cache systems.

You can customize sessions with specific settings. Here are some of the important session-related settings:

- `SESSION_COOKIE_AGE`: The duration of session cookies in seconds. The default value is `1209600` (two weeks).
- `SESSION_COOKIE_DOMAIN`: The domain used for session cookies. Set this to `mydomain.com` to enable cross-domain cookies or use `None` for a standard domain cookie.

- SESSION_COOKIE_SECURE: A boolean indicating that the cookie should only be sent if the connection is an HTTPS connection.
- SESSION_EXPIRE_AT_BROWSER_CLOSE: A boolean indicating that the session has to expire when the browser is closed.
- SESSION_SAVE_EVERY_REQUEST: A boolean that, if True, will save the session to the database on every request. The session expiration is also updated each time it's saved.

You can see all the session settings and their default values at https://docs.djangoproject.com/en/2.0/ref/settings/#sessions.

Session expiration

You can choose to use browser-length sessions or persistent sessions using the SESSION_EXPIRE_AT_BROWSER_CLOSE setting. This is set to False by default, forcing the session duration to the value stored in the SESSION_COOKIE_AGE setting. If you set SESSION_EXPIRE_AT_BROWSER_CLOSE to True, the session will expire when the user closes the browser, and the SESSION_COOKIE_AGE setting will not have any effect.

You can use the set_expiry() method of request.session to overwrite the duration of the current session.

Storing shopping carts in sessions

We need to create a simple structure that can be serialized to JSON for storing cart items in a session. The cart has to include the following data for each item contained in it:

- The ID of a Product instance
- Quantity selected for the product
- Unit price for the product

Since product prices may vary, we take the approach of storing the product's price along with the product itself when it's added to the cart. By doing so, we use the current price of the product when users add it to their cart, no matter if the product's price is changed afterwards.

Now, you have to build functionality to create carts and associate them with sessions. The shopping cart has to work as follows:

- When a cart is needed, we check if a custom session key is set. If no cart is set in the session, we create a new cart and save it in the cart session key.
- For successive requests, we perform the same check and get the cart items from the cart session key. We retrieve the cart items from the session and their related Product objects from the database.

Edit the settings.py file of your project and add the following setting to it:

```
CART_SESSION_ID = 'cart'
```

This is the key that we are going to use to store the cart in the user session. Since Django sessions are managed per-visitor, we can use the same cart session key for all sessions.

Let's create an application for managing shopping carts. Open the Terminal and create a new application, running the following command from the project directory:

```
python manage.py startapp cart
```

Then, edit the settings.py file of your project and add the new application to the INSTALLED_APPS setting as follows:

```
INSTALLED_APPS = [
    # ...
    'shop.apps.ShopConfig',
    'cart.apps.CartConfig',
]
```

Create a new file inside the cart application directory and name it cart.py. Add the following code to it:

```
from decimal import Decimal
from django.conf import settings
from shop.models import Product

class Cart(object):

    def __init__(self, request):
        """
        Initialize the cart.
        """
        self.session = request.session
        cart = self.session.get(settings.CART_SESSION_ID)
        if not cart:
```

```
              # save an empty cart in the session
              cart = self.session[settings.CART_SESSION_ID] = {}
        self.cart = cart
```

This is the `Cart` class that will allow us to manage the shopping cart. We require the cart to be initialized with a `request` object. We store the current session using `self.session = request.session` to make it accessible to the other methods of the `Cart` class. First, we try to get the cart from the current session using `self.session.get(settings.CART_SESSION_ID)`. If no cart is present in the session, we create an empty cart by setting an empty dictionary in the session. We expect our cart dictionary to use product IDs as keys and a dictionary with quantity and price as the value for each key. By doing so, we can guarantee that a product is not added more than once in the cart; this way we also simplify the way to retrieve cart items.

Let's create a method to add products to the cart or update their quantity. Add the following `add()` and `save()` methods to the `Cart` class:

```python
class Cart(object):
    # ...
    def add(self, product, quantity=1, update_quantity=False):
        """
        Add a product to the cart or update its quantity.
        """
        product_id = str(product.id)
        if product_id not in self.cart:
            self.cart[product_id] = {'quantity': 0,
                                     'price': str(product.price)}
        if update_quantity:
            self.cart[product_id]['quantity'] = quantity
        else:
            self.cart[product_id]['quantity'] += quantity
        self.save()

    def save(self):
        # mark the session as "modified" to make sure it gets saved
        self.session.modified = True
```

The `add()` method takes the following parameters as input:

- `product`: The `product` instance to add or update in the cart.
- `quantity`: An optional integer with the product quantity. This defaults to `1`.
- `update_quantity`: This is a boolean that indicates whether the quantity needs to be updated with the given quantity (`True`), or whether the new quantity has to be added to the existing quantity (`False`).

We use the product ID as a key in the cart's content dictionary. We convert the product ID into a string because Django uses JSON to serialize session data, and JSON only allows string key names. The product ID is the key and the value that we persist is a dictionary with quantity and price figures for the product. The product's price is converted from decimal into a string in order to serialize it. Finally, we call the save() method to save the cart in the session.

The save() method marks the session as modified using session.modified = True. This tells Django that the session has changed and needs to be saved.

We also need a method for removing products from the cart. Add the following method to the Cart class:

```
class Cart(object):
    # ...
    def remove(self, product):
        """
        Remove a product from the cart.
        """
        product_id = str(product.id)
        if product_id in self.cart:
            del self.cart[product_id]
            self.save()
```

The remove() method removes a given product from the cart dictionary and calls the save() method to update the cart in the session.

We will have to iterate through the items contained in the cart and access the related Product instances. To do so, you can define an __iter__() method in your class. Add the following method to the Cart class:

```
class Cart(object):
    # ...
    def __iter__(self):
        """
        Iterate over the items in the cart and get the products
        from the database.
        """
        product_ids = self.cart.keys()
        # get the product objects and add them to the cart
        products = Product.objects.filter(id__in=product_ids)

        cart = self.cart.copy()
        for product in products:
            cart[str(product.id)]['product'] = product
```

```
for item in cart.values():
    item['price'] = Decimal(item['price'])
    item['total_price'] = item['price'] * item['quantity']
    yield item
```

In the __iter__() method, we retrieve the Product instances that are present in the cart to include them in the cart items. We copy the current cart in the cart variable and add the Product instances to it. Finally, we iterate over the cart items, converting the item's price back into decimal, and add a total_price attribute to each item. Now, we can easily iterate over the items in the cart.

We also need a way to return the number of total items in the cart. When the len() function is executed on an object, Python calls its __len__() method to retrieve its length. We are going to define a custom __len__() method to return the total number of items stored in the cart. Add the following __len__() method to the Cart class:

```
class Cart(object):
    # ...
    def __len__(self):
        """
        Count all items in the cart.
        """
        return sum(item['quantity'] for item in self.cart.values())
```

We return the sum of the quantities of all the cart items.

Add the following method to calculate the total cost of the items in the cart:

```
class Cart(object):
    # ...
    def get_total_price(self):
        return sum(Decimal(item['price']) * item['quantity'] for item in
self.cart.values())
```

And finally, add a method to clear the cart session:

```
class Cart(object):
    # ...
    def clear(self):
        # remove cart from session
        del self.session[settings.CART_SESSION_ID]
        self.save()
```

Our Cart class is now ready to manage shopping carts.

Creating shopping cart views

Now that we have a `Cart` class to manage the cart, we need to create the views to add, update, or remove items from it. We need to create the following views:

- A view to add or update items in a cart, which can handle current and new quantities
- A view to remove items from the cart
- A view to display cart items and totals

Adding items to the cart

In order to add items to the cart, we need a form that allows the user to select a quantity. Create a `forms.py` file inside the `cart` application directory and add the following code to it:

```
from django import forms

PRODUCT_QUANTITY_CHOICES = [(i, str(i)) for i in range(1, 21)]

class CartAddProductForm(forms.Form):
    quantity = forms.TypedChoiceField(
                            choices=PRODUCT_QUANTITY_CHOICES,
                            coerce=int)
    update = forms.BooleanField(required=False,
                            initial=False,
                            widget=forms.HiddenInput)
```

We will use this form to add products to the cart. Our `CartAddProductForm` class contains the following two fields:

- `quantity`: This allows the user to select a quantity between 1-20. We use a `TypedChoiceField` field with `coerce=int` to convert the input into an integer.
- `update`: This allows you to indicate whether the quantity has to be added to any existing quantity in the cart for this product (`False`), or whether the existing quantity has to be updated with the given quantity (`True`). We use a `HiddenInput` widget for this field since we don't want to display it to the user.

Let's create a view for adding items to the cart. Edit the `views.py` file of the `cart` application and add the following code to it:

```
from django.shortcuts import render, redirect, get_object_or_404
from django.views.decorators.http import require_POST
from shop.models import Product
from .cart import Cart
from .forms import CartAddProductForm

@require_POST
def cart_add(request, product_id):
    cart = Cart(request)
    product = get_object_or_404(Product, id=product_id)
    form = CartAddProductForm(request.POST)
    if form.is_valid():
        cd = form.cleaned_data
        cart.add(product=product,
                 quantity=cd['quantity'],
                 update_quantity=cd['update'])
    return redirect('cart:cart_detail')
```

This is the view for adding products to the cart or updating quantities for existing products. We use the `require_POST` decorator to allow only POST requests, since this view is going to change data. The view receives the product ID as a parameter. We retrieve the `Product` instance with the given ID and validate `CartAddProductForm`. If the form is valid, we either add or update the product in the cart. The view redirects to the `cart_detail` URL that will display the content of the cart. We are going to create the `cart_detail` view shortly.

We also need a view to remove items from the cart. Add the following code to the `views.py` file of the `cart` application:

```
def cart_remove(request, product_id):
    cart = Cart(request)
    product = get_object_or_404(Product, id=product_id)
    cart.remove(product)
    return redirect('cart:cart_detail')
```

The `cart_remove` view receives the product ID as a parameter. We retrieve the `Product` instance with the given ID and remove the product from the cart. Then, we redirect the user to the `cart_detail` URL.

Finally, we need a view to display the cart and its items. Add the following view to the `views.py` file of the `cart` application:

```
def cart_detail(request):
    cart = Cart(request)
    return render(request, 'cart/detail.html', {'cart': cart})
```

The `cart_detail` view gets the current cart to display it.

We have created views to add items to the cart, update quantities, remove items from the cart, and display the cart content. Let's add URL patterns for these views. Create a new file inside the `cart` application directory and name it `urls.py`. Add the following URLs to it:

```
from django.urls import path
from . import views

app_name = 'cart'

urlpatterns = [
    path('', views.cart_detail, name='cart_detail'),
    path('add/<int:product_id>/',
        views.cart_add,
        name='cart_add'),
    path('remove/<int:product_id>/',
        views.cart_remove,
        name='cart_remove'),
]
```

Edit the main `urls.py` file of the `myshop` project and add the following URL pattern to include the cart URLs:

```
urlpatterns = [
    path('admin/', admin.site.urls),
    path('cart/', include('cart.urls', namespace='cart')),
    path('', include('shop.urls', namespace='shop')),
]
```

Make sure that you include this URL pattern before the `shop.urls` pattern, since it's more restrictive than the latter.

Building a template to display the cart

The `cart_add` and `cart_remove` views don't render any templates, but we need to create a template for the `cart_detail` view to display cart items and totals.

Create the following file structure inside the `cart` application directory:

```
templates/
    cart/
        detail.html
```

Edit the `cart/detail.html` template and add the following code to it:

```
{% extends "shop/base.html" %}
{% load static %}

{% block title %}
  Your shopping cart
{% endblock %}

{% block content %}
  <h1>Your shopping cart</h1>
  <table class="cart">
    <thead>
      <tr>
        <th>Image</th>
        <th>Product</th>
        <th>Quantity</th>
        <th>Remove</th>
        <th>Unit price</th>
        <th>Price</th>
      </tr>
    </thead>
    <tbody>
      {% for item in cart %}
        {% with product=item.product %}
          <tr>
            <td>
              <a href="{{ product.get_absolute_url }}">
                <img src="{% if product.image %}{{ product.image.url }}
                {% else %}{% static "img/no_image.png" %}{% endif %}">
              </a>
            </td>
            <td>{{ product.name }}</td>
            <td>{{ item.quantity }}</td>
            <td><a href="{% url "cart:cart_remove" product.id
            %}">Remove</a></td>
            <td class="num">${{ item.price }}</td>
            <td class="num">${{ item.total_price }}</td>
          </tr>
        {% endwith %}
      {% endfor %}
      <tr class="total">
```

```
        <td>Total</td>
        <td colspan="4"></td>
        <td class="num">${{ cart.get_total_price }}</td>
      </tr>
    </tbody>
  </table>
  <p class="text-right">
    <a href="{% url "shop:product_list" %}" class="button
    light">Continue shopping</a>
    <a href="#" class="button">Checkout</a>
  </p>
{% endblock %}
```

This is the template that is used to display the cart content. It contains a table with the items stored in the current cart. We allow users to change the quantity of the selected products using a form that is posted to the cart_add view. We also allow users to remove items from the cart by providing a **Remove** link for each of them.

Adding products to the cart

Now, we need to add an **Add to cart** button to the product detail page. Edit the views.py file of the shop application, and add CartAddProductForm to the product_detail view as follows:

```
from cart.forms import CartAddProductForm

def product_detail(request, id, slug):
    product = get_object_or_404(Product, id=id,
                                          slug=slug,
                                          available=True)
    cart_product_form = CartAddProductForm()
    return render(request,
                  'shop/product/detail.html',
                  {'product': product,
                   'cart_product_form': cart_product_form})
```

Edit the `shop/product/detail.html` template of the `shop` application, and add the following form to the product's price as follows:

```
<p class="price">${{ product.price }}</p>
<form action="{% url "cart:cart_add" product.id %}" method="post">
  {{ cart_product_form }}
  {% csrf_token %}
  <input type="submit" value="Add to cart">
</form>
{{ product.description|linebreaks }}
```

Make sure the development server is running with the command `python manage.py runserver`. Now, open `http://127.0.0.1:8000/` in your browser and navigate to a product's detail page. It now contains a form to choose a quantity before adding the product to the cart. The page will look like this:

Choose a quantity and click on the **Add to cart** button. The form is submitted to the `cart_add` view via `POST`. The view adds the product to the cart in the session, including its current price and the selected quantity. Then, it redirects the user to the cart detail page, which will look like the following screenshot:

Updating product quantities in the cart

When users see the cart, they might want to change product quantities before placing an order. We are going to allow users to change quantities from the cart detail page.

Edit the `views.py` file of the `cart` application and change the `cart_detail` view to this:

```python
def cart_detail(request):
    cart = Cart(request)
    for item in cart:
        item['update_quantity_form'] = CartAddProductForm(
                          initial={'quantity': item['quantity'],
                          'update': True})
    return render(request, 'cart/detail.html', {'cart': cart})
```

We create an instance of `CartAddProductForm` for each item in the cart to allow changing product quantities. We initialize the form with the current item quantity and set the `update` field to `True` so that when we submit the form to the `cart_add` view, the current quantity is replaced with the new one.

Now, edit the `cart/detail.html` template of the `cart` application and find the following line:

```
<td>{{ item.quantity }}</td>
```

Replace the previous line with the following code:

```
<td>
    <form action="{% url "cart:cart_add" product.id %}" method="post">
        {{ item.update_quantity_form.quantity }}
        {{ item.update_quantity_form.update }}
        <input type="submit" value="Update">
        {% csrf_token %}
    </form>
</td>
```

Open `http://127.0.0.1:8000/cart/` in your browser. You will see a form to edit the quantity for each cart item, shown as follows:

Change the quantity of an item and click on the **Update** button to test the new functionality. You can also remove an item from the cart by clicking the **Remove** link.

Creating a context processor for the current cart

You might have noticed that the message **Your cart is empty** is displayed in the header of the site, even when the cart contains items. We should display the total number of items in the cart and the total cost instead. Since this has to be displayed in all pages, we will build a context processor to include the current cart in the request context, regardless of the view that processes the request.

Context processors

A context processor is a Python function that takes the `request` object as an argument and returns a dictionary that gets added to the request context. They come in handy when you need to make something available globally to all templates.

By default, when you create a new project using the `startproject` command, your project contains the following template context processors, in the `context_processors` option inside the `TEMPLATES` setting:

- `django.template.context_processors.debug`: This sets the boolean `debug` and `sql_queries` variables in the context representing the list of SQL queries executed in the request.
- `django.template.context_processors.request`: This sets the `request` variable in the context.
- `django.contrib.auth.context_processors.auth`: This sets the `user` variable in the request.
- `django.contrib.messages.context_processors.messages`: This sets a `messages` variable in the context containing all messages that have been generated using the messages framework.

Django also enables `django.template.context_processors.csrf` to avoid cross-site request forgery attacks. This context processor is not present in the settings, but it is always enabled and cannot be turned off for security reasons.

You can see the list of all built-in context processors at `https://docs.djangoproject.com/en/2.0/ref/templates/api/#built-in-template-context-processors`.

Setting the cart into the request context

Let's create a context processor to set the current cart into the request context. We will be able to access the cart in any template.

Create a new file inside the `cart` application directory and name it `context_processors.py`. Context processors can reside anywhere in your code, but creating them here will keep your code well organized. Add the following code to the file:

```python
from .cart import Cart

def cart(request):
    return {'cart': Cart(request)}
```

A context processor is a function that receives the `request` object as a parameter and returns a dictionary of objects that will be available to all the templates rendered using `RequestContext`. In our context processor, we instantiate the cart using the `request` object and make it available for the templates as a variable named `cart`.

Edit the `settings.py` file of your project and add `cart.context_processors.cart` to the `context_processors` option inside the `TEMPLATES` setting as follows:

```python
TEMPLATES = [
    {
        'BACKEND': 'django.template.backends.django.DjangoTemplates',
        'DIRS': [],
        'APP_DIRS': True,
        'OPTIONS': {
            'context_processors': [
                # ...
                'cart.context_processors.cart',
            ],
        },
    },
]
```

The `cart` context processor will be executed every time a template is rendered using Django's `RequestContext`. The `cart` variable will be set in the context of your templates.

 Context processors are executed in all the requests that use `RequestContext`. You might want to create a custom template tag instead of a context processor if your functionality is not needed in all templates, especially if it involves database queries.

Now, edit the `shop/base.html` template of the `shop` application and find the following lines:

```
<div class="cart">
  Your cart is empty.
</div>
```

Replace the previous lines with the following code:

```
<div class="cart">
  {% with total_items=cart|length %}
    {% if cart|length > 0 %}
      Your cart:
      <a href="{% url "cart:cart_detail" %}">
        {{ total_items }} item{{ total_items|pluralize }},
        ${{ cart.get_total_price }}
      </a>
    {% else %}
      Your cart is empty.
    {% endif %}
  {% endwith %}
</div>
```

Reload your server using the command `python manage.py runserver`. Open `http://127.0.0.1:8000/` in your browser and add some products to the cart. In the header of the website, you can see the total number of items in the cart and the total cost, as follows:

My shop

Your cart: 2 items, $91.0

Registering customer orders

When a shopping cart is checked out, you need to save an order into the database. Orders will contain information about customers and the products they are buying.

Create a new application for managing customer orders using the following command:

```
python manage.py startapp orders
```

Edit the `settings.py` file of your project and add the new application to the `INSTALLED_APPS` setting as follows:

```
INSTALLED_APPS = [
    # ...
    'orders.apps.OrdersConfig',
]
```

You have activated the `orders` application.

Creating order models

You will need a model to store the order details, and a second model to store items bought, including their price and quantity. Edit the `models.py` file of the `orders` application and add the following code to it:

```
from django.db import models
from shop.models import Product

class Order(models.Model):
    first_name = models.CharField(max_length=50)
    last_name = models.CharField(max_length=50)
    email = models.EmailField()
    address = models.CharField(max_length=250)
    postal_code = models.CharField(max_length=20)
    city = models.CharField(max_length=100)
    created = models.DateTimeField(auto_now_add=True)
    updated = models.DateTimeField(auto_now=True)
    paid = models.BooleanField(default=False)

    class Meta:
        ordering = ('-created',)

    def __str__(self):
        return 'Order {}'.format(self.id)

    def get_total_cost(self):
        return sum(item.get_cost() for item in self.items.all())

class OrderItem(models.Model):
    order = models.ForeignKey(Order,
                              related_name='items',
                              on_delete=models.CASCADE)
    product = models.ForeignKey(Product,
```

```
                                   related_name='order_items',
                                   on_delete=models.CASCADE)
        price = models.DecimalField(max_digits=10, decimal_places=2)
        quantity = models.PositiveIntegerField(default=1)

        def __str__(self):
            return '{}'.format(self.id)

        def get_cost(self):
            return self.price * self.quantity
```

The Order model contains several fields to store customer information and a paid boolean field, which defaults to False. Later on, we are going to use this field to differentiate between paid and unpaid orders. We also define a get_total_cost() method to obtain the total cost of the items bought in this order.

The OrderItem model allows us to store the product, quantity, and price paid for each item. We include get_cost() to return the cost of the item.

Run the next command to create initial migrations for the orders application:

```
python manage.py makemigrations
```

You will see the following output:

```
Migrations for 'orders':
  orders/migrations/0001_initial.py
    - Create model Order
    - Create model OrderItem
```

Run the following command to apply the new migration:

```
python manage.py migrate
```

Your order models are now synced to the database.

Including order models in the administration site

Let's add the order models to the administration site. Edit the `admin.py` file of the `orders` application to make it look like this:

```python
from django.contrib import admin
from .models import Order, OrderItem

class OrderItemInline(admin.TabularInline):
    model = OrderItem
    raw_id_fields = ['product']

@admin.register(Order)
class OrderAdmin(admin.ModelAdmin):
    list_display = ['id', 'first_name', 'last_name', 'email',
                    'address', 'postal_code', 'city', 'paid',
                    'created', 'updated']
    list_filter = ['paid', 'created', 'updated']
    inlines = [OrderItemInline]
```

We use a `ModelInline` class for the `OrderItem` model to include it as an *inline* in the `OrderAdmin` class. An inline allows you to include a model on the same edit page its related model.

Run the development server with the command `python manage.py runserver`, and then open `http://127.0.0.1:8000/admin/orders/order/add/` in your browser. You will see the following page:

Add order

First name:

Last name:

Email:

Address:

Postal code:

City:

☐ Paid

ORDER ITEMS

PRODUCT	PRICE	QUANTITY	DELETE?
🔍	◇	1 ◇	
🔍	◇	1 ◇	
🔍	◇	1 ◇	

✦ Add another Order item

Save and add another   Save and continue editing   SAVE

Creating customer orders

We will use the order models we created to persist the items contained in the shopping cart when the user finally places an order. A new order will be created following these steps:

1. Present users an order form to fill in their data
2. Create a new `Order` instance with the data entered, and create an associated `OrderItem` instance for each item in the cart
3. Clear all the cart content and redirect users to a success page

First, we need a form to enter the order details. Create a new file inside the `orders` application directory and name it `forms.py`. Add the following code to it:

```python
from django import forms
from .models import Order

class OrderCreateForm(forms.ModelForm):
    class Meta:
        model = Order
        fields = ['first_name', 'last_name', 'email', 'address',
                  'postal_code', 'city']
```

This is the form that we are going to use for creating new `Order` objects. Now, we need a view to handle the form and create a new order. Edit the `views.py` file of the `orders` application and add the following code to it:

```python
from django.shortcuts import render
from .models import OrderItem
from .forms import OrderCreateForm
from cart.cart import Cart

def order_create(request):
    cart = Cart(request)
    if request.method == 'POST':
        form = OrderCreateForm(request.POST)
        if form.is_valid():
            order = form.save()
            for item in cart:
                OrderItem.objects.create(order=order,
                                         product=item['product'],
                                         price=item['price'],
                                         quantity=item['quantity'])
            # clear the cart
            cart.clear()
            return render(request,
```

```
                      'orders/order/created.html',
                      {'order': order})
    else:
        form = OrderCreateForm()
    return render(request,
                  'orders/order/create.html',
                  {'cart': cart, 'form': form})
```

In the `order_create` view, we will obtain the current cart from the session with `cart = Cart(request)`. Depending on the request method, we will perform the following tasks:

- **GET request**: Instantiates the `OrderCreateForm` form and renders the `orders/order/create.html` template.
- **POST request**: Validates the data sent in the request. If the data is valid, we create a new order in the database using `order = form.save()`. We iterate over the cart items and create an `OrderItem` for each of them. Finally, we clear the cart content and render the template `orders/order/created.html`.

Create a new file inside the `orders` application directory and name it `urls.py`. Add the following code to it:

```
from django.urls import path
from . import views

app_name = 'orders'

urlpatterns = [
    path('create/', views.order_create, name='order_create'),
]
```

This is the URL pattern for the `order_create` view. Edit the `urls.py` file of `myshop` and include the following pattern. Remember to place it before the `shop.urls` pattern:

```
path('orders/', include('orders.urls', namespace='orders')),
```

Edit the `cart/detail.html` template of the `cart` application and edit this line:

```
<a href="#" class="button">Checkout</a>
```

Add the `order_create` URL as follows:

```
<a href="{% url "orders:order_create" %}" class="button">
  Checkout
</a>
```

Users can now navigate from the cart detail page to the order form. We still need to define templates for placing orders. Create the following file structure inside the `orders` application directory:

```
templates/
    orders/
        order/
            create.html
            created.html
```

Edit the `orders/order/create.html` template and include the following code:

```
{% extends "shop/base.html" %}

{% block title %}
  Checkout
{% endblock %}

{% block content %}
  <h1>Checkout</h1>

  <div class="order-info">
    <h3>Your order</h3>
    <ul>
      {% for item in cart %}
        <li>
          {{ item.quantity }}x {{ item.product.name }}
          <span>${{ item.total_price }}</span>
        </li>
      {% endfor %}
    </ul>
    <p>Total: ${{ cart.get_total_price }}</p>
  </div>

  <form action="." method="post" class="order-form">
    {{ form.as_p }}
    <p><input type="submit" value="Place order"></p>
    {% csrf_token %}
  </form>
{% endblock %}
```

This template displays the cart items, including totals, and the form to place an order.

Edit the `orders/order/created.html` template and add the following code:

```
{% extends "shop/base.html" %}
```

```
{% block title %}
  Thank you
{% endblock %}

{% block content %}
  <h1>Thank you</h1>
  <p>Your order has been successfully completed. Your order number is
  <strong>{{ order.id }}</strong>.</p>
{% endblock %}
```

This is the template that we render when the order is successfully created.

Start the web development server to track new files. Open `http://127.0.0.1:8000/` in your browser, add a couple of products to the cart, and continue to the checkout page. You will see a page like the one following:

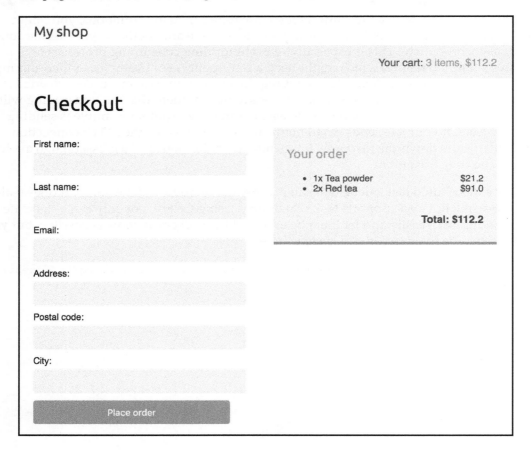

Fill in the form with the valid data and click on the **Place order** button. The order will be created and you will see a success page like this:

Thank you

Your order has been successfully completed. Your order number is **1**.

Now, go to the administration site.

Launching asynchronous tasks with Celery

Everything you execute in a view affects response times. In many situations, you might want to return a response to the user as quickly as possible and let the server execute some process asynchronously. This is especially relevant for time-consuming processes or processes subject to failure, which might need a retry policy. For example, a video sharing platform allows users to upload videos but requires a long time to transcode uploaded videos. The site might return a response to users to inform them that the transcoding will start soon, and start transcoding the video asynchronously. Another example is sending emails to users. If your site sends email notifications from a view, the SMTP connection might fail or slow down the response. Launching asynchronous tasks is essential to avoid blocking the code execution.

Celery is a distributed task queue that can process vast amounts of messages. It does real-time processing but also supports task scheduling. Using Celery, not only can you create asynchronous tasks easily and let them be executed by workers as soon as possible, but you can also schedule them to run at a specific time.

You can find the Celery documentation at `http://docs.celeryproject.org/en/latest/index.html`.

Installing Celery

Let's install Celery and integrate it into our project. Install Celery via `pip` using the following command:

```
pip install celery==4.1.0
```

Celery requires a message broker in order to handle requests from an external source. The broker takes care of sending messages to Celery workers, which process tasks as they receive them. Let's install a message broker.

Installing RabbitMQ

There are several options to choose as a message broker for Celery, including key/value stores such as Redis, or an actual message system such as RabbitMQ. We will configure Celery with RabbitMQ, since it's the recommended message worker for Celery.

If you are using Linux, you can install RabbitMQ from the shell using the following command:

```
apt-get install rabbitmq
```

If you need to install RabbitMQ on macOS X or Windows, you can find standalone versions at `https://www.rabbitmq.com/download.html`.

After installing it, launch RabbitMQ using the following command from the shell:

```
rabbitmq-server
```

You will see output that ends with the following line:

```
Starting broker... completed with 10 plugins.
```

RabbitMQ is running and ready to receive messages.

Adding Celery to your project

You have to provide a configuration for the Celery instance. Create a new file next to the settings.py file of myshop and name it celery.py. This file will contain the Celery configuration for your project. Add the following code to it:

```
import os
from celery import Celery

# set the default Django settings module for the 'celery' program.
os.environ.setdefault('DJANGO_SETTINGS_MODULE', 'myshop.settings')

app = Celery('myshop')

app.config_from_object('django.conf:settings', namespace='CELERY')
app.autodiscover_tasks()
```

In this code, we do the following:

1. We set the DJANGO_SETTINGS_MODULE variable for the Celery command-line program.
2. We create an instance of the application with app = Celery('myshop').
3. We load any custom configuration from our project settings using the config_from_object() method. The namespace attribute specifies the prefix that Celery-related settings will have in our settings.py file. By setting the CELERY namespace, all Celery settings need to include the CELERY_ prefix in their name (for example, CELERY_BROKER_URL).
4. Finally, we tell Celery to auto-discover asynchronous tasks for our applications. Celery will look for a tasks.py file in each application directory of apps added to INSTALLED_APPS in order to load asynchronous tasks defined in it.

You need to import the celery module in the __init__.py file of your project to make sure it is loaded when Django starts. Edit the myshop/__init__.py file and add the following code to it:

```
# import celery
from .celery import app as celery_app
```

Now, you can start programming asynchronous tasks for your applications.

 The CELERY_ALWAYS_EAGER setting allows you to execute tasks locally in a synchronous way instead of sending them to the queue. This is useful for running unit tests or executing the application in your local environment without running Celery.

Adding asynchronous tasks to your application

We are going to create an asynchronous task to send an email notification to our users when they place an order. The convention is to include asynchronous tasks for your application in a tasks module within your application directory.

Create a new file inside the orders application and name it tasks.py. This is the place where Celery will look for asynchronous tasks. Add the following code to it:

```
from celery import task
from django.core.mail import send_mail
from .models import Order

@task
def order_created(order_id):
    """
    Task to send an e-mail notification when an order is
    successfully created.
    """
    order = Order.objects.get(id=order_id)
    subject = 'Order nr. {}'.format(order.id)
    message = 'Dear {},\n\nYou have successfully placed an order.\
            Your order id is {}.'.format(order.first_name,
                                            order.id)
    mail_sent = send_mail(subject,
                            message,
                            'admin@myshop.com',
                            [order.email])
    return mail_sent
```

We define the order_created task by using the task decorator. As you can see, a Celery task is just a Python function decorated with task. Our task function receives an order_id parameter. It's always recommended to pass only IDs to task functions and lookup objects when the task is executed. We use the send_mail() function provided by Django to send an email notification to the user that placed the order.

You learned how to configure Django to use your SMTP server in Chapter 2, *Enhancing Your Blog with Advanced Features*. If you don't want to set up email settings, you can tell Django to write emails to the console by adding the following setting to the settings.py file:

```
EMAIL_BACKEND = 'django.core.mail.backends.console.EmailBackend'
```

 Use asynchronous tasks not only for time-consuming processes, but also for other processes that are subject to failure, which do not take so much time to be executed, but which are subject to connection failures or require a retry policy.

Now we have to add the task to our order_create view. Edit the views.py file of the orders application, import the task, and call the order_created asynchronous task after clearing the cart as follows:

```
from .tasks import order_created

def order_create(request):
    # ...
    if request.method == 'POST':
        # ...
        if form.is_valid():
            # ...
            cart.clear()
            # launch asynchronous task
            order_created.delay(order.id)
        # ...
```

We call the delay() method of the task to execute it asynchronously. The task will be added to the queue and will be executed by a worker as soon as possible.

Open another shell and start the Celery worker from your project directory, using the following command:

```
celery -A myshop worker -l info
```

The Celery worker is now running and ready to process tasks. Make sure the Django development server is also running. Open `http://127.0.0.1:8000/` in your browser, add some products to your shopping cart, and complete an order. In the shell, you started the Celery worker and you will see an output similar to this one:

```
[2017-12-17 17:43:11,462: INFO/MainProcess] Received task:
orders.tasks.order_created[e990ddae-2e30-4e36-b0e4-78bbd4f2738e]
[2017-12-17 17:43:11,685: INFO/ForkPoolWorker-4] Task
orders.tasks.order_created[e990ddae-2e30-4e36-b0e4-78bbd4f2738e] succeeded
in 0.22019841300789267s: 1
```

The task has been executed and you will receive an email notification for your order.

Monitoring Celery

You might want to monitor the asynchronous tasks that are executed. Flower is a web-based tool for monitoring Celery. You can install Flower using this command:

`pip install flower==0.9.2`

Once installed, you can launch Flower by running the following command from your project directory:

`celery -A myshop flower`

Open `http://localhost:5555/dashboard` in your browser. You will be able to see the active Celery workers and asynchronous task statistics:

You can find documentation for Flower at `https://flower.readthedocs.io/`.

Summary

In this chapter, you created a basic shop application. You created a product catalog and built a shopping cart using sessions. You implemented a custom context processor to make the cart available to your templates and created a form for placing orders. You also learned how to launch asynchronous tasks with Celery.

In the next chapter, you will learn how to integrate a payment gateway into your shop, add custom actions to the administration site, export data in CSV format, and generate PDF files dynamically.

8
Managing Payments and Orders

In the previous chapter, you created a basic online shop with a product catalog and a shopping cart. You also learned how to launch asynchronous tasks with Celery. In this chapter, you will learn how to integrate a payment gateway into your site to let users pay by credit card. You will also extend the administration site to export orders to CSV format and you will generate PDF invoices.

In this chapter, you will learn to:

- Integrate a payment gateway into your project
- Export orders to CSV files
- Create custom views for the administration site
- Generate PDF invoices dynamically

Integrating a payment gateway

A payment gateway allows you to process payments online. Using a payment gateway, you can manage customer's orders and delegate payment processing to a reliable, secure third party. You won't have to worry about processing credit cards in your own system.

There are several payment gateway providers to choose from. We are going to integrate Braintree, which is used by popular online services such as Uber or Airbnb. Braintree provides an API that allows you to process online payments with multiple payment methods such as a credit card, PayPal, Android Pay, and Apple Pay. You can learn more about Braintree at `https://www.braintreepayments.com/`.

Braintree provides different integration options. The simplest is the *Drop-in* integration, which contains a pre-formatted payment form. However, in order to customize the behavior and experience of our checkout, we are are going to use the advanced *Hosted Fields* integration. You can learn more about the Hosted Fields integration at `https://developers.braintreepayments.com/guides/hosted-fields/overview/javascript/v3`.

Certain payment fields on the checkout page, such as the credit card number, CVV number, or expiration date, must be hosted securely. The Hosted Fields integration hosts the checkout fields on the payment gateway's domain and renders an iframe to present the fields to the users. This provides you with the ability to customize the look and feel of the payment form, while ensuring that you are compliant with **Payment Card Industry** (**PCI**) requirements. Since you can customize the look and feel of the form fields, users won't notice the iframe.

Creating a Braintree sandbox account

You need a Braintree account to integrate the payment gateway into your site. Let's create a sandbox account to test the Braintree API. Open `https://www.braintreepayments.com/sandbox` in your browser. You will see a form like the following one:

Fill in the details to create a new sandbox account. You will receive an email from Braintree with a link to complete your account setup. Follow the link and complete your account setup. Once you are done, login at `https://sandbox.braintreegateway.com/login`. Your merchant ID and private/public keys will be displayed like this:

Sandbox Keys & Configuration

Here are the keys to your Sandbox Account. Once you're ready to start taking payments with a production Braintree Account you'll have to update your code, replacing these with your production Braintree Account keys.

Merchant ID:	9xtfhm7sv733jznk
Public Key:	q8fxx6fwkjx8dfkw
Private Key:	xxxxxxxxxxxxxxxxxxxxxxxxxxxxxxxx

You will need this information to authenticate requests to the Braintree API. Always keep the private key secret.

Installing the Braintree Python module

Braintree provides a Python module that simplifies dealing with its API. The source code is located at `https://github.com/braintree/braintree_python`. We are going to integrate the payment gateway into our project using the `braintree` module.

Install the `braintree` module from the shell using the following command:

```
pip install braintree==3.45.0
```

Add the following settings to the `settings.py` file of your project:

```
# Braintree settings
BRAINTREE_MERCHANT_ID = 'XXX'  # Merchant ID
BRAINTREE_PUBLIC_KEY = 'XXX'   # Public Key
BRAINTREE_PRIVATE_KEY = 'XXX'  # Private key

from braintree import Configuration, Environment
```

```
Configuration.configure(
    Environment.Sandbox,
    BRAINTREE_MERCHANT_ID,
    BRAINTREE_PUBLIC_KEY,
    BRAINTREE_PRIVATE_KEY
)
```

Replace BRAINTREE_MERCHANT_ID, BRAINTREE_PUBLIC_KEY,
and BRAINTREE_PRIVATE_KEY values with the ones of your account.

 Note that we use Environment.Sandbox for integrating the sandbox.
Once you go live and create a real account, you will need to change this to
Environment.Production. Braintree will provide you with a new
merchant ID and private/public keys for the production environment.

Let's integrate the payment gateway into the checkout process.

Integrating the payment gateway

The checkout process will work as follows:

1. Add items to the shopping cart
2. Check out the shopping cart
3. Enter credit card details and pay

We are going to create a new application to manage payments. Create a new application in
your project using the following command:

```
python manage.py startapp payment
```

Edit the settings.py file of your project and add the new application to the
INSTALLED_APPS setting as follows:

```
INSTALLED_APPS = [
    # ...
    'payment.apps.PaymentConfig',
]
```

The payment application is now active.

After clients place an order, we need to redirect them to the payment process. Edit the `views.py` file of the `orders` application and include the following imports:

```
from django.urls import reverse
from django.shortcuts import render, redirect
```

In the same file, replace the following lines of the `order_create` view:

```
# launch asynchronous task
order_created.delay(order.id)
return render(request,
              'orders/order/created.html',
              locals())
```

Replace them with the following:

```
# launch asynchronous task
order_created.delay(order.id)
# set the order in the session
request.session['order_id'] = order.id
# redirect for payment
return redirect(reverse('payment:process'))
```

With this code, after successfully creating an order, we set the order ID in the current session using the `order_id` session key. Then, we redirect the user to the `payment:process` URL, which we are going to implement later.

Remember that you need to run Celery in order for the `order_created` task to be queued and executed.

Every time an order is created in Braintree, a unique transaction identifier is generated. We will add a new field to the `Order` model of the `orders` application to store the transaction ID. This will allow us to link each order with its related Braintree transaction.

Edit the `models.py` file of the `orders` application and add the following field to the `Order` model:

```
class Order(models.Model):
    # ...
    braintree_id = models.CharField(max_length=150, blank=True)
```

Let's sync this field with the database. Use the following command to generate migrations:

```
python manage.py makemigrations
```

You will see the following output:

```
Migrations for 'orders':
  orders/migrations/0002_order_braintree_id.py
    - Add field braintree_id to order
```

Apply the migration to the database with the following command:

```
python manage.py migrate
```

You will see output that ends with the following line:

```
Applying orders.0002_order_braintree_id... OK
```

The model changes are now synced with the database. Now you are able to store the Braintree transaction ID for each order. Let's integrate the payment gateway.

Integrating Braintree using Hosted Fields

The *Hosted Fields* integration allows you to create your own payment form using custom styles and layout. An iframe is added dynamically to the page using the Braintree JavaScript SDK. The iframe includes the Hosted Fields payment form. When the customer submits the form, Hosted Fields collects the card details securely and attempts to tokenize them. If tokenization succeeds, you can send the generated token nonce to your view to make a transaction using the Python `braintree` module.

We will create a view for processing payments. The whole checkout process will work as follows:

1. In the view, a client token is generated using the `braintree` Python module. This token is used in the next step to instantiate the Braintree JavaScript client; it's not the payment token nonce.
2. The view renders the checkout template. The template loads the Braintree JavaScript SDK using the client token and generates the iframe with the hosted payment form fields.
3. Users enter their credit card details and submit the form. A payment token nonce is generated with the Braintree JavaScript client. We send the token to our view with a `POST` request.
4. The payment view receives the token nonce and we use it to generate a transaction using the `braintree` Python module.

Let's start with the payment checkout view. Edit the `views.py` file of the `payment` application and add the following code to it:

```python
import braintree
from django.shortcuts import render, redirect, get_object_or_404
from orders.models import Order

def payment_process(request):
    order_id = request.session.get('order_id')
    order = get_object_or_404(Order, id=order_id)

    if request.method == 'POST':
        # retrieve nonce
        nonce = request.POST.get('payment_method_nonce', None)
        # create and submit transaction
        result = braintree.Transaction.sale({
            'amount': '{:.2f}'.format(order.get_total_cost()),
            'payment_method_nonce': nonce,
            'options': {
                'submit_for_settlement': True
            }
        })
        if result.is_success:
            # mark the order as paid
            order.paid = True
            # store the unique transaction id
            order.braintree_id = result.transaction.id
            order.save()
            return redirect('payment:done')
        else:
            return redirect('payment:canceled')
    else:
        # generate token
        client_token = braintree.ClientToken.generate()
        return render(request,
                      'payment/process.html',
                      {'order': order,
                       'client_token': client_token})
```

The `payment_process` view manages the checkout process. In this view, take the following actions:

1. We get the current order from the `order_id` session key, which was set previously in the `order_create` view.

2. We retrieve the `Order` object for the given ID or return a `404 Not Found` error if not found.

3. When the view is loaded with a `POST` request, we retrieve the `payment_method_nonce` to generate a new transaction using `braintree.Transaction.sale()`. We pass the following parameters to it:

    - `amount`: The total amount to charge the customer.
    - `payment_method_nonce`: The token nonce generated by Braintree for the payment. It will be generated in the template using the Braintree JavaScript SDK.
    - `options`: We send the `submit_for_settlement` option with `True` so that the transaction is automatically submitted for settlement.

4. If the transaction is successfully processed, we mark the order as paid by setting its `paid` attribute to `True` and we store the unique transaction ID returned by the gateway in the `braintree_id` attribute. We redirect the user to the `payment:done` URL if the payment was successful otherwise to `payment:canceled`.

5. If the view was loaded with a `GET` request, we generate a client token that we will use in the template to instantiate the Braintree JavaScript client.

Let's create basic views to redirect users when the payment has been successful, or when it has been canceled for any reason. Add the following code to the `views.py` file of the `payment` application:

```
def payment_done(request):
    return render(request, 'payment/done.html')

def payment_canceled(request):
    return render(request, 'payment/canceled.html')
```

Create a new file inside the `payment` application directory and name it `urls.py`. Add the following code to it:

```
from django.urls import path
from . import views

app_name = 'payment'

urlpatterns = [
    path('process/', views.payment_process, name='process'),
    path('done/', views.payment_done, name='done'),
    path('canceled/', views.payment_canceled, name='canceled'),
]
```

These are the URLs for the payment workflow. We have included the following URL patterns:

- `process`: The view that processes the payment
- `done`: The view to redirect the user if the payment is successful
- `canceled`: The view to redirect the user if the payment is not successful

Edit the main `urls.py` file of the `myshop` project and include the URL patterns for the `payment` application as follows:

```
urlpatterns = [
    # ...
    path('payment/', include('payment.urls', namespace='payment')),
    path('', include('shop.urls', namespace='shop')),
]
```

Remember to place it before the `shop.urls` pattern to avoid an undesired pattern match.

Create the following file structure inside the `payment` application directory:

```
templates/
    payment/
        process.html
        done.html
        canceled.html
```

Edit the `payment/process.html` template and add the following code to it:

```
{% extends "shop/base.html" %}

{% block title %}Pay by credit card{% endblock %}
```

```
{% block content %}
  <h1>Pay by credit card</h1>
  <form action="." id="payment" method="post">

    <label for="card-number">Card Number</label>
    <div id="card-number" class="field"></div>

    <label for="cvv">CVV</label>
    <div id="cvv" class="field"></div>

    <label for="expiration-date">Expiration Date</label>
    <div id="expiration-date" class="field"></div>

    <input type="hidden" id="nonce" name="payment_method_nonce" value="">
    {% csrf_token %}
    <input type="submit" value="Pay">
  </form>
  <!-- Load the required client component. -->
  <script
src="https://js.braintreegateway.com/web/3.29.0/js/client.min.js"></script>
  <!-- Load Hosted Fields component. -->
  <script src="https://js.braintreegateway.com/web/3.29.0/js/hosted-
  fields.min.js"></script>
  <script>
    var form = document.querySelector('#payment');
    var submit = document.querySelector('input[type="submit"]');

    braintree.client.create({
      authorization: '{{ client_token }}'
    }, function (clientErr, clientInstance) {
      if (clientErr) {
        console.error(clientErr);
        return;
      }

      braintree.hostedFields.create({
        client: clientInstance,
        styles: {
          'input': {'font-size': '13px'},
          'input.invalid': {'color': 'red'},
          'input.valid': {'color': 'green'}
        },
        fields: {
          number: {selector: '#card-number'},
          cvv: {selector: '#cvv'},
          expirationDate: {selector: '#expiration-date'}
        }
      }, function (hostedFieldsErr, hostedFieldsInstance) {
```

```
        if (hostedFieldsErr) {
          console.error(hostedFieldsErr);
          return;
        }

        submit.removeAttribute('disabled');

        form.addEventListener('submit', function (event) {
          event.preventDefault();

          hostedFieldsInstance.tokenize(function (tokenizeErr, payload) {
            if (tokenizeErr) {
              console.error(tokenizeErr);
              return;
            }
            // set nonce to send to the server
            document.getElementById('nonce').value = payload.nonce;
            // submit form
            document.getElementById('payment').submit();
          });
        }, false);
      });
    });
  </script>
{% endblock %}
```

This is the template that displays the payment form and processes the payment. We define `<div>` containers instead of `<input>` elements for the credit card input fields: the credit card number, CVV number, and expiration date. This is how we specify the fields that the Braintree JavaScript client will render in the iframe. We also include an `<input>` element named `payment_method_nonce` that we will use to send the token nonce to our view once generated by the Braintree JavaScript client.

In our template, we load the Braintree JavaScript SDK `client.min.js` and the Hosted Fields component `hosted-fields.min.js`. Then, we execute the following JavaScript code:

1. We instantiate the Braintree JavaScript client with the `braintree.client.create()` method, using the `client_token` generated by the `payment_process` view.
2. We instantiate the Hosted Fields component with the `braintree.hostedFields.create()` method.
3. We specify custom CSS styles for the `input` fields.

4. We specify the `id` selectors for the fields: `card-number`, `cvv`, and `expiration-date`.

5. We add an event listener for the `submit` action of the form. When the form is submitted, the fields are tokenized using the Braintree SDK and the token nonce is set in the `payment_method_nonce` field. Then, the form is submitted so that our view receives the nonce to process the payment.

Edit the `payment/done.html` template and add the following code to it:

```
{% extends "shop/base.html" %}

{% block content %}
  <h1>Your payment was successful</h1>
  <p>Your payment has been processed successfully.</p>
{% endblock %}
```

This is the template for the page that the user is redirected to following a successful payment.

Edit the `payment/canceled.html` template and add the following code to it:

```
{% extends "shop/base.html" %}

{% block content %}
  <h1>Your payment has not been processed</h1>
  <p>There was a problem processing your payment.</p>
{% endblock %}
```

This is the template for the page that the user is redirected to when the transaction is not successful. Let's try the payment process.

Testing payments

Open a shell and run RabbitMQ with the following command:

```
rabbitmq-server
```

Open another shell and start the Celery worker from your project directory with the following command:

```
celery -A myshop worker -l info
```

Open one more shell and start the development server with this command:

```
python manage.py runserver
```

Open `http://127.0.0.1:8000/` in your browser, add some products to the shopping cart, and fill in the checkout form. When you click the **PLACE ORDER** button, the order will be persisted to the database, the order ID will be saved in the current session, and you will be redirected to the payment process page.

The payment process page retrieves the order from the session and renders the Hosted Fields form in an iframe, as follows:

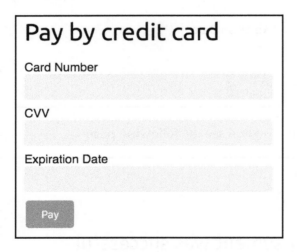

You can take a look at the HTML source code to see the generated HTML.

Braintree provides a list of successful and unsuccessful credit cards so that you can test all possible scenarios. You can find a list of credit cards for testing at `https://developers.` `braintreepayments.com/guides/credit-cards/testing-go-live/python`. We are going to use the VISA test card `4111 1111 1111 1111`, which returns a successful purchase. We are going to use CVV `123` and any future expiration date, such as `12/24`. Enter the credit card details as follows:

Click on the **Pay** button. You will see the following page:

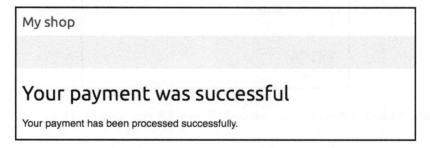

The transaction has been successfully processed. Now you can log in to your account at `https://sandbox.braintreegateway.com/login`. Under **Transactions**, you will be able to see the transaction like this:

ID	Transaction Date	Type	Status	Customer	Payment Information	Amount
2bwkx5b6	02/05/2018 07:45:23 PM CST	Sale	Submitted For Settlement		VISA 411111******1111	21,20 € EUR

Now, open `http://127.0.0.1:8000/admin/orders/order/` in your browser. The order should now be marked as paid and contain the related Braintree transaction ID:

☑ Paid	
Braintree id:	2bwkx5b6

Congratulations! You have implemented a payment gateway to process credit cards.

Going live

Once you have tested your environment, you can create a real Braintree account at `https://www.braintreepayments.com`. Once you are ready for moving into production, remember to change your live environment credentials in the `settings.py` file of your project and use `braintree.Environment.Production` to set up your environment. All steps to go live are summarized at `https://developers.braintreepayments.com/start/go-live/python`.

Exporting orders to CSV files

Sometimes, you might want to export the information contained in a model to a file so that you can import it in any other system. One of the most widely used formats to export/import data is **Comma-Separated Values** (**CSV**). A CSV file is a plain text file consisting of a number of records. There is usually one record per line, and some delimiter character, usually a literal comma, separates the record fields. We are going to customize the administration site to be able to export orders to CSV files.

Adding custom actions to the administration site

Django offers you a wide range of options to customize the administration site. We are going to modify the object list view to include a custom admin action.

An admin action works as follows: a user selects objects from the admin's object list page with checkboxes, then selects an action to perform on all of the selected items, and executes the action. The following screenshot shows where actions are located in the administration site:

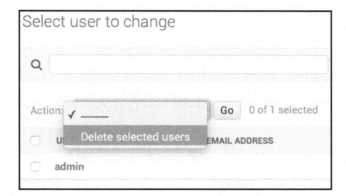

 Create custom admin actions to allow staff users to apply actions to multiple elements at once.

You can create a custom action by writing a regular function that receives the following parameters:

- The current ModelAdmin being displayed
- The current request object as an HttpRequest instance
- A QuerySet for the objects selected by the user

This function will be executed when the action is triggered from the administration site.

We are going to create a custom admin action to download a list of orders as a CSV file. Edit the `admin.py` file of the `orders` application and add the following code before the `OrderAdmin` class:

```python
import csv
import datetime
from django.http import HttpResponse

def export_to_csv(modeladmin, request, queryset):
    opts = modeladmin.model._meta
    response = HttpResponse(content_type='text/csv')
    response['Content-Disposition'] = 'attachment;'\
        'filename={}.csv'.format(opts.verbose_name)
    writer = csv.writer(response)

    fields = [field for field in opts.get_fields() if not
field.many_to_many\
    and not field.one_to_many]
    # Write a first row with header information
    writer.writerow([field.verbose_name for field in fields])
    # Write data rows
    for obj in queryset:
        data_row = []
        for field in fields:
            value = getattr(obj, field.name)
            if isinstance(value, datetime.datetime):
                value = value.strftime('%d/%m/%Y')
            data_row.append(value)
        writer.writerow(data_row)
    return response
export_to_csv.short_description = 'Export to CSV'
```

In this code, we perform the following tasks:

1. We create an instance of `HttpResponse`, including a custom `text/csv` content type, to tell the browser that the response has to be treated as a CSV file. We also add a `Content-Disposition` header to indicate that the HTTP response contains an attached file.
2. We create a CSV `writer` object that will write on the `response` object.
3. We get the `model` fields dynamically using the `get_fields()` method of the model `_meta` options. We exclude many-to-many and one-to-many relationships.
4. We write a header row including the field names.

5. We iterate over the given QuerySet and write a row for each object returned by the QuerySet. We take care of formatting `datetime` objects because the output value for CSV has to be a string.

6. We customize the display name for the action in the template by setting a `short_description` attribute to the function.

We have created a generic admin action that can be added to any `ModelAdmin` class.

Finally, add the new `export_to_csv` admin action to the `OrderAdmin` class as follows:

```
class OrderAdmin(admin.ModelAdmin):
    # ...
    actions = [export_to_csv]
```

Open `http://127.0.0.1:8000/admin/orders/order/` in your browser. The resulting admin action should look like this:

Select some orders and choose the **Export to CSV** action from the select box, then click the **Go** button. Your browser will download the generated CSV file named `order.csv`. Open the downloaded file using a text editor. You should see content with the following format, including a header row and a row for each `Order` object you selected:

```
ID,first name,last name,email,address,postal
code,city,created,updated,paid,braintree id
3,Antonio,Melé,antonio.mele@gmail.com,Bank Street,WS
J11,London,25/02/2018,25/02/2018,True,2bwkx5b6
...
```

As you can see, creating admin actions is pretty straightforward. You can learn more about generating CSV files with Django at `https://docs.djangoproject.com/en/2.0/howto/outputting-csv/`.

Extending the admin site with custom views

Sometimes, you may want to customize the administration site beyond what is possible through configuring `ModelAdmin`, creating admin actions, and overriding admin templates. If this is the case, you need to create a custom admin view. With a custom view, you can build any functionality you need. You just have to make sure that only staff users can access your view and that you maintain the admin look and feel by making your template extend an admin template.

Let's create a custom view to display information about an order. Edit the `views.py` file of the `orders` application and add the following code to it:

```
from django.contrib.admin.views.decorators import staff_member_required
from django.shortcuts import get_object_or_404
from .models import Order

@staff_member_required
def admin_order_detail(request, order_id):
    order = get_object_or_404(Order, id=order_id)
    return render(request,
                  'admin/orders/order/detail.html',
                  {'order': order})
```

The `staff_member_required` decorator checks that both the `is_active` and `is_staff` fields of the user requesting the page are set to `True`. In this view, we get the `Order` object with the given ID and render a template to display the order.

Now, edit the `urls.py` file of the `orders` application and add the following URL pattern to it:

```
path('admin/order/<int:order_id>/', views.admin_order_detail,
name='admin_order_detail'),
```

Create the following file structure inside the `templates/` directory of the `orders` application:

```
admin/
    orders/
        order/
            detail.html
```

Edit the detail.html template and add the following content to it:

```
{% extends "admin/base_site.html" %}
{% load static %}

{% block extrastyle %}
  <link rel="stylesheet" type="text/css" href="{% static "css/admin.css"
%}" />
{% endblock %}

{% block title %}
  Order {{ order.id }} {{ block.super }}
{% endblock %}

{% block breadcrumbs %}
  <div class="breadcrumbs">
    <a href="{% url "admin:index" %}">Home</a> &rsaquo;
    <a href="{% url "admin:orders_order_changelist" %}">Orders</a>
    &rsaquo;
    <a href="{% url "admin:orders_order_change" order.id %}">Order {{
order.id }}</a>
    &rsaquo; Detail
  </div>
{% endblock %}

{% block content %}
<h1>Order {{ order.id }}</h1>
<ul class="object-tools">
  <li>
    <a href="#" onclick="window.print();">Print order</a>
  </li>
</ul>
<table>
  <tr>
    <th>Created</th>
    <td>{{ order.created }}</td>
  </tr>
  <tr>
    <th>Customer</th>
    <td>{{ order.first_name }} {{ order.last_name }}</td>
  </tr>
  <tr>
    <th>E-mail</th>
    <td><a href="mailto:{{ order.email }}">{{ order.email }}</a></td>
  </tr>
  <tr>
    <th>Address</th>
```

```
      <td>{{ order.address }}, {{ order.postal_code }} {{ order.city }}</td>
   </tr>
   <tr>
      <th>Total amount</th>
      <td>${{ order.get_total_cost }}</td>
   </tr>
   <tr>
      <th>Status</th>
      <td>{% if order.paid %}Paid{% else %}Pending payment{% endif %}</td>
   </tr>
</table>

<div class="module">
   <div class="tabular inline-related last-related">
      <table>
         <h2>Items bought</h2>
         <thead>
           <tr>
              <th>Product</th>
              <th>Price</th>
              <th>Quantity</th>
              <th>Total</th>
           </tr>
         </thead>
         <tbody>
            {% for item in order.items.all %}
              <tr class="row{% cycle "1" "2" %}">
                <td>{{ item.product.name }}</td>
                <td class="num">${{ item.price }}</td>
                <td class="num">{{ item.quantity }}</td>
                <td class="num">${{ item.get_cost }}</td>
              </tr>
            {% endfor %}
            <tr class="total">
              <td colspan="3">Total</td>
              <td class="num">${{ order.get_total_cost }}</td>
            </tr>
         </tbody>
      </table>
   </div>
</div>
{% endblock %}
```

This is the template to display an order detail on the administration site. This template extends the `admin/base_site.html` template of Django's administration site, which contains the main HTML structure and CSS styles of the admin. We load the custom static file `css/admin.css`.

In order to use static files, you need to get them from the code that came with this chapter. Copy the static files located in the `static/` directory of `orders application` and add them to the same location in your project.

We use the blocks defined in the parent template to include our own content. We display information about the order and the items bought.

When you want to extend an admin template, you need to know its structure and identify existing blocks. You can find all admin templates at `https://github.com/django/django/tree/2.0/django/contrib/admin/templates/admin`.

You can also override an admin template if you need to. To override an admin template, copy it into your `templates` directory keeping the same relative path and filename. Django's administration site will use your custom template instead of the default one.

Finally, let's add a link to each `Order` object in the list display page of the administration site. Edit the `admin.py` file of the `orders` application and add the following code to it, above the `OrderAdmin` class:

```python
from django.urls import reverse
from django.utils.safestring import mark_safe

def order_detail(obj):
    return mark_safe('<a href="{}">View</a>'.format(
        reverse('orders:admin_order_detail', args=[obj.id])))
```

This is a function that takes an `Order` object as an argument and returns an HTML link for the `admin_order_detail` URL. Django escapes HTML output by default. We have to use the `mark_safe` function to avoid auto-escaping.

 Use the `mark_safe` function to avoid HTML-escaping. When you use `mark_safe`, make sure to escape input that has come from the user to avoid cross-site scripting.

Then, edit the `OrderAdmin` class to display the link:

```
class OrderAdmin(admin.ModelAdmin):
    list_display = ['id',
                    'first_name',
                    # ...
                    'updated',
                    order_detail]
```

Open `http://127.0.0.1:8000/admin/orders/order/` in your browser. Each row now includes a **View** link as follows:

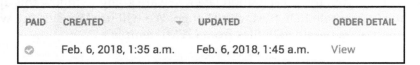

Click on the **View** link for any order to load the custom order detail page. You should see a page like the following one:

Generating PDF invoices dynamically

Now that we have a complete checkout and payment system, we can generate a PDF invoice for each order. There are several Python libraries to generate PDF files. One popular library to generate PDFs with Python code is Reportlab. You can find information about how to output PDF files with Reportlab at `https://docs.djangoproject.com/en/2.0/howto/outputting-pdf/`.

In most cases, you will have to add custom styles and formatting to your PDF files. You will find it more convenient to render an HTML template and convert it into a PDF file, keeping Python away from the presentation layer. We are going to follow this approach and use a module to generate PDF files with Django. We will use WeasyPrint, which is a Python library that can generate PDF files from HTML templates.

Installing WeasyPrint

First, install WeasyPrint's dependencies for your OS, which you will find at `http://weasyprint.org/docs/install/#platforms`. Then, install WeasyPrint via `pip` using the following command:

```
pip install WeasyPrint==0.42.3
```

Creating a PDF template

We need an HTML document as input for WeasyPrint. We are going to create an HTML template, render it using Django, and pass it to WeasyPrint to generate the PDF file.

Create a new template file inside the `templates/orders/order/` directory of the `orders` application and name it `pdf.html`. Add the following code to it:

```html
<html>
<body>
  <h1>My Shop</h1>
  <p>
    Invoice no. {{ order.id }}</br>
    <span class="secondary">
      {{ order.created|date:"M d, Y" }}
    </span>
  </p>

  <h3>Bill to</h3>
```

```html
<p>
  {{ order.first_name }} {{ order.last_name }}<br>
  {{ order.email }}<br>
  {{ order.address }}<br>
  {{ order.postal_code }}, {{ order.city }}
</p>

<h3>Items bought</h3>
<table>
  <thead>
    <tr>
      <th>Product</th>
      <th>Price</th>
      <th>Quantity</th>
      <th>Cost</th>
    </tr>
  </thead>
  <tbody>
    {% for item in order.items.all %}
      <tr class="row{% cycle "1" "2" %}">
        <td>{{ item.product.name }}</td>
        <td class="num">${{ item.price }}</td>
        <td class="num">{{ item.quantity }}</td>
        <td class="num">${{ item.get_cost }}</td>
      </tr>
    {% endfor %}
    <tr class="total">
      <td colspan="3">Total</td>
      <td class="num">${{ order.get_total_cost }}</td>
    </tr>
  </tbody>
</table>
<span class="{% if order.paid %}paid{% else %}pending{% endif %}">
  {% if order.paid %}Paid{% else %}Pending payment{% endif %}
</span>
</body>
</html>
```

This is the template for the PDF invoice. In this template, we display all order details and an HTML `<table>` element including the products. We also include a message to display if the order has been paid or the payment is still pending.

Rendering PDF files

We are going to create a view to generate PDF invoices for existing orders using the administration site. Edit the views.py file inside the orders application directory and add the following code to it:

```python
from django.conf import settings
from django.http import HttpResponse
from django.template.loader import render_to_string
import weasyprint

@staff_member_required
def admin_order_pdf(request, order_id):
    order = get_object_or_404(Order, id=order_id)
    html = render_to_string('orders/order/pdf.html',
                            {'order': order})
    response = HttpResponse(content_type='application/pdf')
    response['Content-Disposition'] = 'filename=\
        "order_{}.pdf"'.format(order.id)
    weasyprint.HTML(string=html).write_pdf(response,
        stylesheets=[weasyprint.CSS(
            settings.STATIC_ROOT + 'css/pdf.css')])
    return response
```

This is the view to generate a PDF invoice for an order. We use the staff_member_required decorator to make sure only staff users can access this view. We get the Order object with the given ID and we use the render_to_string() function provided by Django to render orders/order/pdf.html. The rendered HTML is saved in the html variable. Then, we generate a new HttpResponse object specifying the application/pdf content type and including the Content-Disposition header to specify the filename. We use WeasyPrint to generate a PDF file from the rendered HTML code and write the file to the HttpResponse object. We use the static file css/pdf.css to add CSS styles to the generated PDF file. We load it from the local path by using the STATIC_ROOT setting. Finally, we return the generated response.

If you are missing the CSS styles, remember to copy the static files located in the static/ directory of the shop application to the same location of your project.

Since we need to use the STATIC_ROOT setting, we have to add it to our project. This is the project's path for static files to reside. Edit the settings.py file of the myshop project and add the following setting:

```
STATIC_ROOT = os.path.join(BASE_DIR, 'static/')
```

Then, run the following command:

```
python manage.py collectstatic
```

You should see output that ends likes this:

```
120 static files copied to 'code/myshop/static'.
```

The collectstatic command copies all static files from your applications into the directory defined in the STATIC_ROOT setting. This allows each application to provide its own static files using a static/ directory containing them. You can also provide additional static files sources in the STATICFILES_DIRS setting. All of the directories specified in the STATICFILES_DIRS list will also be copied to the STATIC_ROOT directory when collectstatic is executed. Whenever you execute collectstatic again, you will be asked if you want to override the existing static files.

Edit the urls.py file inside the orders application directory and add the following URL pattern to it:

```
urlpatterns = [
    # ...
    path('admin/order/<int:order_id>/pdf/',
        views.admin_order_pdf,
        name='admin_order_pdf'),
]
```

Now, we can edit the admin list display page for the Order model to add a link to the PDF file for each result. Edit the admin.py file inside the orders application and add the following code above the OrderAdmin class:

```
def order_pdf(obj):
    return mark_safe('<a href="{}">PDF</a>'.format(
        reverse('orders:admin_order_pdf', args=[obj.id])))
order_pdf.short_description = 'Invoice'
```

If you specify a short_description attribute for your callable, Django will use it for the name of the column.

Add `order_pdf` to the `list_display` attribute of the `OrderAdmin` class as follows:

```
class OrderAdmin(admin.ModelAdmin):
    list_display = ['id',
                    # ...
                    order_detail,
                    order_pdf]
```

Open `http://127.0.0.1:8000/admin/orders/order/` in your browser. Each row should now include a PDF link like this:

Click on the **PDF** link for any order. You should see a generated PDF file like the following one for orders that have not been paid yet:

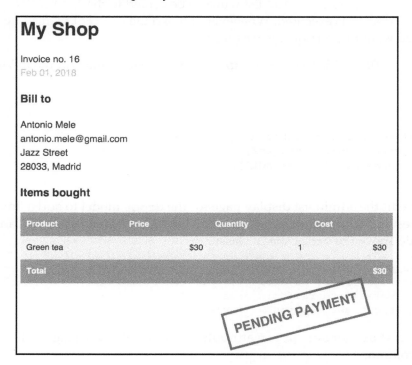

For paid orders, you will see the following PDF file:

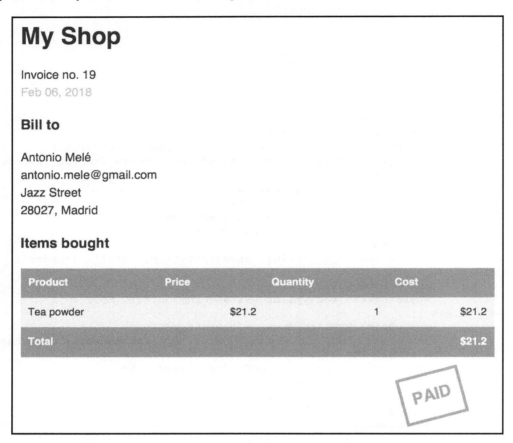

Sending PDF files by email

When a payment is successful, we will send an automatic email to our customers including the generated PDF invoice. Edit the views.py file of the payment application and add the following imports to it:

```
from django.template.loader import render_to_string
from django.core.mail import EmailMessage
from django.conf import settings
import weasyprint
from io import BytesIO
```

Then, in the `payment_process` view, add the following code after the `order.save()` line with the same indentation level as follows:

```python
def payment_process(request):
    # ...
    if request.method == 'POST':
        # ...
        if result.is_success:
            # ...
            order.save()
            # create invoice e-mail
            subject = 'My Shop - Invoice no. {}'.format(order.id)
            message = 'Please, find attached the invoice for your recent\
            purchase.'
            email = EmailMessage(subject,
                                 message,
                                 'admin@myshop.com',
                                 [order.email])
            # generate PDF
            html = render_to_string('orders/order/pdf.html', {'order':
order})
            out = BytesIO()
            stylesheets=[weasyprint.CSS(settings.STATIC_ROOT +
'css/pdf.css')]
            weasyprint.HTML(string=html).write_pdf(out,
                                                   stylesheets=stylesheets)
            # attach PDF file
            email.attach('order_{}.pdf'.format(order.id),
                         out.getvalue(),
                         'application/pdf')
            # send e-mail
            email.send()

            return redirect('payment:done')
        else:
            return redirect('payment:canceled')
    else:
        # ...
```

We use the `EmailMessage` class provided by Django to create an `email` object. Then, we render the template into the `html` variable. We generate the PDF file from the rendered template and we output it to a `BytesIO` instance, which is an in-memory bytes buffer. Then, we attach the generated PDF file to the `EmailMessage` object using the `attach()` method, including the contents of the `out` buffer, and finally we send the email.

Remember to set up your SMTP settings in the `settings.py` file of the project to send emails. You can refer to `Chapter 2`, *Enhancing Your Blog with Advanced Features* to see a working example for an SMTP configuration.

Now, you can complete a new payment process in order to receive the PDF invoice into your email.

Summary

In this chapter, you integrated a payment gateway into your project. You customized the Django administration site and learned how to generate CSV and PDF files dynamically.

The next chapter will give you an insight into the internationalization and localization of Django projects. You will also create a coupon system and build a product recommendation engine.

Extending Your Shop

9

In the previous chapter, you learned how to integrate a payment gateway into your shop. You also learned how to generate CSV and PDF files. In this chapter, you will add a coupon system to your shop. You will learn how internationalization and localization work, and you will build a recommendation engine.

This chapter will cover the following points:

- Creating a coupon system to apply discounts
- Adding internationalization to your project
- Using Rosetta to manage translations
- Translating models using django-parler
- Building a product recommendation engine

Creating a coupon system

Many online shops give out coupons to customers that can be redeemed for discounts on their purchases. An online coupon usually consists of a code that is given to users, valid for a specific time frame. The code can be redeemed one or multiple times.

We are going to create a coupon system for our shop. Our coupons will be valid for clients that enter the coupon in a specific time frame. The coupons will not have any limitations in terms of the number of times they can be redeemed, and they will be applied to the total value of the shopping cart. For this functionality, we will need to create a model to store the coupon code, a valid time frame, and the discount to apply.

Create a new application inside the myshop project using the following command:

```
python manage.py startapp coupons
```

Edit the settings.py file of myshop and add the application to the INSTALLED_APPS setting as follows:

```
INSTALLED_APPS = [
    # ...
    'coupons.apps.CouponsConfig',
]
```

The new application is now active in our Django project.

Building the coupon models

Let's start by creating the Coupon model. Edit the models.py file of the coupons application and add the following code to it:

```python
from django.db import models
from django.core.validators import MinValueValidator, \
                                   MaxValueValidator

class Coupon(models.Model):
    code = models.CharField(max_length=50,
                            unique=True)
    valid_from = models.DateTimeField()
    valid_to = models.DateTimeField()
    discount = models.IntegerField(
                validators=[MinValueValidator(0),
                            MaxValueValidator(100)])
    active = models.BooleanField()

    def __str__(self):
        return self.code
```

This is the model that we are going to use to store coupons. The `Coupon` model contains the following fields:

- `code`: The code that users have to enter in order to apply the coupon to their purchase.
- `valid_from`: The datetime value that indicates when the coupon becomes valid.
- `valid_to`: The datetime value that indicates when the coupon becomes invalid.
- `discount`: The discount rate to apply (this is a percentage, so it takes values from 0 to 100). We use validators for this field to limit the minimum and maximum accepted values.
- `active`: A Boolean that indicates whether the coupon is active.

Run the following command to generate the initial migration for the `coupons` application:

```
python manage.py makemigrations
```

The output should include the following lines:

```
Migrations for 'coupons':
  coupons/migrations/0001_initial.py:
    - Create model Coupon
```

Then, we execute the next command to apply migrations:

```
python manage.py migrate
```

You should see an output that includes the following line:

```
Applying coupons.0001_initial... OK
```

The migrations are now applied in the database. Let's add the `Coupon` model to the administration site. Edit the `admin.py` file of the `coupons` application and add the following code to it:

```
from django.contrib import admin
from .models import Coupon

class CouponAdmin(admin.ModelAdmin):
    list_display = ['code', 'valid_from', 'valid_to',
                    'discount', 'active']
    list_filter = ['active', 'valid_from', 'valid_to']
    search_fields = ['code']
admin.site.register(Coupon, CouponAdmin)
```

The `Coupon` model is now registered in the administration site. Ensure that your local server is running with the command `python manage.py runserver`. Open `http://127.0.0.1:8000/admin/coupons/coupon/add/` in your browser. You should see the following form:

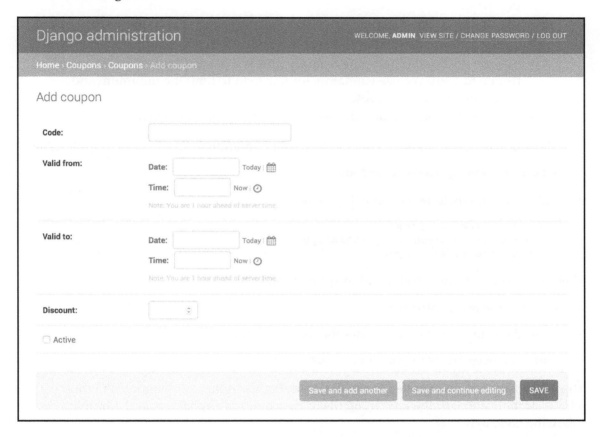

Fill in the form to create a new coupon that is valid for the current date and make sure that you check the **Active** checkbox and click the **SAVE** button.

Applying a coupon to the shopping cart

We can store new coupons and make queries to retrieve existing coupons. Now we need a way for customers to apply coupons to their purchases. The functionality to apply a coupon would be as follows:

1. The user adds products to the shopping cart.
2. The user can enter a coupon code in a form displayed in the shopping cart detail page.
3. When a user enters a coupon code and submits the form, we look for an existing coupon with the given code that is currently valid. We have to check that the coupon code matches the one entered by the user that the `active` attribute is `True`, and that the current datetime is between the `valid_from` and `valid_to` values.
4. If a coupon is found, we save it in the user's session and display the cart, including the discount applied to it and the updated total amount.
5. When the user places an order, we save the coupon to the given order.

Create a new file inside the `coupons` application directory and name it `forms.py`. Add the following code to it:

```python
from django import forms

class CouponApplyForm(forms.Form):
    code = forms.CharField()
```

This is the form that we are going to use for the user to enter a coupon code. Edit the `views.py` file inside the `coupons` application and add the following code to it:

```python
from django.shortcuts import render, redirect
from django.utils import timezone
from django.views.decorators.http import require_POST
from .models import Coupon
from .forms import CouponApplyForm

@require_POST
def coupon_apply(request):
    now = timezone.now()
    form = CouponApplyForm(request.POST)
    if form.is_valid():
        code = form.cleaned_data['code']
        try:
            coupon = Coupon.objects.get(code__iexact=code,
                                        valid_from__lte=now,
```

```
                                        valid_to__gte=now,
                                        active=True)
            request.session['coupon_id'] = coupon.id
        except Coupon.DoesNotExist:
            request.session['coupon_id'] = None
    return redirect('cart:cart_detail')
```

The `coupon_apply` view validates the coupon and stores it in the user's session. We apply the `require_POST` decorator to this view to restrict it to `POST` requests. In the view, we perform the following tasks:

1. We instantiate the `CouponApplyForm` form using the posted data and we check that the form is valid.
2. If the form is valid, we get the `code` entered by the user from the form's `cleaned_data` dictionary. We try to retrieve the `Coupon` object with the given code. We use the `iexact` field lookup to perform a case-insensitive exact match. The coupon has to be currently active (`active=True`) and valid for the current datetime. We use Django's `timezone.now()` function to get the current time zone-aware datetime and we compare it with the `valid_from` and `valid_to` fields performing `lte` (less than or equal to) and `gte` (greater than or equal to) field lookups, respectively.
3. We store the coupon ID in the user's session.
4. We redirect the user to the `cart_detail` URL to display the cart with the coupon applied.

We need a URL pattern for the `coupon_apply` view. Create a new file inside the `coupons` application directory and name it `urls.py`. Add the following code to it:

```
from django.urls import path
from . import views

app_name = 'coupons'

urlpatterns = [
    path('apply/', views.coupon_apply, name='apply'),
]
```

Then, edit the main `urls.py` of the `myshop` project and include the `coupons` URL patterns as follows:

```python
urlpatterns = [
    # ...
    path('coupons/', include('coupons.urls', namespace='coupons')),
    path('', include('shop.urls', namespace='shop')),
]
```

Remember to place this pattern before the `shop.urls` pattern.

Now, edit the `cart.py` file of the `cart` application. Include the following import:

```python
from coupons.models import Coupon
```

Add the following code to the end of the `__init__()` method of the `Cart` class to initialize the coupon from the current session:

```python
class Cart(object):
    def __init__(self, request):
        # ...
        # store current applied coupon
        self.coupon_id = self.session.get('coupon_id')
```

In this code, we try to get the `coupon_id` session key from the current session and store its value in the `Cart` object. Add the following methods to the `Cart` object:

```python
class Cart(object):
    # ...
    @property
    def coupon(self):
        if self.coupon_id:
            return Coupon.objects.get(id=self.coupon_id)
        return None

    def get_discount(self):
        if self.coupon:
            return (self.coupon.discount / Decimal('100')) \
                * self.get_total_price()
        return Decimal('0')

    def get_total_price_after_discount(self):
        return self.get_total_price() - self.get_discount()
```

These methods are as follows:

- `coupon()`: We define this method as `property`. If the cart contains a `coupon_id` attribute, the `Coupon` object with the given ID is returned.
- `get_discount()`: If the cart contains a coupon, we retrieve its discount rate and return the amount to be deducted from the total amount of the cart.
- `get_total_price_after_discount()`: We return the total amount of the cart after deducting the amount returned by the `get_discount()` method.

The `Cart` class is now prepared to handle a coupon applied to the current session and apply the corresponding discount.

Let's include the coupon system in the cart's detail view. Edit the `views.py` file of the `cart` application and add the following import at the top of the file:

```
from coupons.forms import CouponApplyForm
```

Further down, edit the `cart_detail` view and add the new form to it as follows:

```
def cart_detail(request):
    cart = Cart(request)
    for item in cart:
        item['update_quantity_form'] = CartAddProductForm(
                            initial={'quantity': item['quantity'],
                            'update': True})
    coupon_apply_form = CouponApplyForm()

    return render(request,
                    'cart/detail.html',
                    {'cart': cart,
                    'coupon_apply_form': coupon_apply_form})
```

Edit the `cart/detail.html` template of the `cart` application and locate the following lines:

```
<tr class="total">
  <td>Total</td>
  <td colspan="4"></td>
  <td class="num">${{ cart.get_total_price }}</td>
</tr>
```

Replace them with the following:

```
{% if cart.coupon %}
  <tr class="subtotal">
    <td>Subtotal</td>
    <td colspan="4"></td>
    <td class="num">${{ cart.get_total_price|floatformat:"2" }}</td>
  </tr>
  <tr>
    <td>
      "{{ cart.coupon.code }}" coupon
      ({{ cart.coupon.discount }}% off)
    </td>
    <td colspan="4"></td>
    <td class="num neg">
      - ${{ cart.get_discount|floatformat:"2" }}
    </td>
  </tr>
{% endif %}
<tr class="total">
  <td>Total</td>
  <td colspan="4"></td>
  <td class="num">
    ${{ cart.get_total_price_after_discount|floatformat:"2" }}
  </td>
</tr>
```

This is the code for displaying an optional coupon and its discount rate. If the cart contains a coupon, we display a first row, including the total amount of the cart as the subtotal. Then we use a second row to display the current coupon applied to the cart. Finally, we display the total price including any discount by calling the get_total_price_after_discount() method of the cart object.

In the same file, include the following code after the </table> HTML tag:

```
<p>Apply a coupon:</p>
<form action="{% url "coupons:apply" %}" method="post">
  {{ coupon_apply_form }}
  <input type="submit" value="Apply">
  {% csrf_token %}
</form>
```

This will display the form to enter a coupon code and apply it to the current cart.

Open `http://127.0.0.1:8000/` in your browser, add a product to the cart, and apply the coupon you created by entering its code in the form. You should see that the cart displays the coupon discount as follows:

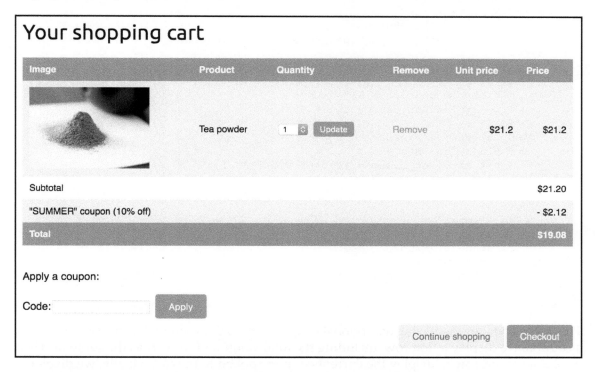

Let's add the coupon to the next step of the purchase process. Edit the `orders/order/create.html` template of the orders application and locate the following lines:

```
<ul>
  {% for item in cart %}
    <li>
      {{ item.quantity }}x {{ item.product.name }}
      <span>${{ item.total_price }}</span>
    </li>
  {% endfor %}
</ul>
```

Replace them with the following code:

```
<ul>
  {% for item in cart %}
    <li>
      {{ item.quantity }}x {{ item.product.name }}
      <span>${{ item.total_price|floatformat:"2" }}</span>
    </li>
  {% endfor %}
  {% if cart.coupon %}
    <li>
      "{{ cart.coupon.code }}" ({{ cart.coupon.discount }}% off)
      <span>- ${{ cart.get_discount|floatformat:"2" }}</span>
    </li>
  {% endif %}
</ul>
```

The order summary should now include the coupon applied, if there is one. Now find the following line:

```
<p>Total: ${{ cart.get_total_price }}</p>
```

Replace it with the following:

```
<p>Total: ${{ cart.get_total_price_after_discount|floatformat:"2" }}</p>
```

By doing so, the total price will also be calculated by applying the discount of the coupon.

Open `http://127.0.0.1:8000/orders/create/` in your browser. You should see that the order summary includes the applied coupon as follows:

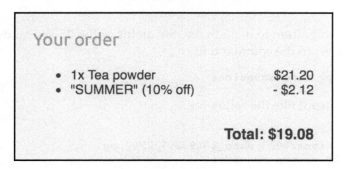

Users can now apply coupons to their shopping cart. However, we still need to store coupon information in the order that is created when users check out the cart.

Applying coupons to orders

We are going to store the coupon that was applied to each order. First, we need to modify the `Order` model to store the related `Coupon` object, if there is any.

Edit the `models.py` file of the `orders` application and add the following imports to it:

```
from decimal import Decimal
from django.core.validators import MinValueValidator, \
                                   MaxValueValidator
from coupons.models import Coupon
```

Then, add the following fields to the `Order` model:

```
class Order(models.Model):
    # ...
    coupon = models.ForeignKey(Coupon,
                               related_name='orders',
                               null=True,
                               blank=True,
                               on_delete=models.SET_NULL)
    discount = models.IntegerField(default=0,
                                   validators=[MinValueValidator(0),
                                               MaxValueValidator(100)])
```

These fields allow us to store an optional coupon for the order and the discount percentage applied with the coupon. The discount is stored in the related `Coupon` object, but we include it in the `Order` model to preserve it if the coupon is modified or deleted. We set `on_delete` to `models.SET_NULL` so that if the coupon gets deleted, the `coupon` field is set to `Null`.

We need to create a migration to include the new fields of the `Order` model. Run the following command from the command line:

```
python manage.py makemigrations
```

You should see an output like the following:

```
Migrations for 'orders':
  orders/migrations/0003_auto_20180307_2202.py:
    - Add field coupon to order
    - Add field discount to order
```

Apply the new migration with the following command:

```
python manage.py migrate orders
```

You should see a confirmation indicating that the new migration has been applied. The `Order` model field changes are now synced with the database.

Go back to the `models.py` file and change the `get_total_cost()` method of the `Order` model as follows:

```
class Order(models.Model):
    # ...
    def get_total_cost(self):
        total_cost = sum(item.get_cost() for item in self.items.all())
        return total_cost - total_cost * \
            (self.discount / Decimal('100'))
```

The `get_total_cost()` method of the `Order` model will now take into account the discount applied if there is one.

Edit the `views.py` file of the `orders` application and modify the `order_create` view to save the related coupon and its discount when creating a new order. Find the following line:

```
order = form.save()
```

Replace it with the following:

```
order = form.save(commit=False)
if cart.coupon:
    order.coupon = cart.coupon
    order.discount = cart.coupon.discount
order.save()
```

In the new code, we create an `Order` object using the `save()` method of the `OrderCreateForm` form. We avoid saving it to the database yet by using `commit=False`. If the cart contains a coupon, we store the related coupon and the discount that was applied. Then we save the `order` object to the database.

Make sure the development server is running with the command `python manage.py runserver`.

Open `http://127.0.0.1:8000/` in your browser and complete a purchase using the coupon you created. When you finish a successful purchase, you can go to `http://127.0.0.1:8000/admin/orders/order/` and check that the order object contains the coupon and the applied discount as follows:

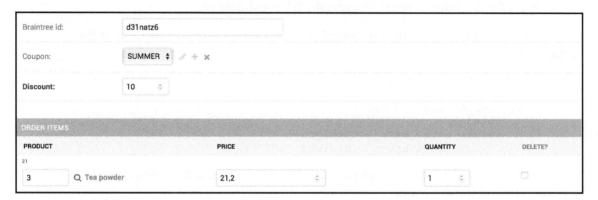

You can also modify the admin order detail template and the order PDF bill to display the applied coupon the same way we did for the cart.

Next, we are going to add internationalization to our project.

Adding internationalization and localization

Django offers full internationalization and localization support. It allows you to translate your application into multiple languages and it handles locale-specific formatting for dates, times, numbers, and time zones. Let's clarify the difference between internationalization and localization. **Internationalization** (frequently abbreviated to **i18n**) is the process of adapting software for the potential use of different languages and locales, so that it isn't hardwired to a specific language or locale. **Localization** (abbreviated to **l10n**) is the process of actually translating the software and adapting it to a particular locale. Django itself is translated into more than 50 languages using its internationalization framework.

Internationalization with Django

The internationalization framework allows you to easily mark strings for translation both in Python code and in your templates. It relies on the GNU gettext toolset to generate and manage message files. A **message file** is a plain text file that represents a language. It contains a part, or all, of the translation strings found in your application and their respective translations for a single language. Message files have the .po extension.

Once the translation is done, message files are compiled to offer rapid access to translated strings. The compiled translation files have the .mo extension.

Internationalization and localization settings

Django provides several settings for internationalization. The following settings are the most relevant ones:

- USE_I18N: A Boolean that specifies whether Django's translation system is enabled. This is True by default.
- USE_L10N: A Boolean indicating whether localized formatting is enabled. When active, localized formats are used to represent dates and numbers. This is False by default.
- USE_TZ: A Boolean that specifies whether datetimes are time zone-aware. When you create a project with the startproject command, this is set to True.
- LANGUAGE_CODE: The default language code for the project. This is in standard language ID format, for example, 'en-us' for American English, or 'en-gb' for British English. This setting requires USE_I18N to be set to True in order to take effect. You can find a list of valid language IDs at http://www.i18nguy.com/unicode/language-identifiers.html.
- LANGUAGES: A tuple that contains available languages for the project. They come in two tuples of a **language code** and **language name**. You can see the list of available languages at django.conf.global_settings. When you choose which languages your site will be available in, you set LANGUAGES to a subset of that list.
- LOCALE_PATHS: A list of directories where Django looks for message files containing translations for this project.
- TIME_ZONE: A string that represents the time zone for the project. This is set to 'UTC' when you create a new project using the startproject command. You can set it to any other time zone, such as 'Europe/Madrid'.

These are some of the internationalization and localization settings available. You can find the full list at `https://docs.djangoproject.com/en/2.0/ref/settings/#globalization-i18n-l10n`.

Internationalization management commands

Django includes the following management commands to manage translations:

- `makemessages`: This runs over the source tree to find all strings marked for translation and creates or updates the `.po` message files in the `locale` directory. A single `.po` file is created for each language.
- `compilemessages`: This compiles the existing `.po` message files to `.mo` files that are used to retrieve translations.

You will need the gettext toolkit to be able to create, update, and compile message files. Most Linux distributions include the gettext toolkit. If you are using macOS X, probably the simplest way to install it is via Homebrew at `https://brew.sh/` with the command `brew install gettext`. You might also need to force link it with the command `brew link gettext --force`. For Windows, follow the steps at `https://docs.djangoproject.com/en/2.0/topics/i18n/translation/#gettext-on-windows`.

How to add translations to a Django project

Let's take a look at the process to internationalize our project. We will need to do the following:

1. Mark strings for translation in our Python code and our templates
2. Run the `makemessages` command to create or update message files that include all translation strings from our code
3. Translate the strings contained in the message files and compile them using the `compilemessages` management command

How Django determines the current language

Django comes with a middleware that determines the current language based on request data. This is the `LocaleMiddleware` middleware that resides in `django.middleware.locale.LocaleMiddleware` performs the following tasks:

1. If you are using `i18_patterns`, that is, you use translated URL patterns, it looks for a language prefix in the requested URL to determine the current language.
2. If no language prefix is found, it looks for an existing `LANGUAGE_SESSION_KEY` in the current user's session.
3. If the language is not set in the session, it looks for an existing cookie with the current language. A custom name for this cookie can be provided in the `LANGUAGE_COOKIE_NAME` setting. By default, the name for this cookie is `django_language`.
4. If no cookie is found, it looks for the `Accept-Language` HTTP header of the request.
5. If the `Accept-Language` header does not specify a language, Django uses the language defined in the `LANGUAGE_CODE` setting.

By default, Django will use the language defined in the `LANGUAGE_CODE` setting unless you are using `LocaleMiddleware`. The process described here only applies when using this middleware.

Preparing our project for internationalization

Let's prepare our project to use different languages. We are going to create an English and a Spanish version for our shop. Edit the `settings.py` file of your project and add the following `LANGUAGES` setting to it. Place it next to the `LANGUAGE_CODE` setting:

```
LANGUAGES = (
    ('en', 'English'),
    ('es', 'Spanish'),
)
```

The `LANGUAGES` setting contains two tuples that consist of a language code and a name. Language codes can be locale-specific, such as `en-us` or `en-gb`, or generic, such as `en`. With this setting, we specify that our application will only be available in English and Spanish. If we don't define a custom `LANGUAGES` setting, the site will be available in all the languages that Django is translated into.

Make your `LANGUAGE_CODE` setting look as follows:

```
LANGUAGE_CODE = 'en'
```

Add `'django.middleware.locale.LocaleMiddleware'` to the `MIDDLEWARE` setting. Make sure that this middleware comes after `SessionMiddleware` because `LocaleMiddleware` needs to use session data. It also has to be placed before `CommonMiddleware` because the latter needs an active language to resolve the requested URL. The `MIDDLEWARE` setting should now look as follows:

```
MIDDLEWARE = [
    'django.middleware.security.SecurityMiddleware',
    'django.contrib.sessions.middleware.SessionMiddleware',
    'django.middleware.locale.LocaleMiddleware',
    'django.middleware.common.CommonMiddleware',
    # ...
]
```

 The order of middleware classes is very important because each middleware can depend on data set by other middleware executed previously. Middleware is applied for requests in order of appearance in `MIDDLEWARE`, and in reverse order for responses.

Create the following directory structure inside the main project directory, next to the `manage.py` file:

```
locale/
    en/
    es/
```

The `locale` directory is the place where message files for your application will reside. Edit the `settings.py` file again and add the following setting to it:

```
LOCALE_PATHS = (
    os.path.join(BASE_DIR, 'locale/'),
)
```

The `LOCALE_PATHS` setting specifies the directories where Django has to look for translation files. Locale paths that appear first have the highest precedence.

When you use the `makemessages` command from your project directory, message files will be generated in the `locale/` path we created. However, for applications that contain a `locale/` directory, message files will be generated in that directory.

Translating Python code

To translate literals in your Python code, you can mark strings for translation using the gettext() function included in django.utils.translation. This function translates the message and returns a string. The convention is to import this function as a shorter alias named _ (underscore character).

You can find all the documentation about translations at https://docs.djangoproject.com/en/2.0/topics/i18n/translation/.

Standard translations

The following code shows how to mark a string for translation:

```
from django.utils.translation import gettext as _
output = _('Text to be translated.')
```

Lazy translations

Django includes **lazy** versions for all of its translation functions, which have the suffix _lazy(). When using the lazy functions, strings are translated when the value is accessed, rather than when the function is called (this is why they are translated **lazily**). The lazy translation functions come in handy when strings marked for translation are in paths that are executed when modules are loaded.

> Using gettext_lazy() instead of gettext(), strings are translated when the value is accessed rather than when the function is called. Django offers a **lazy** version for all translation functions.

Translations including variables

The strings marked for translation can include placeholders to include variables in the translations. The following code is an example of a translation string with a placeholder:

```
from django.utils.translation import gettext as _
month = _('April')
day = '14'
output = _('Today is %(month)s %(day)s') % {'month': month,
                                             'day': day}
```

By using placeholders, you can reorder the text variables. For example, an English translation of the previous example might be *"Today is April 14"*, while the Spanish one is *"Hoy es 14 de Abril"*. Always use string interpolation instead of positional interpolation when you have more than one parameter for the translation string. By doing so, you will be able to reorder the placeholder text.

Plural forms in translations

For plural forms, you can use `ngettext()` and `ngettext_lazy()`. These functions translate singular and plural forms depending on an argument that indicates the number of objects. The following example shows how to use them:

```python
output = ngettext('there is %(count)d product',
                  'there are %(count)d products',
                  count) % {'count': count}
```

Now that you know the basics about translating literals in our Python code, it's time to apply translations to our project.

Translating your own code

Edit the `settings.py` file of your project, import the `gettext_lazy()` function, and change the LANGUAGES setting as follows to translate the language names:

```python
from django.utils.translation import gettext_lazy as _

LANGUAGES = (
    ('en', _('English')),
    ('es', _('Spanish')),
)
```

Here, we use the `gettext_lazy()` function instead of `gettext()` to avoid a circular import, thus translating the languages' names when they are accessed.

Open the shell and run the following command from your project directory:

```
django-admin makemessages --all
```

You should see the following output:

```
processing locale es
processing locale en
```

Take a look at the `locale/` directory. You should see a file structure like the following:

```
en/
     LC_MESSAGES/
          django.po
es/
     LC_MESSAGES/
          django.po
```

A `.po` message file has been created for each language. Open `es/LC_MESSAGES/django.po` with a text editor. At the end of the file, you should be able to see the following:

```
#: myshop/settings.py:117
msgid "English"
msgstr ""

#: myshop/settings.py:118
msgid "Spanish"
msgstr ""
```

Each translation string is preceded by a comment showing details about the file and line where it was found. Each translation includes two strings:

- `msgid`: The translation string as it appears in the source code.
- `msgstr`: The language translation, which is empty by default. This is where you have to enter the actual translation for the given string.

Fill in the `msgstr` translations for the given `msgid` string as follows:

```
#: myshop/settings.py:117
msgid "English"
msgstr "Inglés"

#: myshop/settings.py:118
msgid "Spanish"
msgstr "Español"
```

Save the modified message file, open the shell, and run the following command:

```
django-admin compilemessages
```

If everything goes well, you should see an output like the following:

```
processing file django.po in myshop/locale/en/LC_MESSAGES
processing file django.po in myshop/locale/es/LC_MESSAGES
```

The output gives you information about the message files that are being compiled. Take a look at the `locale` directory of the `myshop` project again. You should see the following files:

```
en/
    LC_MESSAGES/
        django.mo
        django.po
es/
    LC_MESSAGES/
        django.mo
        django.po
```

You can see that a `.mo` compiled message file has been generated for each language.

We have translated the language names themselves. Now let's translate the model field names that are displayed in the site. Edit the `models.py` file of the `orders` application and add names marked for translation for the `Order` model fields as follows:

```python
from django.utils.translation import gettext_lazy as _

class Order(models.Model):
    first_name = models.CharField(_('first name'),
                                  max_length=50)
    last_name = models.CharField(_('last name'),
                                 max_length=50)
    email = models.EmailField(_('e-mail'))
    address = models.CharField(_('address'),
                               max_length=250)
    postal_code = models.CharField(_('postal code'),
                                   max_length=20)
    city = models.CharField(_('city'),
                            max_length=100)
    # ...
```

We have added names for the fields that are displayed when a user is placing a new order. These are `first_name`, `last_name`, `email`, `address`, `postal_code`, and `city`. Remember that you can also use the `verbose_name` attribute to name the fields.

Create the following directory structure inside the `orders` application directory:

```
locale/
    en/
    es/
```

By creating a `locale` directory, translation strings of this application will be stored in a message file under this directory instead of the main messages file. In this way, you can generate separated translation files for each application.

Open the shell from the project directory and run the following command:

```
django-admin makemessages --all
```

You should see the following output:

```
processing locale es
processing locale en
```

Open the `locale/es/LC_MESSAGES/django.po` file of the `order` application using a text editor. You will see the translation strings for the `Order` model. Fill in the following `msgstr` translations for the given `msgid` strings:

```
#: orders/models.py:10
msgid "first name"
msgstr "nombre"

#: orders/models.py:11
msgid "last name"
msgstr "apellidos"

#: orders/models.py:12
msgid "e-mail"
msgstr "e-mail"

#: orders/models.py:13
msgid "address"
msgstr "dirección"

#: orders/models.py:14
msgid "postal code"
msgstr "código postal"

#: orders/models.py:15
msgid "city"
msgstr "ciudad"
```

After you have finished adding the translations, save the file.

Besides a text editor, you can use Poedit to edit translations. Poedit is a software to edit translations, and it uses gettext. It is available for Linux, Windows, and macOS X. You can download Poedit from https://poedit.net/.

Let's also translate the forms of our project. `OrderCreateForm` of the `orders` application does not have to be translated, since it is `ModelForm` and it uses the `verbose_name` attribute of the `Order` model fields for the form field labels. We are going to translate the forms of `cart` and `coupons` applications.

Edit the `forms.py` file inside the `cart` application directory and add a `label` attribute to the `quantity` field of the `CartAddProductForm`, and then mark this field for translation as follows:

```python
from django import forms
from django.utils.translation import gettext_lazy as _

PRODUCT_QUANTITY_CHOICES = [(i, str(i)) for i in range(1, 21)]

class CartAddProductForm(forms.Form):
    quantity = forms.TypedChoiceField(
                            choices=PRODUCT_QUANTITY_CHOICES,
                            coerce=int,
                            label=_('Quantity'))
    update = forms.BooleanField(required=False,
                                initial=False,
                                widget=forms.HiddenInput)
```

Edit the `forms.py` file of the `coupons` application and translate the `CouponApplyForm` form as follows:

```python
from django import forms
from django.utils.translation import gettext_lazy as _

class CouponApplyForm(forms.Form):
    code = forms.CharField(label=_('Coupon'))
```

We have added a label to the `code` field and marked it for translation.

Translating templates

Django offers the `{% trans %}` and `{% blocktrans %}` template tags to translate strings in templates. In order to use the translation template tags, you have to add `{% load i18n %}` at the top of your template to load them.

The {% trans %} template tag

The {% trans %} template tag allows you to mark a string, a constant, or variable content for translation. Internally, Django executes gettext() on the given text. This is how to mark a string for translation in a template:

```
{% trans "Text to be translated" %}
```

You can use as to store the translated content in a variable that you can use throughout your template. The following example stores the translated text in a variable called greeting:

```
{% trans "Hello!" as greeting %}
<h1>{{ greeting }}</h1>
```

The {% trans %} tag is useful for simple translation strings, but it cannot handle content for translation that includes variables.

The {% blocktrans %} template tag

The {% blocktrans %} template tag allows you to mark content that includes literals and variable content using placeholders. The following example shows you how to use the {% blocktrans %} tag, including a name variable in the content for translation:

```
{% blocktrans %}Hello {{ name }}!{% endblocktrans %}
```

You can use with to include template expressions such as accessing object attributes or applying template filters to variables. You always have to use placeholders for these. You cannot access expressions or object attributes inside the blocktrans block. The following example shows you how to use with to include an object attribute to which the capfirst filter is applied:

```
{% blocktrans with name=user.name|capfirst %}
  Hello {{ name }}!
{% endblocktrans %}
```

 Use the {% blocktrans %} tag instead of {% trans %} when you need to include variable content in your translation string.

Translating the shop templates

Edit the `shop/base.html` template of the `shop` application. Make sure that you load the `i18n` tag at the top of the template and mark strings for translation as follows:

```
{% load i18n %}
{% load static %}
<!DOCTYPE html>
<html>
<head>
  <meta charset="utf-8" />
  <title>
    {% block title %}{% trans "My shop" %}{% endblock %}
  </title>
  <link href="{% static "css/base.css" %}" rel="stylesheet">
</head>
<body>
  <div id="header">
    <a href="/" class="logo">{% trans "My shop" %}</a>
  </div>
  <div id="subheader">
    <div class="cart">
      {% with total_items=cart|length %}
        {% if cart|length > 0 %}
          {% trans "Your cart" %}:
          <a href="{% url "cart:cart_detail" %}">
            {% blocktrans with total_items_plural=total_items|pluralize
            total_price=cart.get_total_price %}
              {{ total_items }} item{{ total_items_plural }},
              ${{ total_price }}
            {% endblocktrans %}
          </a>
        {% else %}
          {% trans "Your cart is empty." %}
        {% endif %}
      {% endwith %}
    </div>
  </div>
  <div id="content">
    {% block content %}
    {% endblock %}
  </div>
</body>
</html>
```

Notice the `{% blocktrans %}` tag to display the cart's summary. The cart's summary was previously as follows:

```
{{ total_items }} item{{ total_items|pluralize }},
${{ cart.get_total_price }}
```

We used `{% blocktrans with ... %}` to set up placeholders for `total_items|pluralize` (template tag applied here) and `cart.get_total_price` (object method called here), resulting in the following:

```
{% blocktrans with total_items_plural=total_items|pluralize
 total_price=cart.get_total_price %}
   {{ total_items }} item{{ total_items_plural }},
   ${{ total_price }}
{% endblocktrans %}
```

Next, edit the `shop/product/detail.html` template of the `shop` application and load the `i18n` tags at the top of it, but after the `{% extends %}` tag, which always has to be the first tag in the template:

```
{% load i18n %}
```

Then, find the following line:

```
<input type="submit" value="Add to cart">
```

Replace it with the following:

```
<input type="submit" value="{% trans "Add to cart" %}">
```

Now, translate the `orders` application templates. Edit the `orders/order/create.html` template of the `orders` application and mark text for translation, as follows:

```
{% extends "shop/base.html" %}
{% load i18n %}

{% block title %}
  {% trans "Checkout" %}
{% endblock %}

{% block content %}
  <h1>{% trans "Checkout" %}</h1>

  <div class="order-info">
    <h3>{% trans "Your order" %}</h3>
    <ul>
      {% for item in cart %}
```

```
  <li>
    {{ item.quantity }}x {{ item.product.name }}
    <span>${{ item.total_price }}</span>
  </li>
{% endfor %}
{% if cart.coupon %}
  <li>
    {% blocktrans with code=cart.coupon.code
     discount=cart.coupon.discount %}
      "{{ code }}" ({{ discount }}% off)
    {% endblocktrans %}
    <span>- ${{ cart.get_discount|floatformat:"2" }}</span>
  </li>
{% endif %}
</ul>
<p>{% trans "Total" %}: ${{
cart.get_total_price_after_discount|floatformat:"2" }}</p>
</div>

<form action="." method="post" class="order-form">
  {{ form.as_p }}
  <p><input type="submit" value="{% trans "Place order" %}"></p>
  {% csrf_token %}
</form>
{% endblock %}
```

Take a look at the following files in the code that accompany this chapter to see how strings have been marked for translation:

- The shop application: Template shop/product/list.html
- The orders application: Template orders/order/created.html
- The cart application: Template cart/detail.html

Let's update the message files to include the new translation strings. Open the shell and run the following command:

```
django-admin makemessages --all
```

The .po files are inside the locale directory of the myshop project and you'll see that the orders application now contains all the strings that we marked for translation.

Edit the .po translation files of the project and the orders application and include Spanish translations in the msgstr. You can also use the translated .po files in the source code that accompanies this chapter.

Run the following command to compile the translation files:

```
django-admin compilemessages
```

You will see the following output:

```
processing file django.po in myshop/locale/en/LC_MESSAGES
processing file django.po in myshop/locale/es/LC_MESSAGES
processing file django.po in myshop/orders/locale/en/LC_MESSAGES
processing file django.po in myshop/orders/locale/es/LC_MESSAGES
```

A .mo file containing compiled translations has been generated for each .po translation file.

Using the Rosetta translation interface

Rosetta is a third-party application that allows you to edit translations using the same interface as the Django administration site. Rosetta makes it easy to edit .po files and it updates compiled translation files. Let's add it to our project.

Install Rosetta via `pip` using this command:

```
pip install django-rosetta==0.8.1
```

Then, add `'rosetta'` to the INSTALLED_APPS setting in your project's settings.py file as follows:

```
INSTALLED_APPS = [
    # ...
    'rosetta',
]
```

You need to add Rosetta's URLs to your main URL configuration. Edit the main urls.py file of your project and add the following URL pattern to it:

```
urlpatterns = [
    # ...
    path('rosetta/', include('rosetta.urls')),
    path('', include('shop.urls', namespace='shop')),
]
```

Make sure you place it before the `shop.urls` pattern to avoid undesired pattern match.

Open `http://127.0.0.1:8000/admin/` and log in with a superuser. Then, navigate to `http://127.0.0.1:8000/rosetta/` in your browser. In the **Filter** menu, click **THIRD PARTY** to display all the available message files, including those that belong to the `orders` application. You should see a list of existing languages as follows:

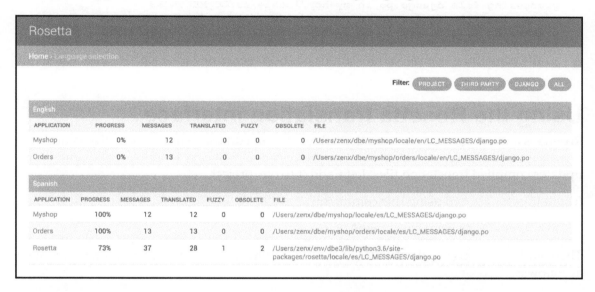

Click the **Myshop** link under the **Spanish** section to edit Spanish translations. You should see a list of translation strings as follows:

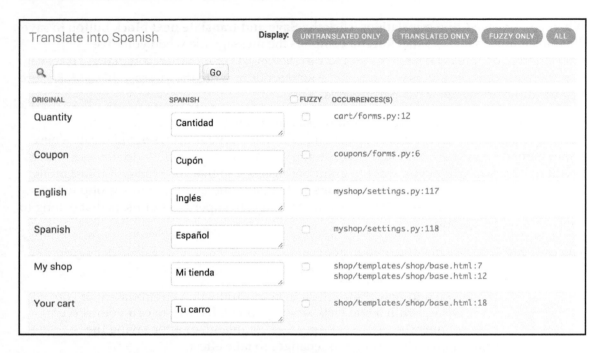

You can enter the translations under the **Spanish** column. The **OCCURRENCES(S)** column displays the files and line of code where each translation string was found.

Translations that include placeholders will appear as follows:

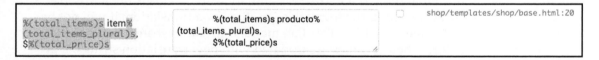

Rosetta uses a different background color to display placeholders. When you translate content, make sure you keep placeholders untranslated. For example, take the following string:

```
%(total_items)s item%(total_items_plural)s, $%(total_price)s
```

It is translated into Spanish as follows:

```
%(total_items)s producto%(total_items_plural)s, $%(total_price)s
```

You can take a look at the source code that comes along with this chapter to use the same Spanish translations for your project.

When you finish editing translations, click the **Save and translate next block** button to save the translations to the `.po` file. Rosetta compiles the message file when you save translations, so there is no need for you to run the `compilemessages` command. However, Rosetta requires write access to the `locale` directories to write the message files. Make sure that the directories have valid permissions.

If you want other users to be able to edit translations, open `http://127.0.0.1:8000/admin/auth/group/add/` in your browser and create a new group named `translators`. Then, access `http://127.0.0.1:8000/admin/auth/user/` to edit the users to whom you want to grant permissions so that they can edit translations. When editing a user, under the **Permissions** section, add the `translators` group to the **Chosen Groups** for each user. Rosetta is only available to superusers or users that belong to the `translators` group.

You can read Rosetta's documentation at `https://django-rosetta.readthedocs.io/en/latest/`.

 When you add new translations in your production environment, if you serve Django with a real web server, you will have to reload your server after running the `compilemessages` command, or after saving the translations with Rosetta for changes to take effect.

Fuzzy translations

You might have noticed that there is a **FUZZY** column in Rosetta. This is not a Rosetta feature; it is provided by gettext. If the fuzzy flag is active for a translation, it will not be included in the compiled message files. This flag marks translation strings that need to be reviewed by a translator. When `.po` files are updated with new translation strings, it is possible that some translation strings are automatically flagged as fuzzy. This happens when `gettext` finds some `msgid` that has been slightly modified. `gettext` pairs it with what it thinks was the old translation and flags it as fuzzy for review. The translator should then review fuzzy translations, remove the fuzzy flag, and compile the translation file again.

URL patterns for internationalization

Django offers internationalization capabilities for URLs. It includes two main features for internationalized URLs:

- **Language prefix in URL patterns**: Adding a language prefix to URLs to serve each language version under a different base URL
- **Translated URL patterns**: Translating URL patterns so that every URL is different for each language

A reason for translating URLs is to optimize your site for search engines. By adding a language prefix to your patterns, you will be able to index a URL for each language instead of a single URL for all of them. Furthermore, by translating URLs into each language, you will provide search engines with URLs that will rank better for each language.

Adding a language prefix to URL patterns

Django allows you to add a language prefix to your URL patterns. For example, the English version of your site can be served under a path starting /en/, and the Spanish version /es/.

To use languages in URL patterns, you have to use the LocaleMiddleware provided by Django. The framework will use it to identify the current language from the requested URL. You added it previously to the MIDDLEWARE setting of your project, so you don't need to do it now.

Let's add a language prefix to our URL patterns. Edit the main urls.py file of the myshop project and add i18n_patterns() as follows:

```
from django.conf.urls.i18n import i18n_patterns

urlpatterns = i18n_patterns(
 path('admin/', admin.site.urls),
 path('cart/', include('cart.urls', namespace='cart')),
 path('orders/', include('orders.urls', namespace='orders')),
 path('payment/', include('payment.urls', namespace='payment')),
 path('coupons/', include('coupons.urls', namespace='coupons')),
 path('rosetta/', include('rosetta.urls')),
 path('', include('shop.urls', namespace='shop')),
)
```

You can combine non-translatable standard URL patterns and patterns under
`i18n_patterns` so that some patterns include a language prefix and others don't.
However, it's best to use translated URLs only to avoid the possibility that a carelessly
translated URL matches a non-translated URL pattern.

Run the development server and open `http://127.0.0.1:8000/` in your browser.
Django will perform the steps described previously in the *How Django determines the current
language* section to determine the current language, and it will redirect you to the requested
URL, including the language prefix. Take a look at the URL in your browser; it should now
look like `http://127.0.0.1:8000/en/`. The current language is the one set by the
`Accept-Language` header of your browser if it is Spanish or English, otherwise the default
`LANGUAGE_CODE` (English) defined in your settings.

Translating URL patterns

Django supports translated strings in URL patterns. You can use a different translation for
each language for a single URL pattern. You can mark URL patterns for translation the
same way you would do with literals, using the `ugettext_lazy()` function.

Edit the main `urls.py` file of the `myshop` project and add translation strings to the regular
expressions of the URL patterns for the `cart`, `orders`, `payment`, and `coupons` applications
as follows:

```
from django.utils.translation import gettext_lazy as _

urlpatterns = i18n_patterns(
 path(_('admin/'), admin.site.urls),
 path(_('cart/'), include('cart.urls', namespace='cart')),
 path(_('orders/'), include('orders.urls', namespace='orders')),
 path(_('payment/'), include('payment.urls', namespace='payment')),
 path(_('coupons/'), include('coupons.urls', namespace='coupons')),
 path('rosetta/', include('rosetta.urls')),
 path('', include('shop.urls', namespace='shop')),
)
```

Edit the `urls.py` file of the `orders` application and mark URL patterns for translation as follows:

```
from django.utils.translation import gettext_lazy as _

urlpatterns = [
    path(_('create/'), views.order_create, name='order_create'),
    # ...
]
```

Edit the `urls.py` file of the `payment` application and change the code to the following:

```
from django.utils.translation import gettext_lazy as _

urlpatterns = [
    path(_('process/'), views.payment_process, name='process'),
    path(_('done/'), views.payment_done, name='done'),
    path(_('canceled/'), views.payment_canceled, name='canceled'),
]
```

We don't need to translate the URL patterns of the `shop` application since they are built with variables and do not include any other literals.

Open the shell and run the next command to update the message files with the new translations:

```
django-admin makemessages --all
```

Make sure the development server is running. Open `http://127.0.0.1:8000/en/rosetta/` in your browser and click the **Myshop** link under the **Spanish** section. Now you will see the URL patterns for translation. You can click on **Untranslated only** to only see the strings that have not been translated yet. You can now translate the URLs.

Allowing users to switch language

Since we are serving content that is available in multiple languages, we should let our users switch the site's language. We are going to add a language selector to our site. The language selector will consist of a list of available languages, which are displayed using links.

Edit the `shop/base.html` template of the `shop` application and find the following lines:

```
<div id="header">
  <a href="/" class="logo">{% trans "My shop" %}</a>
</div>
```

Replace them with the following code:

```
<div id="header">
  <a href="/" class="logo">{% trans "My shop" %}</a>

  {% get_current_language as LANGUAGE_CODE %}
  {% get_available_languages as LANGUAGES %}
  {% get_language_info_list for LANGUAGES as languages %}
  <div class="languages">
    <p>{% trans "Language" %}:</p>
    <ul class="languages">
      {% for language in languages %}
        <li>
          <a href="/{{ language.code }}/"
          {% if language.code == LANGUAGE_CODE %} class="selected"{% endif %}>
            {{ language.name_local }}
          </a>
        </li>
      {% endfor %}
    </ul>
  </div>
</div>
```

This is how we build our language selector:

1. First, we load the internationalization tags using `{% load i18n %}`
2. We use the `{% get_current_language %}` tag to retrieve the current language
3. We get the languages defined in the LANGUAGES setting using the `{% get_available_languages %}` template tag
4. We use the tag `{% get_language_info_list %}` to provide easy access to the language attributes
5. We build an HTML list to display all available languages and we add a `selected` class attribute to the current active language

We use the template tags provided by `i18n`, based on the languages available in the settings of your project. Now open `http://127.0.0.1:8000/` in your browser and take a look. You should see the language selector in the top right-hand corner of the site as follows:

Users can now easily switch to their preferred language.

Translating models with django-parler

Django does not provide a solution for translating models out of the box. You have to implement your own solution to manage content stored in different languages, or use a third-party module for model translation. There are several third-party applications that allow you to translate model fields. Each of them takes a different approach to storing and accessing translations. One of these applications is `django-parler`. This module offers a very effective way to translate models and it integrates smoothly with Django's administration site.

`django-parler` generates a separate database table for each model that contains translations. This table includes all the translated fields and a foreign key for the original object that the translation belongs to. It also contains a language field, since each row stores the content for a single language.

Installing django-parler

Install `django-parler` via `pip` using the following command:

```
pip install django-parler==1.9.2
```

Edit the `settings.py` file of your project and add `'parler'` to the `INSTALLED_APPS` setting as follows:

```
INSTALLED_APPS = [
    # ...
    'parler',
]
```

Also add the following code to your settings:

```
PARLER_LANGUAGES = {
    None: (
        {'code': 'en'},
        {'code': 'es'},
    ),
    'default': {
        'fallback': 'en',
        'hide_untranslated': False,
    }
}
```

This setting defines the available languages `en` and `es` for `django-parler`. We specify the default language `en` and we indicate that `django-parler` should not hide untranslated content.

Translating model fields

Let's add translations for our product catalog. `django-parler` provides a `TranslatedModel` model class and a `TranslatedFields` wrapper to translate model fields. Edit the `models.py` file inside the `shop` application directory and add the following import:

```
from parler.models import TranslatableModel, TranslatedFields
```

Then, modify the `Category` model to make the `name` and `slug` fields translatable as follows:

```
class Category(TranslatableModel):
    translations = TranslatedFields(
        name = models.CharField(max_length=200,
                                db_index=True),
        slug = models.SlugField(max_length=200,
                                db_index=True,
                                unique=True)
    )
```

The `Category` model now inherits from `TranslatedModel` instead of `models.Model` and both the `name` and `slug` fields are included in the `TranslatedFields` wrapper.

Edit the `Product` model to add translations for the `name`, `slug`, and `description` fields as follows:

```
class Product(TranslatableModel):
    translations = TranslatedFields(
        name = models.CharField(max_length=200, db_index=True),
        slug = models.SlugField(max_length=200, db_index=True),
        description = models.TextField(blank=True)
    )
    category = models.ForeignKey(Category,
                                 related_name='products')
    image = models.ImageField(upload_to='products/%Y/%m/%d',
                              blank=True)
    price = models.DecimalField(max_digits=10, decimal_places=2)
    available = models.BooleanField(default=True)
    created = models.DateTimeField(auto_now_add=True)
    updated = models.DateTimeField(auto_now=True)
```

`django-parler` manages translations by generating another model for each translatable model. In the following , you can see the fields of the `Product` model and what the generated `ProductTranslation` model will look like:

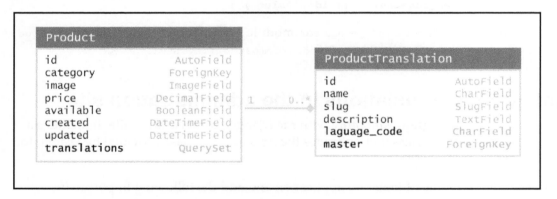

The `ProductTranslation` model generated by `django-parler` includes the `name`, `slug`, and `description` translatable fields, a `language_code` field, and `ForeignKey` for the master `Product` object. There is a one-to-many relationship from `Product` to `ProductTranslation`. A `ProductTranslation` object will exist for each available language of each `Product` object.

Since Django uses a separate table for translations, there are some Django features that we cannot use. It is not possible to use a default ordering by a translated field. You can filter by translated fields in queries, but you cannot include a translatable field in the `ordering` Meta options.

Edit the `models.py` file of the `shop` application and comment out the `ordering` attribute of the `Category` Meta class:

```
class Category(TranslatableModel):
    # ...
    class Meta:
        # ordering = ('name',)
        verbose_name = 'category'
        verbose_name_plural = 'categories'
```

We also have to comment out the `ordering` and `index_together` attributes of the `Product` Meta class. The current version of `django-parler` does not provide support to validate `index_together`. Comment out the `Product` Meta class as follows:

```
class Product(TranslatableModel):
    # ...

    # class Meta:
    #     ordering = ('-name',)
    #     index_together = (('id', 'slug'),)
```

You can read more about `django-parler` module's compatibility with Django at `https://django-parler.readthedocs.io/en/latest/compatibility.html`.

Integrating translations in the administration site

`django-parler` integrates smoothly with the Django administration site. It includes a `TranslatableAdmin` class that overrides the `ModelAdmin` class provided by Django to manage model translations.

Edit the `admin.py` file of the `shop` application and add the following import to it:

```
from parler.admin import TranslatableAdmin
```

Modify the `CategoryAdmin` and `ProductAdmin` classes to inherit from `TranslatableAdmin` instead of `ModelAdmin`. `django-parler` doesn't support the `prepopulated_fields` attribute, but it does support the `get_prepopulated_fields()` method that provides the same functionality. Let's change this accordingly. Edit the `admin.py` file to make it look as follows:

```python
from django.contrib import admin
from .models import Category, Product
from parler.admin import TranslatableAdmin

@admin.register(Category)
class CategoryAdmin(TranslatableAdmin):
    list_display = ['name', 'slug']

    def get_prepopulated_fields(self, request, obj=None):
        return {'slug': ('name',)}

@admin.register(Product)
class ProductAdmin(TranslatableAdmin):
    list_display = ['name', 'slug', 'price',
                    'available', 'created', 'updated']
    list_filter = ['available', 'created', 'updated']
    list_editable = ['price', 'available']

    def get_prepopulated_fields(self, request, obj=None):
        return {'slug': ('name',)}
```

We have adapted the administration site to work with the new translated models. We can now sync the database with the model changes that we made.

Creating migrations for model translations

Open the shell and run the following command to create a new migration for the model translations:

```
python manage.py makemigrations shop --name "translations"
```

You will see the following output:

```
Migrations for 'shop':
  shop/migrations/0002_translations.py
    - Create model CategoryTranslation
    - Create model ProductTranslation
    - Change Meta options on category
    - Change Meta options on product
```

```
- Remove field name from category
- Remove field slug from category
- Alter index_together for product (0 constraint(s))
- Add field master to producttranslation
- Add field master to categorytranslation
- Remove field description from product
- Remove field name from product
- Remove field slug from product
- Alter unique_together for producttranslation (1 constraint(s))
- Alter unique_together for categorytranslation (1 constraint(s))
```

This migration automatically includes the `CategoryTranslation` and `ProductTranslation` models created dynamically by `django-parler`. It's important to note that this migration deletes the previous existing fields from our models. This means that we will lose that data and will need to set our categories and products again in the admin site after running it.

Run the following command to apply the migration:

```
python manage.py migrate shop
```

You will see an output that ends with the following line:

```
Applying shop.0002_translations... OK
```

Our models are now synchronized with the database.

Run the development server using `python manage.py runserver` and open `http://127.0.0.1:8000/en/admin/shop/category/` in your browser. You will see that existing categories lost their name and slug due to deleting those fields and using the translatable models generated by `django-parler` instead. Click on a category to edit it. You will see that the **Change category** page includes two different tabs, one for English and one for Spanish translations:

Make sure to fill in a name and slug for all existing categories. Also add a Spanish translation for each of them and click the **SAVE** button. Make sure to save the changes before you change tabs or you will lose them.

After completing the data for existing categories, open `http://127.0.0.1:8000/en/admin/shop/product/` and edit each of the products providing an English and Spanish name, slug, and description.

Adapting views for translations

We have to adapt our `shop` views to use translation QuerySets. Run the following command to open the Python shell:

```
python manage.py shell
```

Let's take a look at how you can retrieve and query translation fields. To get the object with translatable fields translated in a specific language, you can use Django's `activate()` function as follows:

```
>>> from shop.models import Product
>>> from django.utils.translation import activate
>>> activate('es')
>>> product=Product.objects.first()
>>> product.name
'Té verde'
```

Another way to do this is by using the `language()` manager provided by `django-parler` as follows:

```
>>> product=Product.objects.language('en').first()
>>> product.name
'Green tea'
```

When you access translated fields, they are resolved using the current language. You can set a different current language for an object to access that specific translation as follows:

```
>>> product.set_current_language('es')
>>> product.name
'Té verde'
>>> product.get_current_language()
'es'
```

When performing a QuerySet using `filter()`, you can filter using the related translation objects with the `translations__` syntax as follows:

```
>>> Product.objects.filter(translations__name='Green tea')
<TranslatableQuerySet [<Product: Té verde>]>
```

Let's adapt the product catalog views. Edit the `views.py` file of the `shop` application and in the `product_list` view, find the following line:

```
category = get_object_or_404(Category, slug=category_slug)
```

Replace it with the following ones:

```
language = request.LANGUAGE_CODE
category = get_object_or_404(Category,
                            translations__language_code=language,
                            translations__slug=category_slug)
```

Then, edit the `product_detail` view and find the following lines:

```
product = get_object_or_404(Product,
                            id=id,
                            slug=slug,
                            available=True)
```

Replace them with the following code:

```
language = request.LANGUAGE_CODE
product = get_object_or_404(Product,
                            id=id,
                            translations__language_code=language,
                            translations__slug=slug,
                            available=True)
```

The `product_list` and `product_detail` views are now adapted to retrieve objects using translated fields. Run the development server and open `http://127.0.0.1:8000/es/` in your browser. You should see the product list page, including all products translated into Spanish:

Now each product's URL is built using the `slug` field translated into the current language. For example, the URL for a product in Spanish is `http://127.0.0.1:8000/es/2/te-rojo/`, whereas in English the URL is `http://127.0.0.1:8000/en/2/red-tea/`. If you navigate to a product detail page, you will see the translated URL and the contents of the selected language, as shown in the following example:

If you want to know more about `django-parler`, you can find the full documentation at `https://django-parler.readthedocs.io/en/latest/`.

You have learned how to translate Python code, templates, URL patterns, and model fields. To complete the internationalization and localization process, we need to use localized formatting for dates, times, and numbers as well.

Format localization

Depending on the user's locale, you might want to display dates, times, and numbers in different formats. The localized formatting can be activated by changing the `USE_L10N` setting to `True` in the `settings.py` file of your project.

When USE_L10N is enabled, Django will try to use a locale-specific format whenever it outputs a value in a template. You can see that decimal numbers in the English version of your site are displayed with a dot separator for decimal places, while in the Spanish version they are displayed using a comma. This is due to the locale formats specified for the es locale by Django. You can take a look at the Spanish formatting configuration at https://github.com/django/django/blob/stable/2.0.x/django/conf/locale/es/formats.py.

Normally, you will set the USE_L10N setting to True and let Django apply the format localization for each locale. However, there might be situations in which you don't want to use localized values. This is especially relevant when outputting JavaScript or JSON that has to provide a machine-readable format.

Django offers a {% localize %} template tag that allows you to turn on/off localization for template fragments. This gives you control over localized formatting. You will have to load the l10n tags to be able to use this template tag. The following is an example of how to turn localization on and off in a template:

```
{% load l10n %}

{% localize on %}
  {{ value }}
{% endlocalize %}

{% localize off %}
  {{ value }}
{% endlocalize %}
```

Django also offers the localize and unlocalize template filters to force or avoid localization of a value. These filters can be applied as follows:

```
{{ value|localize }}
{{ value|unlocalize }}
```

You can also create custom format files to specify locale formatting. You can find further information about format localization at https://docs.djangoproject.com/en/2.0/topics/i18n/formatting/.

Using django-localflavor to validate form fields

`django-localflavor` is a third-party module that contains a collection of specific utils, such as form fields or model fields that are specific for each country. It's very useful to validate local regions, local phone numbers, identity card numbers, social security numbers, and so on. The package is organized into a series of modules named after ISO 3166 country codes.

Install `django-localflavor` using the following command:

```
pip install django-localflavor==2.0
```

Edit the `settings.py` file of your project and add `localflavor` to the `INSTALLED_APPS` setting as follows:

```
INSTALLED_APPS = [
    # ...
    'localflavor',
]
```

We are going to add the United States's zip code field so that a valid U.S. zip code is required to create a new order.

Edit the `forms.py` file of the `orders` application and make it look as follows:

```
from django import forms
from .models import Order
from localflavor.us.forms import USZipCodeField

class OrderCreateForm(forms.ModelForm):
    postal_code = USZipCodeField()
    class Meta:
        model = Order
        fields = ['first_name', 'last_name', 'email', 'address',
                  'postal_code', 'city']
```

We import the `USZipCodeField` field from the `us` package of `localflavor` and use it for the `postal_code` field of the `OrderCreateForm` form.

Run the development server and open `http://127.0.0.1:8000/en/orders/create/` in your browser. Fill in all fields, enter a three-letter postal code, and then submit the form. You will get the following validation error that is raised by `USZipCodeField`:

```
Enter a zip code in the format XXXXX or XXXXX-XXXX.
```

This is just a brief example of how to use a custom field from `localflavor` in your own project for validation purposes. The local components provided by `localflavor` are very useful to adapt your application to specific countries. You can read the `django-localflavor` documentation and see all available local components for each country at `https://django-localflavor.readthedocs.io/en/latest/`.

Next, we are going to build a recommendation engine into our shop.

Building a recommendation engine

A recommendation engine is a system that predicts the preference or rating that a user would give to an item. The system selects relevant items for the users based on their behavior and the knowledge it has about them. Nowadays, recommendation systems are used in many online services. They help users by selecting the stuff they might be interested in from the vast amount of available data that is irrelevant to them. Offering good recommendations enhances user engagement. E-commerce sites also benefit from offering relevant product recommendations by increasing their average sale.

We are going to create a simple, yet powerful, recommendation engine that suggests products that are usually bought together. We will suggest products based on historical sales, thus identifying products that are usually bought together. We are going to suggest complementary products in two different scenarios:

- **Product detail page**: We will display a list of products that are usually bought with the given product. This will be displayed as: **Users who bought this also bought X, Y, Z**. We need a data structure that allows us to store the number of times that each product has been bought together with the product being displayed.
- **Cart detail page**: Based on the products users add to the cart, we are going to suggest products that are usually bought together with these ones. In this case, the score we calculate to obtain related products has to be aggregated.

We are going to use Redis to store products that are purchased together. Remember that you already used Redis in `Chapter 6`, *Tracking User Actions*. If you haven't installed Redis yet, you can find installation instructions in that chapter.

Recommending products based on previous purchases

Now, we will recommend products to users based on what they have added to the cart. We are going to store a key in Redis for each product bought on our site. The product key will contain a Redis sorted set with scores. We will increment the score by 1 for each product bought together every time a new purchase is completed.

When an order is successfully paid for, we store a key for each product bought, including a sorted set of products that belong to the same order. The sorted set allows us to give scores for products that are bought together.

Remember to install `redis-py` in your environment using the following command:

```
pip install redis==2.10.6
```

Edit the `settings.py` file of your project and add the following settings to it:

```
REDIS_HOST = 'localhost'
REDIS_PORT = 6379
REDIS_DB = 1
```

These are the settings required to establish a connection with the Redis server. Create a new file inside the `shop` application directory and name it `recommender.py`. Add the following code to it:

```python
import redis
from django.conf import settings
from .models import Product

# connect to redis
r = redis.StrictRedis(host=settings.REDIS_HOST,
                      port=settings.REDIS_PORT,
                      db=settings.REDIS_DB)


class Recommender(object):

    def get_product_key(self, id):
        return 'product:{}:purchased_with'.format(id)

    def products_bought(self, products):
        product_ids = [p.id for p in products]
        for product_id in product_ids:
            for with_id in product_ids:
                # get the other products bought with each product
```

```
if product_id != with_id:
    # increment score for product purchased together
    r.zincrby(self.get_product_key(product_id),
              with_id,
              amount=1)
```

This is the `Recommender` class that will allow us to store product purchases and retrieve product suggestions for a given product or products. The `get_product_key()` method receives an ID of a `Product` object and builds the Redis key for the sorted set where related products are stored, which looks like `product:[id]:purchased_with`.

The `products_bought()` method receives a list of `Product` objects that have been bought together (that is, belong to the same order). In this method, we perform the following tasks:

1. We get the product IDs for the given `Product` objects.
2. We iterate over the product IDs. For each ID, we iterate over the product IDs and skip the same product so that we get the products that are bought together with each product.
3. We get the Redis product key for each product bought using the `get_product_id()` method. For a product with an ID of 33, this method returns the key `product:33:purchased_with`. This is the key for the sorted set that contains the product IDs of products that were bought together with this one.
4. We increment the score of each product ID contained in the sorted set by 1. The score represents the times another product has been bought together with the given product.

So we have a method to store and score the products that were bought together. Now we need a method to retrieve the products that are bought together for a list of given products. Add the following `suggest_products_for()` method to the `Recommender` class:

```
def suggest_products_for(self, products, max_results=6):
    product_ids = [p.id for p in products]
    if len(products) == 1:
        # only 1 product
        suggestions = r.zrange(
                    self.get_product_key(product_ids[0]),
                    0, -1, desc=True)[:max_results]
    else:
        # generate a temporary key
        flat_ids = ''.join([str(id) for id in product_ids])
        tmp_key = 'tmp_{}'.format(flat_ids)
        # multiple products, combine scores of all products
        # store the resulting sorted set in a temporary key
```

```
        keys = [self.get_product_key(id) for id in product_ids]
        r.zunionstore(tmp_key, keys)
        # remove ids for the products the recommendation is for
        r.zrem(tmp_key, *product_ids)
        # get the product ids by their score, descendant sort
        suggestions = r.zrange(tmp_key, 0, -1,
                                 desc=True)[:max_results]
        # remove the temporary key
        r.delete(tmp_key)
    suggested_products_ids = [int(id) for id in suggestions]

    # get suggested products and sort by order of appearance
    suggested_products =
list(Product.objects.filter(id__in=suggested_products_ids))
    suggested_products.sort(key=lambda x:
suggested_products_ids.index(x.id))
    return suggested_products
```

The `suggest_products_for()` method receives the following parameters:

- `products`: This is a list of `Product` objects to get recommendations for. It can contain one or more products.
- `max_results`: This is an integer that represents the maximum number of recommendations to return.

In this method, we perform the following actions:

1. We get the product IDs for the given `Product` objects.
2. If only one product is given, we retrieve the ID of the products that were bought together with the given product, ordered by the total number of times that they were bought together. To do so, we use Redis' ZRANGE command. We limit the number of results to the number specified in the `max_results` attribute (6 by default).
3. If more than one product is given, we generate a temporary Redis key built with the IDs of the products.
4. We combine and sum all scores for the items contained in the sorted set of each of the given products. This is done using the Redis' ZUNIONSTORE command. The ZUNIONSTORE command performs a union of the sorted sets with the given keys, and stores the aggregated sum of scores of the elements in a new Redis key. You can read more about this command at https://redis.io/commands/ ZUNIONSTORE. We save the aggregated scores in the temporary key.

5. Since we are aggregating scores, we might obtain the same products we are getting recommendations for. We remove them from the generated sorted set using the ZREM command.

6. We retrieve the IDs of the products from the temporary key, ordered by their score using the ZRANGE command. We limit the number of results to the number specified in the max_results attribute. Then we remove the temporary key.

7. Finally, we get the Product objects with the given IDs and we order the products in the same order as them.

For practical purposes, let's also add a method to clear the recommendations. Add the following method to the Recommender class:

```
def clear_purchases(self):
    for id in Product.objects.values_list('id', flat=True):
        r.delete(self.get_product_key(id))
```

Let's try our recommendation engine. Make sure you include several Product objects in the database and initialize the Redis server using the following command from the shell in your Redis directory:

src/redis-server

Open another shell, and run the following command to open the Python shell:

python manage.py shell

Make sure to have at least four different products in your database. Retrieve four different products by their name:

```
>>> from shop.models import Product
>>> black_tea = Product.objects.get(translations__name='Black tea')
>>> red_tea = Product.objects.get(translations__name='Red tea')
>>> green_tea = Product.objects.get(translations__name='Green tea')
>>> tea_powder = Product.objects.get(translations__name='Tea powder')
```

Then, add some test purchases to the recommendation engine:

```
>>> from shop.recommender import Recommender
>>> r = Recommender()
>>> r.products_bought([black_tea, red_tea])
>>> r.products_bought([black_tea, green_tea])
>>> r.products_bought([red_tea, black_tea, tea_powder])
>>> r.products_bought([green_tea, tea_powder])
>>> r.products_bought([black_tea, tea_powder])
>>> r.products_bought([red_tea, green_tea])
```

We have stored the following scores:

```
black_tea:  red_tea (2), tea_powder (2), green_tea (1)
red_tea:    black_tea (2), tea_powder (1), green_tea (1)
green_tea:  black_tea (1), tea_powder (1), red_tea(1)
tea_powder: black_tea (2), red_tea (1), green_tea (1)
```

Let's activate a language to retrieve translated products and get product recommendations to buy together with a given single product:

```
>>> from django.utils.translation import activate
>>> activate('en')
>>> r.suggest_products_for([black_tea])
[<Product: Tea powder>, <Product: Red tea>, <Product: Green tea>]
>>> r.suggest_products_for([red_tea])
[<Product: Black tea>, <Product: Tea powder>, <Product: Green tea>]
>>> r.suggest_products_for([green_tea])
[<Product: Black tea>, <Product: Tea powder>, <Product: Red tea>]
>>> r.suggest_products_for([tea_powder])
[<Product: Black tea>, <Product: Red tea>, <Product: Green tea>]
```

You can see that the order for recommended products is based on their score. Let's get recommendations for multiple products with aggregated scores:

```
>>> r.suggest_products_for([black_tea, red_tea])
[<Product: Tea powder>, <Product: Green tea>]
>>> r.suggest_products_for([green_tea, red_tea])
[<Product: Black tea>, <Product: Tea powder>]
>>> r.suggest_products_for([tea_powder, black_tea])
[<Product: Red tea>, <Product: Green tea>]
```

You can see that the order of the suggested products matches the aggregated scores. For example, products suggested for black_tea and red_tea are tea_powder (2+1) and green_tea (1+1).

We have verified that our recommendation algorithm works as expected. Let's display recommendations for products on our site.

Edit the `views.py` file of the `shop` application. Add the functionality to retrieve a maximum of four recommended products in the `product_detail` view as follows:

```python
from .recommender import Recommender

def product_detail(request, id, slug):
    language = request.LANGUAGE_CODE
    product = get_object_or_404(Product,
                                id=id,
                                translations__language_code=language,
                                translations__slug=slug,
                                available=True)
    cart_product_form = CartAddProductForm()

    r = Recommender()
    recommended_products = r.suggest_products_for([product], 4)

    return render(request,
                  'shop/product/detail.html',
                  {'product': product,
                   'cart_product_form': cart_product_form,
                   'recommended_products': recommended_products})
```

Edit the `shop/product/detail.html` template of the `shop` application and add the following code after `{{ product.description|linebreaks }}`:

```html
{% if recommended_products %}
  <div class="recommendations">
    <h3>{% trans "People who bought this also bought" %}</h3>
    {% for p in recommended_products %}
      <div class="item">
        <a href="{{ p.get_absolute_url }}">
          <img src="{% if p.image %}{{ p.image.url }}{% else %}
          {% static  "img/no_image.png" %}{% endif %}">
        </a>
        <p><a href="{{ p.get_absolute_url }}">{{ p.name }}</a></p>
      </div>
    {% endfor %}
  </div>
{% endif %}
```

Run the development server and open `http://127.0.0.1:8000/en/` in your browser. Click on any product to view its details. You should see that recommended products are displayed below the product, as shown in the following screenshot:

We are also going to include product recommendations in the cart. The recommendation will be based on the products that the user has added to the cart.

Edit `views.py` inside the `cart` application, import the `Recommender` class, and edit the `cart_detail` view to make it look as follows:

```python
from shop.recommender import Recommender

def cart_detail(request):
    cart = Cart(request)
    for item in cart:
        item['update_quantity_form'] = CartAddProductForm(
            initial={'quantity': item['quantity'],
            'update': True})

    coupon_apply_form = CouponApplyForm()
```

```
    r = Recommender()
    cart_products = [item['product'] for item in cart]
    recommended_products = r.suggest_products_for(cart_products,
                                                  max_results=4)

return render(request,
              'cart/detail.html',
              {'cart': cart,
               'coupon_apply_form': coupon_apply_form,
               'recommended_products': recommended_products})
```

Edit the `cart/detail.html` template of the `cart` application and add the following code just after the `</table>` HTML tag:

```
{% if recommended_products %}
  <div class="recommendations cart">
    <h3>{% trans "People who bought this also bought" %}</h3>
    {% for p in recommended_products %}
      <div class="item">
        <a href="{{ p.get_absolute_url }}">
          <img src="{% if p.image %}{{ p.image.url }}{% else %}
          {% static "img/no_image.png" %}{% endif %}">
        </a>
        <p><a href="{{ p.get_absolute_url }}">{{ p.name }}</a></p>
      </div>
    {% endfor %}
  </div>
{% endif %}
```

Open `http://127.0.0.1:8000/en/` in your browser and add a couple of products to your cart. When you navigate to `http://127.0.0.1:8000/en/cart/`, you should see the aggregated product recommendations for the items in the cart as follows:

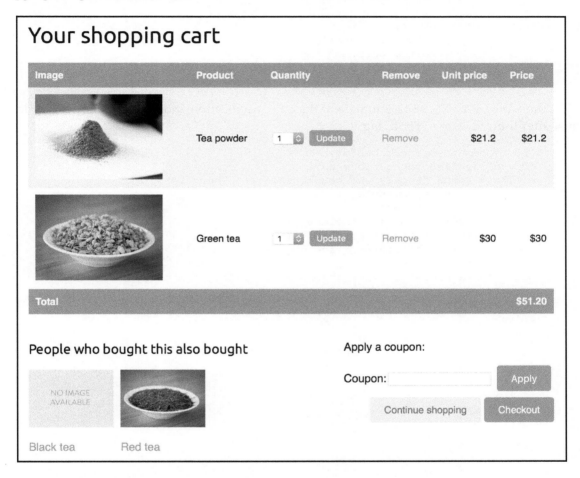

Congratulations! You have built a complete recommendation engine using Django and Redis.

Summary

In this chapter, you created a coupon system using sessions. You learned how internationalization and localization work. You also built a recommendation engine using Redis.

In the next chapter, you will start a new project. You will build an e-learning platform with Django using class-based views and you will create a custom content management system.

Building an E-Learning Platform 10

In the previous chapter, you added internationalization to your online shop project. You also built a coupon system and a product recommendation engine. In this chapter, you will create a new project. You will build an e-learning platform, creating a custom **Content Management System (CMS)**.

In this chapter, you will learn how to:

- Create fixtures for your models
- Use model inheritance
- Create custom model fields
- Use class-based views and mixins
- Build formsets
- Manage groups and permissions
- Create a CMS

Setting up the e-learning project

Our final practical project will be an e-learning platform. In this chapter, we are going to build a flexible CMS that allows instructors to create courses and manage their contents.

First, create a virtual environment for your new project and activate it with the following commands:

```
mkdir env
virtualenv env/educa
source env/educa/bin/activate
```

Install Django in your virtual environment with the following command:

```
pip install Django==2.0.5
```

We are going to manage image uploads in our project, so we also need to install `Pillow` with the following command:

```
pip install Pillow==5.1.0
```

Create a new project using the following command:

```
django-admin startproject educa
```

Enter the new `educa` directory and create a new application using the following commands:

```
cd educa
django-admin startapp courses
```

Edit the `settings.py` file of the `educa` project and add `courses` to the `INSTALLED_APPS` setting as follows:

```
INSTALLED_APPS = [
    'courses.apps.CoursesConfig',
    'django.contrib.admin',
    'django.contrib.auth',
    'django.contrib.contenttypes',
    'django.contrib.sessions',
    'django.contrib.messages',
    'django.contrib.staticfiles',
]
```

The `courses` application is now active for the project. Let's define the models for courses and course contents.

Building the course models

Our e-learning platform will offer courses on various subjects. Each course will be divided into a configurable number of modules, and each module will contain a configurable number of contents. There will be contents of various types: text, file, image, or video. The following example shows what the data structure of our course catalog will look like:

```
Subject 1
  Course 1
    Module 1
```

```
   Content 1 (image)
   Content 2 (text)
Module 2
   Content 3 (text)
   Content 4 (file)
   Content 5 (video)
   ...
```

Let's build the course models. Edit the `models.py` file of the `courses` application and add the following code to it:

```python
from django.db import models
from django.contrib.auth.models import User

class Subject(models.Model):
    title = models.CharField(max_length=200)
    slug = models.SlugField(max_length=200, unique=True)

    class Meta:
        ordering = ['title']

    def __str__(self):
        return self.title

class Course(models.Model):
    owner = models.ForeignKey(User,
                              related_name='courses_created',
                              on_delete=models.CASCADE)
    subject = models.ForeignKey(Subject,
                                related_name='courses',
                                on_delete=models.CASCADE)
    title = models.CharField(max_length=200)
    slug = models.SlugField(max_length=200, unique=True)
    overview = models.TextField()
    created = models.DateTimeField(auto_now_add=True)

    class Meta:
        ordering = ['-created']

    def __str__(self):
        return self.title


class Module(models.Model):
    course = models.ForeignKey(Course,
                               related_name='modules',
                               on_delete=models.CASCADE)
```

```
title = models.CharField(max_length=200)
description = models.TextField(blank=True)

def __str__(self):
    return self.title
```

These are the initial `Subject`, `Course`, and `Module` models. The `Course` model fields are as follows:

- `owner`: The instructor that created this course.
- `subject`: The subject that this course belongs to. A `ForeignKey` field that points to the `Subject` model.
- `title`: The title of the course.
- `slug`: The slug of the course. This will be used in URLs later.
- `overview`: This is a `TextField` column to include an overview of the course.
- `created`: The date and time when the course was created. It will be automatically set by Django when creating new objects because of `auto_now_add=True`.

Each course is divided into several modules. Therefore, the `Module` model contains a `ForeignKey` field that points to the `Course` model.

Open the shell and run the following command to create the initial migration for this app:

```
python manage.py makemigrations
```

You will see the following output:

```
Migrations for 'courses':
  0001_initial.py:
    - Create model Course
    - Create model Module
    - Create model Subject
    - Add field subject to course
```

Then, run the following command to apply all migrations to the database:

```
python manage.py migrate
```

You should see output including all applied migrations, including those of Django. The output will contain the following line:

```
Applying courses.0001_initial... OK
```

The models of our `courses` app have been synced to the database.

Registering the models in the administration site

Let's add the course models to the administration site. Edit the `admin.py` file inside the `courses` application directory and add the following code to it:

```
from django.contrib import admin
from .models import Subject, Course, Module

@admin.register(Subject)
class SubjectAdmin(admin.ModelAdmin):
    list_display = ['title', 'slug']
    prepopulated_fields = {'slug': ('title',)}

class ModuleInline(admin.StackedInline):
    model = Module

@admin.register(Course)
class CourseAdmin(admin.ModelAdmin):
    list_display = ['title', 'subject', 'created']
    list_filter = ['created', 'subject']
    search_fields = ['title', 'overview']
    prepopulated_fields = {'slug': ('title',)}
    inlines = [ModuleInline]
```

The models for the course application are now registered in the administration site. Remember, we use the `@admin.register()` decorator to register models in the administration site.

Using fixtures to provide initial data for models

Sometimes you might want to pre-populate your database with hardcoded data. This is useful to automatically include initial data in the project setup instead of having to add it manually. Django comes with a simple way to load and dump data from the database into files that are called **fixtures**.

Django supports fixtures in JSON, XML, or YAML formats. We are going to create a fixture to include several initial `Subject` objects for our project.

First, create a superuser using the following command:

```
python manage.py createsuperuser
```

Then, run the development server using the following command:

```
python manage.py runserver
```

Open `http://127.0.0.1:8000/admin/courses/subject/` in your browser. Create several subjects using the administration site. The list display page should look as follows:

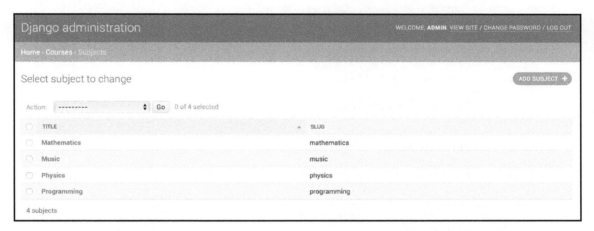

Run the following command from the shell:

```
python manage.py dumpdata courses --indent=2
```

You will see output similar to the following:

```
[
{
  "model": "courses.subject",
  "pk": 1,
  "fields": {
    "title": "Mathematics",
    "slug": "mathematics"
  }
},
{
  "model": "courses.subject",
  "pk": 2,
  "fields": {
    "title": "Music",
    "slug": "music"
  }
},
{
```

```
      "model": "courses.subject",
      "pk": 3,
      "fields": {
        "title": "Physics",
        "slug": "physics"
      }
    },
    {
      "model": "courses.subject",
      "pk": 4,
      "fields": {
        "title": "Programming",
        "slug": "programming"
      }
    }
  }
  ]
```

The `dumpdata` command dumps data from the database into the standard output, serialized in JSON format by default. The resulting data structure includes information about the model and its fields for Django to be able to load it into the database.

You can limit the output to the models of an application by providing the application names to the command or specifying single models for outputting data using the `app.Model` format. You can also specify the format using the `--format` flag. By default, `dumpdata` outputs the serialized data to the standard output. However, you can indicate an output file using the `--output` flag. The `--indent` flag allows you to specify indentation. For more information on `dumpdata` parameters, run `python manage.py dumpdata --help`.

Save this dump to a fixtures file into a `fixtures/` directory in the `orders` application using the following commands:

```
mkdir courses/fixtures
python manage.py dumpdata courses --indent=2 --
output=courses/fixtures/subjects.json
```

Run the development server and use the administration site to remove the subjects you created. Then, load the fixture into the database using the following command:

```
python manage.py loaddata subjects.json
```

All `Subject` objects included in the fixture are loaded into the database.

By default, Django looks for files in the `fixtures/` directory of each application, but you can specify the complete path to the fixture file for the `loaddata` command. You can also use the `FIXTURE_DIRS` setting to tell Django additional directories to look for fixtures.

 Fixtures are not only useful for setting up initial data, but also to provide sample data for your application or data required for your tests.

You can read about how to use fixtures for testing at `https://docs.djangoproject.com/en/2.0/topics/testing/tools/#fixture-loading`.

If you want to load fixtures in model migrations, take a look at Django's documentation about data migrations. You can find the documentation for migrating data at `https://docs.djangoproject.com/en/2.0/topics/migrations/#data-migrations`.

Creating models for diverse content

We plan to add different types of content to the course modules such as texts, images, files, and videos. We need a versatile data model that allows us to store diverse content. In `Chapter 6`, *Tracking User Actions*, you have learned the convenience of using generic relations to create foreign keys that can point to objects of any model. We are going to create a `Content` model that represents the modules' contents and define a generic relation to associate any kind of content.

Edit the `models.py` file of the `courses` application and add the following imports:

```
from django.contrib.contenttypes.models import ContentType
from django.contrib.contenttypes.fields import GenericForeignKey
```

Then, add the following code to the end of the file:

```
class Content(models.Model):
    module = models.ForeignKey(Module,
                               related_name='contents',
                               on_delete=models.CASCADE)
    content_type = models.ForeignKey(ContentType,
                                     on_delete=models.CASCADE)
    object_id = models.PositiveIntegerField()
    item = GenericForeignKey('content_type', 'object_id')
```

This is the `Content` model. A module contains multiple contents, so we define a `ForeignKey` field to the `Module` model. We also set up a generic relation to associate objects from different models that represent different types of content. Remember that we need three different fields to set up a generic relationship. In our `Content` model, these are:

- `content_type`: A `ForeignKey` field to the `ContentType` model
- `object_id`: This is `PositiveIntegerField` to store the primary key of the related object
- `item`: A `GenericForeignKey` field to the related object by combining the two previous fields

Only the `content_type` and `object_id` fields have a corresponding column in the database table of this model. The `item` field allows you to retrieve or set the related object directly, and its functionality is built on top of the other two fields.

We are going to use a different model for each type of content. Our content models will have some common fields, but they will differ in the actual data they can store.

Using model inheritance

Django supports model inheritance. It works in a similar way to standard class inheritance in Python. Django offers the following three options to use model inheritance:

- **Abstract models**: Useful when you want to put some common information into several models. No database table is created for the abstract model.
- **Multi-table model inheritance**: Applicable when each model in the hierarchy is considered a complete model by itself. A database table is created for each model.
- **Proxy models**: Useful when you need to change the behavior of a model, for example, by including additional methods, changing the default manager, or using different meta options. No database table is created for proxy models.

Let's take a closer look at each of them.

Abstract models

An **abstract model** is a base class in which you define fields you want to include in all child models. Django doesn't create any database table for abstract models. A database table is created for each child model, including the fields inherited from the abstract class and the ones defined in the child model.

To mark a model as abstract, you need to include abstract=True in its Meta class. Django will recognize that it is an abstract model and will not create a database table for it. To create child models, you just need to subclass the abstract model.

The following example shows an abstract Content model and a child Text model:

```
from django.db import models

class BaseContent(models.Model):
    title = models.CharField(max_length=100)
    created = models.DateTimeField(auto_now_add=True)

    class Meta:
        abstract = True

class Text(BaseContent):
    body = models.TextField()
```

In this case, Django would create a table for the Text model only, including the title, created, and body fields.

Multi-table model inheritance

In multi-table inheritance, each model corresponds to a database table. Django creates a OneToOneField field for the relationship in the child's model to its parent.

To use multi-table inheritance, you have to subclass an existing model. Django will create a database table for both the original model and the sub-model. The following example shows multi-table inheritance:

```
from django.db import models

class BaseContent(models.Model):
    title = models.CharField(max_length=100)
    created = models.DateTimeField(auto_now_add=True)

class Text(BaseContent):
    body = models.TextField()
```

Django would include an automatically generated `OneToOneField` field in the `Text` model and create a database table for each model.

Proxy models

Proxy models are used to change the behavior of a model, for example, by including additional methods or different meta options. Both models operate on the database table of the original model. To create a proxy model, add `proxy=True` to the `Meta` class of the model.

The following example illustrates how to create a proxy model:

```python
from django.db import models
from django.utils import timezone

class BaseContent(models.Model):
    title = models.CharField(max_length=100)
    created = models.DateTimeField(auto_now_add=True)

class OrderedContent(BaseContent):
    class Meta:
        proxy = True
        ordering = ['created']

    def created_delta(self):
        return timezone.now() - self.created
```

Here, we define an `OrderedContent` model that is a proxy model for the `Content` model. This model provides a default ordering for QuerySets and an additional `created_delta()` method. Both models, `Content` and `OrderedContent`, operate on the same database table, and objects are accessible via the ORM through either model.

Creating the content models

The `Content` model of our `courses` application contains a generic relation to associate different types of content to it. We will create a different model for each type of content. All content models will have some fields in common and additional fields to store custom data. We are going to create an abstract model that provides the common fields for all content models.

Edit the `models.py` file of the `courses` application and add the following code to it:

```python
class ItemBase(models.Model):
    owner = models.ForeignKey(User,
                              related_name='%(class)s_related',
                              on_delete=models.CASCADE)
    title = models.CharField(max_length=250)
    created = models.DateTimeField(auto_now_add=True)
    updated = models.DateTimeField(auto_now=True)

    class Meta:
        abstract = True

    def __str__(self):
        return self.title

class Text(ItemBase):
    content = models.TextField()

class File(ItemBase):
    file = models.FileField(upload_to='files')

class Image(ItemBase):
    file = models.FileField(upload_to='images')

class Video(ItemBase):
    url = models.URLField()
```

In this code, we define an abstract model named `ItemBase`. Therefore, we have set `abstract=True` in its `Meta` class. In this model, we define the `owner`, `title`, `created`, and `updated` fields. These common fields will be used for all types of content. The `owner` field allows us to store which user created the content. Since this field is defined in an abstract class, we need different `related_name` for each sub-model. Django allows us to specify a placeholder for the `model` class name in the `related_name` attribute as `%(class)s`. By doing so, `related_name` for each child model will be generated automatically. Since we use `'%(class)s_related'` as `related_name`, the reverse relation for child models will be `text_related`, `file_related`, `image_related`, and `video_related` respectively.

We have defined four different content models, which inherit from the ItemBase abstract model. These are as follows:

- Text: To store text content
- File: To store files, such as PDF
- Image: To store image files
- Video: To store videos; we use an URLField field to provide a video URL in order to embed it

Each child model contains the fields defined in the ItemBase class in addition to its own fields. A database table will be created for the Text, File, Image, and Video models respectively. There will be no database table associated to the ItemBase model since it is an abstract model.

Edit the Content model you created previously and modify its content_type field as follows:

```
content_type = models.ForeignKey(ContentType,
                    on_delete=models.CASCADE,
                    limit_choices_to={'model__in':(
                                        'text',
                                        'video',
                                        'image',
                                        'file')})
```

We add a limit_choices_to argument to limit the ContentType objects that can be used for the generic relationship. We use the model__in field lookup to filter the query to the ContentType objects with a model attribute that is 'text', 'video', 'image', or 'file'.

Let's create a migration to include the new models we have added. Run the following command from the command line:

```
python manage.py makemigrations
```

You will see the following output:

```
Migrations for 'courses':
  courses/migrations/0002_content_file_image_text_video.py
    - Create model Content
    - Create model File
    - Create model Image
    - Create model Text
    - Create model Video
```

Then, run the following command to apply the new migration:

```
python manage.py migrate
```

The output you see should end with the following line:

```
Applying courses.0002_content_file_image_text_video... OK
```

We have created models that are suitable to add diverse content to the course modules. However, there is still something missing in our models. The course modules and contents should follow a particular order. We need a field that allows us to order them easily.

Creating custom model fields

Django comes with a complete collection of model fields that you can use to build your models. However, you can also create your own model fields to store custom data or alter the behavior of existing fields.

We need a field that allows us to define an order for objects. An easy way to specify an order for objects using existing Django fields is by adding a PositiveIntegerField to your models. Using integers, we can easily specify the order of objects. We can create a custom order field that inherits from PositiveIntegerField and provides additional behavior.

There are two relevant functionalities that we will build into our order field:

- **Automatically assign an order value when no specific order is provided**: When saving a new object with no specific order, our field should automatically assign the number that comes after the last existing ordered object. If there are two objects with order 1 and 2 respectively, when saving a third object, we should automatically assign the order 3 to it if no specific order has been provided.
- **Order objects with respect to other fields**: Course modules will be ordered with respect to the course they belong to and module contents with respect to the module they belong to.

Create a new fields.py file inside the courses application directory and add the following code to it:

```
from django.db import models
from django.core.exceptions import ObjectDoesNotExist

class OrderField(models.PositiveIntegerField):
    def __init__(self, for_fields=None, *args, **kwargs):
```

```
    self.for_fields = for_fields
    super(OrderField, self).__init__(*args, **kwargs)

def pre_save(self, model_instance, add):
    if getattr(model_instance, self.attname) is None:
        # no current value
        try:
            qs = self.model.objects.all()
            if self.for_fields:
                # filter by objects with the same field values
                # for the fields in "for_fields"
                query = {field: getattr(model_instance, field)\
                for field in self.for_fields}
                qs = qs.filter(**query)
            # get the order of the last item
            last_item = qs.latest(self.attname)
            value = last_item.order + 1
        except ObjectDoesNotExist:
            value = 0
        setattr(model_instance, self.attname, value)
        return value
    else:
        return super(OrderField,
                     self).pre_save(model_instance, add)
```

This is our custom `OrderField`. It inherits from the `PositiveIntegerField` field provided by Django. Our `OrderField` field takes an optional `for_fields` parameter that allows us to indicate the fields that the order has to be calculated with respect to.

Our field overrides the `pre_save()` method of the `PositiveIntegerField` field, which is executed before saving the field into the database. In this method, we perform the following actions:

1. We check if a value already exists for this field in the model instance. We use `self.attname`, which is the attribute name given to the field in the model. If the attribute's value is different than `None`, we calculate the order we should give it as follows:
    1. We build a QuerySet to retrieve all objects for the field's model. We retrieve the model class the field belongs to by accessing `self.model`.
    2. We filter the QuerySet by the fields' current value for the model fields that are defined in the `for_fields` parameter of the field, if any. By doing so, we calculate the order with respect to the given fields.

3. We retrieve the object with the highest order with `last_item = qs.latest(self.attname)` from the database. If no object is found, we assume this object is the first one and assign the order 0 to it.

4. If an object is found, we add 1 to the highest order found.

5. We assign the calculated order to the field's value in the model instance using `setattr()` and return it.

2. If the model instance has a value for the current field, we don't do anything.

 When you create custom model fields, make them generic. Avoid hardcoding data that depends on a specific model or field. Your field should work in any model.

You can find more information about writing custom model fields at `https://docs.djangoproject.com/en/2.0/howto/custom-model-fields/`.

Adding ordering to module and content objects

Let's add the new field to our models. Edit the `models.py` file of the `courses` application, and import the `OrderField` class and a field to the `Module` model as follows:

```python
from .fields import OrderField

class Module(models.Model):
    # ...
    order = OrderField(blank=True, for_fields=['course'])
```

We name the new field `order`, and we specify that the ordering is calculated with respect to the course by setting `for_fields=['course']`. This means that the order for a new module will be assigned adding 1 to the last module of the same `Course` object. Now, you can edit the `__str__()` method of the `Module` model to include its order as follows:

```python
class Module(models.Model):
    # ...
    def __str__(self):
        return '{}. {}'.format(self.order, self.title)
```

Module contents also need to follow a particular order. Add an `OrderField` field to the `Content` model as follows:

```python
class Content(models.Model):
    # ...
    order = OrderField(blank=True, for_fields=['module'])
```

This time, we specify that the order is calculated with respect to the `module` field. Finally, let's add a default ordering for both models. Add the following `Meta` class to the `Module` and `Content` models:

```python
class Module(models.Model):
    # ...
    class Meta:
        ordering = ['order']


class Content(models.Model):
    # ...
    class Meta:
        ordering = ['order']
```

The `Module` and `Content` models should now look as follows:

```python
class Module(models.Model):
    course = models.ForeignKey(Course,
                               related_name='modules',
                               on_delete=models.CASCADE)
    title = models.CharField(max_length=200)
    description = models.TextField(blank=True)
    order = OrderField(blank=True, for_fields=['course'])

    class Meta:
        ordering = ['order']

    def __str__(self):
        return '{}. {}'.format(self.order, self.title)

class Content(models.Model):
    module = models.ForeignKey(Module,
                               related_name='contents',
                               on_delete=models.CASCADE)
    content_type = models.ForeignKey(ContentType,
                                     on_delete=models.CASCADE,
                                     limit_choices_to={'model__in':(
                                                       'text',
                                                       'video',
                                                       'image',
```

```
                                                                'file')})
        object_id = models.PositiveIntegerField()
        item = GenericForeignKey('content_type', 'object_id')
        order = OrderField(blank=True, for_fields=['module'])

        class Meta:
                ordering = ['order']
```

Let's create a new model migration that reflects the new order fields. Open the shell and run the following command:

```
python manage.py makemigrations courses
```

You will see the following output:

```
You are trying to add a non-nullable field 'order' to content without a
default; we can't do that (the database needs something to populate
existing rows).
Please select a fix:
 1) Provide a one-off default now (will be set on all existing rows with a
null value for this column)
 2) Quit, and let me add a default in models.py
Select an option:
```

Django is telling us that we have to provide a default value for the new order field for existing rows in the database. If the field had null=True, it would accept null values and Django would create the migration automatically instead of asking for a default value. We can specify a default value or cancel the migration and add a default attribute to the order field in the models.py file before creating the migration.

Enter 1 and press *Ente*r to provide a default value for existing records. You will see the following output:

```
Please enter the default value now, as valid Python
The datetime and django.utils.timezone modules are available, so you can do
e.g. timezone.now
Type 'exit' to exit this prompt
>>>
```

Enter 0 so that this is the default value for existing records and press *Enter*. Django will ask you for a default value for the Module model, too. Choose the first option and enter 0 as the default value again. Finally, you will see an output similar to the following one:

```
Migrations for 'courses':
  courses/migrations/0003_auto_20180326_0704.py
    - Change Meta options on content
    - Change Meta options on module
    - Add field order to content
    - Add field order to module
```

Then, apply the new migrations with the following command:

```
python manage.py migrate
```

The output of the command will inform you that the migration was successfully applied, as follows:

```
Applying courses.0003_auto_20180326_0704... OK
```

Let's test our new field. Open the shell with the following command:

```
python manage.py shell
```

Create a new course as follows:

```
>>> from django.contrib.auth.models import User
>>> from courses.models import Subject, Course, Module
>>> user = User.objects.last()
>>> subject = Subject.objects.last()
>>> c1 = Course.objects.create(subject=subject, owner=user, title='Course
1', slug='course1')
```

We have created a course in the database. Now, let's add modules to the course and see how their order is automatically calculated. We create an initial module and check its order:

```
>>> m1 = Module.objects.create(course=c1, title='Module 1')
>>> m1.order
0
```

OrderField sets its value to 0, since this is the first Module object created for the given course. Now, we create a second module for the same course:

```
>>> m2 = Module.objects.create(course=c1, title='Module 2')
>>> m2.order
1
```

OrderField calculates the next order value adding 1 to the highest order for existing objects. Let's create a third module, forcing a specific order:

```
>>> m3 = Module.objects.create(course=c1, title='Module 3', order=5)
>>> m3.order
5
```

If we specify a custom order, the OrderField field does not interfere and the value given to the order is used.

Let's add a fourth module:

```
>>> m4 = Module.objects.create(course=c1, title='Module 4')
>>> m4.order
6
```

The order for this module has been automatically set. Our OrderField field does not guarantee that all order values are consecutive. However, it respects existing order values and always assigns the next order based on the highest existing order.

Let's create a second course and add a module to it:

```
>>> c2 = Course.objects.create(subject=subject, title='Course 2',
slug='course2', owner=user)
>>> m5 = Module.objects.create(course=c2, title='Module 1')
>>> m5.order
0
```

To calculate the new module's order, the field only takes into consideration existing modules that belong to the same course. Since this is the first module of the second course, the resulting order is 0. This is because we specified for_fields=['course'] in the order field of the Module model.

Congratulations! You have successfully created your first custom model field.

Creating a CMS

Now that we have created a versatile data model, we are going to build the CMS. The CMS will allow instructors to create courses and manage their contents. We need to provide the following functionality:

- Log in to the CMS
- List the courses created by the instructor

- Create, edit, and delete courses
- Add modules to a course and reorder them
- Add different types of content to each module and reorder contents

Adding an authentication system

We are going to use Django's authentication framework in our platform. Both instructors and students will be instances of Django's User model, so they will be able to log in to the site using the authentication views of django.contrib.auth.

Edit the main urls.py file of the educa project and include the login and logout views of Django's authentication framework:

```
from django.contrib import admin
from django.urls import path
from django.contrib.auth import views as auth_views

urlpatterns = [
    path('accounts/login/', auth_views.LoginView.as_view(), name='login'),
    path('accounts/logout/', auth_views.LogoutView.as_view(),
name='logout'),
    path('admin/', admin.site.urls),
]
```

Creating the authentication templates

Create the following file structure inside the courses application directory:

```
templates/
    base.html
    registration/
        login.html
        logged_out.html
```

Before building the authentication templates, we need to prepare the base template for our project. Edit the base.html template file and add the following content to it:

```
{% load staticfiles %}
<!DOCTYPE html>
<html>
<head>
  <meta charset="utf-8" />
  <title>{% block title %}Educa{% endblock %}</title>
```

```
    <link href="{% static "css/base.css" %}" rel="stylesheet">
</head>
<body>
  <div id="header">
    <a href="/" class="logo">Educa</a>
    <ul class="menu">
      {% if request.user.is_authenticated %}
        <li><a href="{% url "logout" %}">Sign out</a></li>
      {% else %}
        <li><a href="{% url "login" %}">Sign in</a></li>
      {% endif %}
    </ul>
  </div>
  <div id="content">
    {% block content %}
    {% endblock %}
  </div>

  <script src="https://ajax.googleapis.com/ajax/libs/jquery/
  3.3.1/jquery.min.js"></script>
  <script>
    $(document).ready(function() {
      {% block domready %}
      {% endblock %}
    });
  </script>
</body>
</html>
```

This is the base template that will be extended by the rest of the templates. In this template, we define the following blocks:

- title: The block for other templates to add a custom title for each page.
- content: The main block for content. All templates that extend the base template should add content to this block.
- domready: Located inside the $document.ready() function of jQuery. It allows us to execute code when the DOM has finished loading.

The CSS styles used in this template are located in the static/ directory of the courses application, in the code that comes along with this chapter. Copy the static/ directory into the same directory of your project to use them.

Edit the `registration/login.html` template and add the following code to it:

```
{% extends "base.html" %}

{% block title %}Log-in{% endblock %}

{% block content %}
  <h1>Log-in</h1>
  <div class="module">
    {% if form.errors %}
      <p>Your username and password didn't match. Please try again.</p>
    {% else %}
      <p>Please, use the following form to log-in:</p>
    {% endif %}
    <div class="login-form">
      <form action="{% url 'login' %}" method="post">
        {{ form.as_p }}
        {% csrf_token %}
        <input type="hidden" name="next" value="{{ next }}" />
        <p><input type="submit" value="Log-in"></p>
      </form>
    </div>
  </div>
{% endblock %}
```

This is a standard login template for Django's `login` view.

Edit the `registration/logged_out.html` template and add the following code to it:

```
{% extends "base.html" %}

{% block title %}Logged out{% endblock %}

{% block content %}
  <h1>Logged out</h1>
  <div class="module">
    <p>You have been successfully logged out.
       You can <a href="{% url "login" %}">log-in again</a>.</p>
  </div>
{% endblock %}
```

This is the template that will be displayed to the user after logout. Run the development server with the following command:

```
python manage.py runserver
```

Open `http://127.0.0.1:8000/accounts/login/` in your browser. You should see the login page like this:

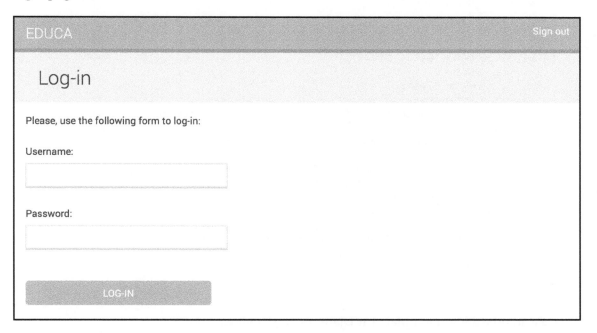

Creating class-based views

We are going to build views to create, edit, and delete courses. We will use class-based views for this. Edit the `views.py` file of the `courses` application and add the following code to it:

```python
from django.views.generic.list import ListView
from .models import Course

class ManageCourseListView(ListView):
    model = Course
    template_name = 'courses/manage/course/list.html'

    def get_queryset(self):
        qs = super(ManageCourseListView, self).get_queryset()
        return qs.filter(owner=self.request.user)
```

This is the `ManageCourseListView` view. It inherits from Django's generic `ListView`. We override the `get_queryset()` method of the view to retrieve only courses created by the current user. To prevent users from editing, updating, or deleting courses they didn't create, we will also need to override the `get_queryset()` method in the create, update, and delete views. When you need to provide a specific behavior for several class-based views, it is recommended to use *mixins*.

Using mixins for class-based views

Mixins are a special kind of multiple inheritance for a class. You can use them to provide common discrete functionality that, added to other mixins, allows you to define the behavior of a class. There are two main situations to use mixins:

- You want to provide multiple optional features for a class
- You want to use a particular feature in several classes

Django comes with several mixins that provide additional functionality to your class-based views. You can learn more about mixins at https://docs.djangoproject.com/en/2.0/topics/class-based-views/mixins/.

We are going to create a mixin class that includes a common behavior and use it for the course's views. Edit the `views.py` file of the `courses` application and modify it as follows:

```
from django.urls import reverse_lazy
from django.views.generic.list import ListView
from django.views.generic.edit import CreateView, UpdateView, \
                                      DeleteView
from .models import Course

class OwnerMixin(object):
    def get_queryset(self):
        qs = super(OwnerMixin, self).get_queryset()
        return qs.filter(owner=self.request.user)

class OwnerEditMixin(object):
    def form_valid(self, form):
        form.instance.owner = self.request.user
        return super(OwnerEditMixin, self).form_valid(form)

class OwnerCourseMixin(OwnerMixin):
    model = Course

class OwnerCourseEditMixin(OwnerCourseMixin, OwnerEditMixin):
```

```
        fields = ['subject', 'title', 'slug', 'overview']
        success_url = reverse_lazy('manage_course_list')
        template_name = 'courses/manage/course/form.html'

    class ManageCourseListView(OwnerCourseMixin, ListView):
        template_name = 'courses/manage/course/list.html'

    class CourseCreateView(OwnerCourseEditMixin, CreateView):
        pass

    class CourseUpdateView(OwnerCourseEditMixin, UpdateView):
        pass

    class CourseDeleteView(OwnerCourseMixin, DeleteView):
        template_name = 'courses/manage/course/delete.html'
        success_url = reverse_lazy('manage_course_list')
```

In this code, we create the `OwnerMixin` and `OwnerEditMixin` mixins. We will use these mixins together with the `ListView`, `CreateView`, `UpdateView`, and `DeleteView` views provided by Django. `OwnerMixin` implements the following method:

- `get_queryset()`: This method is used by the views to get the base QuerySet. Our mixin will override this method to filter objects by the `owner` attribute to retrieve objects that belong to the current user (`request.user`).

`OwnerEditMixin` implements the following method:

- `form_valid()`: This method is used by views that use Django's `ModelFormMixin` mixin, that is, views with forms or modelforms such as `CreateView` and `UpdateView`. `form_valid()` are executed when the submitted form is valid. The default behavior for this method is saving the instance (for modelforms) and redirecting the user to `success_url`. We override this method to automatically set the current user in the `owner` attribute of the object being saved. By doing so, we set the owner for an object automatically when it is saved.

Our `OwnerMixin` class can be used for views that interact with any model that contains an `owner` attribute.

We also define an `OwnerCourseMixin` class that inherits `OwnerMixin` and provides the following attribute for child views:

- `model`: The model used for QuerySets. Used by all views.

We define a `OwnerCourseEditMixin` mixin with the following attributes:

- `fields`: The fields of the model to build the model form of the `CreateView` and `UpdateView` views.
- `success_url`: Used by `CreateView` and `UpdateView` to redirect the user after the form is successfully submitted. We use a URL with the name `manage_course_list` that we are going to create later.

Finally, we create the following views that subclass `OwnerCourseMixin`:

- `ManageCourseListView`: Lists the courses created by the user. It inherits from `OwnerCourseMixin` and `ListView`.
- `CourseCreateView`: Uses a modelform to create a new `Course` object. It uses the fields defined in `OwnerCourseEditMixin` to build a model form and also subclasses `CreateView`.
- `CourseUpdateView`: Allows editing an existing `Course` object. It inherits from `OwnerCourseEditMixin` and `UpdateView`.
- `CourseDeleteView`: Inherits from `OwnerCourseMixin` and the generic `DeleteView`. Defines `success_url` to redirect the user after the object is deleted.

Working with groups and permissions

We have created the basic views to manage courses. Currently, any user could access these views. We want to restrict these views so that only instructors have permission to create and manage courses. Django's authentication framework includes a permission system that allows you to assign permissions to users and groups. We are going to create a group for instructor users and assign permissions to create, update, and delete courses.

Run the development server using the command and open `http://127.0.0.1:8000/admin/auth/group/add/` in your browser to create a new `Group` object. Add the name `Instructors` and choose all permissions of the `courses` application except those of the `Subject` model, as follows:

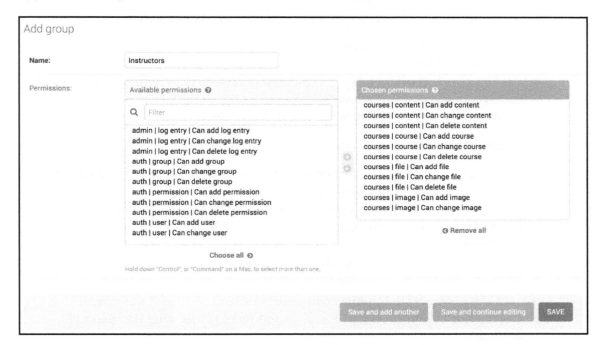

As you can see, there are three different permissions for each model: *can add, can change,* and *can delete*. After choosing permissions for this group, click on the **SAVE** button.

Django creates permissions for models automatically, but you can also create custom permissions. You can read more about adding custom permissions at `https://docs.djangoproject.com/en/2.0/topics/auth/customizing/#custom-permissions`.

Open `http://127.0.0.1:8000/admin/auth/user/add/` and create a new user. Edit the user and add it to the **Instructors** group, as follows:

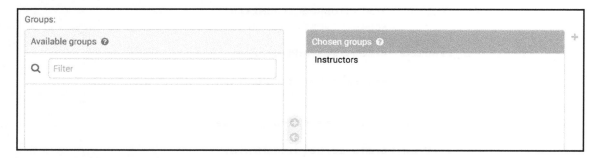

Users inherit the permissions of the groups they belong to, but you can also add individual permissions to a single user using the administration site. Users that have `is_superuser` set to `True` have all permissions automatically.

Restricting access to class-based views

We are going to restrict access to the views so that only users with the appropriate permissions can add, change, or delete `Course` objects. We are going to use the following two mixins provided by `django.contrib.auth` to limit access to views:

- `LoginRequiredMixin`: Replicates the `login_required` decorator's functionality.
- `PermissionRequiredMixin`: Grants access to the view to users that have a specific permission. Remember that superusers automatically have all permissions.

Edit the `views.py` file of the `courses` application and add the following import:

```
from django.contrib.auth.mixins import LoginRequiredMixin, \
                                        PermissionRequiredMixin
```

Make `OwnerCourseMixin` inherit `LoginRequiredMixin` like this:

```
class OwnerCourseMixin(OwnerMixin, LoginRequiredMixin):
    model = Course
    fields = ['subject', 'title', 'slug', 'overview']
    success_url = reverse_lazy('manage_course_list')
```

Then, add a `permission_required` attribute to the create, update, and delete views, as follows:

```
class CourseCreateView(PermissionRequiredMixin,
                       OwnerCourseEditMixin,
                       CreateView):
    permission_required = 'courses.add_course'

class CourseUpdateView(PermissionRequiredMixin,
                       OwnerCourseEditMixin,
                       UpdateView):
    permission_required = 'courses.change_course'

class CourseDeleteView(PermissionRequiredMixin,
                       OwnerCourseMixin,
                       DeleteView):
    template_name = 'courses/manage/course/delete.html'
    success_url = reverse_lazy('manage_course_list')
    permission_required = 'courses.delete_course'
```

`PermissionRequiredMixin` checks that the user accessing the view has the permission specified in the `permission_required` attribute. Our views are now only accessible to users that have proper permissions.

Let's create URLs for these views. Create a new file inside the `courses` application directory and name it `urls.py`. Add the following code to it:

```
from django.urls import path
from . import views

urlpatterns = [
    path('mine/',
         views.ManageCourseListView.as_view(),
         name='manage_course_list'),
    path('create/',
         views.CourseCreateView.as_view(),
         name='course_create'),
    path('<pk>/edit/',
         views.CourseUpdateView.as_view(),
         name='course_edit'),
    path('<pk>/delete/',
         views.CourseDeleteView.as_view(),
         name='course_delete'),
]
```

These are the URL patterns for the list, create, edit, and delete course views. Edit the main `urls.py` file of the `educa` project and include the URL patterns of the `courses` application, as follows:

```
from django.urls import path, include

urlpatterns = [
    path('accounts/login/', auth_views.LoginView.as_view(), name='login'),
    path('accounts/logout/', auth_views.LogoutView.as_view(),
name='logout'),
    path('admin/', admin.site.urls),
    path('course/', include('courses.urls')),
]
```

We need to create the templates for these views. Create the following directories and files inside the `templates/` directory of the `courses` application:

```
courses/
    manage/
        course/
            list.html
            form.html
            delete.html
```

Edit the `courses/manage/course/list.html` template and add the following code to it:

```
{% extends "base.html" %}

{% block title %}My courses{% endblock %}

{% block content %}
  <h1>My courses</h1>

  <div class="module">
    {% for course in object_list %}
      <div class="course-info">
        <h3>{{ course.title }}</h3>
        <p>
          <a href="{% url "course_edit" course.id %}">Edit</a>
          <a href="{% url "course_delete" course.id %}">Delete</a>
        </p>
      </div>
    {% empty %}
      <p>You haven't created any courses yet.</p>
    {% endfor %}
    <p>
      <a href="{% url "course_create" %}" class="button">Create new
```

```
course</a>
    </p>
  </div>
{% endblock %}
```

This is the template for the `ManageCourseListView` view. In this template, we list the courses created by the current user. We include links to edit or delete each course, and a link to create new courses.

Run the development server using the command `python manage.py runserver`. Open `http://127.0.0.1:8000/accounts/login/?next=/course/mine/` in your browser and log in with a user that belongs to the `Instructors` group. After logging in, you will be redirected to the `http://127.0.0.1:8000/course/mine/` URL and you should see the following page:

This page will display all courses created by the current user.

Let's create the template that displays the form for the create and update course views. Edit the courses/manage/course/form.html template and write the following code:

```
{% extends "base.html" %}

{% block title %}
  {% if object %}
    Edit course "{{ object.title }}"
  {% else %}
    Create a new course
  {% endif %}
{% endblock %}

{% block content %}
  <h1>
    {% if object %}
      Edit course "{{ object.title }}"
    {% else %}
      Create a new course
    {% endif %}
  </h1>
  <div class="module">
    <h2>Course info</h2>
    <form action="." method="post">
      {{ form.as_p }}
      {% csrf_token %}
      <p><input type="submit" value="Save course"></p>
    </form>
  </div>
{% endblock %}
```

The form.html template is used for both the CourseCreateView and CourseUpdateView views. In this template, we check whether an object variable is in the context. If object exists in the context, we know that we are updating an existing course, and we use it in the page title. Otherwise, we are creating a new Course object.

Open `http://127.0.0.1:8000/course/mine/` in your browser and click the **CREATE NEW COURSE** button. You will see the following page:

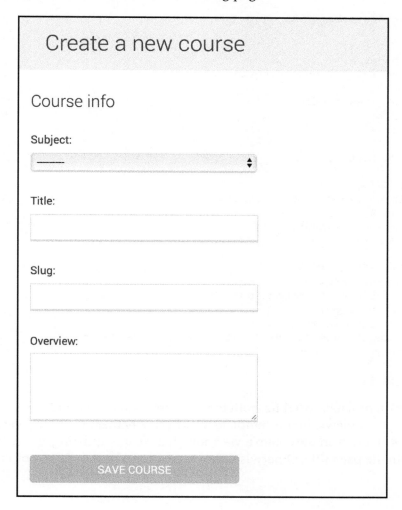

Fill in the form and click the **SAVE COURSE** button. The course will be saved and you will be redirected to the course list page. It should look as follows:

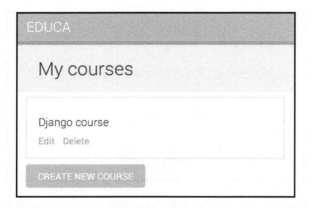

Then, click the **Edit** link for the course you have just created. You will see the form again, but this time you are editing an existing `Course` object instead of creating one.

Finally, edit the `courses/manage/course/delete.html` template and add the following code:

```
{% extends "base.html" %}

{% block title %}Delete course{% endblock %}

{% block content %}
  <h1>Delete course "{{ object.title }}"</h1>

  <div class="module">
    <form action="" method="post">
      {% csrf_token %}
      <p>Are you sure you want to delete "{{ object }}"?</p>
      <input type="submit" class"button" value="Confirm">
    </form>
  </div>
{% endblock %}
```

This is the template for the `CourseDeleteView` view. This view inherits from `DeleteView` provided by Django, which expects user confirmation to delete an object.

Open your browser and click the **Delete** link of your course. You should see the following confirmation page:

Click the **CONFIRM** button. The course will be deleted and you will be redirected to the course list page again.

Instructors can now create, edit, and delete courses. Next, we need to provide them with CMS to add modules and contents to courses. We will start by managing course modules.

Managing course modules and content

We are going to build a system to manage course modules and their contents. We will need to build forms that can be used for managing multiple modules per course and different types of content for each module. Both modules and contents will have to follow a specific order and we should be able to reorder them using the CMS.

Using formsets for course modules

Django comes with an abstraction layer to work with multiple forms on the same page. These groups of forms are known as *formsets*. Formsets manage multiple instances of a certain `Form` or `ModelForm`. All forms are submitted at once and the formset takes care of the initial number of forms to display, limiting the maximum number of forms that can be submitted and validating all the forms.

Formsets include an is_valid() method to validate all forms at once. You can also provide initial data for the forms and specify how many additional empty forms to display.

You can learn more about formsets at https://docs.djangoproject.com/en/2.0/topics/forms/formsets/ and about model formsets at https://docs.djangoproject.com/en/2.0/topics/forms/modelforms/#model-formsets.

Since a course is divided into a variable number of modules, it makes sense to use formsets to manage them. Create a forms.py file in the courses application directory and add the following code to it:

```
from django import forms
from django.forms.models import inlineformset_factory
from .models import Course, Module

ModuleFormSet = inlineformset_factory(Course,
                                      Module,
                                      fields=['title',
                                              'description'],
                                      extra=2,
                                      can_delete=True)
```

This is the ModuleFormSet formset. We build it using the inlineformset_factory() function provided by Django. Inline formsets are a small abstraction on top of formsets that simplify working with related objects. This function allows us to build a model formset dynamically for the Module objects related to a Course object.

We use the following parameters to build the formset:

- fields: The fields that will be included in each form of the formset.
- extra: Allows us to set the number of empty extra forms to display in the formset.
- can_delete: If you set this to True, Django will include a Boolean field for each form that will be rendered as a checkbox input. It allows you to mark the objects you want to delete.

Edit the views.py file of the courses application and add the following code to it:

```
from django.shortcuts import redirect, get_object_or_404
from django.views.generic.base import TemplateResponseMixin, View
from .forms import ModuleFormSet

class CourseModuleUpdateView(TemplateResponseMixin, View):
    template_name = 'courses/manage/module/formset.html'
```

```
    course = None

    def get_formset(self, data=None):
        return ModuleFormSet(instance=self.course,
                             data=data)

    def dispatch(self, request, pk):
        self.course = get_object_or_404(Course,
                                        id=pk,
                                        owner=request.user)
        return super(CourseModuleUpdateView,
                     self).dispatch(request, pk)

    def get(self, request, *args, **kwargs):
        formset = self.get_formset()
        return self.render_to_response({'course': self.course,
                                        'formset': formset})

    def post(self, request, *args, **kwargs):
        formset = self.get_formset(data=request.POST)
        if formset.is_valid():
            formset.save()
            return redirect('manage_course_list')
        return self.render_to_response({'course': self.course,
                                        'formset': formset})
```

The `CourseModuleUpdateView` view handles the formset to add, update, and delete modules for a specific course. This view inherits from the following mixins and views:

- `TemplateResponseMixin`: This mixin takes charge of rendering templates and returning an HTTP response. It requires a `template_name` attribute that indicates the template to be rendered and provides the `render_to_response()` method to pass it a context and render the template.
- `View`: The basic class-based view provided by Django.

In this view, we implement the following methods:

- `get_formset()`: We define this method to avoid repeating the code to build the formset. We create a `ModuleFormSet` object for the given `Course` object with optional data.
- `dispatch()`: This method is provided by the `View` class. It takes an HTTP request and its parameters and attempts to delegate to a lowercase method that matches the HTTP method used: a GET request is delegated to the `get()` method and a POST request to `post()`, respectively. In this method, we use the `get_object_or_404()` shortcut function to get the `Course` object for the given `id` parameter that belongs to the current user. We include this code in the `dispatch()` method because we need to retrieve the course for both GET and POST requests. We save it into the `course` attribute of the view to make it accessible to other methods.
- `get()`: Executed for GET requests. We build an empty `ModuleFormSet` formset and render it to the template together with the current `Course` object using the `render_to_response()` method provided by `TemplateResponseMixin`.
- `post()`: Executed for POST requests. In this method, we perform the following actions:

  1. We build a `ModuleFormSet` instance using the submitted data.
  2. We execute the `is_valid()` method of the formset to validate all of its forms.
  3. If the formset is valid, we save it by calling the `save()` method. At this point, any changes made, such as adding, updating, or marking modules for deletion, are applied to the database. Then, we redirect users to the `manage_course_list` URL. If the formset is not valid, we render the template to display any errors, instead.

Edit the `urls.py` file of the `courses` application and add the following URL pattern to it:

```
path('<pk>/module/',
    views.CourseModuleUpdateView.as_view(),
    name='course_module_update'),
```

Create a new directory inside the `courses/manage/` template directory and name it `module`. Create a `courses/manage/module/formset.html` template and add the following code to it:

```
{% extends "base.html" %}

{% block title %}
  Edit "{{ course.title }}"
{% endblock %}

{% block content %}
  <h1>Edit "{{ course.title }}"</h1>
  <div class="module">
    <h2>Course modules</h2>
    <form action="" method="post">
      {{ formset }}
      {{ formset.management_form }}
      {% csrf_token %}
      <input type="submit" class="button" value="Save modules">
    </form>
  </div>
{% endblock %}
```

In this template, we create a `<form>` HTML element, in which we include `formset`. We also include the management form for the formset with the variable `{{ formset.management_form }}`. The management form includes hidden fields to control the initial, total, minimum, and maximum number of forms. You can see it's very easy to create a formset.

Edit the `courses/manage/course/list.html` template and add the following link for the `course_module_update` URL below the course edit and delete links:

```
<a href="{% url "course_edit" course.id %}">Edit</a>
<a href="{% url "course_delete" course.id %}">Delete</a>
<a href="{% url "course_module_update" course.id %}">Edit
modules</a>
```

We have included the link to edit the course modules. Open
`http://127.0.0.1:8000/course/mine/` in your browser. Create a course and click
the **Edit modules** link for it. You should see a formset as follows:

The formset includes a form for each `Module` object contained in the course. After these,
two empty extra forms are displayed because we set `extra=2` for `ModuleFormSet`. When
you save the formset, Django will include another two extra fields to add new modules.

Adding content to course modules

Now, we need a way to add content to course modules. We have four different types of content: text, video, image, and file. We can consider creating four different views to create content, one for each model. Yet we are going to take a more generic approach and create a view that handles creating or updating objects of any content model.

Edit the `views.py` file of the `courses` application and add the following code to it:

```python
from django.forms.models import modelform_factory
from django.apps import apps
from .models import Module, Content

class ContentCreateUpdateView(TemplateResponseMixin, View):
    module = None
    model = None
    obj = None
    template_name = 'courses/manage/content/form.html'

    def get_model(self, model_name):
        if model_name in ['text', 'video', 'image', 'file']:
            return apps.get_model(app_label='courses',
                                  model_name=model_name)
        return None

    def get_form(self, model, *args, **kwargs):
        Form = modelform_factory(model, exclude=['owner',
                                                 'order',
                                                 'created',
                                                 'updated'])
        return Form(*args, **kwargs)

    def dispatch(self, request, module_id, model_name, id=None):
        self.module = get_object_or_404(Module,
                                        id=module_id,
                                        course__owner=request.user)
        self.model = self.get_model(model_name)
        if id:
            self.obj = get_object_or_404(self.model,
                                         id=id,
                                         owner=request.user)
        return super(ContentCreateUpdateView,
            self).dispatch(request, module_id, model_name, id)
```

This is the first part of `ContentCreateUpdateView`. It will allow us to create and update contents of different models. This view defines the following methods:

- `get_model()`: Here, we check that the given model name is one of the four content models: `Text`, `Video`, `Image`, or `File`. Then, we use Django's `apps module` to obtain the actual class for the given model name. If the given model name is not one of the valid ones, we return `None`.

- `get_form()`: We build a dynamic form using the `modelform_factory()` function of the form's framework. Since we are going to build a form for the `Text`, `Video`, `Image`, and `File` models, we use the `exclude` parameter to specify the common fields to exclude from the form and let all other attributes be included automatically. By doing so, we don't have to know which fields to include depending on the model.

- `dispatch()`: It receives the following URL parameters and stores the corresponding module, model, and content object as class attributes:
  - `module_id`: The ID for the module that the content is/will be associated with.
  - `model_name`: The model name of the content to create/update.
  - `id`: The ID of the object that is being updated. It's `None` to create new objects.

Add the following `get()` and `post()` methods to `ContentCreateUpdateView`:

```
def get(self, request, module_id, model_name, id=None):
    form = self.get_form(self.model, instance=self.obj)
    return self.render_to_response({'form': form,
                                    'object': self.obj})

def post(self, request, module_id, model_name, id=None):
    form = self.get_form(self.model,
                         instance=self.obj,
                         data=request.POST,
                         files=request.FILES)
    if form.is_valid():
        obj = form.save(commit=False)
        obj.owner = request.user
        obj.save()
        if not id:
            # new content
            Content.objects.create(module=self.module,
                                   item=obj)
        return redirect('module_content_list', self.module.id)
```

```
    return self.render_to_response({'form': form,
                                    'object': self.obj})
```

These methods are as follows:

- `get()`: Executed when a `GET` request is received. We build the model form for the `Text`, `Video`, `Image`, or `File` instance that is being updated. Otherwise, we pass no instance to create a new object, since `self.obj` is `None` if no ID is provided.

- `post()`: Executed when a `POST` request is received. We build the modelform passing any submitted data and files to it. Then, we validate it. If the form is valid, we create a new object and assign `request.user` as its owner before saving it to the database. We check for the `id` parameter. If no ID is provided, we know the user is creating a new object instead of updating an existing one. If this is a new object, we create a `Content` object for the given module and associate the new content to it.

Edit the `urls.py` file of the `courses` application and add the following URL patterns to it:

```
path('module/<int:module_id>/content/<model_name>/create/',
    views.ContentCreateUpdateView.as_view(),
    name='module_content_create'),

path('module/<int:module_id>/content/<model_name>/<id>/',
    views.ContentCreateUpdateView.as_view(),
    name='module_content_update'),
```

The new URL patterns are as follows:

- `module_content_create`: To create new text, video, image, or file objects and add them to a module. It includes the `module_id` and `model_name` parameters. The first one allows linking the new content object to the given module. The latter specifies the content model to build the form for.

- `module_content_update`: To update an existing text, video, image, or file object. It includes the `module_id` and `model_name` parameters and an `id` parameter to identify the content that is being updated.

Create a new directory inside the `courses/manage/` template directory and name it `content`. Create the template `courses/manage/content/form.html` and add the following code to it:

```
{% extends "base.html" %}

{% block title %}
  {% if object %}
    Edit content "{{ object.title }}"
  {% else %}
    Add a new content
  {% endif %}
{% endblock %}

{% block content %}
  <h1>
    {% if object %}
      Edit content "{{ object.title }}"
    {% else %}
      Add a new content
    {% endif %}
  </h1>
  <div class="module">
    <h2>Course info</h2>
    <form action="" method="post" enctype="multipart/form-data">
      {{ form.as_p }}
      {% csrf_token %}
      <p><input type="submit" value="Save content"></p>
    </form>
  </div>
{% endblock %}
```

This is the template for the `ContentCreateUpdateView` view. In this template, we check whether an `object` variable is in the context. If `object` exists in the context, we are updating an existing object. Otherwise, we are creating a new object.

We include `enctype="multipart/form-data"` in the `<form>` HTML element; because the form contains a file upload for the `File` and `Image` content models.

Run the development server, open `http://127.0.0.1:8000/course/mine/`, click **Edit modules** for an existing course, and create a module. Open the Python shell with the command `python manage.py shell` and obtain the ID of the most recently created module, as follows:

```
>>> from courses.models import Module
>>> Module.objects.latest('id').id
6
```

Run the development server and open `http://127.0.0.1:8000/course/module/6/content/image/create/` in your browser, replacing the module ID by the one you obtained before. You will see the form to create an `Image` object, as follows:

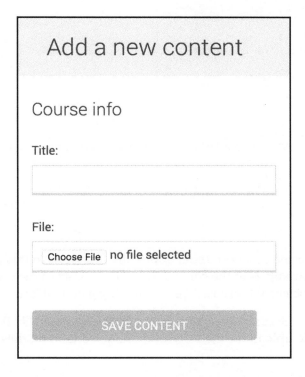

Don't submit the form yet. If you try to do so, it will fail because we haven't defined the `module_content_list` URL yet. We are going to create it in a bit.

We also need a view for deleting contents. Edit the `views.py` file of the `courses` application and add the following code:

```python
class ContentDeleteView(View):

    def post(self, request, id):
        content = get_object_or_404(Content,
                                    id=id,
                                    module__course__owner=request.user)
        module = content.module
        content.item.delete()
        content.delete()
        return redirect('module_content_list', module.id)
```

The `ContentDeleteView` class retrieves the `Content` object with the given ID; it deletes the related `Text`, `Video`, `Image`, or `File` object; and finally, it deletes the `Content` object and redirects the user to the `module_content_list` URL to list the other contents of the module.

Edit the `urls.py` file of the `courses` application and add the following URL pattern to it:

```python
path('content/<int:id>/delete/',
     views.ContentDeleteView.as_view(),
     name='module_content_delete'),
```

Now, instructors can create, update, and delete contents easily.

Managing modules and contents

We have built views to create, edit, and delete course modules and contents. Now, we need a view to display all modules for a course and list contents for a specific module.

Edit the `views.py` file of the `courses` application and add the following code to it:

```python
class ModuleContentListView(TemplateResponseMixin, View):
    template_name = 'courses/manage/module/content_list.html'

    def get(self, request, module_id):
        module = get_object_or_404(Module,
                                   id=module_id,
                                   course__owner=request.user)

        return self.render_to_response({'module': module})
```

This is `ModuleContentListView`. This view gets the `Module` object with the given ID that belongs to the current user and renders a template with the given module.

Edit the `urls.py` file of the `courses` application and add the following URL pattern to it:

```python
path('module/<int:module_id>/',
    views.ModuleContentListView.as_view(),
    name='module_content_list'),
```

Create a new template inside the `templates/courses/manage/module/` directory and name it `content_list.html`. Add the following code to it:

```django
{% extends "base.html" %}

{% block title %}
  Module {{ module.order|add:1 }}: {{ module.title }}
{% endblock %}

{% block content %}
{% with course=module.course %}
  <h1>Course "{{ course.title }}"</h1>
  <div class="contents">
    <h3>Modules</h3>
    <ul id="modules">
      {% for m in course.modules.all %}
        <li data-id="{{ m.id }}" {% if m == module %}
          class="selected"{% endif %}>
          <a href="{% url "module_content_list" m.id %}">
            <span>
              Module <span class="order">{{ m.order|add:1 }}</span>
            </span>
            <br>
            {{ m.title }}
          </a>
        </li>
      {% empty %}
        <li>No modules yet.</li>
      {% endfor %}
    </ul>
    <p><a href="{% url "course_module_update" course.id %}">
    Edit modules</a></p>
  </div>
  <div class="module">
    <h2>Module {{ module.order|add:1 }}: {{ module.title }}</h2>
    <h3>Module contents:</h3>

    <div id="module-contents">
```

```
    {% for content in module.contents.all %}
      <div data-id="{{ content.id }}">
        {% with item=content.item %}
          <p>{{ item }}</p>
          <a href="#">Edit</a>
          <form action="{% url "module_content_delete" content.id %}"
            method="post">
            <input type="submit" value="Delete">
            {% csrf_token %}
          </form>
        {% endwith %}
      </div>
    {% empty %}
      <p>This module has no contents yet.</p>
    {% endfor %}
  </div>
  <h3>Add new content:</h3>
  <ul class="content-types">
    <li><a href="{% url "module_content_create" module.id "text" %}">
    Text</a></li>
    <li><a href="{% url "module_content_create" module.id "image" %}">
    Image</a></li>
    <li><a href="{% url "module_content_create" module.id "video" %}">
    Video</a></li>
    <li><a href="{% url "module_content_create" module.id "file" %}">
    File</a></li>
  </ul>
  </div>
{% endwith %}
{% endblock %}
```

This is the template that displays all modules for a course and the contents of the selected module. We iterate over the course modules to display them in a sidebar. We iterate over the module's contents and access `content.item` to get the related `Text`, `Video`, `Image`, or `File` object. We also include links to create new text, video, image, or file contents.

We want to know which type of object each of the `item` objects is: `Text`, `Video`, `Image`, or `File`. We need the model name to build the URL to edit the object. Besides this, we could display each item in the template differently, based on the type of content it is. We can get the model for an object from the model's `Meta` class, by accessing the object's `_meta` attribute. Nevertheless, Django doesn't allow accessing variables or attributes starting with an underscore in templates to prevent retrieving private attributes or calling private methods. We can solve this by writing a custom template filter.

Create the following file structure inside the `courses` application directory:

```
templatetags/
    __init__.py
    course.py
```

Edit the `course.py` module and add the following code to it:

```python
from django import template

register = template.Library()

@register.filter
def model_name(obj):
    try:
        return obj._meta.model_name
    except AttributeError:
        return None
```

This is the `model_name` template filter. We can apply it in templates as `object|model_name` to get the model name for an object.

Edit the `templates/courses/manage/module/content_list.html` template and add the following line below the `{% extends %}` template tag:

```
{% load course %}
```

This will load the `course` template tags. Then, replace the following lines:

```html
<p>{{ item }}</p>
<a href="#">Edit</a>
```

Replace them with the following ones:

```html
<p>{{ item }} ({{ item|model_name }})</p>
<a href="{% url "module_content_update" module.id item|model_name item.id
%}">Edit</a>
```

Now, we display the item model in the template and use the model name to build the link to edit the object. Edit the `courses/manage/course/list.html` template and add a link to the `module_content_list` URL like this:

```
<a href="{% url "course_module_update" course.id %}">Edit modules</a>
{% if course.modules.count > 0 %}
  <a href="{% url "module_content_list" course.modules.first.id %}">
  Manage contents</a>
{% endif %}
```

The new link allows users to access the contents of the first module of the course, if any.

Open `http://127.0.0.1:8000/course/mine/` and click the **Manage contents** link for a course that contains at least one module. You will see a page like the following one:

When you click on a module in the left sidebar, its contents are displayed in the main area. The template also includes links to add a new text, video, image, or file content for the module being displayed. Add a couple of different types of content to the module and take a look at the result. The contents will appear after **Module contents** like in the following example:

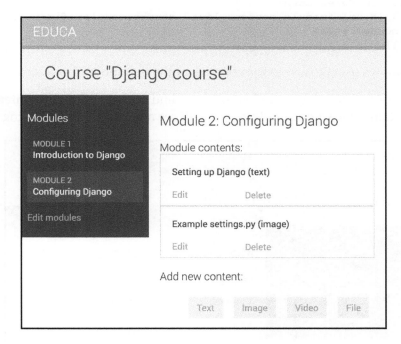

Reordering modules and contents

We need to provide a simple way to reorder course modules and their contents. We will use a JavaScript drag-n-drop widget to let our users reorder the modules of a course by dragging them. When users finish dragging a module, we will launch an asynchronous request (AJAX) to store the new module order.

Using mixins from django-braces

`django-braces` is a third-party module that contains a collection of generic mixins for Django. These mixins provide additional features for class-based views. You can see a list of all mixins provided by `django-braces` at `https://django-braces.readthedocs.io/`.

We will use the following mixins of `django-braces`:

- `CsrfExemptMixin`: To avoid checking the CSRF token in the `POST` requests. We need this to perform AJAX `POST` requests without having to generate a `csrf_token`.
- `JsonRequestResponseMixin`: Parses the request data as JSON and also serializes the response as JSON and returns an HTTP response with the `application/json` content type.

Install `django-braces` via `pip` using the following command:

```
pip install django-braces==1.13.0
```

We need a view that receives the new order of modules' ID encoded in JSON. Edit the `views.py` file of the `courses` application and add the following code to it:

```
from braces.views import CsrfExemptMixin, JsonRequestResponseMixin

class ModuleOrderView(CsrfExemptMixin,
                      JsonRequestResponseMixin,
                      View):
    def post(self, request):
        for id, order in self.request_json.items():
            Module.objects.filter(id=id,
                    course__owner=request.user).update(order=order)
        return self.render_json_response({'saved': 'OK'})
```

This is the `ModuleOrderView` view.

We can build a similar view to order a module's contents. Add the following code to the `views.py` file:

```
class ContentOrderView(CsrfExemptMixin,
                       JsonRequestResponseMixin,
                       View):
    def post(self, request):
        for id, order in self.request_json.items():
            Content.objects.filter(id=id,
                        module__course__owner=request.user) \
                    .update(order=order)
        return self.render_json_response({'saved': 'OK'})
```

Now, edit the `urls.py` file of the `courses` application and add the following URL patterns to it:

```
path('module/order/',
    views.ModuleOrderView.as_view(),
    name='module_order'),

path('content/order/',
    views.ContentOrderView.as_view(),
    name='content_order'),
```

Finally, we need to implement the drag-n-drop functionality in the template. We will use the jQuery UI library for this. jQuery UI is built on top of jQuery and it provides a set of interface interactions, effects, and widgets. We will use its `sortable` element. First, we need to load jQuery UI in the base template. Open the `base.html` file located in the `templates/` directory of the `courses` application, and add jQuery UI below the script to load jQuery as follows:

```
<script
src="https://ajax.googleapis.com/ajax/libs/jquery/3.3.1/jquery.min.js"></script>
<script
src="https://ajax.googleapis.com/ajax/libs/jqueryui/1.12.1/jquery-ui.min.js"></script>
```

We load the jQuery UI library just after the jQuery framework. Now, edit the `courses/manage/module/content_list.html` template and add the following code to it at the bottom of the template:

```
{% block domready %}
$('#modules').sortable({
    stop: function(event, ui) {
        modules_order = {};
        $('#modules').children().each(function(){
            // update the order field
            $(this).find('.order').text($(this).index() + 1);
            // associate the module's id with its order
            modules_order[$(this).data('id')] = $(this).index();
        });
        $.ajax({
            type: 'POST',
            url: '{% url "module_order" %}',
            contentType: 'application/json; charset=utf-8',
            dataType: 'json',
                data: JSON.stringify(modules_order)
            });
```

```
        }
    });

$('#module-contents').sortable({
    stop: function(event, ui) {
        contents_order = {};
        $('#module-contents').children().each(function(){
            // associate the module's id with its order
            contents_order[$(this).data('id')] = $(this).index();
        });

        $.ajax({
            type: 'POST',
            url: '{% url "content_order" %}',
            contentType: 'application/json; charset=utf-8',
            dataType: 'json',
            data: JSON.stringify(contents_order),
        });
    }
});
{% endblock %}
```

This JavaScript code is in the `{% block domready %}` block and therefore it will be
included in the `$(document).ready()` event of jQuery that we defined in the `base.html`
template. This guarantees that our JavaScript code is executed once the page has been
loaded. We define a `sortable` element for the modules list in the sidebar and a different
one for the module's content list. Both work in a similar manner. In this code, we perform
the following tasks:

1. First, we define a `sortable` element for the `modules` HTML element. Remember
   that we use `#modules`, since jQuery uses CSS notation for selectors.

2. We specify a function for the `stop` event. This event is triggered every time the
   user finishes sorting an element.

3. We create an empty `modules_order` dictionary. The keys for this dictionary will
   be the modules' ID, and the values will be the assigned order for each module.

4. We iterate over the `#module` children elements. We recalculate the displayed
   order for each module and get its `data-id` attribute, which contains the
   module's ID. We add the ID as the key of the `modules_order` dictionary and the
   new index of the module as the value.

5. We launch an AJAX `POST` request to the `content_order` URL, including the
   serialized JSON data of `modules_order` in the request. The corresponding
   `ModuleOrderView` takes care of updating the modules' order.

The `sortable` element to order contents is quite similar to this one. Go back to your browser and reload the page. Now, you will be able to click and drag both modules and contents to reorder them like the following example:

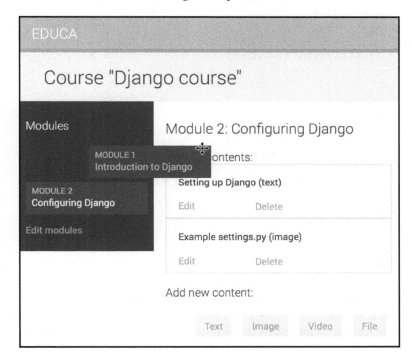

Great! Now you can reorder both course modules and module contents.

Summary

In this chapter, you learned how to create a versatile CMS. You used model inheritance and created a custom model field. You also worked with class-based views and mixins. You created formsets and a system to manage diverse types of content.

In the next chapter, you will create a student registration system. You will also render different kinds of content, and you will learn how to work with Django's cache framework.

11
Rendering and Caching Content

In the previous chapter, you used model inheritance and generic relationships to create flexible course content models. You also built a course management system using class-based views, formsets, and AJAX ordering for contents. In this chapter, you will:

- Create public views for displaying course information
- Build a student registration system
- Manage student enrollment in courses
- Render diverse course contents
- Cache content using the cache framework

We will start by creating a course catalog for students to browse existing courses and be able to enroll in them.

Displaying courses

For our course catalog, we have to build the following functionality:

- List all available courses, optionally filtered by subject
- Display a single course overview

Edit the views.py file of the courses application and add the following code:

```
from django.db.models import Count
from .models import Subject

class CourseListView(TemplateResponseMixin, View):
    model = Course
    template_name = 'courses/course/list.html'
```

```
def get(self, request, subject=None):
    subjects = Subject.objects.annotate(
                    total_courses=Count('courses'))
    courses = Course.objects.annotate(
                    total_modules=Count('modules'))
    if subject:
        subject = get_object_or_404(Subject, slug=subject)
        courses = courses.filter(subject=subject)
    return self.render_to_response({'subjects': subjects,
                                    'subject': subject,
                                    'courses': courses})
```

This is the `CourseListView` view. It inherits from `TemplateResponseMixin` and `View`. In this view, we perform the following tasks:

1. We retrieve all subjects, including the total number of courses for each of them. We use the ORM's `annotate()` method with the `Count()` aggregation function to include the total number of courses for each subject.
2. We retrieve all available courses, including the total number of modules contained in each course.
3. If a subject slug URL parameter is given, we retrieve the corresponding subject object and we limit the query to the courses that belong to the given subject.
4. We use the `render_to_response()` method provided by `TemplateResponseMixin` to render the objects to a template and return an HTTP response.

Let's create a detail view for displaying a single course overview. Add the following code to the `views.py` file:

```
from django.views.generic.detail import DetailView

class CourseDetailView(DetailView):
    model = Course
    template_name = 'courses/course/detail.html'
```

This view inherits from the generic `DetailView` provided by Django. We specify the `model` and `template_name` attributes. Django's `DetailView` expects a primary key (`pk`) or slug URL parameter to retrieve a single object for the given model. Then, it renders the template specified in `template_name`, including the object in the context as object.

Edit the main `urls.py` file of the `educa` project and add the following URL pattern to it:

```python
from courses.views import CourseListView

urlpatterns = [
    # ...
    path('', CourseListView.as_view(), name='course_list'),
]
```

We add the `course_list` URL pattern to the main `urls.py` file of the project because we want to display the list of courses in the URL `http://127.0.0.1:8000/` and all other URLs for the `courses` application have the `/course/` prefix.

Edit the `urls.py` file of the `courses` application and add the following URL patterns:

```python
path('subject/<slug:subject>)/',
    views.CourseListView.as_view(),
    name='course_list_subject'),

path('<slug:slug>/',
    views.CourseDetailView.as_view(),
    name='course_detail'),
```

We define the following URL patterns:

- `course_list_subject`: For displaying all courses for a subject
- `course_detail`: For displaying a single course overview

Let's build templates for the `CourseListView` and `CourseDetailView` views. Create the following file structure inside the `templates/courses/` directory of the courses application:

```
course/
    list.html
    detail.html
```

Edit the `courses/course/list.html` template and write the following code:

```django
{% extends "base.html" %}

{% block title %}
    {% if subject %}
        {{ subject.title }} courses
    {% else %}
        All courses
    {% endif %}
```

```
    {% endblock %}

    {% block content %}
    <h1>
        {% if subject %}
            {{ subject.title }} courses
        {% else %}
            All courses
        {% endif %}
    </h1>
    <div class="contents">
        <h3>Subjects</h3>
        <ul id="modules">
            <li {% if not subject %}class="selected"{% endif %}>
                <a href="{% url "course_list" %}">All</a>
            </li>
            {% for s in subjects %}
                <li {% if subject == s %}class="selected"{% endif %}>
                    <a href="{% url "course_list_subject" s.slug %}">
                        {{ s.title }}
                        <br><span>{{ s.total_courses }} courses</span>
                    </a>
                </li>
            {% endfor %}
        </ul>
    </div>
    <div class="module">
        {% for course in courses %}
            {% with subject=course.subject %}
                <h3><a href="{% url "course_detail" course.slug %}">
                {{ course.title }}</a></h3>
                <p>
                    <a href="{% url "course_list_subject" subject.slug %}">
                    {{ subject }}</a>.
                    {{ course.total_modules }} modules.
                    Instructor: {{ course.owner.get_full_name }}
                </p>
            {% endwith %}
        {% endfor %}
    </div>
    {% endblock %}
```

This is the template for listing the available courses. We create an HTML list to display all Subject objects and build a link to the course_list_subject URL for each of them. We add a selected HTML class to highlight the current subject, if any. We iterate over every Course object, displaying the total number of modules and the instructor name.

Run the development server and open `http://127.0.0.1:8000/` in your browser. You should see a page similar to the following one:

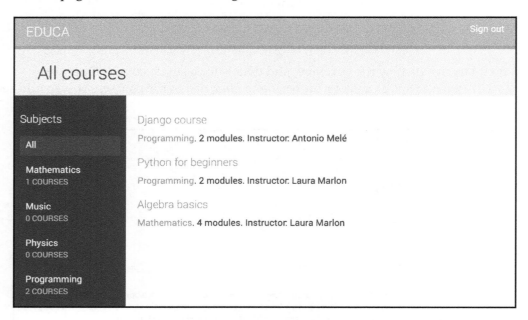

The left sidebar contains all subjects, including the total number of courses for each of them. You can click any subject to filter the courses displayed.

Edit the `courses/course/detail.html` template and add the following code to it:

```
{% extends "base.html" %}

{% block title %}
    {{ object.title }}
{% endblock %}

{% block content %}
    {% with subject=course.subject %}
        <h1>
            {{ object.title }}
        </h1>
        <div class="module">
            <h2>Overview</h2>
            <p>
                <a href="{% url "course_list_subject" subject.slug %}">
                {{ subject.title }}</a>.
                {{ course.modules.count }} modules.
```

```
                Instructor: {{ course.owner.get_full_name }}
          </p>
          {{ object.overview|linebreaks }}
        </div>
     {% endwith %}
  {% endblock %}
```

In this template, we display the overview and details for a single course. Open `http://127.0.0.1:8000/` in your browser and click one of the courses. You should see a page with the following structure:

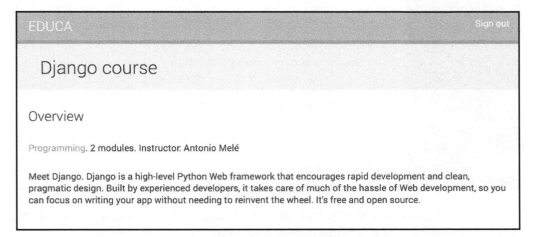

We have created a public area for displaying courses. Next, we need to allow users to register as students and enroll in courses.

Adding student registration

Create a new application using the following command:

```
python manage.py startapp students
```

Edit the `settings.py` file of the `educa` project and add the new application to the `INSTALLED_APPS` setting, as follows:

```
INSTALLED_APPS = [
    # ...
    'students.apps.StudentsConfig',
]
```

Creating a student registration view

Edit the `views.py` file of the `students` application and write the following code:

```python
from django.urls import reverse_lazy
from django.views.generic.edit import CreateView
from django.contrib.auth.forms import UserCreationForm
from django.contrib.auth import authenticate, login

class StudentRegistrationView(CreateView):
    template_name = 'students/student/registration.html'
    form_class = UserCreationForm
    success_url = reverse_lazy('student_course_list')

    def form_valid(self, form):
        result = super(StudentRegistrationView,
                        self).form_valid(form)
        cd = form.cleaned_data
        user = authenticate(username=cd['username'],
                            password=cd['password1'])
        login(self.request, user)
        return result
```

This is the view that allows students to register on our site. We use the generic `CreateView`, which provides the functionality for creating model objects. This view requires the following attributes:

- `template_name`: The path of the template to render this view.
- `form_class`: The form for creating objects, which has to be `ModelForm`. We use Django's `UserCreationForm` as the registration form to create `User` objects.
- `success_url`: The URL to redirect the user to when the form is successfully submitted. We reverse the `student_course_list` URL, which we are going to create in the *Accessing the course contents* section for listing the courses students are enrolled in.

The `form_valid()` method is executed when valid form data has been posted. It has to return an HTTP response. We override this method to log the user in after successfully signing up.

Create a new file inside the `students` application directory and name it `urls.py`. Add the following code to it:

```python
from django.urls import path
from . import views
```

```
urlpatterns = [
    path('register/',
         views.StudentRegistrationView.as_view(),
         name='student_registration'),
]
```

Then, edit the main `urls.py` of the `educa` project and include the URLs for the `students` application by adding the following pattern to your URL configuration:

```
urlpatterns = [
    # ...
    path('students/', include('students.urls')),
]
```

Create the following file structure inside the `students` application directory:

```
templates/
    students/
        student/
            registration.html
```

Edit the `students/student/registration.html` template and add the following code to it:

```
{% extends "base.html" %}

{% block title %}
    Sign up
{% endblock %}

{% block content %}
    <h1>
        Sign up
    </h1>
    <div class="module">
        <p>Enter your details to create an account:</p>
        <form action="" method="post">
            {{ form.as_p }}
            {% csrf_token %}
            <p><input type="submit" value="Create my account"></p>
        </form>
    </div>
{% endblock %}
```

Run the development server and open `http://127.0.0.1:8000/students/register/` in your browser. You should see the registration form like this:

Note that the `student_course_list` URL specified in the `success_url` attribute of the `StudentRegistrationView` view doesn't exist yet. If you submit the form, Django won't find the URL to redirect you after a successful registration. We will create this URL in the *Accessing the course contents* section.

Enrolling in courses

After users create an account, they should be able to enroll in courses. In order to store enrollments, we need to create a many-to-many relationship between the Course and User models.

Edit the models.py file of the courses application and add the following field to the Course model:

```
students = models.ManyToManyField(User,
                                  related_name='courses_joined',
                                  blank=True)
```

From the shell, execute the following command to create a migration for this change:

```
python manage.py makemigrations
```

You will see an output similar to this:

```
Migrations for 'courses':
  courses/migrations/0004_course_students.py
    - Add field students to course
```

Then, execute the next command to apply pending migrations:

```
python manage.py migrate
```

You should see output that ends with the following line:

```
Applying courses.0004_course_students... OK
```

We can now associate students with the courses in which they are enrolled. Let's create the functionality for students to enroll in courses.

Create a new file inside the students application directory and name it forms.py. Add the following code to it:

```python
from django import forms
from courses.models import Course

class CourseEnrollForm(forms.Form):
    course = forms.ModelChoiceField(queryset=Course.objects.all(),
                                    widget=forms.HiddenInput)
```

We are going to use this form for students to enroll in courses. The course field is for the course in which the user gets enrolled. Therefore, it's a ModelChoiceField. We use a HiddenInput widget because we are not going to show this field to the user. We are going to use this form in the CourseDetailView view to display a button to enroll.

Edit the views.py file of the students application and add the following code:

```
from django.views.generic.edit import FormView
from django.contrib.auth.mixins import LoginRequiredMixin
from .forms import CourseEnrollForm

class StudentEnrollCourseView(LoginRequiredMixin, FormView):
    course = None
    form_class = CourseEnrollForm

    def form_valid(self, form):
        self.course = form.cleaned_data['course']
        self.course.students.add(self.request.user)
        return super(StudentEnrollCourseView,
                     self).form_valid(form)

    def get_success_url(self):
        return reverse_lazy('student_course_detail',
                            args=[self.course.id])
```

This is the StudentEnrollCourseView. view. It handles students enrolling in courses. The view inherits from the LoginRequiredMixin mixin so that only logged in users can access the view. It also inherits from Django's FormView view since we handle a form submission. We use the CourseEnrollForm form for the form_class attribute and also define a course attribute for storing the given Course object. When the form is valid, we add the current user to the students enrolled in the course.

The get_success_url() method returns the URL the user will be redirected to if the form was successfully submitted. This method is equivalent to the success_url attribute. We reverse the student_course_detail URL, which we will create in the next *Accessing the course contents* section in order to display the course contents.

Edit the urls.py file of the students application and add the following URL pattern to it:

```
path('enroll-course/',
     views.StudentEnrollCourseView.as_view(),
     name='student_enroll_course'),
```

Let's add the enroll button form to the course overview page. Edit the `views.py` file of the `courses` application and modify `CourseDetailView` to make it look as follows:

```python
from students.forms import CourseEnrollForm

class CourseDetailView(DetailView):
    model = Course
    template_name = 'courses/course/detail.html'

    def get_context_data(self, **kwargs):
        context = super(CourseDetailView,
                        self).get_context_data(**kwargs)
        context['enroll_form'] = CourseEnrollForm(
                                    initial={'course':self.object})
        return context
```

We use the `get_context_data()` method to include the enrollment form in the context for rendering the templates. We initialize the hidden course field of the form with the current `Course` object, so that it can be submitted directly.

Edit the `courses/course/detail.html` template and find the following line:

```html
{{ object.overview|linebreaks }}
```

Replace it with the following code:

```html
{{ object.overview|linebreaks }}
{% if request.user.is_authenticated %}
    <form action="{% url "student_enroll_course" %}" method="post">
        {{ enroll_form }}
        {% csrf_token %}
        <input type="submit" class="button" value="Enroll now">
    </form>
{% else %}
    <a href="{% url "student_registration" %}" class="button">
        Register to enroll
    </a>
{% endif %}
```

This is the button for enrolling in courses. If the user is authenticated, we display the enrollment button, including the hidden form that points to the `student_enroll_course` URL. If the user is not authenticated, we display a link to register in the platform.

Make sure the development server is running, open `http://127.0.0.1:8000/` in your browser and click a course. If you are logged in, you should see an **ENROLL NOW** button placed below the course overview, as follows:

Overview

Programming. **2 modules. Instructor: Antonio Melé**

Meet Django. Django is a high-level Python Web framework that encourages rapid development and clean, pragmatic design. Built by experienced developers, it takes care of much of the hassle of Web development, so you can focus on writing your app without needing to reinvent the wheel. It's free and open source.

ENROLL NOW

If you are not logged in, you will see a **REGISTER TO ENROLL** button instead.

Accessing the course contents

We need a view for displaying the courses the students are enrolled in, and a view for accessing the actual course contents. Edit the `views.py` file of the `students` application and add the following code to it:

```python
from django.views.generic.list import ListView
from courses.models import Course

class StudentCourseListView(LoginRequiredMixin, ListView):
    model = Course
    template_name = 'students/course/list.html'

    def get_queryset(self):
        qs = super(StudentCourseListView, self).get_queryset()
        return qs.filter(students__in=[self.request.user])
```

This is the view for students to list the courses they are enrolled in. It inherits from `LoginRequiredMixin` to make sure that only logged in users can access the view. It also inherits from the generic `ListView` for displaying a list of `Course` objects. We override the `get_queryset()` method for retrieving only the courses the user is enrolled in; we filter the QuerySet by the student's `ManyToManyField` field for doing so.

Then, add the following code to the `views.py` file:

```python
from django.views.generic.detail import DetailView

class StudentCourseDetailView(DetailView):
    model = Course
    template_name = 'students/course/detail.html'

    def get_queryset(self):
        qs = super(StudentCourseDetailView, self).get_queryset()
        return qs.filter(students__in=[self.request.user])

    def get_context_data(self, **kwargs):
        context = super(StudentCourseDetailView,
                        self).get_context_data(**kwargs)
        # get course object
        course = self.get_object()
        if 'module_id' in self.kwargs:
            # get current module
            context['module'] = course.modules.get(
                                    id=self.kwargs['module_id'])
        else:
            # get first module
            context['module'] = course.modules.all()[0]
        return context
```

This is `StudentCourseDetailView`. We override the `get_queryset()` method to limit the base QuerySet to courses in which the user is enrolled. We also override the `get_context_data()` method to set a course module in the context if the `module_id` URL parameter is given. Otherwise, we set the first module of the course. This way, students will be able to navigate through modules inside a course.

Edit the `urls.py` file of the `students` application and add the following URL patterns to it:

```python
path('courses/',
     views.StudentCourseListView.as_view(),
     name='student_course_list'),

path('course/<pk>/',
     views.StudentCourseDetailView.as_view(),
     name='student_course_detail'),

path('course/<pk>/<module_id>/',
     views.StudentCourseDetailView.as_view(),
     name='student_course_detail_module'),
```

Create the following file structure inside the `templates/students/` directory of the `students` application:

```
course/
    detail.html
    list.html
```

Edit the `students/course/list.html` template and add the following code to it:

```
{% extends "base.html" %}

{% block title %}My courses{% endblock %}

{% block content %}
    <h1>My courses</h1>

    <div class="module">
        {% for course in object_list %}
            <div class="course-info">
                <h3>{{ course.title }}</h3>
                <p><a href="{% url "student_course_detail" course.id %}">
                Access contents</a></p>
            </div>
        {% empty %}
            <p>
                You are not enrolled in any courses yet.
                <a href="{% url "course_list" %}">Browse courses</a>
                to enroll in a course.
            </p>
        {% endfor %}
    </div>
{% endblock %}
```

This template displays the courses the user is enrolled in. Remember that when a new student successfully registers with the platform, they will be redirected to the `student_course_list` URL. Let's also redirect students to this URL when they log in to the platform.

Edit the `settings.py` file of the `educa` project and add the following code to it:

```
from django.urls import reverse_lazy
LOGIN_REDIRECT_URL = reverse_lazy('student_course_list')
```

This is the setting used by the `auth` module to redirect the user to after a successful login if no next parameter is present in the request. After successful login, students will be redirected to the `student_course_list` URL to view the courses that they are enrolled in.

Edit the `students/course/detail.html` template and add the following code to it:

```
{% extends "base.html" %}

{% block title %}
    {{ object.title }}
{% endblock %}

{% block content %}
    <h1>
        {{ module.title }}
    </h1>
    <div class="contents">
        <h3>Modules</h3>
        <ul id="modules">
        {% for m in object.modules.all %}
            <li data-id="{{ m.id }}" {% if m == module
            %}class="selected"
            {% endif %}>
                <a href="{% url "student_course_detail_module"
                object.id m.id %}">
                    <span>
                        Module <span class="order">{{ m.order|add:1 }}
                    </span>
                    </span>
                    <br>
                    {{ m.title }}
                </a>
            </li>
        {% empty %}
            <li>No modules yet.</li>
        {% endfor %}
        </ul>
    </div>
    <div class="module">
        {% for content in module.contents.all %}
            {% with item=content.item %}
                <h2>{{ item.title }}</h2>
                {{ item.render }}
            {% endwith %}
        {% endfor %}
    </div>
{% endblock %}
```

This is the template for enrolled students to access the contents of a course. First, we build an HTML list including all course modules and highlighting the current module. Then, we iterate over the current module contents and access each content item to display it using {{ item.render }}. We are going to add the render() method to the content models next. This method will take care of rendering the content properly.

Rendering different types of content

We need to provide a way to render each type of content. Edit the models.py file of the courses application and add the following render() method to the ItemBase model:

```python
from django.template.loader import render_to_string
from django.utils.safestring import mark_safe

class ItemBase(models.Model):
    # ...

    def render(self):
        return render_to_string('courses/content/{}.html'.format(
                    self._meta.model_name), {'item': self})
```

This method uses the render_to_string() function for rendering a template and returning the rendered content as a string. Each kind of content is rendered using a template named after the content model. We use self._meta.model_name to generate the appropriate template name for each content model dynamically. The render() method provides a common interface for rendering diverse content.

Create the following file structure inside the templates/courses/ directory of the courses application:

```
content/
    text.html
    file.html
    image.html
    video.html
```

Edit the `courses/content/text.html` template and write this code:

```
{{ item.content|linebreaks|safe }}
```

Edit the `courses/content/file.html` template and add the following:

```
<p><a href="{{ item.file.url }}" class="button">Download file</a></p>
```

Edit the `courses/content/image.html` template and write:

```
<p><img src="{{ item.file.url }}"></p>
```

For files uploaded with `ImageField` and `FileField` to work, we need to set up our project to serve media files with the development server. Edit the `settings.py` file of your project and add the following code to it:

```
MEDIA_URL = '/media/'
MEDIA_ROOT = os.path.join(BASE_DIR, 'media/')
```

Remember that `MEDIA_URL` is the base URL to serve uploaded media files and `MEDIA_ROOT` is the local path where the files are located.

Edit the main `urls.py` file of your project and add the following imports:

```
from django.conf import settings
from django.conf.urls.static import static
```

Then, write the following lines at the end of the file:

```
if settings.DEBUG:
    urlpatterns += static(settings.MEDIA_URL,
                          document_root=settings.MEDIA_ROOT)
```

Your project is now ready to upload and serve media files. The Django development server will be in charge of serving the media files during development (that is, when the `DEBUG` setting is set to `True`). Remember that the development server is not suitable for production use. You will learn how to set up a production environment in `Chapter 13`, *Going Live*.

We also have to create a template for rendering `Video` objects. We will use `django-embed-video` for embedding video content. `django-embed-video` is a third-party Django application that allows you to embed videos in your templates, from sources such as YouTube or Vimeo, by simply providing the video's public URL.

Install the package with the following command:

```
pip install django-embed-video==1.1.2
```

Edit the `settings.py` file of your project and add the app to the `INSTALLED_APPS`, setting as follows:

```
INSTALLED_APPS = [
    # ...
    'embed_video',
]
```

You can find `django-embed-video` application's documentation at `https://django-embed-video.readthedocs.io/en/latest/`.

Edit the `courses/content/video.html` template and write the following code:

```
{% load embed_video_tags %}
{% video item.url "small" %}
```

Now run the development server and access `http://127.0.0.1:8000/course/mine/` in your browser.

Access the site with a user that belongs to the `Instructors` group, and add multiple contents to a course. To include video content, you can just copy any YouTube URL, such as `https://www.youtube.com/watch?v=bgV39DlmZ2U`, and include it in the `url` field of the form.

After adding contents to the course open `http://127.0.0.1:8000/`, click the course and click on the **ENROLL NOW** button. You should be enrolled in the course and redirected to the `student_course_detail` URL. The following screenshot shows a sample course content:

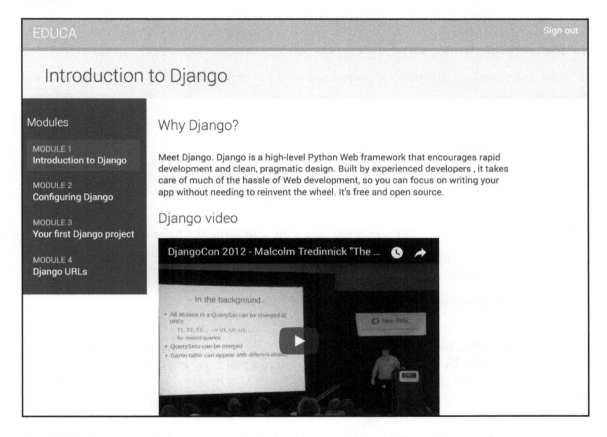

Great! You have created a common interface for rendering different types of course contents.

Using the cache framework

HTTP requests to your web application usually entail database access, data processing, and template rendering. This is much more expensive in terms of processing than serving a static website.

The overhead in some requests can be significant when your site starts getting more and more traffic. This is where caching becomes precious. By caching queries, calculation results, or rendered content in an HTTP request, you will avoid cost-expensive operations in the following requests. This translates into shorter response times and less processing on the server side.

Django includes a robust cache system that allows you to cache data with different levels of granularity. You can cache a single query, the output of a specific view, parts of rendered template content, or your entire site. Items are stored in the cache system for a default time. You can specify the default timeout for cached data.

This is how you will usually use the cache framework when your application gets an HTTP request:

1. Try to find the requested data in the cache
2. If found, return the cached data
3. If not found, perform the following steps:
    1. Perform the query or processing required to obtain the data
    2. Save the generated data in the cache
    3. Return the data

You can read detailed information about Django's cache system at `https://docs.djangoproject.com/en/2.0/topics/cache/`.

Available cache backends

Django comes with several cache backends. These are the following:

- `backends.memcached.MemcachedCache` or
  `backends.memcached.PyLibMCCache`: A Memcached backend. Memcached is a fast and efficient memory-based cache server. The backend to use depends on the Memcached Python bindings you choose.
- `backends.db.DatabaseCache`: Use the database as cache system.
- `backends.filebased.FileBasedCache`: Use the file storage system. Serializes and stores each cache value as a separate file.

- `backends.locmem.LocMemCache`: Local memory cache backend. This the default cache backend.
- `backends.dummy.DummyCache`: A dummy cache backend intended only for development. It implements the cache interface without actually caching anything. This cache is per-process and thread-safe.

 For optimal performance, use a memory-based cache backend such as the Memcached backend.

Installing Memcached

We are going to use the Memcached backend. Memcached runs in memory and it is allotted a specified amount of RAM. When the allotted RAM is full, Memcached starts removing the oldest data to store new data.

Download Memcached from `https://memcached.org/downloads`. If you are using Linux, you can install Memcached using the following command:

```
./configure && make && make test && sudo make install
```

If you are using macOS X, you can install Memcached with the Homebrew package manager using the command `brew install memcached`. You can download Homebrew from `https://brew.sh/`.

After installing Memcached, open a shell and start it using the following command:

```
memcached -l 127.0.0.1:11211
```

Memcached will run on port `11211` by default. However, you can specify a custom host and port by using the `-l` option. You can find more information about Memcached at `https://memcached.org`.

After installing Memcached, you have to install its Python bindings. You can do it with the following command:

```
pip install python-memcached==1.59
```

Cache settings

Django provides the following cache settings:

- CACHES: A dictionary containing all available caches for the project.
- CACHE_MIDDLEWARE_ALIAS: The cache alias to use for storage.
- CACHE_MIDDLEWARE_KEY_PREFIX: The prefix to use for cache keys. Set a prefix to avoid key collisions if you share the same cache between several sites.
- CACHE_MIDDLEWARE_SECONDS: The default number of seconds to cache pages.

The caching system for the project can be configured using the CACHES setting. This setting is a dictionary that allows you to specify the configuration for multiple caches. Each cache included in the CACHES dictionary can specify the following data:

- BACKEND: The cache backend to use.
- KEY_FUNCTION: A string containing a dotted path to a callable that takes a prefix, version, and key as arguments and returns a final cache key.
- KEY_PREFIX: A string prefix for all cache keys, to avoid collisions.
- LOCATION: The location of the cache. Depending on the cache backend, this might be a directory, a host and port, or a name for the in-memory backend.
- OPTIONS: Any additional parameters to be passed to the cache backend.
- TIMEOUT: The default timeout, in seconds, for storing the cache keys. 300 seconds by default, which is five minutes. If set to None, cache keys will not expire.
- VERSION: The default version number for the cache keys. Useful for cache versioning.

Adding Memcached to your project

Let's configure the cache for our project. Edit the settings.py file of the educa project and add the following code to it:

```
CACHES = {
    'default': {
        'BACKEND': 'django.core.cache.backends.memcached.MemcachedCache',
        'LOCATION': '127.0.0.1:11211',
    }
}
```

We are using the `MemcachedCache` backend. We specify its location using the `address:port` notation. If you have multiple Memcached instances, you can use a list for `LOCATION`.

Monitoring Memcached

In order to monitor Memcached, we will use a third-party package called `django-memcache-status`. This app displays statistics for your Memcached instances in the administration site. Install it with the following command:

```
pip install django-memcache-status==1.3
```

Edit the `settings.py` file and add `'memcache_status'` to the `INSTALLED_APPS` setting:

```
INSTALLED_APPS = [
    # ...
    'memcache_status',
]
```

Make sure Memcached is running, start the development server in another shell window, and open `http://127.0.0.1:8000/admin/` in your browser. Log in to the administration site using a superuser. You should see the following block:

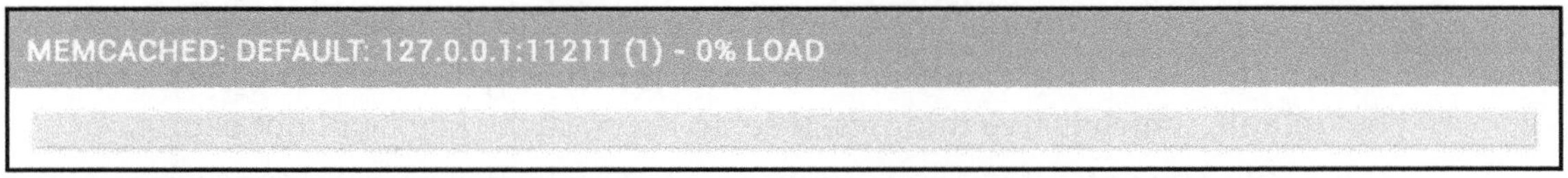

MEMCACHED: DEFAULT: 127.0.0.1:11211 (1) - 0% LOAD

This graph shows the cache usage. The green color represents free cache while red indicates used space. If you click the title of the box, it shows detailed statistics of your Memcached instance.

We have set up Memcached for our project and are able to monitor it. Let's start caching data!

Cache levels

Django provides the following levels of caching listed here by ascending order of granularity:

- **Low-level cache API**: Provides the highest granularity. Allows you to cache specific queries or calculations.
- **Per-view cache**: Provides caching for individual views.
- **Template cache**: Allows you to cache template fragments.
- **Per-site cache**: The highest-level cache. It caches your entire site.

 Think about your cache strategy before implementing caching. Focus first on expensive queries or calculations, which are not calculated on a per-user basis.

Using the low-level cache API

The low-level cache API allows you to store objects in the cache with any granularity. It is located at `django.core.cache`. You can import it like this:

```
from django.core.cache import cache
```

This uses the default cache. It's equivalent to `caches['default']`. Accessing a specific cache is also possible via its alias:

```
from django.core.cache import caches
my_cache = caches['alias']
```

Let's take a look at how the cache API works. Open the shell with the command `python manage.py shell` and execute the following code:

```
>>> from django.core.cache import cache
>>> cache.set('musician', 'Django Reinhardt', 20)
```

We access the default cache backend and use `set(key, value, timeout)` to store a key named `'musician'` with a value that is the string `'Django Reinhardt'` for 20 seconds. If we don't specify a timeout, Django uses the default timeout specified for the cache backend in the CACHES setting. Now, execute the following code:

```
>>> cache.get('musician')
'Django Reinhardt'
```

We retrieve the key from the cache. Wait for 20 seconds and execute the same code:

```
>>> cache.get('musician')
```

No value is returned this time. The `'musician'` cache key expired and the `get()` method returns None because the key is not in the cache anymore.

 Always avoid storing a None value in a cache key because you won't be able to distinguish between the actual value and a cache miss.

Let's cache a QuerySet with the following code:

```
>>> from courses.models import Subject
>>> subjects = Subject.objects.all()
>>> cache.set('all_subjects', subjects)
```

We perform a QuerySet on the `Subject` model and store the returned objects in the `'all_subjects'` key. Let's retrieve the cached data:

```
>>> cache.get('all_subjects')
<QuerySet [<Subject: Mathematics>, <Subject: Music>, <Subject: Physics>,
<Subject: Programming>]>
```

We are going to cache some queries in our views. Edit the `views.py` file of the `courses` application and add the following import:

```
from django.core.cache import cache
```

In the `get()` method of the `CourseListView`, replace the following line:

```
subjects = Subject.objects.annotate(
             total_courses=Count('courses'))
```

Replace it with the following ones:

```
subjects = cache.get('all_subjects')
if not subjects:
    subjects = Subject.objects.annotate(
                    total_courses=Count('courses'))
    cache.set('all_subjects', subjects)
```

In this code, we try to get the `all_students` key from the cache using `cache.get()`. This returns `None` if the given key is not found. If no key is found (not cached yet or cached but timed out), we perform the query to retrieve all `Subject` objects and their number of courses, and we cache the result using `cache.set()`.

Run the development server and open `http://127.0.0.1:8000/` in your browser. When the view is executed, the cache key is not found and the QuerySet is executed. Open `http://127.0.0.1:8000/admin/` in your browser and expand the Memcached statistics. You should see usage data for the cache similar to the following screen:

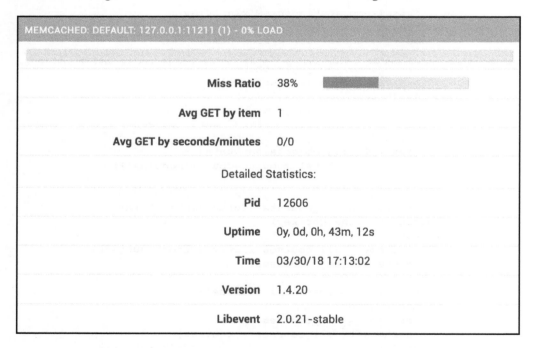

Take a look at **Curr Items**, which should be **1**. This shows that there is one item currently stored in the cache. **Get Hits** shows how many get commands were successful and **Get Misses** shows the get requests for keys that are missing. The **Miss Ratio** is calculated using both of them.

Now, navigate back to `http://127.0.0.1:8000/` using your browser and reload the page several times. If you take a look at the cache statistics now, you will see several more reads (**Get Hits** and **Cmd Get** will increase).

Caching based on dynamic data

Many times you will want to cache something that is based on dynamic data. In these cases, you have to build dynamic keys that contain all information required to uniquely identify the cached data. Edit the `views.py` file of the `courses` application and modify the `CourseListView` view to make it look like this:

```python
class CourseListView(TemplateResponseMixin, View):
    model = Course
    template_name = 'courses/course/list.html'

    def get(self, request, subject=None):
        subjects = cache.get('all_subjects')
        if not subjects:
            subjects = Subject.objects.annotate(
                        total_courses=Count('courses'))
            cache.set('all_subjects', subjects)
        all_courses = Course.objects.annotate(
                        total_modules=Count('modules'))
        if subject:
            subject = get_object_or_404(Subject, slug=subject)
            key = 'subject_{}_courses'.format(subject.id)
            courses = cache.get(key)
            if not courses:
                courses = all_courses.filter(subject=subject)
                cache.set(key, courses)
        else:
            courses = cache.get('all_courses')
            if not courses:
                courses = all_courses
                cache.set('all_courses', courses)
        return self.render_to_response({'subjects': subjects,
                                        'subject': subject,
                                        'courses': courses})
```

In this case, we also cache both all courses and courses filtered by subject. We use the `all_courses` cache key for storing all courses if no subject is given. If there is a subject, we build the key dynamically with `'subject_{}_courses'.format(subject.id)`.

It is important to note that you cannot use a cached QuerySet to build other QuerySets, since what you cached are actually the results of the QuerySet. So you cannot do the following:

```
courses = cache.get('all_courses')
courses.filter(subject=subject)
```

Instead, you have to create the base QuerySet `Course.objects.annotate(total_modules=Count('modules'))`, which is not going to be executed until it is forced, and use it to further restrict the QuerySet with `all_courses.filter(subject=subject)` in case the data was not found in the cache.

Caching template fragments

Caching template fragments is a higher-level approach. You need to load the cache template tags in your template using `{% load cache %}`. Then, you will be able to use the `{% cache %}` template tag to cache specific template fragments. You will usually use the template tag as follows:

```
{% cache 300 fragment_name %}
    ...
{% endcache %}
```

The `{% cache %}` tag has two required arguments: the timeout, in seconds, and a name for the fragment. If you need to cache content depending on dynamic data, you can do so by passing additional arguments to the `{% cache %}` template tag to uniquely identify the fragment.

Edit the `/students/course/detail.html` of the `students` application. Add the following code at the top of it, just after the `{% extends %}` tag:

```
{% load cache %}
```

Then, replace the following lines:

```
{% for content in module.contents.all %}
  {% with item=content.item %}
    <h2>{{ item.title }}</h2>
    {{ item.render }}
  {% endwith %}
{% endfor %}
```

Replace them with the following ones:

```
{% cache 600 module_contents module %}
  {% for content in module.contents.all %}
    {% with item=content.item %}
      <h2>{{ item.title }}</h2>
      {{ item.render }}
    {% endwith %}
  {% endfor %}
{% endcache %}
```

We cache this template fragment using the name `module_contents` and passing the current `Module` object to it. Thus, we uniquely identify the fragment. This is important to avoid caching a module's contents and serving the wrong content when a different module is requested.

 If the `USE_I18N` setting is set to `True`, the per-site middleware cache will respect the active language. If you use the `{% cache %}` template tag you have to use one of the translation-specific variables available in templates to achieve the same result, such as `{% cache 600 name request.LANGUAGE_CODE %}`.

Caching views

You can cache the output of individual views using the `cache_page` decorator located at `django.views.decorators.cache`. The decorator requires a `timeout` argument (in seconds).

Let's use it in our views. Edit the `urls.py` file of the `students` application and add the following import:

```
from django.views.decorators.cache import cache_page
```

Then, apply the `cache_page` decorator to the `student_course_detail` and `student_course_detail_module` URL patterns, as follows:

```
path('course/<pk>/',
    cache_page(60 * 15)(views.StudentCourseDetailView.as_view()),
    name='student_course_detail'),

path('course/<pk>/<module_id>/',
    cache_page(60 * 15)(views.StudentCourseDetailView.as_view()),
    name='student_course_detail_module'),
```

Now, the result for the `StudentCourseDetailView` is cached for 15 minutes.

 The per-view cache uses the URL to build the cache key. Multiple URLs pointing to the same view will be cached separately.

Using the per-site cache

This is the highest-level cache. It allows you to cache your entire site.

To allow the per-site cache, edit the `settings.py` file of your project and add the `UpdateCacheMiddleware` and `FetchFromCacheMiddleware` classes to the `MIDDLEWARE` setting, as follows:

```
MIDDLEWARE = [
    'django.middleware.security.SecurityMiddleware',
    'django.contrib.sessions.middleware.SessionMiddleware',
    'django.middleware.cache.UpdateCacheMiddleware',
    'django.middleware.common.CommonMiddleware',
    'django.middleware.cache.FetchFromCacheMiddleware',
    # ...
]
```

Remember that middlewares are executed in the given order during the request phase, and in reverse order during the response phase. `UpdateCacheMiddleware` is placed before `CommonMiddleware` because it runs during response time, when middlewares are executed in reverse order. `FetchFromCacheMiddleware` is placed after `CommonMiddleware` intentionally because it needs to access request data set by the latter.

Then, add the following settings to the `settings.py` file:

```
CACHE_MIDDLEWARE_ALIAS = 'default'
CACHE_MIDDLEWARE_SECONDS = 60 * 15   # 15 minutes
CACHE_MIDDLEWARE_KEY_PREFIX = 'educa'
```

In these settings, we use the default cache for our cache middleware and we set the global cache timeout to 15 minutes. We also specify a prefix for all cache keys to avoid collisions in case we use the same Memcached backend for multiple projects. Our site will now cache and return cached content for all `GET` requests.

We have done this to test the per-site cache functionality. However, the per-site cache is not suitable for us, since the course management views need to show updated data to instantly reflect any changes. The best approach to follow in our project is to cache the templates or views that are used to display course contents to students.

We have seen an overview of the methods provided by Django to cache data. You should define your cache strategy wisely and prioritize the most expensive QuerySets or calculations.

Summary

In this chapter, we created public views for the courses and you have built a system for students to register and enroll in courses. We installed Memcached and implemented different cache levels.

In the next chapter, we will build a RESTful API for your project.

12
Building an API

In the previous chapter, you built a system of student registration and enrollment in courses. You created views to display course contents and learned how to use Django's cache framework. In this chapter, you will learn how to do the following:

- Build a RESTful API
- Handle authentication and permissions for API views
- Create API view sets and routers

Building a RESTful API

You might want to create an interface for other services to interact with your web application. By building an API, you can allow third parties to consume information and operate with your application programmatically.

There are several ways you can structure your API but following REST principles is encouraged. The **REST** architecture comes from **Representational State Transfer**. RESTful APIs are resource-based. Your models represent resources and HTTP methods such as GET, POST, PUT, or DELETE are used to retrieve, create, update, or delete objects. HTTP response codes are also used in this context. Different HTTP response codes are returned to indicate the result of the HTTP request, for example, 2XX response codes for success, 4XX for errors, and so on.

The most common formats to exchange data in RESTful APIs are JSON and XML. We will build a REST API with JSON serialization for our project. Our API will provide the following functionality:

- Retrieve subjects
- Retrieve available courses
- Retrieve course contents
- Enroll in a course

We can build an API from scratch with Django by creating custom views. However, there are several third-party modules that simplify creating an API for your project, the most popular among them being Django REST framework.

Installing Django REST framework

Django REST framework allows you to easily build REST APIs for your project. You can find all information about REST framework at `https://www.django-rest-framework.org/`.

Open the shell and install the framework with the following command:

```
pip install djangorestframework==3.8.2
```

Edit the `settings.py` file of the `educa` project and add `rest_framework` to the `INSTALLED_APPS` setting to activate the application, as follows:

```
INSTALLED_APPS = [
    # ...
    'rest_framework',
]
```

Then, add the following code to the `settings.py` file:

```
REST_FRAMEWORK = {
    'DEFAULT_PERMISSION_CLASSES':
'rest_framework.permissions.DjangoModelPermissionsOrAnonReadOnly'
    ]
}
```

You can provide a specific configuration for your API using the `REST_FRAMEWORK` setting. REST framework offers a wide range of settings to configure default behaviors. The `DEFAULT_PERMISSION_CLASSES` setting specifies the default permissions to read, create, update, or delete objects. We set `DjangoModelPermissionsOrAnonReadOnly` as the only default permission class. This class relies on Django's permissions system to allow users to create, update, or delete objects, while providing read-only access for anonymous users. You will learn more about permissions later in the *Adding permissions to views* section.

For a complete list of available settings for REST framework, you can visit `https://www.django-rest-framework.org/api-guide/settings/`.

Defining serializers

After setting up REST framework, we need to specify how our data will be serialized. Output data has to be serialized in a specific format, and input data will be de-serialized for processing. The framework provides the following classes to build serializers for single objects:

- `Serializer`: Provides serialization for normal Python class instances
- `ModelSerializer`: Provides serialization for model instances
- `HyperlinkedModelSerializer`: The same as `ModelSerializer`, but it represents object relationships with links rather than primary keys

Let's build our first serializer. Create the following file structure inside the `courses` application directory:

```
api/
    __init__.py
    serializers.py
```

We will build all the API functionality inside the `api` directory to keep everything well organized. Edit the `serializers.py` file and add the following code:

```python
from rest_framework import serializers
from ..models import Subject

class SubjectSerializer(serializers.ModelSerializer):
    class Meta:
        model = Subject
        fields = ['id', 'title', 'slug']
```

This is the serializer for the `Subject` model. Serializers are defined in a similar fashion to Django's `Form` and `ModelForm` classes. The `Meta` class allows you to specify the model to serialize and the fields to be included for serialization. All model fields will be included if you don't set a `fields` attribute.

Let's try our serializer. Open the command line and start the Django shell with the following command:

```
python manage.py shell
```

Run the following code:

```
>>> from courses.models import Subject
>>> from courses.api.serializers import SubjectSerializer
>>> subject = Subject.objects.latest('id')
>>> serializer = SubjectSerializer(subject)
>>> serializer.data
{'id': 4, 'title': 'Programming', 'slug': 'programming'}
```

In this example, we get a `Subject` object, create an instance of `SubjectSerializer`, and access the serialized data. You can see that the model data is translated into Python native data types.

Understanding parsers and renderers

The serialized data has to be rendered in a specific format before you return it in an HTTP response. Likewise, when you get an HTTP request, you have to parse the incoming data and de-serialize it before you can operate with it. REST framework includes renderers and parsers to handle that.

Let's see how to parse incoming data. Execute the following code in the Python shell:

```
>>> from io import BytesIO
>>> from rest_framework.parsers import JSONParser
>>> data = b'{"id":4,"title":"Programming","slug":"programming"}'
>>> JSONParser().parse(BytesIO(data))
{'id': 4, 'title': 'Programming', 'slug': 'programming'}
```

Given a JSON string input, you can use the `JSONParser` class provided by REST framework to convert it to a Python object.

REST framework also includes `Renderer` classes that allow you to format API responses. The framework determines which renderer to use through content negotiation. It inspects the request's `Accept` header to determine the expected content type for the response. Optionally, the renderer is determined by the format suffix of the URL. For example, accessing will trigger the `JSONRenderer` in order to return a JSON response.

Go back to the shell and execute the following code to render the `serializer` object from the previous serializer example:

```
>>> from rest_framework.renderers import JSONRenderer
>>> JSONRenderer().render(serializer.data)
```

You will see the following output:

```
b'{"id":4,"title":"Programming","slug":"programming"}'
```

We use the `JSONRenderer` to render the serialized data into JSON. By default, REST framework uses two different renderers: `JSONRenderer` and `BrowsableAPIRenderer`. The latter provides a web interface to easily browse your API. You can change the default renderer classes with the `DEFAULT_RENDERER_CLASSES` option of the `REST_FRAMEWORK` setting.

You can find more information about renderers and parsers at https://www.django-rest-framework.org/api-guide/renderers/ and https://www.django-rest-framework.org/api-guide/parsers/, respectively.

Building list and detail views

REST framework comes with a set of generic views and mixins that you can use to build your API views. These provide functionality to retrieve, create, update, or delete model objects. You can see all generic mixins and views provided by REST framework at https://www.django-rest-framework.org/api-guide/generic-views/.

Let's create list and detail views to retrieve `Subject` objects. Create a new file inside the `courses/api/` directory and name it `views.py`. Add the following code to it:

```
from rest_framework import generics
from ..models import Subject
from .serializers import SubjectSerializer

class SubjectListView(generics.ListAPIView):
    queryset = Subject.objects.all()
    serializer_class = SubjectSerializer

class SubjectDetailView(generics.RetrieveAPIView):
    queryset = Subject.objects.all()
    serializer_class = SubjectSerializer
```

In this code, we are using the generic `ListAPIView` and `RetrieveAPIView` views of REST framework. We include a `pk` URL parameter for the detail view to retrieve the object for the given primary key. Both views have the following attributes:

- `queryset`: The base `QuerySet` to use to retrieve objects
- `serializer_class`: The class to serialize objects

Let's add URL patterns for our views. Create a new file inside the `courses/api/` directory, name it `urls.py`, and make it look as follows:

```
from django.urls import path
from . import views

app_name = 'courses'

urlpatterns = [
    path('subjects/',
        views.SubjectListView.as_view(),
        name='subject_list'),

    path('subjects/<pk>/',
        views.SubjectDetailView.as_view(),
        name='subject_detail'),
]
```

Edit the main `urls.py` file of the `educa` project and include the API patterns as follows:

```
urlpatterns = [
    # ...
    path('api/', include('courses.api.urls', namespace='api')),
]
```

We use the `api` namespace for our API URLs. Ensure that your server is running with the command `python manage.py runserver`. Open the shell and retrieve the URL `http://127.0.0.1:8000/api/subjects/` with `curl` as follows:

```
curl http://127.0.0.1:8000/api/subjects/
```

You will get a response similar to the following one:

```
[
    {"id":1,"title":"Mathematics","slug":"mathematics"},
    {"id":2,"title":"Music","slug":"music"},
    {"id":3,"title":"Physics","slug":"physics"},
    {"id":4,"title":"Programming","slug":"programming"}
]
```

The HTTP response contains a list of `Subject` objects in JSON format. If your operating system doesn't come with `curl` installed, you can download it from `https://curl.haxx.se/dlwiz/`. Instead of `curl`, you can also use any other tool to send custom HTTP requests, such as a browser extension, such as Postman, which you can get at `https://www.getpostman.com/`.

Open `http://127.0.0.1:8000/api/subjects/` in your browser. You will see REST framework's browsable API as follows:

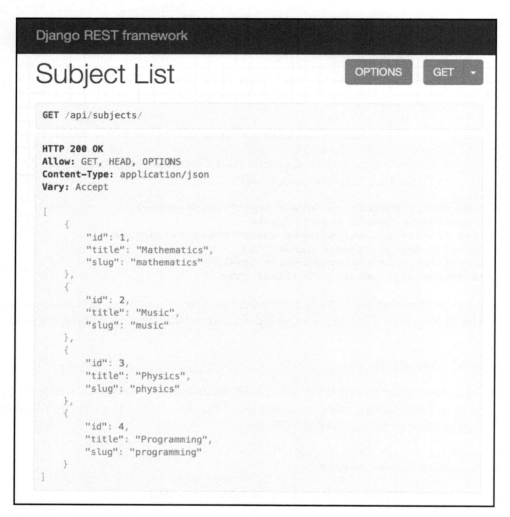

This HTML interface is provided by the `BrowsableAPIRenderer` renderer. It displays the result headers and content and allows you to perform requests. You can also access the API detail view for a `Subject` object by including its ID in the URL. Open `http://127.0.0.1:8000/api/subjects/1/` in your browser. You will see a single `Subject` object rendered in JSON format.

Creating nested serializers

We are going to create a serializer for the `Course` model. Edit the `api/serializers.py` file of the `courses` application and add the following code to it:

```
from ..models import Course

class CourseSerializer(serializers.ModelSerializer):
    class Meta:
        model = Course
        fields = ['id', 'subject', 'title', 'slug', 'overview',
                  'created', 'owner', 'modules']
```

Let's take a look at how a `Course` object is serialized. Open the shell, run `python manage.py shell`, and run the following code:

```
>>> from rest_framework.renderers import JSONRenderer
>>> from courses.models import Course
>>> from courses.api.serializers import CourseSerializer
>>> course = Course.objects.latest('id')
>>> serializer = CourseSerializer(course)
>>> JSONRenderer().render(serializer.data)
```

You will get a JSON object with the fields we included in `CourseSerializer`. You can see that the related objects of the `modules` manager are serialized as a list of primary keys, as follows:

```
"modules": [6, 7, 9, 10]
```

We want to include more information about each module, so we need to serialize `Module` objects and nest them. Modify the previous code of the `api/serializers.py` file of the `courses` application to make it look as follows:

```
from rest_framework import serializers
from ..models import Module

class ModuleSerializer(serializers.ModelSerializer):
    class Meta:
        model = Module
        fields = ['order', 'title', 'description']

class CourseSerializer(serializers.ModelSerializer):
    modules = ModuleSerializer(many=True, read_only=True)

    class Meta:
        model = Course
```

```
fields = ['id', 'subject', 'title', 'slug', 'overview',
          'created', 'owner', 'modules']
```

We define `ModuleSerializer` to provide serialization for the `Module` model. Then we add a `modules` attribute to `CourseSerializer` to nest the `ModuleSerializer` serializer. We set `many=True` to indicate that we are serializing multiple objects. The `read_only` parameter indicates that this field is read-only and should not be included in any input to create or update objects.

Open the shell and create an instance of `CourseSerializer` again. Render the serializer's `data` attribute with `JSONRenderer`. This time, the listed modules are being serialized with the nested `ModuleSerializer` serializer, as follows:

```
"modules": [
    {
        "order": 0,
        "title": "Introduction to overview",
        "description": "A brief overview about the Web Framework."
    },
    {
        "order": 1,
        "title": "Configuring Django",
        "description": "How to install Django."
    },
    ...
]
```

You can read more about serializers at `https://www.django-rest-framework.org/api-guide/serializers/`.

Building custom views

REST framework provides an `APIView` class, which builds API functionality on top of Django's `View` class. The `APIView` class differs from `View` in using REST framework's custom `Request` and `Response` objects and handling `APIException` exceptions to return the appropriate HTTP responses. It also has a built-in authentication and authorization system to manage access to views.

We are going to create a view for users to enroll in courses. Edit the `api/views.py` file of the `courses` application and add the following code to it:

```python
from django.shortcuts import get_object_or_404
from rest_framework.views import APIView
from rest_framework.response import Response
from ..models import Course

class CourseEnrollView(APIView):
    def post(self, request, pk, format=None):
        course = get_object_or_404(Course, pk=pk)
        course.students.add(request.user)
        return Response({'enrolled': True})
```

The `CourseEnrollView` view handles user enrollment in courses. The preceding code is as follows:

1. We create a custom view that subclasses `APIView`.
2. We define a `post()` method for POST actions. No other HTTP method will be allowed for this view.
3. We expect a `pk` URL parameter containing the ID of a course. We retrieve the course by the given `pk` parameter and raise a `404` exception if it's not found.
4. We add the current user to the `students` many-to-many relationship of the `Course` object and return a successful response.

Edit the `api/urls.py` file and add the following URL pattern for the `CourseEnrollView` view:

```python
path('courses/<pk>/enroll/',
    views.CourseEnrollView.as_view(),
    name='course_enroll'),
```

Theoretically, we could now perform a POST request to enroll the current user in a course. However, we need to be able to identify the user and prevent unauthenticated users from accessing this view. Let's see how API authentication and permissions work.

Handling authentication

REST framework provides authentication classes to identify the user performing the request. If authentication is successful, the framework sets the authenticated User object in request.user. If no user is authenticated, an instance of Django's AnonymousUser is set instead.

REST framework provides the following authentication backends:

- BasicAuthentication: This is HTTP basic authentication. The user and password are sent by the client in the Authorization HTTP header encoded with Base64. You can learn more about it at https://en.wikipedia.org/wiki/Basic_access_authentication.
- TokenAuthentication: This is token-based authentication. A Token model is used to store user tokens. Users include the token in the Authorization HTTP header for authentication.
- SessionAuthentication: This one uses Django's session backend for authentication. This backend is useful to perform authenticated AJAX requests to the API from your website's frontend.
- RemoteUserAuthentication: This allows you to delegate authentication to your web server, which sets a REMOTE_USER environment variable.

You can build a custom authentication backend by subclassing the BaseAuthentication class provided by REST framework and overriding the authenticate() method.

You can set authentication on a per-view basis, or set it globally with the DEFAULT_AUTHENTICATION_CLASSES setting.

 Authentication only identifies the user performing the request. It won't allow or deny access to views. You have to use permissions to restrict access to views.

You can find all the information about authentication at https://www.django-rest-framework.org/api-guide/authentication/.

Let's add `BasicAuthentication` to our view. Edit the `api/views.py` file of the `courses` application and add an `authentication_classes` attribute to `CourseEnrollView` as follows:

```
from rest_framework.authentication import BasicAuthentication

class CourseEnrollView(APIView):
    authentication_classes = (BasicAuthentication,)
    # ...
```

Users will be identified by the credentials set in the `Authorization` header of the HTTP request.

Adding permissions to views

REST framework includes a permission system to restrict access to views. Some of the built-in permissions of REST framework are:

- `AllowAny`: Unrestricted access, regardless of if a user is authenticated or not.
- `IsAuthenticated`: Allows access to authenticated users only.
- `IsAuthenticatedOrReadOnly`: Complete access to authenticated users. Anonymous users are only allowed to execute read methods such as `GET`, `HEAD`, or `OPTIONS`.
- `DjangoModelPermissions`: Permissions tied to `django.contrib.auth`. The view requires a `queryset` attribute. Only authenticated users with model permissions assigned are granted permission.
- `DjangoObjectPermissions`: Django permissions on a per-object basis.

If users are denied permission, they will usually get one of the following HTTP error codes:

- `HTTP 401`: Unauthorized
- `HTTP 403`: Permission denied

You can read more information about permissions at `https://www.django-rest-framework.org/api-guide/permissions/`.

Edit the `api/views.py` file of the `courses` application and add a `permission_classes` attribute to `CourseEnrollView` as follows:

```python
from rest_framework.authentication import BasicAuthentication
from rest_framework.permissions import IsAuthenticated

class CourseEnrollView(APIView):
    authentication_classes = (BasicAuthentication,)
    permission_classes = (IsAuthenticated,)
    # ...
```

We include the `IsAuthenticated` permission. This will prevent anonymous users from accessing the view. Now we can perform a POST request to our new API method.

Make sure the development server is running. Open the shell and run the following command:

```
curl -i -X POST http://127.0.0.1:8000/api/courses/1/enroll/
```

You will get the following response:

```
HTTP/1.1 401 Unauthorized
...
{"detail": "Authentication credentials were not provided."}
```

We get a `401` HTTP code as expected, since we are not authenticated. Let's use basic authentication with one of our users. Run the following command, replacing `student:password` with the credentials of an existing user:

```
curl -i -X POST -u student:password
http://127.0.0.1:8000/api/courses/1/enroll/
```

You will get the following response:

```
HTTP/1.1 200 OK
...
{"enrolled": true}
```

You can access the administration site and check that the user is now enrolled in the course.

Creating view sets and routers

ViewSets allow you to define the interactions of your API and let REST framework build the URLs dynamically with a Router object. By using view sets, you can avoid repeating logic for multiple views. View sets include actions for the typical create, retrieve, update, delete operations, which are list(), create(), retrieve(), update(), partial_update(), and destroy().

Let's create a view set for the Course model. Edit the api/views.py file and add the following code to it:

```
from rest_framework import viewsets
from .serializers import CourseSerializer

class CourseViewSet(viewsets.ReadOnlyModelViewSet):
    queryset = Course.objects.all()
    serializer_class = CourseSerializer
```

We subclass ReadOnlyModelViewSet, which provides the read-only actions list() and retrieve() to both list objects or retrieve a single object. Edit the api/urls.py file and create a router for our view set as follows:

```
from django.urls import path, include
from rest_framework import routers
from . import views

router = routers.DefaultRouter()
router.register('courses', views.CourseViewSet)

urlpatterns = [
    # ...
    path('', include(router.urls)),
]
```

We create a DefaultRouter object and register our view set with the courses prefix. The router takes charge of generating URLs automatically for our view set.

Open http://127.0.0.1:8000/api/ in your browser. You will see that the router lists all view sets in its base URL, as shown in the following screenshot:

Api Root

OPTIONS   GET ▾

The default basic root view for DefaultRouter

GET /api/

HTTP 200 OK
Allow: GET, HEAD, OPTIONS
Content-Type: application/json
Vary: Accept

```
{
    "courses": "http://127.0.0.1:8000/api/courses/"
}
```

You can access http://127.0.0.1:8000/api/courses/ to retrieve the list of courses.

You can learn more about view sets at https://www.django-rest-framework.org/api-guide/viewsets/. You can also find more information about routers at https://www.django-rest-framework.org/api-guide/routers/.

Adding additional actions to view sets

You can add extra actions to view sets. Let's change our previous CourseEnrollView view into a custom view set action. Edit the api/views.py file and modify the CourseViewSet class to look as follows:

```python
from rest_framework.decorators import detail_route

class CourseViewSet(viewsets.ReadOnlyModelViewSet):
    queryset = Course.objects.all()
    serializer_class = CourseSerializer

    @detail_route(methods=['post'],
                  authentication_classes=[BasicAuthentication],
                  permission_classes=[IsAuthenticated])
    def enroll(self, request, *args, **kwargs):
```

```
course = self.get_object()
course.students.add(request.user)
return Response({'enrolled': True})
```

We add a custom `enroll()` method that represents an additional action for this view set. The preceding code is as follows:

1. We use the `detail_route` decorator of the framework to specify that this is an action to be performed on a single object.
2. The decorator allows us to add custom attributes for the action. We specify that only the `post` method is allowed for this view and set the authentication and permission classes.
3. We use `self.get_object()` to retrieve the `Course` object.
4. We add the current user to the `students` many-to-many relationship and return a custom success response.

Edit the `api/urls.py` file and remove the following URL, since we don't need it anymore:

```
path('courses/<pk>/enroll/',
    views.CourseEnrollView.as_view(),
    name='course_enroll'),
```

Then edit the `api/views.py` file and remove the `CourseEnrollView` class.

The URL to enroll in courses is now automatically generated by the router. The URL remains the same, since it's built dynamically using our action name `enroll`.

Creating custom permissions

We want students to be able to access the contents of the courses they are enrolled in. Only students enrolled in a course should be able to access its contents. The best way to do this is with a custom permission class. Django provides a `BasePermission` class that allows you to define the following methods:

- `has_permission()`: View-level permission check
- `has_object_permission()`: Instance-level permission check

These methods should return `True` to grant access or `False` otherwise. Create a new file inside the `courses/api/` directory and name it `permissions.py`. Add the following code to it:

```
from rest_framework.permissions import BasePermission

class IsEnrolled(BasePermission):
    def has_object_permission(self, request, view, obj):
        return obj.students.filter(id=request.user.id).exists()
```

We subclass the `BasePermission` class and override the `has_object_permission()`. We check that the user performing the request is present in the `students` relationship of the `Course` object. We are going to use the `IsEnrolled` permission next.

Serializing course contents

We need to serialize course contents. The `Content` model includes a generic foreign key that allows us to associate objects of different content models. Yet, we have added a common `render()` method for all content models in the previous chapter. We can use this method to provide rendered contents to our API.

Edit the `api/serializers.py` file of the `courses` application and add the following code to it:

```
from ..models import Content

class ItemRelatedField(serializers.RelatedField):
    def to_representation(self, value):
        return value.render()

class ContentSerializer(serializers.ModelSerializer):
    item = ItemRelatedField(read_only=True)

    class Meta:
        model = Content
        fields = ['order', 'item']
```

In this code, we define a custom field by subclassing the `RelatedField` serializer field provided by REST framework and overriding the `to_representation()` method. We define the `ContentSerializer` serializer for the `Content` model and use the custom field for the `item` generic foreign key.

We need an alternate serializer for the `Module` model that includes its contents, and an extended `Course` serializer as well. Edit the `api/serializers.py` file and add the following code to it:

```
class ModuleWithContentsSerializer(serializers.ModelSerializer):
    contents = ContentSerializer(many=True)

    class Meta:
        model = Module
        fields = ['order', 'title', 'description', 'contents']

class CourseWithContentsSerializer(serializers.ModelSerializer):
    modules = ModuleWithContentsSerializer(many=True)

    class Meta:
        model = Course
        fields = ['id', 'subject', 'title', 'slug',
                  'overview', 'created', 'owner', 'modules']
```

Let's create a view that mimics the behavior of the `retrieve()` action, but it includes the course contents. Edit the `api/views.py` file and add the following method to the `CourseViewSet` class:

```
from .permissions import IsEnrolled
from .serializers import CourseWithContentsSerializer

class CourseViewSet(viewsets.ReadOnlyModelViewSet):
    # ...
    @detail_route(methods=['get'],
                  serializer_class=CourseWithContentsSerializer,
                  authentication_classes=[BasicAuthentication],
                  permission_classes=[IsAuthenticated,
                                      IsEnrolled])
    def contents(self, request, *args, **kwargs):
        return self.retrieve(request, *args, **kwargs)
```

The description of this method is as follows:

- We use the `detail_route` decorator to specify that this action is performed on a single object.
- We specify that only the `GET` method is allowed for this action.
- We use the new `CourseWithContentsSerializer` serializer class that includes rendered course contents.
- We use both the `IsAuthenticated` and our custom `IsEnrolled` permissions. By doing so, we make sure that only users enrolled in the course are able to access its contents.
- We use the existing `retrieve()` action to return the `Course` object.

Open `http://127.0.0.1:8000/api/courses/1/contents/` in your browser. If you access the view with the right credentials, you will see that each module of the course includes the rendered HTML for course contents, as follows:

```
{
    "order": 0,
    "title": "Introduction to Django",
    "description": "Brief introduction to the Django Web Framework.",
    "contents": [
        {
            "order": 0,
            "item": "<p>Meet Django. Django is a high-level
            Python Web framework
            ...</p>"
        },
        {
            "order": 1,
            "item": "\n<iframe width=\"480\" height=\"360\"
            src=\"http://www.youtube.com/embed/bgV39DlmZ2U?
            wmode=opaque\"
            frameborder=\"0\" allowfullscreen></iframe>\n"
        }
    ]
}
```

You have built a simple API that allows other services to access the course application programmatically. REST framework also allows you to handle creating and editing objects with the `ModelViewSet` view set. We have covered the main aspects of Django REST framework, but you will find further information about its features in its extensive documentation at `https://www.django-rest-framework.org/`.

Summary

In this chapter, you created a RESTful API for other services to interact with your web application.

The next chapter will teach you how to build a production environment using uWSGI and NGINX. You will also learn how to implement a custom middleware and create custom management commands.

13
Going Live

In the previous chapter, you created a RESTful API for your project. In this chapter, we will learn how to create a production environment for our project by covering the following topics:

- Configuring a production environment
- Creating a custom middleware
- Implementing custom management commands

Creating a production environment

It's time to deploy your Django project in a production environment. We are going to follow these steps to get our project live:

1. Configure project settings for a production environment
2. Use a PostgreSQL database
3. Set up a web server with uWSGI and NGINX
4. Serve static assets
5. Secure our site with SSL

Managing settings for multiple environments

In real-world projects you will have to deal with multiple environments. You will have at least a local and a production environment, but you could have other environments as well, such as testing or pre-production environments. Some project settings will be common to all environments, but others will have to be overridden per environment. Let's set up project settings for multiple environments while keeping everything neatly organized.

Create a `settings/` directory next to the `settings.py` file of the `educa` project. Rename the `settings.py` file to `base.py` and move it into the new `settings/` directory. Create the following additional files inside the `setting/` folder so that the new directory looks as follows:

```
settings/
    __init__.py
    base.py
    local.py
    pro.py
```

These files are as follows:

- `base.py`: The base settings file that contains common settings (previously `settings.py`)
- `local.py`: Custom settings for your local environment
- `pro.py`: Custom settings for the production environment

Edit the `settings/base.py` file and replace the following line:

```
BASE_DIR = os.path.dirname(os.path.dirname(os.path.abspath(__file__)))
```

With the following one:

```
BASE_DIR =
os.path.dirname(os.path.dirname(os.path.abspath(os.path.join(__file__,
os.pardir))))
```

We have moved our settings files to a directory one level lower, so we need `BASE_DIR` to point to the parent directory to be correct. We achieve this by pointing to the parent directory with `os.pardir`.

Edit the `settings/local.py` file and add the following lines of code:

```
from .base import *

DEBUG = True

DATABASES = {
    'default': {
        'ENGINE': 'django.db.backends.sqlite3',
        'NAME': os.path.join(BASE_DIR, 'db.sqlite3'),
    }
}
```

This is the settings file for our local environment. We import all settings defined in the base.py file and we only define specific settings for this environment. We have copied the DEBUG and DATABASES settings from the base.py file, since these will be set per environment. You can remove the DATABASES and DEBUG settings from the base.py settings file.

Edit the settings/pro.py file and make it look as follows:

```
from .base import *

DEBUG = False

ADMINS = (
    ('Antonio M', 'email@mydomain.com'),
)

ALLOWED_HOSTS = ['*']

DATABASES = {
    'default': {
    }
}
```

These are the settings for the production environment. Let's take a closer look at each of them:

- DEBUG: Setting DEBUG to False should be mandatory for any production environment. Failing to do so will result in traceback information and sensitive configuration data exposed to everyone.
- ADMINS: When DEBUG is False and a view raises an exception, all information will be sent by email to the people listed in the ADMINS setting. Make sure to replace the name/email tuple with your own information.
- ALLOWED_HOSTS: Django will only allow the hosts included in this list to serve the application. This is a security measure. We include the asterisk symbol * to refer to all hostnames. We will limit the hostnames that can be used for serving the application later.
- DATABASES: We just keep this setting empty. We are going to cover database setup for production hereafter.

When handling multiple environments, create a base settings file and a settings file for each environment. Environment settings files should inherit the common settings and override environment-specific settings.

We have placed the project settings in a different location than the default `settings.py` file. You will not be able to execute any commands with the `manage.py` tool unless you specify the settings module to use. You will need to add a `--settings` flag when you run management commands from the shell or set a `DJANGO_SETTINGS_MODULE` environment variable.

Open the shell and run the following command:

```
export DJANGO_SETTINGS_MODULE=educa.settings.pro
```

This will set the `DJANGO_SETTINGS_MODULE` environment variable for the current shell session. If you want to avoid executing this command for each new shell, add this command to your shell's configuration in the `.bashrc` or `.bash_profile` files. If you don't set this variable you will have to run management commands, including the `--settings` flag, as follows:

```
python manage.py migrate --settings=educa.settings.pro
```

You have successfully organized settings for handling multiple environments.

Using PostgreSQL

Throughout this book, we have mostly used the SQLite database. SQLite is simple and quick to set up, but for a production environment you will need a more powerful database, such as PostgreSQL, MySQL, or Oracle. You already learned how to install PostgreSQL and set up a PostgreSQL database in Chapter 3, *Extending Your Blog Application*. If you need to install PostgreSQL, you can read the *Installing PostgreSQL* section of Chapter 3, *Extending Your Blog Application*.

Let's create a PostgreSQL user. Open the shell and run the following commands to create a database user:

```
su postgres
createuser -dP educa
```

You will be prompted for a password and permissions you want to give to this user. Enter the desired password and permissions and then create a new database with the following command:

```
createdb -E utf8 -U educa educa
```

Then edit the `settings/pro.py` file and modify the `DATABASES` setting to make it look as follows:

```
DATABASES = {
    'default': {
        'ENGINE': 'django.db.backends.postgresql',
        'NAME': 'educa',
        'USER': 'educa',
        'PASSWORD': '*****',
    }
}
```

Replace the preceding data with the database name and credentials for the user you created. The new database is empty. Run the following command to apply all database migrations:

```
python manage.py migrate
```

Finally, create a superuser with the following command:

```
python manage.py createsuperuser
```

Checking your project

Django includes the `check` management command for checking your project anytime. This command inspects the apps installed in your Django project and outputs any errors or warnings. If you include the `--deploy` option, additional checks only relevant for production use will be triggered. Open the shell and run the following command to perform a check:

```
python manage.py check --deploy
```

You will see an output with no errors but several warnings. This means the check was successful, but you should go through the warnings to see if there is anything more you can do to make your project safe for production. We are not going to go deeper into this, but keep in mind that you should check your project before production use to look for any relevant issues.

Serving Django through WSGI

Django's primary deployment platform is WSGI. **WSGI** stands for **Web Server Gateway Interface** and it is the standard for serving Python applications on the web.

When you generate a new project using the `startproject` command, Django creates a `wsgi.py` file inside your project directory. This file contains a WSGI application callable, which is an access point to your application. WSGI is used for both running your project with the Django development server, and deploying your application with the server of your choice in a production environment.

You can learn more about WSGI at `https://wsgi.readthedocs.io/en/latest/`.

Installing uWSGI

Throughout this book, you have been using the Django development server to run projects in your local environment. However, you need a real web server for deploying your application in a production environment.

uWSGI is an extremely fast Python application server. It communicates with your Python application using the WSGI specification. uWSGI translates web requests into a format that your Django project can process.

Install uWSGI using the following command:

```
pip install uwsgi==2.0.17
```

In order to build uWSGI, you will need a C compiler, such as `gcc` or `clang`. In a Linux environment you can install it with the command `apt-get install build-essential`.

If you are using macOS X, you can install uWSGI with the Homebrew package manager using the command `brew install uwsgi`. If you want to install uWSGI on Windows, you will need Cygwin `https://www.cygwin.com`. However, it's desirable to use uWSGI in UNIX-based environments.

You can read uWSGI's documentation at `https://uwsgi-docs.readthedocs.io/en/latest/`.

Configuring uWSGI

You can run uWSGI from the command line. Open the shell and run the following command from the `educa` project directory:

```
sudo uwsgi --module=educa.wsgi:application \
--env=DJANGO_SETTINGS_MODULE=educa.settings.pro \
--master --pidfile=/tmp/project-master.pid \
--http=127.0.0.1:8000 \
--uid=1000 \
--virtualenv=/home/env/educa/
```

You might have to prepend `sudo` to this command if you don't have the required permissions.

With this command, we run uWSGI on our localhost with the following options:

- We use the `educa.wsgi:application` WSGI callable.
- We load the settings for the production environment.
- We use our virtual environment. Replace the path in the `virtualenv` option with your actual virtual environment directory. If you are not using a virtual environment, you can skip this option.

If you are not running the command within the project directory, include the option `--chdir=/path/to/educa/` with the path to your project.

Open `http://127.0.0.1:8000/` in your browser. You should see the generated HTML without any CSS style sheets or images being loaded. This makes sense since we didn't configure uWSGI to serve static files.

uWSGI allows you to define a custom configuration in a `.ini` file. This is more convenient than passing options through the command line.

Create the following file structure inside the main `educa/` directory:

```
config/
    uwsgi.ini
```

Edit the `uwsgi.ini` file and add the following code to it:

```
[uwsgi]
# variables
projectname = educa
base = /home/projects/educa
```

```
# configuration
master = true
virtualenv = /home/env/%(projectname)
pythonpath = %(base)
chdir = %(base)
env = DJANGO_SETTINGS_MODULE=%(projectname).settings.pro
module = educa.wsgi:application
socket = /tmp/%(projectname).sock
```

In the `.ini` file we define the following variables:

- `projectname`: The name of our Django project, which is `educa`.
- `base`: The absolute path to the `educa` project. Replace it with the absolute path to your project.

These are custom variables that we will use in the uWSGI options. You can define any other variables you like as long as the name is different than uWSGI options.

We set the following options:

- `master`: Enable master process.
- `virtualenv`: The path to your virtual environment. Replace this path with the appropriate path.
- `pythonpath`: The paths to add to your Python path.
- `chdir`: The path to your project directory, so that uWSGI changes to that directory before loading the application.
- `env`: Environment variables. We include the `DJANGO_SETTINGS_MODULE` variable pointing to the settings for the production environment.
- `module`: The WSGI module to use. We set this to the `application` callable contained in the `wsgi` module of our project.
- `socket`: The UNIX/TCP socket to bind the server.

The `socket` option is intended for communication with some third-party router, such as NGINX, while the `http` option is for uWSGI to accept incoming HTTP requests and route them by itself. We are going to run uWSGI using a socket, since we are going to configure NGINX as our web server, and communicate with uWSGI through the socket.

You can find the list of available uWSGI options at `https://uwsgi-docs.readthedocs.io/en/latest/Options.html`.

Now you can run uWSGI with your custom configuration using this command:

```
uwsgi --ini config/uwsgi.ini
```

You will not be able to access your uWSGI instance from your browser now, since it's running through a socket. Let's complete the production environment.

Installing NGINX

When you are serving a website, you have to serve dynamic content, but you also need to serve static files, such as CSS, JavaScript files, and images. While uWSGI is capable of serving static files, it adds an unnecessary overhead to HTTP requests and therefore, it is encouraged to set up a web server, such as NGINX in front of it.

NGINX is a web server focused on high concurrency, performance, and low memory usage. NGINX also acts as a reverse proxy, receiving HTTP requests, and routing them to different backends. Generally, you will use a web server, such as NGINX in front, for serving static files efficiently and quickly, and you will forward dynamic requests to uWSGI workers. By using NGINX, you can also apply rules and benefit from its reverse proxy capabilities.

Install NGINX with the following command:

```
sudo apt-get install nginx
```

If you are using macOS X, you can install NGINX using the command `brew install nginx`. You can find NGINX binaries for Windows at `https://nginx.org/en/download.html`.

The production environment

The following diagram shows how our final production environment will look:

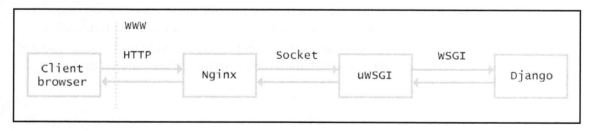

The following will happen when the client browser launches an HTTP request:

1. NGINX receives the HTTP request.
2. If a static file is requested, NGINX serves the static file directly. If a dynamic page is requested, NGINX delegates the request to uWSGI through a socket.
3. uWSGI passes the request to Django for processing. The resulting HTTP response is passed back to NGINX, which in turn passes it back to the client browser.

Configuring NGINX

Create a new file inside the `config/` directory and name it `nginx.conf`. Add the following code to it:

```
# the upstream component nginx needs to connect to
upstream educa {
    server unix:///tmp/educa.sock;
}

server {
    listen      80;
    server_name  www.educaproject.com educaproject.com;

    location / {
        include     /etc/nginx/uwsgi_params;
        uwsgi_pass  educa;
    }
}
```

This is the basic configuration for NGINX. We set up an upstream named `educa`, which points to the socket created by uWSGI. We use the `server` directive and add the following configuration:

- We tell NGINX to listen on port `80`.
- We set the server name to both `www.educaproject.com` and `educaproject.com`. NGINX will serve incoming requests for both domains.
- We specify that everything under the / path has to be routed to the `educa` socket (uWSGI). We also include the default uWSGI configuration params that come with NGINX.

You can find NGINX documentation at `https://nginx.org/en/docs/`.

The primary NGINX configuration file is located at `/etc/nginx/nginx.conf`. It includes any configuration files found under `/etc/nginx/sites-enabled/`. To make NGINX load your custom configuration file, open the shell and create a symbolic link as follows:

```
sudo ln -s /home/projects/educa/config/nginx.conf /etc/nginx/sites-enabled/educa.conf
```

Replace `/home/projects/educa/` with your project's absolute path. Then open a shell and run uWSGI if you are not running it yet:

```
uwsgi --ini config/uwsgi.ini
```

Open a second shell and run NGINX with the following command:

```
service nginx start
```

Since we are using a sample domain name, we need to redirect it to our local host. Edit your `/etc/hosts` file and add the following lines to it:

```
127.0.0.1 educaproject.com
127.0.0.1 www.educaproject.com
```

By doing so, we are routing both hostnames to our local server. In a production server you won't need to do this, since you will have a fixed IP address and you will point your hostname to your server in your domain's DNS configuration.

Open `http://educaproject.com/` in your browser. You should be able to see your site, still without any static assets being loaded. Our production environment is almost ready.

Now you can restrict the hosts that can serve your Django project. Edit the production settings file `settings/pro.py` of your project and change the ALLOWED_HOSTS setting as follows:

```
ALLOWED_HOSTS = ['educaproject.com', 'www.educaproject.com']
```

Django will now only serve your application if it's running under any of these hostnames. You can read more about the allowed setting at `https://docs.djangoproject.com/en/2.0/ref/settings/#allowed-hosts`.

Serving static and media assets

NGINX is very good at serving static content. For best performance we will use NGINX to serve the static files in our production environment. We will set up NGINX to serve both static files of our application and media files uploaded for course contents.

Edit the `settings/base.py` file and add the following code to it:

```
STATIC_ROOT = os.path.join(BASE_DIR, 'static/')
```

We need to export static assets with Django. The `collectstatic` command copies static files from all applications and stores them in the `STATIC_ROOT` directory. Open the shell and run the following command:

```
python manage.py collectstatic
```

You will see this output:

```
160 static files copied to '/educa/static'.
```

Now edit the `config/nginx.conf` file and add the following code inside the `server` directive:

```
location /static/ {
    alias /home/projects/educa/static/;
}
location /media/ {
    alias /home/projects/educa/media/;
}
```

Remember to replace the `/home/projects/educa/` path with the absolute path to your project directory. These directives tell NGINX to serve static assets located under `/static/` and `/media/` paths directly. These paths are as follows:

- `/static/`: This path matches the one set in the `STATIC_URL` setting and its target path corresponds to the value of the `STATIC_ROOT` setting. We use it to serve the static files of our application.
- `/media/`: This path matches the one set in the `MEDIA_URL` setting and its target path corresponds to the value of the `MEDIA_ROOT` setting. We use it to serve the media files uploaded to the course contents.

Reload NGINX's configuration with the following command to keep track of the new paths:

```
service nginx reload
```

Open `http://educaproject.com/` in your browser. You should be able to see your site correctly loading static resources such as CSS style sheets and images. NGINX is now serving the static files directly instead of forwarding static files' requests to uWSGI.

Great! You have successfully configured NGINX for serving static files.

Securing connections with SSL

The **Secure Sockets Layer** protocol (**SSL**), is becoming the norm for serving websites through a secure connection. It's strongly encouraged that you serve your websites under HTTPS. We are going to configure an SSL certificate in NGINX to serve our site securely.

Creating an SSL certificate

Create a new directory inside the `educa` project directory and name it `ssl`. Then generate an SSL certificate from the command line with the following command:

```
sudo openssl req -x509 -nodes -days 365 -newkey rsa:2048 -keyout
ssl/educa.key -out ssl/educa.crt
```

We are generating a private key and a 2048-bit SSL certificate valid for one year. You will be asked to enter data as follows:

```
Country Name (2 letter code) [AU]:
State or Province Name (full name) [Some-State]:
Locality Name (eg, city) []:
Organization Name (eg, company) [Internet Widgits Pty Ltd]:
Organizational Unit Name (eg, section) []:
Common Name (e.g. server FQDN or YOUR name) []: educaproject.com
Email Address []: email@domain.com
```

You can fill in the requested data with your own information. The most important field is the **Common Name**. You have to specify the domain name for the certificate. We use `educaproject.com`.

This will generate, inside the `ssl/` directory, an `educa.key` private key file and an `educa.crt` file, which is the actual certificate.

Configuring NGINX to use SSL

Edit the `nginx.conf` file and edit the `server` directive to include SSL as follows:

```
server {
    listen              80;
    listen              443 ssl;
    ssl_certificate     /home/projects/educa/ssl/educa.crt;
    ssl_certificate_key /home/projects/educa/ssl/educa.key;
    server_name         www.educaproject.com educaproject.com;
    # ...
}
```

With the preceding code, our server now listens both to HTTP through port 80 and HTTPS through port 443. We indicate the path to the SSL certificate with `ssl_certificate` and the certificate key with `ssl_certificate_key`.

Restart NGINX with the following command:

```
sudo service nginx restart
```

NGINX will load the new configuration. Open `https://educaproject.com/` with your browser. You should see a warning message similar to the following one:

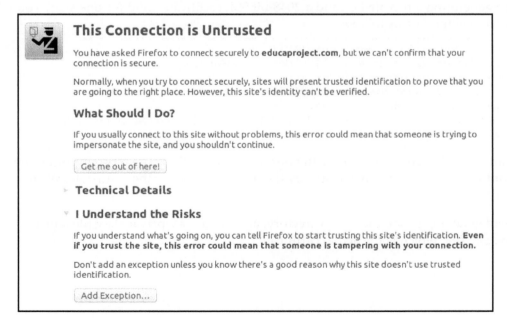

The message might be different depending on your browser. It alerts you that your site is not using a trusted certificate: the browser cannot verify the identity of your site. This is because we signed our own certificate instead of obtaining one from a trusted **Certification Authority (CA)**. When you own a real domain, you can apply for a trusted CA to issue an SSL certificate for it, so that browsers can verify its identity.

If you want to obtain a trusted certificate for a real domain, you can refer to the *Let's Encrypt* project created by the Linux Foundation. It is a collaborative project that aims to simplify obtaining and renewing trusted SSL certificates for free. You can find more information at `https://letsencrypt.org`.

Click on the **Add Exception** button to let your browser know that you trust this certificate. You will see that the browser displays a lock icon next to the URL as follows:

If you click the lock icon, SSL certificate details will be displayed.

Configuring our project for SSL

Django comes with specific settings for SSL support. Edit the `settings/pro.py` settings file and add the following settings to it:

```
SECURE_SSL_REDIRECT = True
CSRF_COOKIE_SECURE = True
```

These settings are as follows:

- `SECURE_SSL_REDIRECT`: Whether HTTP requests have to be redirected to HTTPS
- `CSRF_COOKIE_SECURE`: Has to be set for establishing a secure cookie for the cross-site request forgery protection

Congratulations! You have configured a production environment that will offer great performance for serving your project.

Creating a custom middleware

You already know the MIDDLEWARE setting, which contains the middlewares for your project. You can think of it as a low-level plugin system, allowing you to implement hooks that get executed in the request/response process. Each middleware is responsible for some specific action that will be executed for all HTTP requests or responses.

 Avoid adding expensive processing to middlewares, since they are executed in every single request.

When an HTTP request is received, middlewares are executed in order of appearance in the MIDDLEWARE setting. When an HTTP response has been generated by Django, the response passes through all middlewares back in reverse order.

A middleware can be written as a function as follows:

```
def my_middleware(get_response):

    def middleware(request):
        # Code executed for each request before
        # the view (and later middleware) are called.

        response = get_response(request)

        # Code executed for each request/response after
        # the view is called.

        return response

    return middleware
```

A middleware factory is a callable that takes a get_response callable and returns a middleware. A middleware is a callable that takes a request and returns a response, just like a view. The get_response callable might be the next middleware in the chain or the actual view in case of the last listed middleware.

If any middleware returns a response without calling its get_response callable, it short-circuits the process, no further middlewares get executed (also not the view), and the response returns through the same layers that the request passed in through.

The order of middlewares in the MIDDLEWARE setting is very important because a middleware can depend on data set in the request by other middlewares that have been executed previously.

 When adding a new middleware to the MIDDLEWARE setting, make sure to place it in the right position. Middlewares are executed in order of appearance in the setting during the request phase, and in reverse order for responses.

You can find more information about middleware at https://docs.djangoproject.com/en/2.0/topics/http/middleware/.

Creating a subdomain middleware

We are going to create a custom middleware to allow courses to be accessible through a custom subdomain. Each course detail URL, which looks like https://educaproject.com/course/django/, will also be accessible through the subdomain that makes use of the course slug, such as https://django.educaproject.com/. Users will be able to use the subdomain as a shortcut to access the course details. Any requests to subdomains will be redirected to each corresponding course detail URL.

Middlewares can reside anywhere within your project. However, it's recommended to create a middleware.py file in your application directory.

Create a new file inside the courses application directory and name it middleware.py. Add the following code to it:

```python
from django.urls import reverse
from django.shortcuts import get_object_or_404, redirect
from .models import Course

def subdomain_course_middleware(get_response):
    """
    Provides subdomains for courses
    """
    def middleware(request):
        host_parts = request.get_host().split('.')
        if len(host_parts) > 2 and host_parts[0] != 'www':
            # get course for the given subdomain
            course = get_object_or_404(Course, slug=host_parts[0])
            course_url = reverse('course_detail',
                                 args=[course.slug])
```

```
        # redirect current request to the course_detail view
        url = '{}://{}{}'.format(request.scheme,
                                 '.'.join(host_parts[1:]),
                                 course_url)
        return redirect(url)

    response = get_response(request)
    return response

return middleware
```

When an HTTP request is received, we perform the following tasks:

1. We get the hostname that is being used in the request and divide it into parts. For example, if the user is accessing mycourse.educaproject.com we generate the list ['mycourse', 'educaproject', 'com'].
2. We check if the hostname includes a subdomain by checking whether the split generated more than two elements. If the hostname includes a subdomain, and this is not www we try to get the course with the slug provided in the subdomain.
3. If a course is not found, we raise an HTTP 404 exception. Otherwise, we redirect the browser to the course detail URL.

Edit the settings.py file of the project and add 'courses.middleware.SubdomainCourseMiddleware' at the bottom of the MIDDLEWARE list as follows:

```
MIDDLEWARE = [
    # ...
    'courses.middleware.subdomain_course_middleware',
]
```

Our middleware will now be executed in every request.

Remember that the hostnames allowed to serve our Django project are specified in the ALLOWED_HOSTS setting. Let's change this setting so that any possible subdomain of educaproject.com is allowed to serve our application.

Edit the settings/pro.py file and modify the ALLOWED_HOSTS setting as follows:

```
ALLOWED_HOSTS = ['.educaproject.com']
```

A value that begins with a period is used as a subdomain wildcard: '.educaproject.com' will match educaproject.com and any subdomain for this domain, for example course.educaproject.com and django.educaproject.com.

Serving multiple subdomains with NGINX

We need NGINX to be able to serve our site with any possible subdomain. Edit the `config/nginx.conf` file and replace this line:

```
server_name   www.educaproject.com educaproject.com;
```

With the following one:

```
server_name   *.educaproject.com educaproject.com;
```

By using the asterisk, this rule applies to all subdomains of `educaproject.com`. In order to test our middleware locally, we need to add any subdomains we want to test to `/etc/hosts`. For testing the middleware with a `Course` object with the slug `django`, add the following line to your `/etc/hosts` file:

```
127.0.0.1  django.educaproject.com
```

Then open `https://django.educaproject.com/` in your browser. The middleware will find the course by the subdomain and redirect your browser to `https://educaproject.com/course/django/`.

Implementing custom management commands

Django allows your applications to register custom management commands for the `manage.py` utility. For example, we used the management commands `makemessages` and `compilemessages` in `Chapter 9`, *Extending Your Shop* to create and compile translation files.

A management command consists of a Python module containing a `Command` class that inherits from `django.core.management.base.BaseCommand` or one of its subclasses. You can create simple commands or make them take positional and optional arguments as input.

Django looks for management commands in the `management/commands/` directory for each active application in the `INSTALLED_APPS` setting. Each module found is registered as a management command named after it.

You can learn more about custom management commands at `https://docs.djangoproject.com/en/2.0/howto/custom-management-commands/`.

We are going to create a custom management command to remind students to enroll at least in one course. The command will send an email reminder to users that have been registered for longer than a specified period that aren't enrolled in any course yet.

Create the following file structure inside the `students` application directory:

```
management/
    __init__.py
    commands/
        __init__.py
        enroll_reminder.py
```

Edit the `enroll_reminder.py` file and add the following code to it:

```
import datetime
from django.conf import settings
from django.core.management.base import BaseCommand
from django.core.mail import send_mass_mail
from django.contrib.auth.models import User
from django.db.models import Count

class Command(BaseCommand):
    help = 'Sends an e-mail reminder to users registered more \
            than N days that are not enrolled into any courses yet'

    def add_arguments(self, parser):
        parser.add_argument('--days', dest='days', type=int)

    def handle(self, *args, **options):
        emails = []
        subject = 'Enroll in a course'
        date_joined = datetime.date.today() - \
        datetime.timedelta(days=options['days'])
        users =
User.objects.annotate(course_count=Count('courses_joined'))\
            .filter(course_count=0, date_joined__lte=date_joined)
        for user in users:
            message = 'Dear {},\n\n We noticed that you didn't\
            enroll in any courses yet. What are you waiting\
            for?'.format(user.first_name)
            emails.append((subject,
                            message,
                            settings.DEFAULT_FROM_EMAIL,
                            [user.email]))
        send_mass_mail(emails)
        self.stdout.write('Sent {} reminders'.format(len(emails)))
```

This is our `enroll_reminder` command. The preceding code is as follows:

- The `Command` class inherits from `BaseCommand`.
- We include a `help` attribute. This attribute provides a short description of the command that is printed if you run the command `python manage.py help enroll_reminder`.
- We use the `add_arguments()` method to add the `--days` named argument. This argument is used to specify the minimum number of days a user has to be registered, without having enrolled in any course, in order to receive the reminder.
- The `handle()` command contains the actual command. We get the `days` attribute parsed from the command line. We retrieve the users that have been registered for more than the specified days, which are not enrolled in any courses yet. We achieve this by annotating the QuerySet with the total number of courses each user is enrolled in. We generate the reminder email for each user and append it to the `emails` list. Finally, we send the emails using the `send_mass_mail()` function, which is optimized to open a single SMTP connection for sending all emails, instead of opening one connection per email sent.

You have created your first management command. Open the shell and run your command:

```
python manage.py enroll_reminder --days=20
```

If you don't have a local SMTP server running, you can take a look at Chapter 2, *Enhancing Your Blog with Advanced Features* where we configured SMTP settings for our first Django project. Alternatively, you can add the following setting to the `settings.py` file to make Django output emails to the standard output during development:

```
EMAIL_BACKEND = 'django.core.mail.backends.console.EmailBackend'
```

Let's schedule our management command so that the server runs it every day at 8 a.m. If you are using a UNIX-based system such as Linux or macOS X, open the shell and run `crontab -e` to edit your `crontab`. Add the following line to it:

```
0 8 * * * python /path/to/educa/manage.py enroll_reminder --days=20 --settings=educa.settings.pro
```

If you are not familiar with **cron** you can find an introduction to cron at http://www.unixgeeks.org/security/newbie/unix/cron-1.html.

If you are using Windows, you can schedule tasks using the Task Scheduler. You can find more information about it at `https://msdn.microsoft.com/en-us/library/windows/desktop/aa383614(v=vs.85).aspx`.

Another option for executing actions periodically is to create tasks and schedule them with Celery. Remember that we used Celery in `Chapter 7`, *Building an Online Shop* to execute asynchronous tasks. Instead of creating management commands and scheduling them with cron, you can create asynchronous tasks and execute them with the Celery beat scheduler. You can learn more about scheduling periodic tasks with Celery at `https://celery.readthedocs.io/en/latest/userguide/periodic-tasks.html`.

 Use management commands for standalone scripts that you want to schedule with cron or the Windows scheduler control panel.

Django also includes a utility to call management commands using Python. You can run management commands from your code as follows:

```
from django.core import management
management.call_command('enroll_reminder', days=20)
```

Congratulations! You can now create custom management commands for your applications and schedule them when needed.

Summary

In this chapter, you configured a production environment using uWSGI and NGINX. You have also implemented a custom middleware and you have learned how to create custom management commands.

You have reached the end of this book. Congratulations! You have learned the skills required to build successful web applications with Django. This book has guided you through the process of developing real-life projects and integrating Django with other technologies. Now you are ready to create your own Django project, whether it is a simple prototype or a large-scale web application.

Good luck with your next Django adventure!

Other Books You May Enjoy

If you enjoyed this book, you may be interested in these other books by Packt:

Python Programming Blueprints
Daniel Furtado, Marcus Pennington

ISBN: 978-1-78646-816-1

- Learn object-oriented and functional programming concepts while developing projects
- The dos and don'ts of storing passwords in a database
- Develop a fully functional website using the popular Django framework
- Use the Beautiful Soup library to perform web scrapping
- Get started with cloud computing by building microservice and serverless applications in AWS
- Develop scalable and cohesive microservices using the Nameko framework
- Create service dependencies for Redis and PostgreSQL

Django RESTful Web Services
Gastón C. Hillar

ISBN: 978-1-78883-392-9

- The best way to build a RESTful Web Service or API with Django and the Django REST Framework
- Develop complex RESTful APIs from scratch with Django and the Django REST Framework
- Work with either SQL or NoSQL data sources
- Design RESTful Web Services based on application requirements
- Use third-party packages and extensions to perform common tasks
- Create automated tests for RESTful web services
- Debug, test, and profile RESTful web services with Django and the Django REST Framework

Leave a review - let other readers know what you think

Please share your thoughts on this book with others by leaving a review on the site that you bought it from. If you purchased the book from Amazon, please leave us an honest review on this book's Amazon page. This is vital so that other potential readers can see and use your unbiased opinion to make purchasing decisions, we can understand what our customers think about our products, and our authors can see your feedback on the title that they have worked with Packt to create. It will only take a few minutes of your time, but is valuable to other potential customers, our authors, and Packt. Thank you!

Leave a review - let other readers know what you think

Index

Table of Contents

About the reviewers

Norbert Máté is a web developer. He started his career back in 2008. His first programming language as a professional web developer was PHP, then he moved on to JavaScript/Node.js and Python/Django/Django REST framework. He is passionate about software architecture, design patterns, and clean code. Norbert was the reviewer of another Django book *Django RESTful Web Services* by Packt Publishing.

> *I would like to thank my wife for her support.*

Packt is searching for authors like you

If you're interested in becoming an author for Packt, please visit `authors.packtpub.com` and apply today. We have worked with thousands of developers and tech professionals, just like you, to help them share their insight with the global tech community. You can make a general application, apply for a specific hot topic that we are recruiting an author for, or submit your own idea.

Contributors

About the author

Antonio Melé is the CTO of Exo Investing and the founder of Zenx IT. Antonio has been developing Django projects since 2006 for clients in several industries. He has been working as the CTO and as a technology consultant for multiple technology-based start-ups, and he has managed development teams building projects for large digital businesses. Antonio holds a master's in computer science from Universidad Pontificia Comillas. His father inspired his passion for computers and programming.

`mapt.io`

Mapt is an online digital library that gives you full access to over 5,000 books and videos, as well as industry leading tools to help you plan your personal development and advance your career. For more information, please visit our website.

Why subscribe?

- Spend less time learning and more time coding with practical eBooks and Videos from over 4,000 industry professionals

- Improve your learning with Skill Plans built especially for you

- Get a free eBook or video every month

- Mapt is fully searchable

- Copy and paste, print, and bookmark content

PacktPub.com

Did you know that Packt offers eBook versions of every book published, with PDF and ePub files available? You can upgrade to the eBook version at `www.PacktPub.com` and as a print book customer, you are entitled to a discount on the eBook copy. Get in touch with us at `service@packtpub.com` for more details.

At `www.PacktPub.com`, you can also read a collection of free technical articles, sign up for a range of free newsletters, and receive exclusive discounts and offers on Packt books and eBooks.

To my sister

Django 2 by Example

Content Development Editor: Arun Nadar
Technical Editor: Prajakta Mhatre
Copy Editor: Dhanya Baburaj and Safis Editing
Project Coordinator: Sheejal Shah
Proofreader: Safis Editing
Indexer: Rekha Nair
Production Coordinator: Nilesh Mohite

First published: May 2018

Production reference: 1250518

Published by Packt Publishing Ltd.
Livery Place
35 Livery Street
Birmingham
B3 2PB, UK.

ISBN 978-1-78847-248-7

www.packtpub.com

Django 2 by Example

Build powerful and reliable Python web applications from scratch

Antonio Melé

BIRMINGHAM - MUMBAI